Praise for *The Georgetown Ladies' Social Club*

"[A] winning combination of sex, scandal, and political escapade."

—*Publishers Weekly*

"Heymann pulls out all the stops . . . a well-researched, fast-paced, and fascinating look at dinner-party power-brokering."

—*Booklist*

"[A] massively researched study of five of Washington's leading grandes dames."

—*The Washington Times*

"Heymann reveals Washington's most enduring power brokers . . . to be a circle of wealthy, connected, and ambitious women."

—*Elle*

"[A] fascinating look into a hierarchical world that ultimately governs our own small slices of life."

—*The Kingston Observer* (MA)

THE
GEORGETOWN
LADIES'
SOCIAL CLUB

POWER, PASSION, AND POLITICS
IN THE NATION'S CAPITAL

BY C. DAVID HEYMANN

ATRIA BOOKS
NEW YORK   LONDON   TORONTO   SYDNEY

ATRIA BOOKS

1230 Avenue of the Americas
New York, NY 10020

Copyright © 2003 by C. David Heymann

ISBN: 0-7434-2856-0
0-7434-2857-9 (Pbk)

First Atria Books trade paperback edition November 2004

10 9 8 7 6 5 4 3 2 1

ATRIA BOOKS is a trademark of Simon & Schuster, Inc.

Manufactured in the United States of America

For information regarding special discounts for bulk purchases,
please contact Simon & Schuster Special Sales at 1-800-456-6798
or business@simonandschuster.com.

TO MY GOOD FRIEND,

LESTER PERSKY,

1925–2001

CONTENTS

were bound together not only by their hard-won successes and victories but also by their losses and defeats. At the center of each of their lives can be found secrets so deep and dark that they threaten to destroy everything these women worked so long and diligently to achieve. What these Georgetown ladies ultimately share is their ability to maintain a public pose, to protect the image they sought to create, no matter what the cost, no matter what the burden.

"The Georgetown Ladies' Social Club" was actually a term coined by none other than Ronald Reagan to identify an elite corps of prominent and powerful Washington women whose connections, courage, wealth, vision, intelligence, and ambition afforded them an abundance of social and political clout in a town traditionally and historically run by men. Richard Nixon, brought down by one of them, referred to all as "a shadow conspiracy of women." The description is biased but apt. The ladies in question emerged from the shadows into the light. Their parties, their personalities, and their presence forged change and lent shape to the human drama of the twentieth century and are still being felt in the twenty-first century.

AUTHOR'S NOTE

THE WHITE HOUSE, Capitol Hill, the Pentagon, and the Supreme Court immediately come to mind when considering the major spheres of influence in the nation's capital, but the true seat of power in Washington, D.C., may well be Georgetown, a tiny, picturesque, eighteenth-century village cozily nestled in the oldest section of the city. Lyndon Baines Johnson, while serving in the Oval Office, noted that "every student of Washington's political process ought to know that the business of government is often transacted during evening hours, sometimes over a drink and sometimes over a meal—but almost always in Georgetown."

What President Johnson did not say is that these evening transactions are largely conceived, created, produced, and directed by women. On the pages that follow I attempt to trace and chronicle the evolution, over the last fifty years, of female power in Georgetown through the public as well as the personal lives of five women—Katharine Graham, Evangeline Bruce, Lorraine Cooper, Pamela Harriman, and Sally Quinn—and through the lifestyles of a sizeable constituency of supporting players—both male and female.

This is the story then of a group of highly motivated and independent women who all happened to reside in the same place at roughly the same time. They pursued common goals and common interests. Their paths frequently intersected and overlapped. They socialized with many of the same people. They were married to well-educated, successful, power-driven men whose careers in almost every instance took precedence over the careers of their wives. Marriage and children aside, these women

CHAPTER ONE

THE LAST PARTY

FOR MANY YEARS two invitations were particularly cherished in Washington. One was to the White House, the other to Washington Post Company owner Katharine Graham's home at 2020 R Street on the edge of fashionable Georgetown. Of the many Graham gatherings, none surpassed in terms of impact or poignancy the private funeral reception given for her at her residence on Monday, July 23, 2001, six days after her death from injuries sustained in a fall while attending an international business conference at Sun Valley, Idaho, with her son Donald, current publisher of *The Washington Post*. On July 14, after collapsing and striking her head on the sidewalk outside her Sun Valley living quarters, Graham had been airlifted by helicopter to a hospital in Boise, where she underwent emergency surgery for a brain hemorrhage. For three days, while her family gathered around her, Graham lingered on a life-support system, never regaining consciousness. Finally, in accordance with the dictates of her living will, doctors disconnected her from the respirator. Within minutes the eighty-four-year-old publishing giant was dead.

The nostalgia and sadness that marked the otherwise coolly orchestrated, nationally televised funeral services held the morning of July 23 continued long after the recessional march, as a half-dozen pallbearers shouldered the dark walnut coffin out of Washington's National Cathedral and into a waiting hearse to be transported to Oak Hill, the nineteenth-

1

century garden park cemetery located directly across the street from Graham's home. Her husband, Philip L. Graham, victim of a self-inflicted gunshot wound to the right temple, had been buried there in 1963. Katharine's Episcopal graveside ceremony, attended solely by members of her immediate family and presided over by Reverend and former Republican Missouri Senator John C. Danforth ("earth to earth, ashes to ashes, dust to dust"), took less than twenty minutes.

The gloom was palpable among the roughly five hundred mourners who arrived—some on foot, many by limousine, all by invitation—at the early afternoon reception, a posthumous gathering that *The Washington Post* dubbed "Kay Graham's Last Party," as opposed to "The Last Cocktail Party," the title bestowed by the same newspaper upon the 1997 National Cathedral funeral of Pamela Harriman, another Georgetown royal. As at her past parties, Kay had managed, even in death, to bring together notables from both sides of the political aisle, business leaders, media monarchs, press lords, foreign dignitaries, old-line dowagers, reclusive Georgetown cave dwellers, bluebloods, and well-connected socialites. "Wall-to-wall everybody rich and famous . . ." read the random notes of one journalist assigned to cover the affair. The turnout of such a star-studded cast came as no great surprise. The passing of Katharine Graham had been reported in every newspaper and on every radio and television news broadcast from Maine to California, heralded by a stream of headlines and sound bites that bespoke her universal prominence: "The Most Powerful Woman in Washington," "The Most Powerful Woman in the World," "America's Queen," "The Queen Is Dead, Long Live the Queen."

Kay Graham's house, a substantial, square-fronted, cream-colored brick structure, with green shutters, sat well back from the street behind a high wrought-iron fence. Kay had owned it since 1947, when her father paid $125,000 to acquire it for his daughter and son-in-law from William J. ("Wild Bill") Donovan, director of the OSS (Office of Strategic Services), the high-risk World War II espionage organization that, after the war, evolved into the Central Intelligence Agency. The nine-bedroom, 9,000-plus-square-foot, multilevel mansion's size made it stand out like Gulliver in a land of Lilliputian Georgetown dollhouses. Although it had simple lines and looked like a comfortable sort of country dwelling that the city had grown up around—the central part of the house dated back to 1784—it had at first seemed too large and grand for Phil and Kay. Yet it boasted enough features—an old-fashioned back porch, a separate carriage house that had been converted into a garage, a multitude of trees—to make it a worthwhile investment. Despite the alterations and changes Kay Graham made over the years, including the installation of an outdoor heated swimming pool, the house retained much of its original character.

A semicircular pebbled driveway led guests past stone gate posts and a police checkpoint to the main entrance, then round again to an electronically controlled exit gate. An extensive tree-shaded front lawn, partially obscured from view by thick summer foliage, was site to a large party tent that had been set up the day before. Within the confines of the tent, tables had been laid out buffet-style with finger sandwiches, sliced ham and beef tenderloin, chicken salad, fancy breads, cookies, chocolates, tarts, and fresh fruit. Coffee, tea, milk (for the children), cold drinks, and alcoholic beverages were available at any of several service bars spread across the property.

In front of the tent, surrounded by a cluster of Graham admirers, stood Ben Bradlee, executive editor of *The Washington Post* from 1968 to 1991 and one of Katharine's closest confidants. Having delivered a stirring eulogy at her morning funeral ("She was a spectacular dame, and I loved her very much"), Bradlee now regaled his captive audience with tales charting the life of the *real* Kay Graham—her love of news, movies, the grandeur of celebrity, and ice cream; her flirtatious nature with men and her interest in clothes and perfume when it came to other women; her loyalty, devotion, essential decency, and sense of humor. Above all, her sense of humor.

"I will miss her laugh," said Bradlee.

"She had a formidable laugh," agreed another member of the group. "It came from somewhere deep inside her belly and rolled across the room like thunder. It was absolutely infectious."

The contingent surrounding Bradlee included Watergate reporters Bob Woodward and Carl Bernstein; former Defense Secretary William Cohen; Senator John Kerry with his wife, Teresa Heinz; fashion designer Oscar de la Renta; movie director Mike Nichols and his wife, Diane

Sawyer; magazine editor Tina Brown; and Alan Greenspan, chairman of the Federal Reserve Board.

Sally Quinn—Ben Bradlee's wife and a longtime writer for *The Washington Post*—reflected on the significance of Katharine Graham's death, telling a reporter from her own newspaper that "so many people have thought of the White House as the center of Washington, but the fact is it was Kay's house that has been the center of Washington for so many years, and now it seems as if the center has gone."

There were hugs, kisses, greetings from people who hadn't seen one another in a long time. Reminiscences were rampant. Stories were told of a woman whose life had been full and meaningful. Former Secretary of Defense Robert McNamara, an intimate for more than forty years, spoke of Kay's contribution in advancing the role of women in the life of the nation, her ability to override challenges, the Pentagon Papers, Richard Nixon, and Watergate, her determination to make the *Post* one of the two or three best periodicals in the country. No wonder that every U.S. president from John F. Kennedy through George W. Bush, with the exception of Richard Nixon, had insisted at one time or another on visiting the home of Katharine Graham.

In lieu of a formal receiving line, Katharine's great-granddaughter, ten grandchildren, and four children—Elizabeth ("Lally"), Donald ("Donny"), William, and Stephen—mingled freely with the guests, shaking hands and embracing those they considered old friends. Lally, credited by the press with having organized and orchestrated a good deal of the funeral and reception, had argued so vociferously about certain details of the funeral with officials at the National Cathedral that they requested she find a replacement to represent the family. Only then did Lally compose herself. Now, assuming the mantle of the oldest child, she seemed more animated and outgoing than any of her brothers. Donald, the next oldest sibling, appeared his usual low-key self.

At one point during the reception, investments sage Warren E. Buffett, Microsoft chairman Bill Gates, and Steve Case, then chairman of AOL Time Warner, were spotted standing together by the side of the house, deeply immersed in conversation. "There's two hundred billion dollars over there," quipped one attendee, gesturing in their direction.

All three had been at the international business conference in Sun Valley when Kay Graham collapsed; two days before her accident she joined the threesome in what had become (after she grew too old and lame for tennis) her favorite pastime: a passionate game of bridge. (Her favorite moments at the conference had reportedly been an informal meeting with actor Tom Hanks and a power breakfast with Vicente Fox, president of Mexico.)

Behind the R Street house and along the driveway were figures no less celebrated than Vice President Dick Cheney and his wife, Lynne; former president Bill Clinton and his wife, Democratic New York Senator Hillary Rodham Clinton; former Clinton cabinet members Madeleine Albright, Donna Shalala, and Robert Rubin; Clinton friend and adviser Vernon Jordan; local politicians Anthony A. Williams, Walter E. Washington, and Marion Barry; financier Ronald Perelman; Rupert Murdoch; Barbara Walters; Tom Brokaw; Arthur Sulzberger; New York State Governor George Pataki and his wife, Libby; Senators Edward Kennedy, Orrin Hatch, John McCain, and Bob Graham, the younger half-brother of the late Phil Graham. It was a name dropper's paradise.

Inside the house, seated in a high-ceilinged, well-appointed, coral red drawing room, one of several on the first floor, were other Graham associates, among them Mike Wallace, Art Buchwald, Jim Lehrer, Barry Diller, and William Styron. Yo-Yo Ma, who had played the cello at her funeral, put in a brief appearance but left early because of a previous engagement. Henry Kissinger and Arthur Schlesinger Jr., both of whom had that morning joined Ben Bradlee at the lectern to eulogize Kay, were ensconced in the library, a room of modest proportions whose walls were lined with brown fabric and leather-bound books.

"She died with her boots on," marveled Kissinger. "She remained active to the very end. And although I didn't know her in the early days, she has to be admired for transforming herself from an insecure homemaker into the head of one of the nation's top communications operations. McGeorge Bundy once said of Kay that she is next in line after Queen Victoria as the world's most powerful woman."

For Jack Valenti, president of the Motion Picture Association of America and one-time White House press secretary to Lyndon Johnson,

Graham's demise signaled the end of an epoch. Wandering from room to room, parlor to parlor, pausing here and there to examine a Tiffany-framed photograph or some other telling memento, he recalled previous visits to the house. "The history that emanates from this place can never be re-created," he said. "Kay's soirées represented the epitome of great talk and great debate. She was the doyenne of Washington, the only person whose invitations were a command performance." It is true. Kay Graham's bipartisan get-togethers resembled a salon in the more traditional sense. In the warm reflection of a blazing fireplace, by the glow of candlelight on fine Georgian silver, conversation flourished. The discourse was witty and intelligent. Toasts were clever and articulate. Insights were exchanged, information bartered. The dialogue was never trivial or boring. The guest lists routinely included a cross-section of the country's best-informed, most influential governmental, business, and multimedia figures. Those who attended knew they were glimpsing a slice of cultivated life, an increasingly rare commodity in contemporary America.

Valenti recalled an evening in 1965, a Graham dinner party attended by President Johnson: "The president had been very attached to Phil Graham. As a matter of fact, Phil was a major instrument in convincing John F. Kennedy to select LBJ as his running mate in 1960. So there was an inherent closeness between the president and Phil's widow. And on the night in question, after the other guests had gone home, LBJ sat down with Kay and three of her children and began to tell them stories about their father. All sorts of warm little anecdotes about him. Always in a positive vein. And these kids, who ranged in age from eight to fourteen, something like that, were absolutely transfixed by it all. And Kay told me later, it was one of the nicest things that had ever happened to her—for the president to take time out to talk to those children about their father, who of course had taken his own life. And it wasn't the only time the president did that. At another point he brought along letters he'd gotten from their father and read them aloud to the kids, and told them how much Phil had meant to him. It was Lyndon Johnson at his best."

If Valenti's recollections seemed somehow sentimental, they nevertheless conferred a sense of finality. Without Kay Graham, there appeared to be little reason to return to her house, a feeling her children must have experienced as well. Ten weeks after Kay's death, they placed her residence on the sales block for a formidable $8.35 million. Because it had belonged to Katharine Graham for more than fifty years, the property (known in the marketplace as the Beall-Washington House) had gained what realtors call "historic presence." Its book value, according to the latest Georgetown tax listings, came to $3.47 million, some $5 million less than the family's asking price. The cost of the house, coupled with high maintenance fees and the need for considerable refurbishing, made it an investment that few house hunters could hope to afford. It would not sell until March 2002, when Mark Ein, a thirty-seven-year-old venture capitalist, paid what newspapers called an "undisclosed sum" to acquire the property. Also sold was a house Kay owned on Martha's Vineyard and a cooperative apartment she maintained in Manhattan. Her furniture, personal possessions, books, and artwork (featuring a Renoir and a Marsden Hartley) were auctioned in separate lots at Weschler's in Washington and Sotheby's in New York.

"This is Kay Graham's final party," commented *New Yorker* writer Ken Auletta, who attended both the funeral and reception with his wife, the New York literary agent Amanda "Binky" Urban. "Kay was known for bringing people together. We've come back to her house today for a last meal and a last chat. She would've loved this party."

There was more than a modicum of truth in Auletta's contention. Kay Graham had a passion for parties. Parties were fundamental to her personality. Anybody who knew her knew this to be the case. Even when she didn't feel well, she would be there with bells on her feet and rings on her toes. Parties provided access not just to the right people but also to the social palaver and hard news items that, once processed, filled the pages of her two major publications: *Newsweek* and *The Washington Post*. Giving and attending parties were simply part of her job. And since the day of her husband's death, her job had been the focus of her life.

Nobody seemed more aware of Kay's absence from the afternoon's proceedings than the once sturdy, now frail eighty-nine-year-old Polly Wisner Fritchey, Katharine's Georgetown neighbor and one of her dearest friends. Polly, whose maiden name was Mary Ellis Knowles, outlived

Kay by almost a year, passing away on July 9, 2002, at age ninety. Born into a family of means in Pensacola, Florida, she grew up in Greenwich, Connecticut, and attended St. Timothy's, an exclusive boarding school in Stevenson, Maryland. She and Kay initially met in New York during World War II. Their friendship blossomed in 1947 when Polly and her first husband, Frank Wisner, a future chief of covert operations for the CIA, moved from New York to Washington, where he worked for two years in the U.S. State Department before switching to Central Intelligence. In *Personal History*, Kay Graham's 1997 Pulitzer Prize–winning autobiography, she writes: "On the social front . . . Phil [Graham] noticed that there was always a three-way morning conversation among Polly Wisner, Evangeline Bruce, and me. He dubbed this the 'nine o'clock network' and said he was going to buy time in it."

Evangeline Bruce, the third peg of this early-morning telephone triumvirate, had known Kay Graham for some time before her own marriage in 1945 to David K. E. Bruce, the distinguished future ambassador to France, West Germany, Great Britain, and other politically charged ports of call. Vangie, as her pals called her, and Polly had been introduced by Kay Graham. Like Kay, they both lived in old and opulent Georgetown dwellings only blocks apart. Both had children and both were married to wellborn, successful gentlemen from the South whose careers started with law degrees—Frank Wisner's from the University of Virginia School of Law and David Bruce's from the University of Maryland—and led in the 1930s to positions as attorneys with first-rate Wall Street investment firms. During World War II, Bruce and Wisner both worked for the OSS, the former as operations chief in England, the latter as operations chief in the Balkans. Both men reported directly to "Wild Bill" Donovan. As fate would later have it, Frank Wisner, who was manic-depressive, would take his own life in 1965, two years after Phil Graham's tragic suicide. David Bruce died in 1977, Vangie in 1995. At Oak Hill Cemetery, the Bruce and Graham family plots were located next to each other, a scant fifteen yards apart.

Evangeline Bruce attended a dinner party hosted by Phil and Kay Graham at their Georgetown home in the late spring of 1951, the year of Georgetown's bicentennial. Vangie, whose husband was then the American ambassador to France, had flown alone from Paris for a brief stateside visit. The Graham celebration of Georgetown's 200th birthday represented a departure from their usual fireside entertainments, which in those days consisted of informal, twice-monthly Sunday brunches and an annual Christmas Eve fête to which they invited mostly *Washington Post* staffers. Their bicentennial gathering was significant in that it became the first black-tie dinner party they had attempted since moving into the R Street residence. Given Phil's aversion to overcrowded, stuffy affairs and Kay's relative inexperience at hosting such dinners, the evening loomed as something of an anomaly in the Graham household.

Among the guests that night were George Kennan, chief of the State Department's Policy Planning Staff; Secretary of State Dean Acheson; Speaker of the House Sam Rayburn; Edward Burling, cofounder of Covington and Burling, one of Washington's largest and most respected law firms; future National Gallery of Art director John Walker and his wife, Margaret; actress-socialite Constance Bennett and her fifth husband, Air Force Brigadier General John Theron Coulter; and Phil Graham's old boss, U.S. Supreme Court Justice Felix Frankfurter. There were twenty-four guests in all. The guests of honor were Henri Bonnet, French ambassador to the United States, and his wife, whom the Grahams had met at a New Year's Eve party given that same year by journalist Walter Lippmann. Almost everybody at the dinner either lived or partied in Georgetown.

As Evangeline Bruce recalled the evening, Phil Graham—having consumed his fill of champagne—held forth from his soapbox in high good humor, delivering a rambling predinner peroration on the life and times of "the tiny kingdom of Georgetown." The village, one square mile in size and a mile from the White House, had been patented in 1703 as the Rock of Dunbarton by Ninan Beall, a Scottish immigrant who became commander in chief of the Provincial Forces of Maryland. Beall and his military troop bore responsibility for driving out and relocating the Native Americans who had originally settled the area. By 1751, the Rock had burgeoned into a booming tobacco port, and it was then incorporated and named in honor of King George II of England. After the Revolution, in 1791, George Washington met with major land owners and commissioners at Sutter's Tavern, in Georgetown, to sign the proclamation creating the federal city, the permanent seat of government in the United States, a place called Washington, D.C. Yet Georgetown always retained a separate identity, with a relatively small population, its own citizens council, and its own distinct geographical boundaries. It stretched from Oak Hill Cemetery on the northern edge of the district to the Potomac at the south, and from Rock Creek on the eastern edge to Georgetown University at the west.

A patchwork of gardens, meandering tree-lined lanes, and redbrick Federalist and Victorian town houses, Georgetown was not so much a place as a state of mind. It was, as Philip Graham put it, "home to the great, the near great and the once great in government and in journalism." But only the cognoscenti, in 1951, were aware of the social and financial importance of Georgetown, a community that until 1950—and the passing of the Old Georgetown Act—remained fully integrated, populated by as many blacks as whites. Many of the houses currently inhabited by cabinet officers, members of Congress, intelligence agency officials, and retired ambassadors had once belonged to poor but proud black families, whose economic eviction from the area had led to a sweeping reconstruction program and a feeding frenzy among Georgetown Realtors desperate for home and property sales in what very rapidly had become Washington's most desirable and unaffordable neighborhood. As blacks fled to outlying parts of Washington or to Anacostia in the southeast quadrant of the city, a crop of young, financially stable, highly employed individuals rushed in. Real estate values soared to the point where a row house built in 1800 (not far from a house once occupied by writer Sinclair Lewis), with exterior dimensions of thirteen by eighteen feet, had recently sold for a small fortune, only to be torn down, rebuilt, and resold for a greater fortune. The value of commercial real estate in Georgetown also skyrocketed. A storefront on Wisconsin Avenue, where slaves were once bought and sold, gave way to a high-priced beauty salon. A section of seedy shacks located along the C & O Canal were razed and replaced with a multiple-unit, six-story office building. Urban renewal had come to stay.

"Georgetown is an entity unto itself," declared Graham, pausing only long enough to down another glass of bubbly. "In other cities, people go to parties primarily to have fun. In Georgetown, people who have fun at parties probably aren't getting much work done. That's because parties in Georgetown aren't really parties in the true sense of the word. They're business after business hours, a form of government by invitation. Georgetown works even when it plays. Given the composition of its populace, the place is perfectly designed for such 'noble' pursuits as the exchange of political confidences, the sowing of ideological seeds, the establishment of contacts and alliances. It's fair to say that more political decisions get made at Georgetown suppers than anywhere else in the nation's capital, including the Oval Office."

On that hyperbolic note, dinner was served. Guests sat at three round tables of eight each and began their repast with a dish southerners call "angels on horseback"—grilled oysters wrapped in bacon. In those days, Katharine Graham rarely served soup as an appetizer, her mother, Agnes Meyer, having once admonished her to "never start your meal in a swamp—it's bad for the digestive tract!" (Mrs. Meyer also never allowed salt on the table, a culinary dictate her daughter studiously ignored.) The next course was a baked brook trout with cucumbers and tomatoes vinaigrette, followed by the main entrée, roast leg of lamb with sautéed mushrooms and side dishes of wild rice and carrots, which the hostess herself served from monogrammed silver platters. A pair of waiters, hired for the evening, poured dinner wines and cleared dishes.

Dinner table conversation, according to Vangie Bruce, centered on the events of the day: the Korean War, the Alger Hiss case, the Red menace, the presidential candidacy of Dwight David Eisenhower. Eschewing his usual Democratic Party leanings, Phil Graham had declared himself an early Eisenhower supporter, authorizing the publication of several pro-Ike editorials in the *Post*. Kay Graham, on the other hand, would emerge as an ardent backer of Adlai Stevenson, contributing large sums (in tandem with her mother) to the Democrat's war chest. Once Stevenson became the Democratic Party's presidential nominee, Phil Graham reversed himself and also supported Adlai.

When the salad plates appeared, each came with a lace doily, a finger bowl, and a fork and spoon for dessert, although the latter was still two courses away. An endive salad with diced beets and walnut shavings preceded an assorted cheese platter. Marrons glacés crème (glazed cream of chestnut dessert) topped off the menu.

After dinner the men and women separated, a ritual inherited from the British, the women repairing noiselessly either to an upstairs bedroom or, in the present instance, to the backyard where, in the warm glow of a bright moon, they exchanged recipes and discussed their children. The men retired to the same drawing room that Kay Graham later painted red but which at the time boasted eggshell-white walls, blue velvet draperies, heavy, masculine furniture, and a valuable collection of Oriental art, much of it given to the Grahams by Agnes Meyer. Scattered comfortably about the room, the men talked politics over brandy and Cuban cigars.

Kay Graham walked around the room pouring coffee for the men before joining the rest of the ladies in the garden. There she pulled Vangie aside and reported on the clandestine conversations she had just overheard, the language oblique, a kind of verbal Morse code, vague whispered references to the Cold War, to political dealings in other countries, plots and subplots to influence foreign as well as domestic elections, encourage revolutions, overthrow governments, defeat the Communists, or defeat the man who most wanted to defeat the Communists—Senator Joseph McCarthy, not yet quite the witch-hunter he would soon become.

"They were speaking English," said Kay, "but I didn't understand a word they were saying. In any case, I'm certain it was more interesting than what's being said out here."

A subject that evidently arose among the men that evening had to do with the French-Indochina War, which started in 1946 and was gradually transmogrifying into a battle that would soon incorporate America and become known as the Vietnam War. To date, President Truman had sent France eight transport planes and millions of dollars in emergency funds. That evening, when French Ambassador Henri Bonnet insisted that the United States could do more, Phil Graham began to deride him about the French campaign, portraying it as nothing less than an attempt on the part of the French military to recolonize Vietnam. The derision escalated into acrimony, the acrimony into accusations, much of it the probable result of Phil's semiinebriated state. Over the course of the evening he had imbibed far too much alcohol.

"The party ended on a truly dank note," said Evangeline Bruce. "By the time the women rejoined them, the men had divided into two camps, one in support of American intervention in France's efforts, the other opposed. There were some harsh words about France's lackadaisical performance during World War II, their rolling over like a dog the moment the Nazis appeared on the horizon. At some point I looked out the window and caught sight of Phil Graham squaring off with Bonnet on the front lawn. No punches were thrown, but it was clear that the evening had run its course. Kay purposely knocked over the tea tray to distract the men from getting drawn further into an already unpleasant situation. Suddenly, as if on cue, everyone stood and headed for the door. Some days later, at Kay's urging, Phil Graham apologized to Bonnet and the two men reconciled."

After the departure of their guests, Phil and Kay Graham seem to have become embroiled in an altercation of their own, this one somewhat violent in nature. Details of the fracas are not known, but on seeing her friend again a few days later, Evangeline Bruce noticed that Kay's arms and legs looked swollen and bruised. The subject of the bicentennial dinner never arose, neither in conversation with Vangie nor in Graham's often painfully candid *Personal History,* which, for the year 1951, reveals only that Kay suffered a miscarriage at some point between January and August, her second miscarriage since marrying Phil Graham ten years earlier.

"We never discussed what happened that evening," Evangeline Bruce told the current author. "At another juncture, Kay did talk to me about the despair she experienced in her role as a housewife. She didn't like living intellectually off Phil, asking that dreadful question whenever he came home at night: 'Darling, what did you do today?' She found it utterly demeaning to be an appendage, to subsist in her husband's shadow. But as for her battle scars, the perceived violence—she never mentioned it.

"The closest Kay came to disclosing the true story behind her marriage was when she told me that she and Phil had endured more than their share of confrontations. Evidently, with the passage of time, especially after Phil began to develop symptoms of manic-depressive illness, these confrontations became more pronounced. Although I can't prove it and even though Phil Graham could be extremely sweet and exceedingly charming, my guess is that Kay suffered physical as well as emotional abuse. I knew about the emotional abuse—his insults, his affairs with other women, his attempt to leave Kay for another woman and take control of *The Washington Post*—but she never revealed anything about his violent side."

On another front, Evangeline Bruce noted that Kay Graham's best parties were those she gave when she was alone, following her husband's suicide: "By the late 1960s, Kay's house had become a magnet for every power broker in captivity. You had to be invited to Kay Graham's to know you had arrived. To be granted an audience with her, at a dinner party or on any other occasion, was tantamount to being enshrined. You didn't exist until you'd broken bread with Kay Graham."

CHAPTER TWO

PHIL AND KAY

THE LEAD STORY on the front page of *The Washington Post* for June 5, 1940, concerned British Prime Minister Winston Churchill's "We Shall Never Surrender" speech, in which he exhorted his fellow countrymen to resist the Blitz, the unrelenting onslaught of an enemy bent on mass destruction. The same edition's society page carried an announcement that Eugene Isaac Meyer's third daughter, Katharine, twenty-two, was being married that day to Philip Leslie Graham, twenty-four, at the 350-acre Meyer family estate in Mount Kisco (Westchester County, N.Y.). Eugene Meyer was the owner of the *Post*, having acquired it at a bankruptcy sale from the McLean family in 1933. The auction price of $825,000 included the keys to the dilapidated, rat-infested building on E Street that served as publishing headquarters for the paper, at that time the worst of Washington's five dailies.

In terms of their backgrounds and upbringing, Philip Graham and his new bride had little in common. He was born on July 18, 1915, in a town called Terry in the Black Hills of South Dakota. His father, Ernest, a mining engineer, was of Scottish ancestry, born and raised on a farm in Michigan. His mother, Florence Morris Graham, taught grade school in South Dakota before she married Ernest and had three children. As a young boy, Philip moved with his family first to Michigan, where his father managed the family's general store and dairy herd, then to the

Florida Everglades, where he became resident manager of a sugarcane plantation. For several years the Grahams resided on a houseboat in the Miami Canal, a mosquito-ridden body of water twenty miles from downtown Miami. A small tribe of Seminole Indians lived nearby. Phil Graham credited the Seminoles with teaching him how to hunt and fish. He credited his mother with instilling in him a love of the written word. Even in the leanest of times, she subscribed to magazines such as *The New Yorker* and *Time;* she frequently talked to him about books and the theater, telling him that these were part of "an important and attainable world."

During the Depression the sugarcane plantation went out of business and Ernest Graham turned back to dairy farming as a livelihood, acquiring a sizable spread outside Miami, naming it Ten Circle Farms, and starting a commercial cow-calf enterprise. A stern, hard-driven, ambitious man, he made money as a dairy farm operator, sank his profits into real estate, and ran successfully for the state senate, though he later failed in his bid to become governor of Florida.

George Smathers, future Democratic senator from Florida, attended Miami Junior High and High School with Phil and then the University of Florida, where they were dormitory roommates before joining the same fraternity. "We both pledged SAE, Sigma Alpha Epsilon," noted Smathers. "We were great buds. We did everything together that kids do in college: double-dated, drank, partied, studied. What I mean is that I studied, and Phil didn't. He rarely cracked a book. He didn't have to. He was brighter and quicker than anyone around. He earned straight A's, but despite his academic achievements his father appeared in Gainesville one afternoon and took him out of school for a semester because he was doing too much partying. He spent four months working on his father's farm and returned to college a chastened young man, more serious than he'd been before. Another important factor in Phil's development was the death, when he turned nineteen, of his mother and the remarriage of his father to Hilda, a much younger woman with whom he had a son named Bob. Phil graduated magna cum laude and was admitted to Harvard Law School, which is where his mother had long wanted him to go.

So he went off to Cambridge, Massachusetts, to become a lawyer, while I opted for Washington, D.C., and a career in politics."

At Harvard Law School, it was Phil who spoke about going into politics, announcing to faculty members and classmates alike that once he passed the bar exam he planned to return to Florida and either work for the state attorney general or run for elective office. Tall and gaunt, at six foot two and 135 pounds, he possessed the kind of commanding and charismatic presence that instantly attracted followers. Well suited to the arena of public affairs, he had merely to enter a room and heads swiveled in his direction. He could charm anyone he wanted. He could dominate a crowd. At Harvard he continued demonstrating not only a winning personality but also the same intellectual capabilities that had served him so well at the University of Florida. His only failing had to be his tendency to drink too much, a liability that dogged him his entire life.

One of the people whose attention he captured was fellow law school student Edward F. Prichard Jr., a native of Bourbon County, Kentucky, and a graduate of Princeton University. Fat, funny, eloquent, blessed with a photographic memory, a claptrap legal mind, and a backcountry slickness, "Prich" found a ready ally in the person of Phil Graham. The two men bonded not only with each other but also with Felix Frankfurter, the preeminent Harvard Law School professor whose 1939 appointment to the U.S. Supreme Court, by President Franklin D. Roosevelt, would cosmically link Cambridge and Washington, D.C. Choosing the brainiest, feistiest young men he could find at Harvard, Frankfurter guided them to the nation's capital. Graham and Prichard were no exception. So impressed with Phil and Prich was the recently appointed justice that he asked them to serve as law clerks—Prichard in 1940, Graham a year later. What set Frankfurter apart from other justices was the close working relationship he maintained with the youthful attorneys who constituted his support staff. For Frankfurter, divergence and dissent were the lifeblood of a democracy. He loved debating political and legal issues with the members of his staff. He cultivated and encouraged the forthright exchange of views and ideas. It didn't bother him when his law clerks disagreed with his legal opinions. It didn't even disturb him that they could be condescending of him at such times. Particularly fond of Ed Prichard and Phil Graham, he once noted that "Prich and Phil are men in whose company it is impossible to be bored." He thought of them as the sons he never had; they considered him their friend and mentor.

In his third and final year of law school, Phil Graham was named editor of the *Harvard Law Review*. Graduating third in a class of four hundred, he decided not to pursue a political career in Florida but instead to go to Washington, where he would serve a year-long clerkship under U.S. Supreme Court Justice Stanley Reed, while awaiting the Frankfurter appointment. Washington, then still a quaint and somnambulant southern town, had not yet developed into the citadel of bustle and bureaucracy it would become during the war years, when thousands of federal and military personnel flocked into town, giving rise to an unprecedented construction boom. When Phil Graham arrived he joined Ed Prichard and ten others, mostly Harvard Law School graduates, at Hockley House in nearby Arlington, Virginia. A redbrick, turn-of-the-century mansion with white columns, commanding views of Washington in the distance, and a lawn that sloped down to the Potomac, the rented house contained six bedrooms, seven bathrooms, a large formal dining room that easily seated twenty, a library, a billiards room, and an institutional-size kitchen. Each man contributed fifty dollars per month for room and board as well as the services of a gardener, a cook, a maid, and a valet named Johnson. Previously employed for twenty-five years by Dean Acheson, the valet and maid had been summarily dismissed by Acheson's wife, Alice, after she discovered them in "a compromising situation"—they claimed to be married but in fact weren't. The duo diligently attended to the divergent needs of their new bosses, ironing their shirts, pressing their suits, polishing their shoes and silverware, changing their bed linens, and serving their meals.

Jane Swarthmore, the girlfriend of one of Hockley's residents, described the setting. "They lived like kings," she said of the Hockley House dozen. "They worked hard and played hard. On Friday and Saturday nights they gave dinner parties, and on Sundays they held brunches that started at noon and ran well beyond the cocktail hour. There were always plenty of girls around, vying for male attention. Because there were usually more women than men at these gatherings, the guys tended to be a bit on the arrogant side. They would date a girl for several weeks or months, tire of her, then pawn her off on some of the other guys in the house. They traded names and telephone numbers. It wasn't unusual for the same girl to be asked out by as many as three or four of the boys. It was all very incestuous and chauvinistic. The place had the air of a glorified fraternity house, the main difference being that instead of college students it was occupied by a cadre of New Dealers, all of them extremely bright and eligible."

Another frequent visitor, Helga Moss, remembered Hockley House as "a uniquely exciting place to be because it was tied directly to the great events and activities of Washington through the up-and-coming young lawyers who lived there. Dinners were like colloquia in current affairs. You never knew who might turn up as a houseguest or for dinner. One evening you'd find yourself seated next to Walter Reuther, Adlai Stevenson, or Archibald MacLeish; the next night, J. Robert Oppenheimer, future director of the Manhattan Project at Los Alamos, New Mexico, would be at the table, expounding on the vices and virtues of what would soon become known as atomic energy. You quickly learned that unless you'd read the day's newspapers before dinner, you were out of the conversation and therefore out of the loop. Every theme and issue—from FDR and the New Deal to Hitler and the pernicious threat of Nazism—was discussed and argued in debates that seemed to go on forever. And when they weren't engaged in debate, the fellows at Hockley amused themselves with marathon games of chess, bridge, or touch football. They weren't happy unless locked in some form of intellectual or athletic competition.

"I also recollect their valet, Johnson, a convivial black man of about fifty who doubled as bartender at their parties and whose stock-in-trade was a mint julep, which he made to perfection. But beyond this, he'd invented a cocktail of his own, a lethal concoction without a name, whose ingredients were known only to him. The drink was pink in color and tasted as mild and sweet as fruit punch. It was deceiving, because two or three glasses of this diabolical potion and you were out for the count. On Sunday mornings as you walked around the house, you'd invariably find two or three victims passed out on a sofa or in an easy chair from the night before."

It was at such a party that Katharine Meyer first encountered Phil Graham. Since his arrival in Washington, he had dated a number of young ladies, including Phyllis Asher, a Georgetown University Law School student, and Alice Barry, a friend of Kay's and a member of an old Washington family. Kay, while writing occasional editorials for *The Washington Post* and editing the paper's "Letters to the Editor" section, had also been playing the field, going out on dates with some of the cub reporters she'd met at the *Post*. One of her escorts, John Oakes, a nephew of Arthur Sulzberger, publisher of *The New York Times,* happened to live at Hockley House, and it was he who finally introduced Phil and Kay, setting in motion the chain of events that would soon bring them together as husband and wife.

George Smathers, then living in Washington with his wife, Rosemary, recalled meeting Kay for the first time in early February 1940, when the two couples went out to Henry's, a seafood restaurant next door to the Mayflower Hotel. "Kay was tall at about five feet, nine inches, pretty, a bit shy, a little awkward, had bright eyes, dark curly hair, and seemed to possess a sense of the world well beyond her young years," said Smathers. "She was clearly dazzled by Phil—the golden boy in a glittering world— and he appeared to be equally taken with her. What she liked best about him, she later told me, was that he made her laugh. It was only their third or fourth date, but that was the night, following dinner, when he proposed to her, insisting that he would never accept a penny of her old man's money and that they would have to move to Florida and subsist— she with no more than two dresses—on whatever he could eke out as either a neophyte politician or a country lawyer working for the local attorney general. Kay accepted the marriage proposal but insisted on two provisos—they should wait a month before announcing, and they would have to stay put in Washington, as she had no intention of settling in Florida."

Ed Prichard, who shared a room with Phil at Hockley, also met Kay at this juncture and, as she reveals in *Personal History,* developed a "temporary interest" in her. In addition, Prich had been introduced to Kay's sister, Elizabeth, nicknamed "Bis," a slightly older, more glamorous version of Kay. Instantly attracted to her, he visited Bis in New York one weekend and took her to an expensive East Side restaurant, but in typical Prich fashion he forgot to bring his wallet, leaving his date to pay for both of them. The relationship ended before it began. Twice rebuffed, Prich reacted adversely to Phil's newfound love, greeting the news of his engagement to Kay with an expletive: "You son of a bitch, you've got her!" For several weeks he refused to speak to either one. Another time he spat a drink into Phil's face, then told him that the marriage would never work, that the two of them—Phil and Kay—came from disparate backgrounds and were therefore incompatible. Although Prich eventually apologized for his childish behavior, his ominous warning would one day come back to haunt his roommate.

Two years younger than Philip Graham, Katharine Meyer was born on June 16, 1917, in New York City into a wealthy family oriented to philanthropy and public service. Her father—the son of a well-to-do Alsatian Jewish merchant and banker who had emigrated from France to California—graduated from Yale and made a fortune on Wall Street before marrying Katharine's mother, Agnes Elizabeth Ernst, the daughter of German Lutheran immigrants. He was twelve years her senior.

Tom Kelly, an early Katharine Graham biographer, described Agnes Meyer in terms befitting the classic "Mommie Dearest" figure, a woman he found "impetuous, brash, self-confident, bitter, beautiful, difficult, and determined." She grew up in the Bronx, attended local public schools, and as a young girl nearly died when her brother accidentally shot her in the forehead with a .32-caliber pistol the family kept hidden in the house. She recovered, earned high grades, and won a full scholarship to Barnard College, which she promptly lost after a difference of opinion with one of her professors—or so she claimed. Because her father, a small-time New York businessman, had gone into debt, Agnes had to finance the remainder of her Barnard education by procuring a series of part-time jobs, including a reporter's position at the New York *Sun*, a post she retained for eighteen months following her graduation. In later years, after attaining wealth and position as the wife of Eugene Meyer, she served as a member of Barnard College's board of trustees. Yet her resentment of the school persisted. When Eleanor Elliott, an editor at *Vogue* and chairwoman of the board of trustees for many years, approached her for a contribution, Agnes refused. "I have more important things to do with my money than give it to Barnard College," she said. Eleanor Elliott summed up her reaction to Agnes in the most succinct terms: "Mrs. Meyer was a really tough broad."

Strict and pious Lutherans, Agnes's parents objected when she disclosed her intention to wed a man of Jewish descent, no less a man whose forebears included a number of Orthodox rabbis. As far as the Ernst family elders were concerned, Eugene Meyer's most impressive feature was the size of his bankroll. Among other money-making ventures, he had put together what became the giant Allied Chemical Company, and by age forty, his net worth was estimated at nearly 60 million. Once married to Agnes, he took it upon himself to bolster her family's sagging finances. He paid off her debts as well as her father's.

In her autobiography, *Out of These Roots,* Agnes Meyer traces her relationship with Eugene to 1908, a year in which she was being pursued by several suitors. Although he represented a solution to her monetary problems, she deferred marriage until 1910 in favor of a European junket. In Paris, she dazzled sculptor Constantin Brancusi, delighted the poet Paul Claudel, and became the "untouched" darling of "the lecherous" Auguste Rodin. Art, particularly eleventh-century Chinese painting, a subject about which she went on to write a book, became a lifelong passion. Portrayed in some quarters as a "culture vulture" with nothing but a dilettante's passing interest in Democratic Party politics, Agnes was lionized in others. Lindy Boggs, highly respected wife of the late Louisiana congressman Hale Boggs, the mother of Washington lobbyist Tommy Boggs and National Public Radio correspondent Cokie Roberts, celebrates Agnes Meyer as a "role model for future generations of superbright American women, having established a reputation as a journalist, lecturer, translator of Thomas Mann, intrepid warrior on behalf of public education and, second only to her friendships with John Dewey, Toscanini, Eleanor Roosevelt, and Adlai Stevenson, a leader in social welfare causes and prefeminist issues of all kinds. She was an individualist.

From the beginning she opposed the Red Scare machinations of Joseph McCarthy, a man whose cause and tactics she utterly despised."

When Agnes wasn't storming the ramparts, she lived the life of an overprivileged wife with homes in New York, Mount Kisco (a 700-acre estate), Jackson Hole (Wyoming), Washington, D.C., and the foothills of Virginia, all five amply stocked with Cézannes and Chippendales, Monets and Ming vases, and many of the other accouterments of great prosperity. For her five children, four of them girls, there were governesses, servants, tutors, horseback riding and tennis instructors, dance classes (which Kay hated), household retainers, as well as frequent trips abroad and to the West Coast. But if Agnes Meyer overindulged her children in terms of luxury, she tended to ignore their other needs. Kay, in particular, experienced only limited emotional support from her mother, a woman who resented the demands of domestic life, had never really wanted children in the first place, and often left them in the indifferent hands of caretakers while traveling the world in search of new interests. Of her own efforts as a parent, Agnes wrote in her autobiography: "I was a dutiful, but not a loving mother." In fact, she was more an absentee mother than anything else, a woman who delighted in relegating responsibility for raising her offspring to almost anybody. Katharine's childhood was thus lavish but incredibly lonely.

Stories abound of Agnes Meyer's bizarre behavior, her lack of maternal instincts, her alcoholism, her harsh and at times cruel nature. "She seemed like a character out of a Wagnerian opera," said Joan Braden, the Washington hostess who befriended Phil and Kay Graham in the early 1950s. "Kay called her 'the Viking' and told stories of how her mother constantly denigrated her for not being intelligent or attractive enough, for not meeting her expectations and for not knowing how to organize a household or throw a proper social function. It was not just Phil Graham who had systematically eroded Kay's confidence. The process began much earlier with her mother, who so intimidated and frightened Katharine that she could reduce her to tears merely by giving her a disapproving look. Agnes was glamorous, I suppose, but I would not have wanted her as a mother.

"I recall a detail which somehow symbolizes how Kay felt about Agnes. In the 1960s my husband and I owned a pet boa constrictor that would devour live mice for dinner. When she first witnessed this Darwinian feeding frenzy, Kay covered her eyes and winced. She asked whether the snake had a name. When I said it was named Alice, she suggested changing it to Agnes."

Cynthia Helms, wife of former CIA director Richard Helms and a longtime bridge partner of Kay Graham, had heard similar tales from Kay about her mother. "Agnes was very mean and condescending to all her children, but particularly so to Kay," said Helms. "As a child she wanted nothing more than to please her mother. She would come home from school and say, 'Look, Mother, I won this literary prize for an essay I wrote,' and Agnes would respond, 'You're wearing an awful dress. It looks terribly unflattering on you.' In no uncertain terms, Kay's mother made her feel like an ugly duckling—and it took years before she began to believe otherwise."

Another friend of Kay's, Sally Reston, widow of James "Scotty" Reston, Washington bureau chief for *The New York Times*, knew Agnes Meyer and found her to be "a cold, abrasive woman who took out her frustrations on her children. She communicated to them the feeling that they were not worthy of her, that somewhere, somehow they had let her down. Also, she was an unrelenting party person, and the impression I derived was that she preferred her career and dinner guests to her husband and children. It reached the point where if any of the kids wanted to see their mom, they had to make a formal appointment through her secretary. Arthur Krock, Scotty's predecessor at the *Times*, told me Agnes once said to him she wished she'd never married or had any children. That was her big regret in life.

"It was Kay's father who instilled in her the basic belief in herself that enabled her ultimately to cope with life's vicissitudes. Eugene Meyer seemed much more supportive of the children than Agnes, though at the same time he appeared to be opinionated, stuffy, and remote. After Kay married Phil Graham, her father referred to her simply as 'Mrs. Graham'—no longer 'Kay'—as if she were merely an extension of her husband. He might say, for instance, 'Phil Graham and his wife are coming over for dinner tonight,' reinforcing the notion that capable women in those days were only expected to become wives and mothers. This rather limited perspective was shared by Agnes Meyer. I recall Kay telling me about the day she came upon her mother and Phil Graham in a deep discussion on the deployment by President Truman, in 1945, of atomic bombs at Hiroshima and Nagasaki. Shooing her daughter away, Agnes said, 'Pardon us dear. We're having an intellectual conversation.' Mrs. Meyer always considered Kay her inferior in terms of intellect and social prowess."

In one regard it may have come as a blessing to their children that the Meyers were absent with such frequency. According to David Halberstam's *The Powers That Be*, a history of *The Washington Post*, Agnes's marriage to Eugene Meyer "had not been a calm or happy one, the sense of erosion and discord was powerful." There were problems and disappointments almost from the start. She had married him not for love but for money—and he knew it. He once showed some of her letters to a friend. "Very intelligent, aren't they? But there's no love there," he said. For the most part, her letters to him document Agnes's frequent meetings with former male admirers—men, she insisted, "whose hearts still leap at the sight of me." Throughout her marriage, Agnes maintained a string of such relationships on the side, never consummating any of them physically (with the possible exception of Bill Ward, a friend and political mentor of hers, who, according to *Personal History*, may well have been Agnes's lover) but forever flaunting them for the benefit of her frustrated husband. Returning to their ostentatious Crescent Place home one evening, Eugene Meyer found his wife in her bedroom entertaining an old flame. "They weren't in a compromising position," Meyer told the same friend to whom he'd previously shown his wife's letters, "but almost." The truth of the matter is that as she aged, Agnes put on considerable weight, the result of a glandular malady compounded by a drinking problem. Her fading beauty, according to those who knew her, added to her growing insecurity, her need to demonstrate to the world that she was still an attractive and desirable woman.

Another facet of Kay's upbringing was anti-Semitism. Agnes Meyer had discovered early in her marriage that no amount of success on her husband's part could eradicate it. The discrimination she experienced, particularly in Mount Kisco where the Meyers were never very popular, distressed her to no end. She blamed her husband for it, insisted that he renounce his religion and that the Meyer household be made to seem thoroughly Protestant. As a student at Madeira, the progressive boarding and day school for girls outside Washington, Katharine Meyer had no idea that she was half Jewish. Her father, as remote in certain ways as her mother, had never discussed the matter with her or with any of her siblings. Not until her freshman year at Vassar College, when a classmate inquired of her what it felt like to be Jewish, did Kay begin to pose questions of her parents—not just about religion but also about sex and money.

By the time she found answers, Kay—after two years at Vassar—had transferred as an American history major into the academically rigorous Great Books program at the University of Chicago, a center of radical thought and philosophy in the 1930s. Unlike Vassar, which Kay found cold and confining, the atmosphere at the University of Chicago, with its large, heterogeneous, financially uncertain student body, was intellectual and intense. Katharine shared a two-bedroom suite in the International House—a coed dormitory largely reserved for foreign students—with Taylor Churchill, a transfer student from Sarah Lawrence College, and drove herself around town in an old Buick convertible. At Vassar, not knowing how to wash her own clothes, she had worn the same cardigan for months; at Chicago, having mastered the ins and outs of student laundries, she dressed appropriately. Within a matter of months, she had become active in the student movement, picketing against sweatshop labor policies and in support of the International Ladies Garment Workers Union. She discussed Marx and Stalin with fellow students over beer and popcorn at Hanley's, the campus drinking parlor, took a course in labor relations with Paul Douglas (later the U.S. senator from Illinois), and witnessed a confrontation between striking steel workers and the Chicago police, which left seven strikers dead and dozens injured. When she graduated from Chicago with a B.A. in June 1938, neither her mother nor father attended the ceremony. Carol Felsenthal, another of Katharine Graham's biographers, commented, "a congratulatory note arrived instead, signed by Agnes Meyer's secretary and with Katharine's first name misspelled. Friends at the university, who saw her burst into tears, threw her a graduation party."

Having been editor in chief of the school literary magazine at Madeira and on the staff of the student newspaper during her sophomore year at Vassar, and having worked for brief periods at *The Washington Post*, Kay now moved to the West Coast to become a reporter at $21 per week for the San Francisco *News*, a Scripps Howard afternoon paper. Her father procured the position for her and arranged her stay with a wealthy aunt and uncle, Rosalie and Sigmund Stern. Joining the Newspaper Guild, Kay worked at the *News* for seven and a half months and showed—in Carol Felsenthal's words—"a remarkable grasp of the issues at hand." In a letter to her sister Bis, she reflected on her intention to become a labor reporter, "possibly working up to political reporting later." She had no desire to work for their father, who "wants and needs someone . . . willing to go through the whole mill, from reporting, to circulation management, to editorial writing, and eventually to be his assistant. . . . I detest beyond description advertising and circulation, and that is what a newspaper executive spends most of his time doing." She ended the letter by adding that working for the *Post* would be nothing less than a "first-class dog's life."

Kay's long-term assignment in San Francisco was to cover the violent dockworkers' strike, an ongoing struggle between the International Labor Workers Union, which was the longshoremen's union, and the shipping firms that controlled the docks. While reporting on the strike Kay met Harry Bridges, head of the longshoremen's union and Eugene Patton, a fiery, ruggedly handsome union organizer whose romantic exterior fueled her imagination. She became infatuated with Patton. The two hung out together, frequenting the cheap bars and restaurants along San Francisco's waterfront, imbibing boilermakers and hot fish chowder, spending an occasional night in a seedy Market Street hotel, where they would sign in as husband and wife. On weekends Kay would put on evening clothes and attend the opera or the opening of some new Nob

Hill art gallery. She found the combination of the two contrasting lifestyles exhilarating. But when she discovered that Patton already had a long-standing wife as well as several children, she ended the affair.

Disappointed by the failed romance, her first, and perhaps a bit homesick, Kay felt relieved when her father offered to raise her salary by four dollars a week if she would return to Washington and "learn the newspaper trade" by working for him at the *Post*. Years later he told friends that of his children, "Kate's the only one like me. She's got a hard mind. She'd make a good businessman." Although she'd promised herself never to work for her father, Kay returned to the East Coast, purchased a new wardrobe, and began her career at the *Post*. In retrospect it would be both the best and worst thing she could have done. Following her arrival in Washington, she would meet Phil Graham.

✑

PHILIP GRAHAM'S FATHER was stunned to learn that his "ultraliberal" son planned on marrying into a family as well off as the Meyers. When Phil assured him that his motivation had been pure, that he had simply fallen in love, Ernest Graham wished him the best. He wanted to know, however, how his son intended to support his new family. Phil patiently explained that they would live within their means—he earned $3,600 a year as law clerk to Felix Frankfurter, while Kay made $25 per week at *The Washington Post*. And in the event of a shortfall, they could always take out a bank loan. Phil Graham had it all mapped out.

The wedding ceremony took place, as the *Post* said it would, on June 5, 1940, in the gardens of the Meyer family's Mount Kisco compound. Horses grazed in the meadow and the Olympic-size swimming pool glistened in the bright sunlight. Master photographer Edward Steichen, an acquaintance of Agnes Meyer, took the wedding pictures. But the afternoon did not go as expected. The wedding luncheon was disrupted by a violent row between Felix Frankfurter and the groom over a recent Supreme Court decision requiring public school students to salute the American flag regardless of their religious affiliation or convictions. Frankfurter, having written the High Court's opinion in the case, strongly supported the ruling; Phil Graham was opposed, accusing Frankfurter of having betrayed the Bill of Rights. The altercation mushroomed when Phil's best man, Ed Prichard, joined the battle in support of his former roommate. What started as the kind of intellectual exchange that Frankfurter generally encouraged among his acolytes had suddenly deteriorated into a war of words. Joseph L. Rauh Jr., a Harvard Law School graduate who had also briefly clerked for Frankfurter, felt that Graham and Prichard had gone too far for once, provoking and tormenting their mentor until he could no longer tolerate it. Rising to his feet, the furious Supreme Court justice took hold of Kay's hand and marched off with her for a long trek in the woods—"to calm down," he said.

Prichard's companion during this period was the stunning Evangeline Bruce, at the time still Evangeline Bell, an administrative assistant in the offices of Francis Biddle, solicitor general of the United States and future U.S. attorney general. "When I met him, Prich was about to go to work for the executive branch of the government," recalled Vangie. "We dated only briefly but remained lifelong friends. He used to take me along whenever he visited with Phil and Kay Graham. I seem to remember Felix Frankfurter being around a lot, so I can't imagine that he entertained any lingering resentment from the wedding ceremony.

"Prich and I saw Phil and Kay shortly after their honeymoon in Bermuda and Florida, where they stayed with Phil's family. They were talking about the honeymoon, and Phil playfully complained that while he was a late-night person, Kay liked to retire early. 'That's because you and your father spent endless hours discussing local Dade County politics,' she said. 'What else was I supposed to do?' I later learned that she'd read the whole of War and Peace during their Miami sojourn."

The Grahams had purchased a secondhand Oldsmobile and rented a modest, two-story row house at 1814 Thirty-seventh Street, just outside Georgetown. Kay's parents furnished the place, while the boys at Hockley House presented the couple with all the kitchenware they would ever need. They hired a maid, Mattie Jeffress, who for fifteen dollars a week arrived daily before breakfast and stayed through dinner, with two half-days off. She cooked, cleaned, and did the laundry while Kay worked on feature articles for the Post's weekend news supplement. Not until Mattie became ill and had to be hospitalized did Kay bother to learn the rudiments of food preparation. Purchasing a copy of *Fanny Farmer* and heeding Phil's admonition to "keep it simple," she tried her hand at such standards as meat loaf, pot roast, and spaghetti with meat sauce. A few notable dinners were interspersed among any number of successive failures.

In the fall of 1941, Kay suffered a miscarriage but soon became pregnant again, and on July 3, 1942, she gave birth to Elizabeth ("Lally") Morris Graham, the first of four children. Kay's father drove down to see the newborn, but her mother remained behind in Mount Kisco, bestowing upon her granddaughter the same inattention she had earlier afforded her own progeny. The Meyers did agree to pay for a full-time baby nurse, and Mary Bishop, described by Katharine as "a Scots lady of great warmth," joined the slowly expanding household staff. Mary remained with the Grahams as nurse and nanny through the birth of all four of their children.

After Pearl Harbor, Phil Graham, who had briefly worked as a lawyer for the Lend-Lease Administration and then the Office of Emergency Management, joined the U.S. Army Air Corps as a private. After basic training at a military post in South Dakota, he entered the Air Intelligence School in Harrisburg, Pennsylvania, to be trained in military intelligence. Again graduating high in his class, he received his commission and remained in Harrisburg to teach in the program, an advantageous situation, considering that he could send for his wife and infant daughter. Finally, in October 1944, having temporarily returned with his family to Washington, where he continued to work in army intelligence decoding secret Japanese messages (with the Office of Economic Warfare), Phil was shipped off to the Southwest Pacific to serve as a staff officer under General George C. Kenney. It was during this phase that he decided once the war ended to accept a long-standing offer from his father-in-law to join him at the helm of *The Washington Post.*

Chalmers M. Roberts, a star political reporter and editor at the *Post*, regarded Phil's presence at the paper as "a natural progression, considering that Eugene Meyer hailed from a generation that believed businesses were meant to be run by men. He had four daughters and one son, Eugene III ("Bill"), and the son turned out to be a psychiatrist—he was not interested in the newspaper business. So Meyer had to pick up a son-in-law, and when Kay married Phil Graham, he was the ideal solution to the problem, from her father's standpoint. And also from Phil's, since it guaranteed him immediate access to a position of power and influence.

"I don't know that Phil necessarily represented the ideal choice. He'd been trained as a lawyer and still harbored dreams of one day entering politics. But Meyer was determined to keep the paper within the family circle. I imagine he envisioned Kay as playing an essential role in the paper's future but always as a subordinate to her husband. She at least had some newspaper experience, and he had none. Toward the end of the war when she was pregnant with her second child, Donald, and Phil was away in the Pacific, she worked in the circulation department. Just a little something to keep her hand in the till. And from 1947 to 1953, she wrote a weekly column for the paper called "The Magazine Rack," reviewing and highlighting the best and worst articles she could find in the plethora of weekly and monthly magazines that could either be had by subscription or purchased at the newsstand. But once Phil stepped in, she remained in the background and concentrated on raising her children. Although she did some fund-raising and belonged to several boards, her main interest, perhaps her only interest in those years, was Phil Graham."

Phil started at the *Post* as associate editor on January 2, 1946. "I had a feeling," said Eugene Meyer in an oral history he conducted for Columbia University, "that he would have been on the paper three years earlier if it hadn't been for the service." Commenting in the same document on the current status of the paper, Meyer pointed out that "a lot of things had to be done . . . which couldn't be done during the war because of the scarcity of manpower. . . . A lot of our own people had gone into the service. The men that you would like to get of the age group that we wanted to strengthen the organization were all in the service as well."

Despite the wartime manpower shortage, the *Post* for the first time since Meyer acquired it in 1933 began to operate in the black, showing a net profit for the years 1942 to 1945 of just under $250,000. In May 1946, President Truman asked Eugene Meyer, who had served four previous administrations in appointed government positions, to become the first chairman of the newly established World Bank. Phil Graham's apprenticeship came to an abrupt halt. After less than six months on the job, the boss's thirty-year-old son-in-law was about to become the boss. Undeterred by lack of newspaper experience—or modesty, for that matter—the *Post*'s new publisher stood to make far more in his present position than what he would have earned had he continued to work as a lawyer in the public sector. Phil's personal fortunes continued to soar when, in 1947, he and Kay moved into the R Street mansion Eugene Meyer had recently purchased for them and which, at great added expense, had been redecorated and refurbished. The large house necessitated an equally large staff. A part-time driver, a gardener, and a second maid were appended to the list of household employees. Not too much later the Grahams, on Phil's suggestion, acquired Glen Welby, a weekend retreat on 350 acres outside Marshall, Virginia. In 1950, the Washington Post Company, having recently purchased two radio and two television stations in Florida, moved its headquarters from E Street into a larger building on L. As an indication of his growing confidence in the *Post*'s chief executive, Eugene Meyer transferred five thousand shares of the paper's voting stock to the Grahams, the majority (3,500 shares) in Phil's name, the remainder in Kay's. Another, more substantial stock transfer took place in 1954, the year Meyer paid $8.5 million to purchase (and close down) the *Washington Times-Herald,* a conservative daily newspaper formerly run by the late Eleanor ("Cissy") Patterson and currently owned by her cousin, Colonel Robert R. McCormick, right-wing publisher of the *Chicago Tribune.* The elimination of a rival publication placed the *Post* on a solid footing and paved the way for a promising economic future. Phil Graham announced his intention to transform the family-owned paper (which for several years was called *The Washington Post and Times-Herald*) from a periodical that featured predominantly local news into an international vehicle that could compete favorably with *The New York Times.*

Reexamining that period, *Washington Post* editor Richard Harwood observed that "once Phil Graham became publisher, he quickly made a name for himself. Unlike his father-in-law, he gave the paper an identity, leading it squarely into the liberal political camp, making it an instrument of social change in the city of Washington as well as a voice in Democratic politics on a national level. During the McCarthy era he wrote editorials against 'witch-hunting' and 'the mad-dog mentality of McCarthyism,' which became key elements in the courageous campaign waged in the 1950s by the *Post* against anti-Communist hysteria. As a result of his stance, Phil developed a reputation as a gunslinger. If, in the decades after World War II, Georgetown emerged as the Cold War capital—the epicenter of the foreign policy, journalism, and Intelligence Agency establishments—then Phil Graham was its crown prince."

༒

POLLY WISNER FRITCHEY, wife of senior CIA official Frank Wisner, remembered the McCarthy era as "a defining moment in all our lives. Hardly a dinner party went by when McCarthy's name didn't pop up in conversation. Our collective exposure to McCarthy, our distaste for him, and our shared Second World War experiences were major factors in bringing together the individuals who, as a group, came to be known as the Georgetown set."

It was in the shadow of the Cold War that the Georgetown set came into being. Its first clubhouse was at 3327 P Street, the home of the Wisners, hosts of a weekly dinner party unofficially called the Sunday Night Supper Club. Original members of the group included the Wisners, the Grahams, the Bohlens, and the Joyces. "The Grahams were, of course, Phil and Kay Graham," said Polly Fritchey, "and the Bohlens were Avis and Charles ('Chip') Bohlen, United States ambassador to the Soviet Union in 1953 and, during the Kennedy administration, ambassador to France. Robert Joyce was the State Department liaison to the CIA, and Jane was his wife." The way the potluck suppers worked is that the host or hosts usually furnished a hot dish, while the others brought salads, side dishes, and desserts. The dinners took place on Sundays because that was servants' night off. The evenings proved so popular that the regulars soon started inviting their friends. Tracy and Janet Barnes, Richard and Annie Bissell, and Desmond FitzGerald, who had once been married to Democratic Party lioness Marietta Tree (a member of the historic Peabody family), were next to join. All of them, like most of the others, resided in Georgetown. And all—Barnes, Bissell, and FitzGerald—at one time or another worked for the CIA. Another, more occasional visitor was Allen Dulles, the sophisticated, mustachioed director of the CIA, whose brother, John Foster Dulles, served as secretary of state. Both men lived in Georgetown and often used Georgetown social gatherings as a means of harvesting information. Allen Dulles, although married and afflicted with an uncorrected clubfoot, had a well-deserved reputation as a womanizer. When he attended the Sunday night potlucks, it was often in the company of one or another of his many mistresses. And then there were the Frankfurters, the Achesons, the Restons, Bill Walton (an editor and painter), John and Margaret Walker, George Kennan, W. Averell Harriman, the John McCloys (he was assistant secretary of war and future chairman of Chase Bank), the Robert Lovetts (he was chief operating officer of the State Department), Tommy Thompson (another high-ranking State Department official), and the Alsop Brothers, Joe and Stewart, political journalists who eventually took over the Sunday night dinners and were instrumental in running them. Tom Braden, a former CIA operative and newspaper publisher from California, and his wife, Joan, came aboard a bit later, as did the columnist Joseph Kraft, a speechwriter for John F. Kennedy in the 1960 presidential campaign, and his wife, Polly, an accomplished artist. Others came and went according to the year and political climate. Isaiah Berlin, for instance, a Russian-born Intelligence officer with the British embassy in Washington during World War II, subsequently a professor of philosophy at Oxford, attended whenever he found himself back in the United States.

In their way the Sunday dinners were not unlike the suppers conducted at Hockley House during Phil Graham's residency there. They were loud, informal, combative affairs with an abundance of smoking, drinking, and shrieking about the role America should play as a postwar world power. Quite often the gatherings didn't break up until 3 or 4 A.M., and then only because everyone had to go to work Monday morning. "A predominant topic at every dinner had to do with the Russians," said Evan Thomas, Washington correspondent for *Newsweek*. " 'What should we do about the Soviets?' Another prevalent theme was McCarthy, the scourge of a Georgetown composed mainly of Democratic liberals, all of whom feared and loathed the senator from Wisconsin. In any case, the parties became so raucous and there was so much liquor that Joe Alsop renamed the event, calling it 'the Sunday Night Drunk.' At points the members of the group grew so weary of one another that they would suspend the dinner for several weeks. But then they would resume again, and the altercations would grow even louder."

"A typical 1950s Sunday Night dinner," said Sally Reston, "might include, in addition to the regulars, a Supreme Court justice, a couple of newspaper or magazine editors, several ambassadors, some senior think tank official, and a few Defense Department types. And they'd be all around the same table, breaking the same bread and speaking with great candor. Social life and politics were inextricable and indistinguishable at Georgetown dinners. We were liberal anti-Communists, intellectuals, precisely the class and breed that Joe McCarthy hated and whose careers he wanted to ruin. It was that same old battle: the Republican right versus the Democratic left.

"There was also the matter of the press, whose presence at these get-togethers was expected and welcomed. In those days, the meter wasn't running. In other words, nobody cared if a reporter formed an opinion based on a conversation he overheard at a dinner party and then pursued certain sources on his own. Nobody cared if somebody like my husband or Joe Alsop proffered theories on government goings-on in hopes of eliciting information from invited officials. But if you went beyond these entitlements, if you quoted actual comments made at these dinners, you were persona non grata. Nobody trusted Drew Pearson, for example, and nobody invited him to group dinners. Pearson wrote his 'Washington Merry-Go-Round' column from 1932 to 1969, but I don't remember ever seeing him at any of these functions. Which isn't to say that he wasn't close friends on an individual basis with at least several of us. He and his wife, Luvie, were quite social. Among others, they often dined with Phil and Kay Graham, because they ran Drew's column in their paper. Luvie

Pearson had a sense of humor. She'd don a pair of roller skates to walk her dogs, and the dogs would pull her along, sometimes at a rather rapid clip. But you had to watch yourself around Drew. The term 'off-the-record' meant nothing to him. 'It's off-the-record,' he'd say, 'unless it's a newsworthy story.' "

Frank George Wisner, a former ambassador and the eldest son of Frank Wisner and Polly Wisner Fritchey, came of age in the late 1940s. "One notable feature about Washington at that time," he said, "is that there wasn't anything to do. There was virtually no theater, there was no Kennedy Center. We did have the National Theater, which picked up occasional road shows here and there. But that was about it. We had a second-rate baseball and football team. There were no restaurants to speak of, very few hotels, the Mayflower being one. No nightclubs. There was Laura Gross's 1925 F Street Club for benefits or receptions, but it was impersonal and much too public. There were a couple of riverside eateries. I recall a place called the Rawbean and a lobster joint on some pier in the river, but there were no real places to go. People sometimes met at Morgan's Pharmacy on P Street, which had a marble-topped soda fountain, or at Scheele's, a small market with a large food inventory, or even at Stambuck's, a saddle shop. Dog owners, of which there were many in Georgetown, walked their canines either in Montrose Park or Rock Creek Park, depending on where they lived. But essentially, for dinner and conversation, you moved around from house to house. The dinner table became the place of social intercourse, and the old cave dweller families, whose prominence had mostly to do with birthright, were replaced with a social hierarchy more closely tied to real accomplishment and proximity to power.

"But if your primary form of extracurricular entertainment and intellectual exchange and the way you enrich your mind and stay current transpired around the dinner table, then Georgetown dinners became extraordinarily important events. They were not just trifling social affairs. They became the very lifeblood of the way the government thought, fought, worked, compared notes, made up its mind, and reached consensus. All these people—journalists, CIA operatives, State Department officials, diplomats—were seated around a table making policy recommendations that more often than not got implemented. Georgetown became a code name in Washington. It was at the center of things. Truman, Eisenhower, Kennedy, and Johnson would regularly ask: 'What does Georgetown think?' And Georgetown's women were the glue that held it all together. It was the women who set the pace, and decided who was acceptable and who wasn't, who was amusing and who wasn't, who sat next to whom, who could make the evening sizzle and who got excluded."

The Sunday Night Supper Club represented only one component of the increasingly complex sociopolitical substructure that pervaded the nation's capital. Lunches, brunches, dinners, cocktail parties, and receptions were a logical extension of normal working hours and took place every day of the week. Such had long been Washington's way. Dolley Madison had mastered the art of parlor politics and made the White House an entertainment and cultural center—always seating men and women alternately at the dinner table, separating husbands from their wives—long before Jacqueline Kennedy came along. Henry James dubbed Washington "the city of conversation," referring to the social circle he encountered in the late 1870s at 1607 H Street, across Lafayette Park from the White House, while visiting Henry Adams and his wife, Clover, the "it" couple of their day.

Another seminal social figure, Alice Roosevelt Longworth, the eldest daughter of Theodore Roosevelt and the wife of Nicholas Longworth, speaker of the house from 1925 to 1931, gave parties at her Massachusetts Avenue town house (off Dupont Circle) to which only the crème de la crème were invited. Extraordinarily insightful, incredibly funny, and very mean, Princess Alice, as she was known, was eminently quotable. When she lacerated another human being, which she did with great frequency, that person remained fixed in one's mind exactly as she had described them. She detested her cousins Eleanor and Franklin Roosevelt, both politically and personally. At her parties, she often performed merciless burlesques of Eleanor and aped Franklin's sometimes tiresome public speeches. James Roosevelt Jr., a grandson of Franklin and Eleanor, labeled Alice "a grande dame with a grand salon." She didn't invite people to her house simply because she liked them but because she found them interesting, and she found them interesting partly because they were intelligent and partly because they were powerful.

Alice's acid tongue and love of the put-down ("If you don't have something nice to say about somebody, come sit next to me") were legendary. George Plimpton visited her home only once. "Alice owned a Victorian dollhouse," he said, "which I remember with great distinction. It must have been five feet high, every room and stick of furniture designed perfectly to scale. There were Persian rugs, chandeliers, mirrors, candelabras. The dollhouse was in better condition than her home, which seemed to be rather raggedy. She had a lion's skin mounted against a wall, and half of it had come undone and it hung there like a bat in a barn. Anyway, in the course of the evening, I accidentally bumped up against her dollhouse and knocked something over, a miniature table or chair. Alice became enormously exercised. 'You moron,' she screeched. 'Watch what you're doing!' Her anger far exceeded any actual damage I'd done, since I'd done none."

Above all, Alice disliked the competition, particularly Perle Mesta ("the hostess with the mostess") and Gwen Cafritz, two of the leading social arbiters of Cold War Washington. Mesta, a smallish but very vocal Oklahoman who settled in the District of Columbia following the death of her multimillionaire husband, had become a major supporter of Harry Truman. Truman reciprocated by pounding the piano keys and belting out songs at her parties. But what truly rankled Alice was Truman's appointment of the lady, in 1949, to the post of American minister to the Grand Duchy of Luxembourg. "The only benefit to Old Perle's new position," sniffed Longworth, "is that she's no longer in Washington."

No Washington hostess, however, including Mesta, was held in greater contempt by Alice than Gwendolyn Detre de Surary Cafritz, the wife of Morris Cafritz, an unassuming but inordinately prosperous real estate developer. Born in Budapest, Hungary, Gwen Cafritz lived out her social fantasies not in Georgetown—an area her husband deemed "inhospitable to Jews"—but on a sprawling Foxhall Road estate, not far from the home occupied by Perle Mesta after she returned from Luxembourg in 1953. Championed early in her career by newspaper publisher and power hostess Cissy Patterson, Mrs. Cafritz rapidly ascended the Washington social ladder. "I started out entertaining little attachés," said Gwen, "and worked my way up to the Supreme Court." Although Alice actually attended several Cafritz extravaganzas, she regarded Gwendolyn as nothing more than a social climber, an arriviste. "The only published work I ever glimpsed in Mrs. Cafritz's library was a copy of the Washington *Green Book*," remarked Alice. "Other than that, the shelves were as barren as her mind."

Alice's barbed comments paled before the disparaging remarks uttered by the two ladies themselves. Cafritz and Mesta regularly insulted each other in the press. The only hostess whose parties they attended at the same time were those of Marjorie Merriweather Post, the decadently wealthy cereal heiress whose Washington estate, Hillwood, featured an intricate maze of Japanese gardens, gold dinner settings for a hundred, Russian Imperial porcelain and crystal, an army of liveried servants (two per dinner guest), museum-quality Russian art, and eighteenth-century French antique collections, and the spacious Pavilion Room where Marjorie showed first-run movies and held postdinner square dances (women were issued rubber tips to place over their heels). Among her other prized possessions: Mar-A-Lago, a Palm Beach mansion that ranked among the most expensive private residences in the country, and the *Sea Cloud*, one of the world's most elegant yachts. Her outrageous lifestyle encompassed five other mansions spread indiscriminately across the United States and a stable of deposed or deceased husbands, including investment banker E. F. Hutton and Joseph E. Davies, ambassador to the Soviet Union from 1936 to 1938. There were those, such as the widow of Woodrow Wilson, who accused her of being nothing but a manhunter.

Marjorie's natural taste for luxury failed to impress Washington's old guard, though rival hostesses Perle Mesta and Gwen Cafritz turned up at Hillwood whenever invited. Ernest Lowy, an eighteenth-century French antiques dealer from New York who often visited Marjorie in Washington, recalled a Hillwood dinner party followed by a formal dance at which "Perle and Gwen practically fox-trotted with one another." Lowy further acknowledged that the "bluebloods and the cave dwellers couldn't stomach Marjorie's lavish ways. There were stories, for example, that she had an annual fashion budget in excess of $300,000, which is probably an exaggeration but not too far off. She had no compunction about spending money, but didn't spend it in direct proportion to her true wealth. The Georgetown crowd considered her an idle curiosity. They occasionally attended her parties but almost never invited her to theirs."

CHAPTER THREE

THE P AND Q STREET AXIS

MIMI CROCKER, a Washington socialite, described the tranquil atmosphere to be found in Georgetown in the mid-1950s. "It was a strolling time," she said. "People were on the street a great deal and they were extremely friendly. Felix Frankfurter and Dean Acheson, who had started as Louis Brandeis's law clerk, met for breakfast every morning and then they would walk to work together, crossing the Montgomery Meigs Memorial Bridge into Washington. You couldn't miss them because Acheson towered over Frankfurter—they looked like Mutt and Jeff, each carrying a bulky briefcase and the morning newspaper. You would see all sorts of important people on the streets of Georgetown: Paul Mellon, Herman Wouk, Robert Taft. Doors were left open, or at the very least unlocked. We didn't have security concerns in those days. You could park your car on the street in the evening—provided you were lucky enough to find a space—and it would still be there the next day. The congenial social environment of Georgetown belied the hostile political climate of Washington proper. Everything seemed very placid. There were parties almost every day. You got to know everybody, and everybody got to know you."

In this seemingly placid setting, the female members of the Sunday Night Supper Club undertook a new venture, forming a subgroup called the Cooking Class, which met for more than a year at 2706 Olive Street,

41

the Georgetown home of a rising young culinary expert named Julia Child. An OSS agent during World War II, Child stood a gangly six feet two inches and spoke in the halting high-pitched nasal voice that became so familiar to her legions of television fans. Attendees of the class included Kay Graham, Polly Wisner, Margaret Walker, Avis Bohlen, Janet Barnes, and Annie Bissell. The women gathered every Monday afternoon to prepare a sumptuous meal, usually based on one of Julia Child's latest creations, such as her twenty-eight-page pheasant recipe, and frequently they would invite their husbands over in the evening to sample the results. The one ground rule, according to Alsop family biographer Robert Merry, was that "the men couldn't belittle their wives' efforts or criticize the food." Frank Wisner was permanently banished from the festivities when he complained that a certain dish—a chicken filled with juniper berries—tasted dry because it hadn't been properly basted. Chip Bohlen came close to getting the boot. His baggy suits, stained ties, and cigarette habit (he chain-smoked Camels, even over dinner) didn't exactly endear him to Julia Child. She allowed him to stay but only after he promised to abstain from smoking, at least until dessert and coffee were served.

The sole bachelor at the food samplings was Joseph Wright Alsop, the older brother of Stewart Alsop, whose British-born wife Patricia ("Tish") had recently joined the class. A central figure in the formation of the Georgetown set, Joe Alsop, member of an old Connecticut Yankee clan, arrived in Washington in 1935 with a degree from Harvard and a reporter's job with the *New York Herald Tribune*. Two years later, at the age of twenty-seven, he and fellow journalist Robert Kintner began writing a nationally syndicated political column for the *Herald Tribune*. The column proved popular; so, too, did Joe Alsop. Related on his mother's side of the family to Franklin and Eleanor Roosevelt—he was the son of Teddy Roosevelt's niece Connie Robinson—Alsop soon received an invitation to attend a New Year's Eve party at the White House. His cousin Alice Roosevelt Longworth, with whom he shared a wonderfully observant view of the world, took him under her wing and introduced him to her many friends and admirers. Other Washington hostesses of note followed suit. For his part, Joe Alsop seemed to prefer the select group of public servants who had come to Washington to serve as FDR's Brain Trust. Many of these men—Tommy Corcoran, Harry Hopkins, Ben Cohen, and William O. Douglas, to name a few—had procured inexpensive housing in Georgetown, still very much a black community dotted with pockets of great poverty. In that regard, the Brain Trust represented the first wave to arrive in Georgetown during its gentrification process, its transformation from "a black ghetto," as Washington society referred to it, into the city's most historic district. Felix Frankfurter and the New Dealers who appeared during the 1930s (and into the early 1940s) represented the second wave. And those couples, like Phil and Kay Graham, who bought Georgetown property after World War II, represented the third (and largest) wave. Joe Alsop's career spanned all three waves and continued to flourish well into the dire years of the Vietnam War.

In 1940, with the Nazis about to overrun France, Alsop published his first book, *American White Papers*, detailing the difficulties encountered by Franklin Roosevelt in rousing prointernationalist sentiment in a nation severely oppressed by the isolationist opponents of America's intervention in the war. During the war, while Stewart Alsop joined the famed Jedburgh division of the OSS, Joe languished for nine months as a prisoner of war in Hong Kong and, after his release, was posted to the lend-lease mission in China, where he became acquainted with Chiang Kai-shek. By early 1946, Joe and Stewart Alsop were back in Washington, collaborating on their own twice-weekly column for the *Herald Tribune* syndicate and penning longer opinion pieces for the *Saturday Evening Post*. Outspoken critics of the Red-baiting tactics of Senators Joe McCarthy and Pat McCaran as well as other congressional inquisitors, the brothers nevertheless supported the Cold War doctrine that cast the Soviet Union in the role of public enemy number one. Exponents of a policy calling for the aggressive containment of communism, their frame of reference encompassed six American statesmen who emerged in 1945 with one common goal: to bring order to postwar chaos, and to help limit Soviet expansionism by any means possible.

The half-dozen officials—Averell Harriman, Dean Acheson, Robert Lovett, John McCloy, George Kennan, and Chip Bohlen—were the original "best and brightest," men whose breeding and training enabled them to band together and create a game plan that would shape the course their country would pursue for years to come. Joe Alsop called this group "the WASP Ascendancy;" his brother termed it "the WASP Conspiracy." "They were responsible," said Robert Merry, "for bringing America out of World War II and into the world, as it were, formulating relationships with various countries in Europe as well as, in a negative sense, the Soviet Union. The Marshall Plan was an idea that originated with the group. Alsop considered himself an adjunct and follower of the group. He identified with them. His views, expressed both in writing and verbally, reflected their views. He was their leading chronicler. He supported the Vietnam War because they supported it. After traveling to Vietnam in 1961 as a member of a fact-finding commission formed by President Kennedy, Alsop became an outspoken advocate of U.S. commitment of troops there, a position he maintained to the bitter end."

✑

JOE ALSOP HAD KNOWN Kay Graham since 1935, the same year he arrived in Washington. In *Personal History,* Graham describes a coming-out party given for her that year by her parents, to which Agnes Meyer suggested inviting the brilliant, young reporter for the *Herald Tribune,* whom she had recently had the good fortune to meet. Impressed by his credentials, Kay arranged for him to be seated next to her, only to find the combination of his physique—five feet, seven inches, 250 pounds—and erudition overwhelming. "I was appalled by his appearance and unable to cope with his mature mind and presence," she wrote. "Later, we became lifelong, devoted friends, but this was an odd and inauspicious beginning." It no doubt helped that along the way, Alsop managed to shed nearly a hundred pounds—and this, despite his participation in the caloric eating sessions of the Cooking Class.

"The one subject you could not talk about with Joe Alsop," said Joan Braden, "was homosexuality. He was gay, and like so many gay men of his generation, he never came out of the closet. There was a great stigma attached to being gay, especially in a one-company town like Washington. I know his brother Stew realized the situation and so did Isaiah Berlin, be-

cause Joe admitted it to him. But I'm convinced that his own family didn't
know. Stew's five children were in the dark about their uncle. For a long
time Stew's wife, Tish Alsop, suspected nothing. It's just something that
didn't come up in conversation with him."

Although he never discussed his sexual proclivities, a number of people seem to have been aware of Joe Alsop's preference for men. Robert
Devaney, editor in chief of *The Georgetowner*, had a friend, Everson
Duncan, now dead, who once encountered Alsop at a Georgetown dinner party. "Joe did his utmost to convince Everson to return to his house
that night, despite the fact that Everson had his wife with him," said Devaney. "It didn't seem to bother Alsop that Everson was evidently as
straight as an arrow. They would simply drop off Mrs. Duncan by cab and
then continue on to Alsop's place. That, in a nutshell, was Alsop's modus
operandi. It's called persistence. Of course, Everson declined."

Wearing his tortoiseshell eyeglasses and a fake beard, Joe Alsop frequently cruised a section of Georgetown called the P Street Beach, not
far from the local tennis courts, a stretch of several blocks frequented by
male prostitutes. Or he would try to meet men at the gay bars and
pornography shops spread along Fourteenth Street, within striking distance of the White House. In 1952 he was arrested by the San Francisco
police for frequenting a park well known as a hangout for gays and drug
dealers. Stewart Alsop used the full power of his influence to have the
case dismissed.

There were occasional longer lasting relationships. In the early 1940s
he met a sailor, Frank Merlo, with whom he remained on close terms
until 1947, when Merlo became involved with playwright Tennessee
Williams, who nicknamed him "The Little Horse." For a time, he was
also somewhat serious about a young lady, Lily Emmett, a British painter
living in New York. But almost always his romantic attachments were
furtive and short-lived, exemplified by a fling he had with an unemployed
male actor while visiting West Germany in 1954. Because a German official had introduced Alsop to the impecunious thespian, the brief entan-
glement eventually came to the attention of J. Edgar Hoover, who made
note of it in his voluminous personal files. Although Hoover himself did
nothing further with the information, he apparently leaked it to Joseph

McCarthy, who hinted at Joe's homosexuality in an irate letter he fired off to the *Saturday Evening Post* in response to an anti-HUAC (House Un-American Activities Committee) article by Alsop.

J. Edgar Hoover and the FBI were soon apprised of another Alsop escapade. In 1957, while on a trip to the Soviet Union, he propositioned a young Russian Army officer. Their rendezvous, which took place in a Moscow hotel room, was secretly photographed by the KGB. Several days later, two KGB agents approached Alsop bearing copies of the sexually explicit snapshots. Unless Joe agreed to provide the KGB with inside information on certain high-ranking U.S. government officials, the photographs would be released to members of the American press. Alsop's career would be obliterated. Bewildered and embarrassed, he made an appointment with his friend Chip Bohlen, the American ambassador to the Soviet Union. On hearing the story, Bohlen urged Alsop to leave Russia at once and to cooperate with U.S. Intelligence investigators, who would want to interrogate him upon his return to Washington. Alsop did as told. Once the CIA finished debriefing him, a detailed report went to J. Edgar Hoover and the FBI for possible follow-up, a rare (if minor) example of information being shared between these two major Washington agencies.

The only other person from whom Alsop sought advice regarding the Russian scandal was Frank Wisner, who over the years had helped recruit a number of friends into the folds of the CIA. Wisner, too, his devotion to the anti-Communist cause notwithstanding, had long been a target of Hoover and McCarthy-initiated barbs, most notably the disclosure by the latter that in 1951—his first year as head of covert operations for the CIA—he had sponsored the immigration into the United States of an accused former Nazi war criminal. What McCarthy failed to acknowledge was that the purported war criminal possessed extensive firsthand knowledge of the inner workings of the Soviet military establishment, information that proved invaluable to the Cold War needs of the Agency. In addition, McCarthy and Hoover somehow learned that in 1945, while still in the OSS, Wisner had become involved in an extramarital affair with Princess Caraja of Romania, a romantic figure whose ties to the Eastern bloc countries lent credence to Hoover's false claim that she was a Communist sympathizer and spy. Hoover's public disclosure of the assignation nearly ended Frank Wisner's marriage to Polly. Based on these experiences, Wisner cautioned Alsop to confer with the CIA but to steer clear of the FBI.

Despite the guidance provided by Chip Bohlen and Frank Wisner, Joe Alsop's problems continued to mount. Washington political columnist Charles Bartlett received an envelope in the mail one day containing a collection of photographs of Alsop engaged in a sexual encounter with another man—the photos taken by KGB agents during Alsop's ill-fated trip to Moscow. Bartlett, who also lived in Georgetown and knew Alsop, telephoned a friend, Cord Meyer Jr., a CIA official often involved in covert operations, to determine what action to take. After conferring with several of his associates in the Agency, Meyer prodded Bartlett to mail the snapshots directly to Alsop. This Bartlett did, and there the matter rested until it became clear, some months later, that copies of the candid black-and-whites had been sent by the KGB to a number of newsmen in the area, among them such unlikely choices as humorist Art Buchwald and Herb Block ("Herblock"), the popular political cartoonist for *The Washington Post*. Like Alsop, Buchwald and Herblock both lived in Georgetown.

On the surface an often prissy and obdurate soul, Joe Alsop was also a man of great sensitivity and tenderness. In October 1964, Walter Jenkens, a family man and White House aide to Lyndon Johnson, was arrested for performing oral sex on another man in the basement pay toilet of a Washington Y.M.C.A. Forced to resign, Jenkens received scant public or private support. Placing his own reputation on the line, Joe Alsop published a commentary on the scandal in support of Jenkens and wrote him privately in terms that were both understanding and moving. Jenkens, who had never met Alsop, told intimates that Joe's letter had helped sustain him; it had been instrumental in encouraging him to go on.

"Whatever Joe's sexual leanings," said Evangeline Bruce, "he never allowed them to interfere with his friendships." Indeed, his friendship with CIA operative Tracy Barnes's wife, Janet—"one of the great ladies of Georgetown," attested Elizabeth Winthrop, a children's book author and daughter of Stewart Alsop—resulted in Joe's joining the Dancing Class, a Washington tradition since 1910 that many Washingtonians dismissed as "snobbish" and "elitist." Entrance requirements for the once-a-month formal dance sessions were extremely rigid. Alben Barkley, vice president during the Truman administration, and his young bride, Jane, were barred from joining the group. Actress Gertrude Lawrence and her producer husband, Richard Aldrich, were likewise turned away. Yet Janet Barnes, a member of the Dancing Class's executive board, managed to usher in not only Joe Alsop but also Phil and Kay Graham. By her own admission, Kay had wanted to join mainly because her mother had been denied membership. Given what she once referred to as "the mundane drudgery" of homemaking and child rearing, Kay cherished the glamour and elegance associated with the Dancing Class and the idea of donning a floor-length evening gown and mingling, even fox-trotting, with some of the capital's oldest bloodlines. Joe Alsop appreciated the organization for much the same reason and soon became friends with Meyer Davis, whose orchestra had played at nearly every party since World War I. Even Phil Graham, not necessarily one who liked to dress up, found something appealing about the elegant veneer of the Dancing Class.

In the early 1950s, Alsop designed and built his own home on the 2700 block of Dumbarton Avenue in Georgetown, the same street where he had first rented after arriving in Washington in 1935. Predominantly occupied by blacks at that time, the immediate neighborhood included an undertaker, a brothel, a Baptist church, a Catholic church, and the abandoned mistress of Senator Reed Smoot of Utah, chairman, during Herbert Hoover's administration, of the Senate Finance Committee.

Although not yet the glossy fortress of the rich it would soon become, Georgetown in 1952 was nevertheless the place to live. As such, Joe Alsop's newly constructed abode, a wacky hodgepodge of building styles, proved nearly as controversial as his sexual orientation. For more than a year he argued about the design plans for his house with the Georgetown Citizens Association, of which Phil Graham was a member, as well as with the Fine Arts Commission, which also had a say in the matter. Sally Reston described the exterior of the finished product as "something you'd expect to find in Sioux City, Iowa, rather than in the privileged, homogenized outreaches of Georgetown. It looked like a midwestern motel, completely out of synch with the traditional Federalist and Victorian architecture so much in evidence in Georgetown. David E. Finley, who lived in Georgetown and helped get the legislation passed that became known as the Old Georgetown Act of 1950, groaned whenever he passed the place. The interior of the house, on the other hand, was a flag of a different color. It exuded charm. It had a warm and homey quality with lots of plants, books, tapestries, paintings, and artifacts that Joe had acquired during his trips abroad and to the Far East. He was truly a bon vivant. The food at his parties tasted great and he had a profound knowledge of wines. He knew how to create a wonderful setting, the perfect mise-en-scène."

Joe Alsop's residence also had the advantage of being within walking distance of Dumbarton Oaks, the majestic Georgetown estate that gained prominence as the first meetinghouse of what would later emerge as the United Nations in New York. Because it currently belonged to Harvard, his alma mater, Joe had been granted use of the Dumbarton Oaks swimming pool. "Most of those invited to swim there were diplomats," he wrote in *I've Seen the Best of It*, his posthumously published autobiography. "The guests would cluster around the pool, talking what I can only call light 'cambric tea' politics." Alsop had little patience for prattle. When his cousin Dottie Robinson moved to Washington with her husband, Randolph Kidder, a foreign service officer, he invited them to one of his dinner parties, which by the mid-1950s had expanded well beyond the Sunday night format and now took place at least three times a week, in addition to smaller, more frequent luncheons. "Randolph yattered on and on," recalled Sally Reston, a guest at the same gathering. "After they left, Joe swore that as much as he loved his cousin, he would never again invite her husband to his house for dinner. He simply could not tolerate boring people."

"The bore factor," as Alsop called it, played a more vital role in Washington than it did anyplace else. "It's important in Washington," he wrote, "because most dinner guests here wish to see men in high office, and men in high office have a tendency to retain their wives, often very boring, whom they married when they had no office at all." Alsop further expounded on his theory by stipulating that he "counted as half a bore a very dull but powerful man or a very stupid but pretty woman. The mindless rich, if very rich, also count as half bores."

Margot Hahn, a generation younger than Alsop, remarked that she and her husband, Gil, "went to dinner at Joe's quite a lot. It was scary as hell. You had to have memorized that morning's *New York Times,* because Joe imposed this ghastly ritual on his guests whereby he asked 'the question of the day,' usually concerning some recent political event, and he'd go around the table and everybody had to say something about it. And you had to be fast and terse and clever, or extremely funny. You had to offer something memorable. It was very nervous making. You were there with all of these pundits, anyway, and you were probably there because you were young and attractive and a woman. But they still expected you to say something smart-assed, and it was hard. Joe would say, 'Margot, darling, beautiful Mrs. Hahn, what do you have to add to tonight's discussion?' He could be absolutely adorable or a true monster—you never knew which one you were going to get.

"But there were also positive aspects to these gatherings. They were all very heady and chic. You felt you were living at the top of the world, breaking bread with the most powerful people on earth. My husband and I befriended all those leading CIA officials who were so involved in the Georgetown dinner scene. In those days—the 1950s and 1960s—the Agency was an old boys' network. They all had gone to Groton, with Joe and Stewart Alsop, and then on to Harvard, Yale, or Princeton. And then there were always a number of VIP politicians at the dinners. It's easier to get a line on the character of a person in power by seeing him or her informally at a dinner table. It's also easier to build a sense of trust if you meet somebody on a congenial basis, which in turn lays a foundation for future dealings with that person. So there were several benefits to being part of the Georgetown set, especially if you were either in the media or held public office. Even that strange business of having the men and women separate after dinner didn't seem so bad at the time. It does in retrospect, but it didn't then."

There were those who appeared to be far less prepared for the heightened atmosphere of Joe Alsop's social events. Nora Cameron, an aide to Senator John Sherman Cooper before becoming a reporter for *The Washington Post,* depicted a scene in which her husband, Juan Cameron, attended a party at Joe Alsop's house and, much to his chagrin, found himself in the middle of a major fracas—a pushing match had broken out between the host and one of his guests, "and the two men were soon rolling around on the floor, kicking and flailing." The apparent cause of the fight was the guest's charge that both Joe and Stewart Alsop, being friends with so many CIA operatives, had more and more come to reflect the CIA's viewpoint on political affairs in their newspaper columns.

Although fisticuffs were not the norm, abrasive verbal exchanges were commonplace. Henry Kissinger, having befriended Joe Alsop in the mid-1960s, marveled at the journalist's "ability to bring together interesting and powerful people with divergent political views and agendas. His dinner table was a place where ideas were tested and debated, often in a rather hostile manner. Joe frequently argued with his guests, but no matter what he said about or to them, they almost always came back for more."

Within the context of Joe McCarthy's heyday, Kay Graham (in *Personal History)* describes an era when "friends fell out with each other" and "rows erupted on every side." Nowhere was this more apparent than at Joe Alsop's luncheons and dinner parties. Of the numerous examples provided by Kay Graham, two seem particularly apropos. In late March 1952 Alsop invited several associates, including Phil Graham and Isaiah Berlin, to an intimate luncheon, the kind at which the "difficult" questions of the day were asked and answered on a more regular basis than at larger and less personal dinner parties. When the subject of Joe McCarthy came up, as it invariably did at every Alsop gathering, Berlin took the opportunity to denounce the senator as "nothing, if not a virulent anti-Semite." Although Phil Graham considered McCarthy's methods the work of an incipient fascist dictator, he did not agree with Berlin's characterization of the man. To buttress his position, Graham cited the close connection that existed between McCarthy and Roy Cohn, the young and brash Jewish lawyer from New York who had been named chief counsel to McCarthy's investigations committee. When Alsop took Berlin's side in the discussion, tempers flared until Phil eventually threw his linen napkin on the table and stomped out of the house. A week later he sent both men the same letter of apology, ending it with an almost flip observation: "I am an occasional sufferer from . . . a tendency to get one's mouth in high [gear] before one's brain turns over."

More offended by the note than mollified, Berlin presently wrote to Alsop: "As usual, Phil misses the point. It's not what he said, but rather what he did. He may even have been correct concerning McCarthy, but he was wrong to have simply walked out."

Hostilities were renewed the following year at an Alsop dinner party when Phil and Joe again wrangled, this time over the issue of the Fifth Amendment, specifically the question of invoking the Fifth at a trial or hearing to avoid having to testify. Again Phil Graham walked out, but on this occasion only after Alsop asked him to leave. Now it was Joe's turn to apologize. "As nearly as I can disentangle our discussion," he wrote to Graham, "you may perhaps have thought I was teasing you because you are now a successful man. Well, in a minor way, I suppose I am too."

Commenting on Joe's letter to her husband, Kay Graham noted that Alsop "obviously touched on a more sensitive nerve than any of us understood at the time." It was, according to Kay, Phil's insecurity over the origins of his success, the supposition that he had earned it by way of marriage as opposed to merit, which came out so viciously in the illness that later caused him to commit suicide.

∽

THE INTERRELATIONSHIP between Georgetown society and the Intelligence community manifested itself in several different ways and for several different reasons. E. J. Applewhite, one of eight Yale graduates from the class of 1941 to sign on with the CIA, settled in Georgetown during the same period as many of the other CIA officials who subsequently joined the Sunday Night Supper Club. "After World War II," said Applewhite, "at the time of the Marshall Plan and the resistance to communism in Europe, a lot of ambitious, attractive people who might otherwise have gone to Wall Street or some major New York law firm came to Washington to become part of this new organization, the CIA, because they thought they could make a difference in the world. At the beginning the Agency established several temporary installations in and about Washington, including one at Foggy Bottom, within walking distance of Georgetown. Georgetown was one of the few places in Washington where you could still procure desirable housing in those years. Generally speaking, it was easier to find a bride than a rental property. But if you were in the Agency or the Company, as it was sometimes called, the place to live after the war was 2500 Q Street, a large Georgetown house subdivided into separate units. New agents with wives and kids who wanted to live near 2500 Q bought or rented houses up and down the same thoroughfare. Q Street in Georgetown became synonymous with the CIA. By happenstance, many of the journalists of the day had homes on nearby P Street. The proximity of the two, and the social connections that then linked the CIA to the world of Washington journalists, gave rise to a code name: the P and Q Street Axis."

Philip Graham, through his hiring practices at *The Washington Post*, gave further resonance and meaning to the so-called P and Q Street Axis. Influenced by his World War II service in Army Intelligence as well as his friendships with Frank Wisner, Dick Bissell, and other CIA officials, Phil went to unprecedented lengths to employ former members of the Intelligence community to fill new staff positions at the newspaper. Alfred Friendly Jr., managing editor at the *Post*, attended Army Intelligence School; James Truitt, a personal assistant to Graham, had been a longtime CIA informant; editorial page editor (James) Russell Wiggins worked in Army Intelligence during the war; Phil Geyelin, also an editorial page editor, had been a CIA agent; John Hayes, head of the Post Company's broadcasting division, spent the war with the Armed Forces Radio Network, a division of the OSS; senior editor Alan Barth served with the Office of War Information, a section of Army Intelligence; Stewart Alsop, a contributor to the paper, had served with the OSS. The list went on. The *Post* masthead was filled from top to bottom with the names of editors and reporters who had spent time, either during the war or afterward, working in some facet of intelligence gathering. Moreover, almost all the new staff members lived in Georgetown, many on P Street. The CIA regularly tapped senior reporters and editors at the *Post* for confidential information, and in turn routinely supplied the paper with classified material they wanted to see in print. During Phil Graham's tenure, *The Washington Post* developed a reputation as a publication that frequently ran items and stories leaked to them by the Agency, often full of dis- and misinformation. The word within the inner sanctum of the CIA was that Phil Graham could always be counted on to accommodate their needs, but that in return he expected to be compensated with newsworthy leads and leaks.

Russ Wiggins confirmed Phil Graham's preference for employing former Intelligence agency personnel at the *Post.* "One of the essential functions of the CIA operative is intelligence gathering," said Wiggins. "An effective political journalist performs basically the same task, though for a different purpose. But there are certain overlaps—journalists, like CIA agents, need to know how to get hold of certain documents, how to convince people to talk, how to develop tips and informants. The Fourth Estate and the Agency were natural allies. The heads of the CIA and Phil Graham had something else in common: both wanted to reshape the world, a sort of game that had proved popular among the British aristocracy in the days of the Empire. The *Post*'s alliance with the Agency continued long after 1962, when they moved their headquarters to Langley. It didn't change much even after Kay Graham took over the newspaper. What changed was the composition of the CIA, as did the way they conducted business."

By the early 1950s Georgetown had become a major CIA listening post. It made good sense. Georgetown, by virtue of those who lived and socialized in the tiny kingdom, had become as much a seat of power as the White House, only far more accessible. "Georgetown was crawling with spooks," declared historian Dick McLellan, whose wife, Diana, wrote the "Ear" column for several Washington newspapers, including the *Post.* "They were everywhere, under every rock. You couldn't attend a Georgetown function during that era without finding yourself seated next to a spook, usually some Ivy League type in an imported three-piece suit, sipping a martini and discussing the necessity of overthrowing some inconvenient Third World banana republic."

Eloise R. Page, one-time personal assistant to "Wild Bill" Donovan and later an operative for the CIA, belonged to Georgetown's Christ Church and recalled that "half the congregation worked for the CIA. The other half were employed by either *The Washington Post* or the *Washington Star.* The Agency's presence in Georgetown never flagged. Cord Meyer moved to Georgetown in 1964. CIA directors Richard Helms and William Colby lived there as well, to say nothing of all those agents who had lived there since the late 1940s."

The CIA wasn't the only intelligence-gathering unit to be found in Georgetown. Gordon Thomas, a specialist in the field, observed that many foreign powers with intelligence agents in the United States "made a point of sending their operatives to Georgetown parties. Agents for MI6 and the Mossad, for example, were frequent guests at the dinners of Phil and Kay Graham, where they would pick up bits and pieces of gossip as well as exposure to leading American politicians. Agents for the Mossad, often in the guise of Israeli diplomats, adhered religiously to one cardinal rule: no drinking on the job." John White, a reporter for the *Washington Times-Herald,* noted that you could always tell the Mossad agents, "because they were the only ones at the party still on their feet by the end of the evening."

J. Edgar Hoover, spurred on by his determination "to keep tabs" on everyone, including the Georgetown crowd, set in motion a private project he informally called "Operation G-town," whereby he registered a number of FBI agents with an exclusive domestic employment agency to serve as per diem waiters and bartenders at Georgetown get-togethers. "Their main objective," said John White, "was to amass data on both the CIA and the Georgetown social set. The CIA, of course, knew that Hoover was spying on them. They, in return, were spying on him. And both were spying on Georgetown. At a certain point Hoover stopped using FBI agents to do his undercover work in Georgetown and turned to the Pentagon for would-be domestics, utilizing armed forces personnel to fill the temporary positions, a tactic also followed at a later date by CIA Director William Casey." It was Evangeline Bruce in 1985 who would write to a friend: "The best pastry chef I ever employed turned out to be an FBI agent."

Although he never lived in Georgetown, James Jesus Angleton,

America's legendary spy catcher and in many respects the last great Cold Warrior, recognized the village's importance as a hub of power and influence. After graduating from Yale in 1943, where he acquired a reputation as a brilliant, creative student and a first-rate poet, Angleton joined the OSS, transferring to the recently established Central Intelligence Agency in 1947. He spent the next seven years predominantly in Rome, Italy (where he had also been stationed as an OSS officer), with an assignment entailing the administration and distribution of American funds to anti-Communist causes throughout Europe. It was during his residency abroad that he developed a gloomily conservative stance about many foreign affairs issues, including the Soviet Union's ominous military might and the need to counter their expansionist efforts with an effective Intelligence program.

Eloise Page had an acquaintance, Neva Gingleblock, who worked as Angleton's secretary in Rome. "Neva used to tell the story of meeting Angleton for the first time," said Page. "He lived in a villa on the outskirts of the city and worked in a high-ceilinged office on the Via Veneto. The drapes were always drawn and the office was immersed in perpetual darkness, save a single light that shined brightly on Angleton's cavernous face. On her first day, Neva sat opposite him in a chair so low that it hurt her back as she stared up at her boss. He was a narrow-shouldered, gaunt man with thick glasses and protruding ears. His visage flooded in white light, he looked to Neva like a gray-skinned Rembrandt portrait. Like everybody else who ever met him, she found Angleton terribly intimidating."

In 1954 Angleton returned to Washington to establish the CIA's counterintelligence section (often referred to as the "dirty tricks" department), which he would oversee for the next twenty years. During this period he played an important role in organizing U.S. attempts at infiltrating KGB Intelligence strategies, interfacing the Agency's counterintelligence efforts with their covert operations division (at the time run by Frank Wisner), managing the CIA's illegal intercepts and monitoring of mail between American residents and those living in Eastern Europe, and developing close ties with the Mossad and several other select foreign Intelligence outfits.

Angleton's closest colleague in the Agency, Cord Meyer, had graduated from Yale a year before Angleton. "The two men," according to former CIA agent Bill Koplowitz, "greatly respected each other's character and mental capacities," and in addition demonstrated a shared enthusiasm for alcohol, Realpolitik, and fly-fishing. They lunched and attended Georgetown cocktail parties together. They shared a fiercely anti-Communist, often reactionary philosophy. "They were a couple of old drunks," claimed Washington Realtor and club owner C. Wyatt Dickerson. "It's hard to believe that America's future security lay almost exclusively in their hands. But it did." Dickerson's scathing assessment, especially of Angleton, reflected the sentiments of many toward the end of his tenure. The prevailing opinion concerning the chief of counterintelligence was that he had retained his position for an excessive period of time.

With his secretive manner, eccentric behavior, and complex personality, Angleton established an early reputation as the quintessential spymaster, a real-life model for countless fictionalized CIA protagonists. Attired in a well-worn khaki trench coat and a monochromatic business suit—his "uniform"—he amassed a medley of sobriquets, including "Mother," "Fly," "The Gray Ghost," "The Invisible Man," and "The Locksmith." Allowing himself to become brainwashed by his own paranoid suspicions of Russian duplicity and wrongdoing, Angleton began to see the postwar Sino-Soviet split as nothing but a ruse, a plot devised to lull the West, and viewed a number of high-ranking Soviet defectors as decoys sent over to spread KGB disinformation. Convinced that a KGB mole had somehow invaded the country's central governmental power structure, Angleton took it upon himself to expose the traitor. He felt that the CIA itself had likewise been penetrated by the KGB, that a double agent had betrayed them, and he set out to cure the situation by instituting the Special Investigation Group (SIG), an internal affairs commission that created a great deal of dissension within the ranks. Ultimately, many of his critics condemned his compulsive search for a Soviet deep-penetration agent—both in government as well as in the Intelligence community—to have done far more harm than good.

"Ironically," remarked Arthur Schlesinger, an adviser to John F. Kennedy, "one of the few people James Angleton did not suspect until it was too late was his friend Kim Philby, the notorious Soviet mole within British Intelligence. He told Philby everything. When Philby turned out to be a spy, Angleton went berserk. Thereafter, he suspected everybody of being a turncoat. McGeorge Bundy, a classmate of Angleton's at Yale, told me years later that Angleton had fingered me as a mole, a Russian mole at the White House. He also accused Averell Harriman of being a Soviet agent. Despite his nutty notions, he wielded a great deal of power."

In many respects James Angleton wielded more power than any Intelligence or investigations operative in the country, including J. Edgar Hoover. With his photographic memory and appreciation for detail, Angleton's accounts of Georgetown dinner party conversations were so explicit that there were those in the Agency who suspected him of being wired while in attendance; others believed he had bugged the dining rooms of the elite, having planted a tiny microphone inside the salt shaker. Although the image of Angleton walking around taping conversations often elicited laughter, his stubborn individualism and overzealous ways lent a degree of credence to the possibility. "His power," as Evan Thomas put it, "derived in large measure from the same source as J. Edgar Hoover's—an implicit threat of blackmail."

Eloise Page's office at CIA headquarters was located a few doors down from Angleton's. "He looked like a spook," she said. "When he walked down the street in that old trench coat of his, his collar drawn up and his hands dug deep into his pockets, it was difficult to mistake him for anything else.

"Although a veil of secrecy has always hung over the Agency, Angleton took it a step further. He wouldn't allow anyone to take his photograph. His name appeared in no telephone book or Agency directory. Whereas the rest of us had either our names or titles embossed on our office doors, he had nothing on his. In fact, if you confronted the office receptionist and asked for a Mr. Angleton, she would tell you that nobody by that name worked there."

Page had a friend who worked on Angleton's staff. "She complained," said Page, "that you never knew what project he was working on. He never trusted anyone enough to divulge anything he felt might compromise his efforts. Nor did you know what the person at the desk next to yours was doing. If you worked for Angleton in CI, as it was called, you weren't permitted to discuss the nature of your work with anyone, not even your family.

"One day my friend marched into Angleton's office and began asking questions about some of the projects that were crossing her desk. Angleton refused to answer. 'You don't have proper clearance,' he told her. She had the same clearance he did, or she wouldn't have been there. A few weeks later she approached him again and this time asked to be transferred to another department. 'You may leave the Agency,' he told her, 'but you may not leave counterintelligence and work anywhere else in the Agency.' She eventually quit and wound up with a great job at CBS-TV."

Another of Angleton's esoteric interests (or obsessions) had to do with orchids. "He cultivated rare, one-of-a-kind orchids," said CIA agent Elizabeth P. ("Betty") McIntosh, "and he knew more about them than any horticulturist or botanist. So when an orchid plant I owned began to wilt, somebody in the Agency suggested I show it to Angleton. It took several days to get an appointment. When I finally went in to see him, he was seated behind a raised desk engulfed in a thick cloud of cigarette smoke. The room was dark and cool. He stood up and walked toward me. I held out the orchid, my fingers trembling ever so slightly. I'd seen Angleton around the office before but had never spoken with him. 'Do you have any suggestions what can be done about this poor orchid?' I asked him. He took the wilting flower and held it up for a better look. He touched the plant, ran his fingers lightly along a petal, then handed it back to me. 'Bury it!' he rasped, turning away and retreating to his desk."

Although James Angleton kept a respectful distance from the Washington press corps, he managed to befriend at least one journalist, Ben Bradlee, at the time head of the Washington bureau of *Newsweek*. Born on August 26, 1921, in Boston, Benjamin Crowninshield Bradlee—related to the wealthy New England publishing family from which he derived his middle name—conquered polio as a child, graduated Harvard in three years, joined the navy in the Pacific during World War II, co-founded a newspaper in New Hampshire, began his first stint at *The*

Washington Post as a city beat and police reporter, became press attaché in 1951 at the American embassy in Paris (he spoke fluent French), joined the Paris bureau of *Newsweek* in 1954, then transferred to the Washington bureau in 1957. Divorced from Boston socialite Jean Saltonstall in 1953 after eleven years of marriage (they had one son, Benjamin Jr.), he wed Antoinette ("Tony") Pinchot in 1956. Previously married to Stuart Pittman, a Washington lawyer with whom she had four children, Tony had two more with Ben Bradlee. The entire brood, including "his" children, "hers," and "theirs," moved into a Georgetown town house at 3325 N Street, a few doors from the home—at 3321 N Street—of Senator and Mrs. John F. Kennedy. Bradlee and Kennedy literally crossed paths for the first time in 1958 while wheeling their respective newborns down N Street in opposite directions. They solidified their friendship by playing touch football together on Saturday afternoons in nearby Montrose Park. Being ultracompetitive, both men played to win.

On Saturday nights the Bradlees often gave impromptu parties, crowded gatherings attended by an odd assortment of informally attired politicos, intellectuals, and journalists at which guests danced to rock-and-roll records while feasting on beer and pizza. An avid fan of Elvis Presley, James Angleton frequented these functions almost without fail. Tom Mangold, Angleton's biographer, has ably described the wiry CI chief at these social evenings as both participant and voyeur, dancing by himself in the center of the room, shimmying and shaking to the beat of the music, at other times standing on the sidelines absorbing and observing the scene. "According to Ben Bradlee," writes Mangold, "Angleton never felt at home in the slightly Bohemian atmosphere of Georgetown during those days." More to the point, he evidently felt as conflicted about Georgetown society as the Agency felt about him. Angleton's daughter, Helen, is quoted by Mangold as stating that her father "was dying to be accepted," at the same time that he felt "socially uncomfortable with the Georgetown group and scorned all of it. He would always joke about it to us when we were teenagers and we told him we wanted to move to Georgetown. He would say he didn't want to move because there were no parking spaces in Georgetown."

Sally Reston, an occasional guest in the Bradlee household, remembered it differently. "James Angleton," she said, "wasn't at all out of place in Georgetown. He turned up at almost every Georgetown party. He wasn't going to learn anything from the newspapers or in the halls of Congress, but he did pick up information while on the cocktail party circuit. I used to see him all the time at the homes of Evangeline Bruce and Lorraine Cooper, busily assaying the lay of the land, taking mental notes, listening in on conversations, issuing directives, gathering intelligence. It was no different for Frank Wisner, Dick Bissell, Allen Dulles, or any of the other CIA bigwigs. Everybody was spying on everybody else.

"Those smoke-filled living rooms and parlors were truly where the business of Washington got done. You would walk around and hear people whispering. 'Go see the president about this.' 'I think you ought to see the secretary of state about that.' Polly Wisner Fritchey once told me that the CIA encouraged the wives of agents to throw parties so their husbands could gather information. She said that when she was married to Frank Wisner, the Agency would pay the cost of these social gatherings, to the time of $100 per guest. The checks would arrive via the State Department. The money supposedly covered the cost of the party with a little inducement on the side. If it's true, all this strikes me as enormously bizarre."

Cord Meyer, who regularly accompanied Angleton to these affairs, acknowledged that Georgetown parties provided a perfect opportunity to gain valuable knowledge in a nonofficial capacity. "If we could get something out of somebody, we'd do it," he said. "That's why we were there. The most common method was to issue an inflammatory statement, say something to the mark you knew he'd oppose. You'd make it up. If you were lucky, the mark would start to argue with you. People are more apt to let their guard down in a moment of ire than when they're composed. You ignite a spark and watch it build into a bonfire."

CHAPTER FOUR

THE TURNING POINT

LOOKING BACK ON HER LIFE, Kay Graham would point to 1954 as a turning point in terms of her marriage. For the first time she began to notice that despite her unswerving devotion to Phil Graham, the relationship had problems that were becoming increasingly insurmountable. In *Personal History* she notes that "there were moments of strain between us, mostly when he drank too much, after which—almost inevitably—another violent quarrel would ensue, followed by abject apologies and diminished drinking." The pattern is familiar to anyone who has ever been involved with a physically or verbally abusive alcoholic. Without identifying herself as such, without using the clinical term, Katharine Graham had become a codependent, an enabler, whose inaction and silent suffering only exacerbated the situation. "Whenever I saw the drinking begin," she continues, "I started to freeze; dreading the inevitable fight, I grew over-worried." She became so concerned and worried, testified Timothy Dickinson, a Georgetown social figure, that "at this stage she had begun to throw up before every party." Her other defensive response involved turning down party invitations altogether, using her four young children as an excuse to stay home.

One party she did attend took place during the spring of 1954 at the home of Tom and Joan Braden. The Bradens, Washington's newest "fun" couple, had leased an interim house for themselves and the first of their eight offspring on the Virginia side of the Potomac. Among the party's guests were the Grahams, the Wisners, Stewart and Tish Alsop, and Paul and Phyllis Nitze. ("Paul Nitze," said Georgetown denizen Oatsie Charles, "has been at one time or another the secretary of everything.") Each couple anteed up $400 and invited thirty of their closest confederates. There were more than 150 guests at the party. Because the nation's economy had taken an unexpected (but short-lived) nosedive and because so many couples were funding the affair, they called it the Bankruptcy Ball. At least that was the explanation posited by one of the invitees. By way of contrast, Kay Graham perceived the evening simply as another example of the impending bankruptcy of her marriage. By her own account, Phil again had too much to drink. On the way home, with Katharine driving, they had a violent disagreement, Phil suddenly bolting out of the car and trudging most of the way back on foot. Nina Sturgeon, a student at a nearby college who rented a room in a neighboring house, spotted Kay Graham a day or two later on the sidewalk in front of her home. According to the witness, Kay appeared frazzled and unsteady. "She looked," Sturgeon declared, "as though she'd been run over by a tank. Among other facial marks, she bore a very painful-looking black eye."

In addition to the alcoholic binges, incessant rows with his wife, and occasional mood swings, Phil suffered from almost constant health problems—flus, viruses, colds, sore throats, and a host of indefinable maladies that at times kept him housebound. As with his drinking, Kay blamed Phil's delicate health issues on the strain and tension that derived from his position as chief executive officer of the upwardly mobile Washington Post Company.

There were other tension-provoking activities as well. Toward the end of 1954, Phil founded a wide-sweeping organization he called the Federal City Council, whose stated purpose, as revealed in a *Post* editorial, was to help "minimize the procrastination and the buck passing in public agencies, to mobilize community opinion and to interest private capital in rebuilding some of the areas to be cleared of existing slums." The group, composed predominantly of wealthy businessmen, local civic leaders, and elected federal officials, operated more along the lines of a paternal cabal than a council. The names of its then roughly one hundred members, 98 percent of them male, were never made public. The organization's written records proved almost impossible to procure, even by members of the group. The secrecy surrounding the Federal City Council, on whose board Katharine and her son Donald Graham also sat in later years, has persisted to the present day. "Nobody knows who belongs or what the group actually does," said Anthony Mizzer, a Washington real estate journalist. "True or not, the general presumption among the public is that there's something nefarious about it, that it's all very self-serving, a testimonial to cronyism." Although Phil Graham may originally have had only the most noble of intentions, those intentions were never fully realized. On too many occasions contracts for jobs, such as the remodeling of Washington's Union Station or the upgrading of Pennsylvania Avenue, were awarded either to members of the council or to insiders: friends of members. The true benefactors of Phil Graham's solution to Washington's gentrification process were the architects, Realtors, contractors, bankers, builders, construction supply manufacturers, and city planners whose involvement with the council only inflated their personal bankrolls. As usual, the rich became richer.

Despite Phil Graham's alcohol-tinged episodes and Katharine's growing awareness of the perils of marriage, she remained dazzled by him and everything about him: "his wit, great energy, soaring imagination and fervent desire for excellence—in himself and in others." What Kay failed to recognize—or refused to acknowledge until years after the fact—was that Phil often used his wit at her expense. Ella Poe Burling, the first wife of Edward Burling Jr., the son of Covington and Burling's cofounder, recalled how cutting and critical Phil Graham could be toward his wife. "I'd known Kay since her childhood," said Ella. "Her mother had convinced her that she was undesirable, and Phil Graham only reinforced that notion, undermining what little self-confidence she'd been able to amass by constantly reminding her that she knew nothing about either fashion or housekeeping. He lambasted and ridiculed her in public. At a dinner party he once asked the guests, 'Do you know the first thing Kay does every morning?' There was a pause and then he said, 'She looks in the mirror and says how lucky she is to be married to me.' On another occasion, when they had Adlai Stevenson over to dinner, Phil went down to get a bottle of wine from the cellar. When he discovered it was sour, he blamed Kay. He used to call her 'Porky,' because she'd put on a little weight after the birth of their children. He kept reminding her how dumb and dowdy and ungainly he found her, how she couldn't set a proper dinner table by herself, and had no idea how to dress. At one point he hired Nancy White at *Harper's Bazaar* to spruce up her wardrobe. Phil Graham struck me as extremely temperamental, whereas Kay was the picture of restraint. He made her feel unattractive and therefore undesirable."

Aware of her own fashion shortcomings, Kay Graham in 1955 told *Women's Wear Daily:* "I do admire pretty clothes and often wish I had the knack. Evangeline Bruce has a special individual look. Babe Paley [the wife of CBS founder William Paley] does it beautifully. It takes an inner flair. I don't think it can really be learned. Some people, like Lorraine Cooper, just have it."

Tyler Abell, the son of Luvie Pearson (and the stepson of Drew Pearson), remarked, "Washington is a small town, one in which people talk. And they loved to talk about the Grahams, particularly when it became known that they weren't exactly the happiest couple in the neighborhood. Kay used to follow Phil around like a little puppy dog. For his part, Phil misbehaved. He was rude to Kay at dinner parties, poked fun at her and generally embarrassed and humiliated her. He could be an exceedingly intimidating figure, a man with a sharp tongue and a fertile imagination."

Although few of Katharine Graham's friends had the courage to openly express to her their views on her marriage, they banded together in early 1956 to give a party in her honor, dubbing it "A Salute to Katharine Graham." According to Polly Wisner Fritchey, one of the party's organizers, "We wanted to help her regain her equilibrium, her sense of self." Kay, though pleased by the effort, remained puzzled as to the real reason for such an event.

In retrospect, it appears that the more sadistic, the nastier Phil became, the more his wife idolized him. His not-so-gentle insults and putdowns seemed only to increase her determination to please. Almost always she described him in only the most glowing terms. "Phil was the fizz in our lives," she remarks in her autobiography. "He was . . . fun at the dinner table and in our country life. He had the ideas, the jokes, the games. . . . His ideas dominated our lives. Everything rotated around him, and I willingly participated at keeping him in the center of things. In fact, I agreed with almost all his ideas."

Attempting to explore the masochistic quality that drove her existence with Phil forward, Kay depicts herself (in *Personal History*) as something of a Stepford wife: "I adopted the assumption of many of my generation that women were intellectually inferior to men, that we were not capable of governing, leading, managing anything but our home and our children. Once married, we were confined to running houses, providing a smooth atmosphere, dealing with children, supporting our husbands. Pretty soon this kind of thinking . . . took its toll: most of us became somehow inferior."

Aside from being an enabler, Kay Graham appears to have been either in complete denial or totally oblivious to the fact that her rambunctious husband, almost from the beginning of their marriage, had been unfaithful to her. One witness to his treachery, Nancy Hanschman Dickerson, a wide-eyed, idealistic twenty-four-year-old, had moved to Washington in 1952 from America's Heartland (Wawatosa, Wisconsin, "where nothing ever happened"), because she "wanted to change the world." Nancy, whose later marriage to Wyatt Dickerson ended in divorce, emerged as the first female national network (CBS-TV) news correspondent as well as a successful independent TV news producer. Before acquiring Merrywood, Jacqueline Kennedy's childhood home in McLean, Virginia, which the Dickersons purchased with joint funds, the budding news correspondent owned a town house in Georgetown, where she entertained lavishly, throwing frequent parties for the express purpose, she said, of "meeting Washington kingpins and picking up news-breaking stories that helped advance my career."

A young lady of dark good looks and quiet charm, Nancy Dickerson first met Phil Graham at a British embassy reception in the early 1950s. "At the time," she recalled, "I was working as a staff assistant with the Senate Foreign Relations Committee. The embassy reception had been arranged to welcome the newly crowned chief of Britain's Foreign Trade Commission. Phil Graham and I found ourselves standing next to each other in a long hall filled with people sipping drinks and making muted conversation. He introduced himself by handing me his business card. He had a healthy laugh and a crisp, confident manner. White-gloved waiters buzzed about armed with trays of cocktails and teasers, those crunchy little hors d'oeuvres that have been served at such affairs since time immemorial. Kay Graham, having absented herself from the occasion, was nowhere to be found. Phil made no mention of her. Instead, he invited me to visit him in his offices at *The Washington Post*, making some vague reference to the possibility of my coming to work for him at a salary far in excess of what I'd been earning at the Senate Committee."

Two weeks later Nancy went in to see Graham. Their meeting turned into an unmitigated disaster. After a few minutes of idle chatter, the newspaper magnate revealed his true (amorous) intentions by gently trying to coax Nancy into starting an affair; when that strategy failed, he took a more direct approach. After pouncing on her and watching her wriggle free, he proceeded to chase her around his desk, up a corridor, into a stairwell, down three flights of stairs, and out the revolving lobby door to a taxi stand on the corner. Their fleeting dialogue, as she recounted it, comprised a series of thrusts and parries.

"I thought you were married," she panted.

"I am but only metaphysically."

"What does that mean?"

"It means I'm available romantically."

"But I'm not," Nancy countered.

Graham's pursuit of his prey went on. "For several months he continued to call me up, repeatedly insisting that we rendezvous," she noted. "I soon learned that he gave every attractive woman the rush. He met them everywhere—on airplanes, at parties, simply in the course of his daily regimen at the *Post*. And to their detriment, most of them eventually succumbed."

Of Phil Graham's numerous extramarital relationships, the one that lasted the longest was a fourteen-year liaison he had with Constance

Noel, a former model and actress from Norfolk, Virginia, whose legal name had been changed to Noel-Noel, the stage moniker of a French film actor. Discovered by Otto Preminger at Neiman Marcus in Dallas, where she worked as a fashion model, Noel-Noel became Preminger's mistress and made cameo appearances in several of his films. She left Preminger for comedic actor Danny Kaye, moved to Washington, D.C., and after a variety of administrative positions in government offices began working as a legal secretary at Howrey, Simon, Arnold and White, an international law firm. It was in Washington, in 1949, that she met Phil Graham.

Margaret E. Cheney, a cousin of Vice President Dick Cheney, likewise worked at Howrey, Simon and became chummy with Noel-Noel— "or as chummy as anyone could become with her," said Cheney. "There was an air of mystery about her. She had a teenage daughter who didn't reside with her, and she evidently had another source of income because she lived rather well. She had floor-to-ceiling bookshelves in her living room and was very well read. The walls of her bedroom were lined with dozens of framed photographs of Noel in her youthful days. She strongly resembled Vivien Leigh as Scarlett O'Hara in Gone With the Wind. She had high cheekbones, great facial structure, long lustrous hair, lovely features. Her bedroom also contained several large pictures of Phil Graham. And on a bulletin board in her kitchen were smaller snapshots of John F. Kennedy, with whom she'd also been involved, though for a far shorter duration. She met Kennedy through Graham. Evidently the two men frequently sent their girlfriends back and forth. Kennedy had been her lover, but Phil Graham had been the love of her life.

"Noel tended to be solicitous of men and seemed to gravitate mostly toward important, powerful men. Another of her paramours was Jim Henson, inventor of the Muppets. But Phil Graham definitely stole her heart. When he killed himself in August 1963, I looked for Noel at the law firm. She wasn't there. Out of curiosity, I suppose, I peeked into one of her desk drawers and came across some photos of Graham and a very sweet, endearing letter he'd written to Noel, presumably during a happier period in his life."

In late 1990, Noel-Noel, aware that she had terminal cancer, rented a hotel suite at the Four Seasons Hotel in Georgetown and, true to her calling as a member of the Hemlock Society, took her own life by swallowing an overdose of sleeping pills. She left no suicide note. On a nightstand next to the queen-size bed lay a 1956 copy of *Time*, featuring a cover story on Phil Graham.

Graham began to show signs of his own impending doom as early as the mid-to-late 1950s. In 1956, the year of the *Time* story, Scotty and Sally Reston joined the Grahams on a ten-day vacation in the south of Florida, where they all rented a house together. Sally remembered that Herbert Elliston, editor of *The Washington Post*'s editorial page, had suffered a debilitating heart attack, and Phil wanted Scotty to quit his position with *The New York Times* and take over for Elliston at the *Post*. "For ten days," said Sally, "Phil could talk of nothing but the prospect of having Scotty join his newspaper's editorial staff. This wasn't going to happen, but Phil wouldn't let go. It became a mania with him, what Ph.D. candidates in English literature call an objective correlative. Now and again he would change the subject, posing imaginary questions such as 'What would have happened had the South won the Civil War?' or 'Should Congress be abolished?' Yet for the most part, he spent the vacation badgering Scotty for an answer. It reached the point where Kay had to intervene, telling her husband to desist—'or Scotty will return early to Washington.'"

By 1959, Phil's aberrational behavior had deteriorated into full-blown manic-depressive illness. During one quiet moment that year, when he no doubt sensed the world closing in on him, Phil asked the Restons if they would take care of his children in the event he "didn't make it," and Kay "needed help." The Restons, who had children of their own, agreed.

Hearing of Graham's touching request, Evangeline Bruce, by now the mother of three, telephoned Sally Reston and volunteered her own services as surrogate parent to the Graham children in case the Restons weren't up to it. Sally passed on Vangie's offer to Phil, whose response was quick and to the point. "Tell her, 'thanks, but no thanks.' She can't look after her own children—what makes her think she'd do any better with mine?"

CHAPTER FIVE

THE AMBASSADOR'S WIFE

"EVANGELINE BRUCE WAS EXQUISITE, a monument from a different time," remarked Henry Kissinger. "She had all the makings of a great lady: class, style, wit, intelligence, beauty, refinement, and impeccable taste. She was a bit shyer than, say, Lorraine Cooper or Pamela Harriman, but she had tremendous drawing power. She also had the ability to create an atmosphere, a setting where politicians, intellectuals, and statesmen from all over the world could gather and exchange ideas and points of view. Vangie was the classic ambassador's wife, the ultimate ambassador's wife."

Historian Ronald Steel, a loyal friend of Evangeline Bruce, found her glamorous and fascinating: "She was girlish in an effervescent sense. Long and willowy, she had dark hair and piercing eyes and a lightness that was timeless. She embodied the enthusiasm of youth. She was grand, yet accessible. What's more, she loved oysters. She had a wonderful sunken living room in her Georgetown home where it would not be unusual to find fifty to sixty people milling around eating oysters. Her house was wonderful. She always had an enthusiastic crowd and was the only woman I knew who could break into song at any given moment. Once when R. W. ('Johnny') Apple Jr., Washington bureau chief for *The New York Times,* successor to Scotty Reston, was about to leave Vangie's home with his wife after one of her parties, she started singing in German a

Marlene Dietrich rendition of 'Oh Johnny!' She had that kind of robust theatrical humor."

Alan Simpson, the former Republican senator from Wyoming, thought Vangie Bruce "a gorgeous apparition—she had spirit and energy and, of course, was tall and elegant. I'm six feet, seven inches, and she was nearly five feet, ten inches, and we'd occasionally swing around the dance floor, until in her later years she couldn't do it any longer. But she was still beautiful with her delicate oval face, amber eyes, cloud of tawny hair, and that low, quiet voice of hers. She possessed beauty without self-consciousness. She was what the French call *racée*—patrician."

Taller even than Kay Graham, more imperious and certainly more flirtatious, Vangie Bruce—whose husband David K. E. Bruce had been the U.S. ambassador to France, West Germany, Great Britain, and NATO as well as envoy to China—became best known for her legendary evenings both in the countries where the couple served and at their Georgetown town house, at once properly old-fashioned and glitteringly up to the moment. With her big hair and multipatterned, black-and-white stockings, Mrs. Bruce not only appeared on multiple best-dressed lists but also looked like a high-salaried fashion model for *Vogue* or *Harper's Bazaar*. Diana Vreeland, an editor of both magazines, pronounced her "one of the most fashionable women I've ever known." Jacqueline Kennedy, who counted Vangie as one of her primary role models, sent her a note in the mid-1960s praising "the bright path you cut through an age where so few people have grace and imagination and the virtues of another time." To these words she added: "One was so proud as an American to think that other countries recognized you as our very best."

Evangeline Bruce's typical guest list included a whole spectrum of personalities, names culled from the *Green Book,* from diplomatic cables, from campaign-contribution reports, and from the literary and entertainment sections of the daily press. Paul and Bunny Mellon, Barbara Walters, Gore Vidal, Vernon E. Jordan, Robert Strauss, David Brinkley, Arthur Schlesinger Jr., Averell and Pamela Harriman, Kitty Carlisle Hart, Clare Boothe Luce, Marietta Tree, Truman Capote, Christian Herter, Henry and Nancy Kissinger, John and Lorraine Cooper, and Katharine Graham were among her favorites. Often she organized dinner parties and brunches around a guest speaker who would present an informal lecture in his or her field of expertise: Elizabeth Drew on journalism in the nation's capital; George Weidenfeld on recent literary developments in Great Britain; John Huston on film and Hollywood. Despite her undisputed place at the center of the Georgetown social whirl, she shunned what she called "the dreaded *h* word." "I'm not a hostess," she told a reporter for the London *Times*. "Presumably the word means you have people in for food and drink. By those standards most women have been hostesses at one time or another."

"I'm an ambassador's wife," Vangie observed in the course of another newspaper interview. That phrase became a refrain to be offered up again and again. "What I do is run the social wing of the embassy. I entertain. I organize. That doesn't make me a hostess. There's a difference." She informed Lucy Moorhead, author of the book *Entertaining in Washington,* that people in government never understood that entertaining was "an important tool" of the job of successful diplomacy and that it was "hard work to entertain often and do it well. Or that entertaining has a purpose—it's not for personal pleasure or relaxation at all. It is for a reason."

As Evangeline Bruce saw it, the most notable element of entertaining was "the cast of characters," that is, the invitees and where they were seated. To the current author she remarked: "You never have a dinner of nothing but people you owe. That's fatal. You must mix and match your guests. Different types love to gape at one another. Mix ages, mix professions, mix nationalities, invite several beautiful young women, some wealthy older men—seat a struggling but well-received artist or author in the proximity of a Greek shipping magnate, a conservative next to a liberal. That's when it's a private party. When it's an ambassadorial function, you must adhere to the rules of protocol—there's less room for creativity, and the challenge is therefore greater.

"You have to be reared, schooled, and trained to comprehend the fine art of entertaining. I like to compare it to being an architect in that you must design and structure a setting where deals can be made and information exchanged. To do it successfully you have to have the right props. You need the friendships, the contacts, the house, the staff, the silverware and china. To be blunt about it, you need the finances. But the point is that if you do it well, you can make a difference. In my day, if you were able to bring together interesting, powerful men, those in charge of running the government, to trade ideas and opinions in the privacy of your living room, you could find the solution to any of a number of problems."

Evangeline performed her job with such panache and aplomb that she became the country's standard bearer so far as diplomacy went. Whenever a new American ambassador (to any country) received an appointment, he and his wife were directed first to speak with Mrs. Bruce as to comportment and local customs. Additionally, in anticipation of official state dinners or dinners for visiting foreign dignitaries, the White House chief of protocol invariably turned to Evangeline for advice and counsel. She had become the State Department's last word on good taste.

Sylvia Clark, a former foreign service officer, suggested that what Evangeline stressed in the advice she gave to future American diplomats was that when an American citizen visited an American embassy in another country, he or she had to be made to feel at home. "You have got to always remember," Vangie would say, "that the American embassy and the American ambassador's residence belong to every American. 'It's yours. This is your place.' The visitor must feel totally comfortable. Introduce him to the right guests. Make the introductions yourself. Don't rely on your staff to make the introductions." Clark further observed that Vangie's greatest strength was her ability to charm. "She could charm a baboon in a baboon cage," said Clark.

Evangeline had been bred to the position of ambassador's wife. Born in London, England, on November 27, 1914, she was the daughter of Edward ("Ned") Bell, member of an old New York family and a Harvard classmate of Franklin D. Roosevelt, though the Bells themselves were staunch Republicans. A foreign service officer, Bell's brief first marriage to a Manhattan socialite ended in divorce. Following diplomatic assignments in Egypt, Persia, Cuba, and France, he passed World War I as a second secretary at the American embassy in London. It was there he met and married the beguilingly beautiful Etelka Surtees, an English-woman whose forebears included Tory members of Parliament, writers, and actors. Evangeline Bruce's great-grandmother (on her mother's side), Ruth Herbert, had been the lover and favorite model of Dante Gabriel Rossetti. According to Nelson D. Lankford, David Bruce's official biographer, it was Herbert who passed on to Vangie "some of the ethereal beauty that had captivated the Pre-Raphaelite artist and poet."

With the end of World War I, Ned Bell, his wife, and their two young daughters were transferred to the American embassy, first in Japan and then China, where Bell took over as chargé d'affaires. Vangie's early childhood memories of Peking were limited to walks along the Great Wall with her nanny and pony rides with an armed military escort in a park adjacent to the Temple of Heaven. Virginia Surtees, Vangie's younger sister, had several additional recollections. "We had our rickshaws," she noted, "and when we went out to a tea party we always took our own boiled milk with us, as I expect all the other Western children did too, China's hygiene not being up to snuff in those days."

It was an age of civility, one in which privileged little girls like the Bell sisters were taught to curtsey or "bob" whenever they shook hands with an adult. Virginia also recalled her sister "coming down after dessert at Mother's lunch parties for select circles of women and reciting in French Victor Hugo's 'Waterloo, Waterloo.'" Too shy to participate, Virginia stood in the doorway "with Mademoiselle" and observed. "My sister," she remarked, "would have had her hair in cold water rags the evening before so it was nice and curly when she came down. . . . Mother was very proud of her."

Vangie's father died on October 26, 1924, from what Virginia Surtees maintained was a heart attack: "He and Mother had been out to dinner . . . and on their return he fell on the tall flight of steps leading up to the front door of our house. I remember very clearly (my sister didn't) the next day when he died. . . . I remember a bit of the funeral too. We were devoted to our grandmother Bell. She came over every summer from roughly 1926 to 1933 and took us to Switzerland."

William Xavier Cross, an associate of Ned Bell, attributed his untimely death not to heart failure but to alcohol. "He had a severe drinking problem," said Cross. "Alcohol ruined his diplomatic career. Had he stopped drinking he could have risen to the top of his field. He was a bril-

liant but unhappy man. He was drunk the night he died. He lost his balance, fell, struck his head on the stone steps, and never regained consciousness." After Evangeline Bruce became a well-known international
social figure, an article in *Life* made the apocryphal claim that Etelka had
pushed her husband down the steps and to his death. "She didn't have to
push him," Cross countered. "He toppled over on his own."

The widow and her daughters moved to Paris, where in July 1927
Etelka married British diplomat Sir James Dodds. "I can't remember
whether my sister and I discussed our stepfather at the time, probably
not," Virginia mused. "You know how one accepts things when one is
younger: He was *there*. Much later when we thought about him we
agreed it must have been something of a burden to have taken on two
rather hulking creatures. He didn't mean a great deal in our lives but we
loved his mother, Lady Dodds, who was angelic to us. It was she who took
me to my first *Hamlet* [performance] and to Stratford-on-Avon."

Over much of the next decade Evangeline and Virginia spent time in
nearly every European country, including England, France, Italy, Switzerland, Sweden, Hungary, Spain, and the Netherlands. They attended
so many boarding schools and moved so often that in 1949 Vangie, in an
interview with David Schoenbrun of the New York *Herald Tribune*, described her childhood in terms of "never having a home, frequent heart-
wrenching farewells to friends, struggling to learn new languages, always
[being] the foreigner, the outsider wherever you were landed." She did in
fact master several foreign languages, spoke fluent French—she and her
sister sometimes conversed with each other in French—but she also
grew rebellious, particularly toward her mother. "They argued incessantly," observed William Cross. Said Virginia Surtees: "The relationship
between them became one of irritation on Mother's part at my sister's un-
tidiness in her room and the fact that she was always late for everything.
And my sister has never liked to be criticized. (Who does?) One way and
another they grew apart and things deteriorated."

The tensions between mother and daughter were increased by
Etelka's refusal to allow Evangeline to invite classmates home from
school, complaining they made too much noise, coupled with her de-

mand that all her dates with boys be chaperoned. "There were [constant] rows," stated Virginia. "Often Mother was right, but of course I always sided with my sister." The final break took place on the occasion of Evangeline's eighteenth birthday. "Mother," said Virginia, "had done nothing to help my sister when she 'came out' in the way of entertaining for her, although our [Bell] grandmother gave money for that purpose and Mother preferred to use it on living at a 'good address.' "

Moving out of the house, Vangie gained employment as organizing secretary with the Anglo-French Art and Travel Society in London. In 1937 she visited with her uncle, Harold Bell, in Boston. She had stayed with relatives in the United States on previous trips but only briefly. Determined to remain in Boston—because of their father's nationality, both Vangie and her sister were considered American citizens—she registered as a part-time student at Radcliffe, taking courses in French literature and Oriental art. Arthur Schlesinger Jr., an undergraduate at Harvard in the late 1930s, recalled her as "excruciatingly attractive. But there were great areas of privacy that surrounded her, a line that one simply didn't cross." Vangie retained her part-time student status for three semesters, moving to New York in 1940 and then to Washington, D.C., to take a job arranged by her uncle as private secretary to Francis Biddle in the Justice Department. She and her mother, however, never made up. Evangeline rarely wrote to her and for years refused to see her. "The odd thing," said Virginia, "was that my sister felt bitter about Mother right to the end. . . . I could put it all behind me and . . . rarely thought about it; it wasn't so for my sister."

Marie Ridder, a journalist and former head (through marriage) of the Ridder Newspaper Group, whose mother had been a great friend of Etelka, found it equally difficult to understand why the bond between Etelka and Evangeline had ruptured to the extent that it did: "Their relationship was tempestuous. Vangie couldn't bring herself to so much as speak about her mother. I found the woman lovely and charming, but Vangie hated her. Etelka made plans to come to Georgetown to visit with her on one occasion, and Vangie became so anxious and upset she began to tremble. Her relationship with her mother affected the way in which she related to her own three children. When they were little, she was a caring mother but always nervous, uncertain. Later, when the children matured, her ties to them came unraveled."

∽

STARTING IN HER LATE TEENAGE YEARS, Evangeline Bell developed a keen and appreciative eye for older men. Christopher Ogden, a biographer and *Time* magazine correspondent, has written and spoken of Evangeline as being a temptress and sexual adventuress. In *Legacy*, Ogden's biography of Moses and Walter Annenberg, the author recounts the scandalous details of two of Vangie's early affairs. Both took place after her 1937 arrival in Boston. "A Philadelphia matron," writes Ogden, "threw her out of the house when she found the visiting Evangeline sleeping with her husband. A Washingtonian grande dame described how as a young woman on a Maine camping trip with her father, brothers, and Evangeline, when both were twenty-four, she awoke to find Evangeline in a sleeping bag with her father." Looking ahead to her partnership with David Bruce, Ogden—in the same volume—reveals that "they . . , maintained a European marriage; each had a lover." The same claim has been made by other friends and acquaintances of the couple.

Peter Rivers, a Boston business executive who knew Vangie during her student days at Radcliffe, remembered an affair she had with an American history professor at Harvard. "It went on for the better part of a year," said Rivers. "The professor, married and a grandfather, was forty-five years Evangeline's senior. Every undergraduate at Harvard, which had an all-male student body in those days, lusted after her. She, on the other hand, had a deep and abiding affinity for elderly gentlemen. Her affair with the historian ultimately became public knowledge in the Cambridge community."

Vangie's penchant for older men soon brought her into contact, if only circuitously, with her future husband. In 1942, while living and working in Washington, she accompanied her friend Ed Prichard to a dinner party at the home of William Phillips. Phillips, like Evangeline's father and stepfather, was a distinguished, old-time career diplomat whose appointment as American ambassador to Italy had ended in 1940 with his unsuccessful bid to dissuade Mussolini from entering the war. Others at the same dinner included Franklin Roosevelt's son Jimmy and actress Myrna Loy, both of them residents of Georgetown. But the guest who most captured Evangeline's interest that evening was OSS director William "Wild Bill" Donovan. Donovan had recently asked Phillips to become the first operations (or station) chief for the OSS in London. By dinner's end, Vangie Bell had succeeded in convincing both men that, having spent a good deal of time in Britain as well as on the Continent, she could be of value to Phillips as an administrative assistant in helping to organize the English office. The position carried with it, Donovan told her, an annual salary of $1,200.

On July 18, 1942, Ambassador Phillips flew to London to begin his OSS assignment. He was accompanied by his special assistant, David Williamson, and by Evangeline Bell, his new office administrator. Fisher Howe, an OSS officer already posted in London, recalled that Vangie took a flat with two other young ladies at Berkeley Square. "They threw frequent parties," he said, "and just as frequently attended our bachelor soirées in the apartment several of us shared at One Gore Street. The nightly bombing raids by the Germans only heightened the experience of living in wartime London." By July 1943 Vangie, while continuing as administrative aide and secretary to Phillips, had started working part-time for the Censorship and Documents Division of the OSS, or C & O as it was called. Her major responsibility involved concocting cover stories and preparing bogus documentation for agents about to be dropped behind enemy lines. "A minor mistake," said French OSS agent Michel de Bourbon, "could prove fatal if an alert Nazi border guard spotted an error or incongruity in the OSS agent's papers."

"She also outfitted the agents," said Elizabeth McIntosh. "Jack Hemingway, for example, Ernest Hemingway's eldest son, had joined the OSS, and since he spoke fluent French he was parachuted into German-occupied France disguised as a local fisherman. Evangeline had to make certain he looked the part and had papers to match. She was very emotionally involved in the process, aware that if a button wasn't sewn on correctly or if something didn't jive, the results could be a death sentence."

Evangeline, who found the work exhilarating as well as nerve-wracking, remembered the day in late July when William Donovan came to visit her in her office at 72 Grosvenor Street. With him were Fisher Howe and a man Howe introduced to her as David Bruce. "Ambassador Phillips had just been assigned by President Roosevelt to go on a secret mission to India, and David Bruce had been chosen to succeed him," said Howe. "Donovan gave Evangeline a choice: she could either accompany Phillips to New Delhi or remain in London and work as personal assistant to Bruce. 'I'll serve wherever I'm needed,' she responded. David Bruce evidently told her later in the week that going to India was a preposterous idea—she must stay in London."

Despite David Bruce's conviction that Evangeline Bell was more needed in London than New Delhi, he at first resisted the temptation of employing her as his personal secretary. He didn't need a secretary, and in any event she would be better off working full-time with C & O. It was Fisher Howe—Vangie later dubbed him "Stupid Cupid"—who kept after Bruce to at least interview her for the job.

Although he consented to the interview, Bruce seemed reluctant (as Evangeline remembered their meeting) to take on a secretary.

"I take it that you speak French?" he said to her.

"Not as well as I would like," she replied, "but I do broadcast to Occupied France twice a week."

While somewhat set back by her rejoinder, Bruce rallied by saying that of course there were many young women in London who spoke perfect French, but what particularly interested him were the languages of Central and Eastern Europe.

"Would Hungarian do?" asked Evangeline.

Not yet undone, Bruce remarked that one must also look ahead to the possible occupation of Japan.

"Oh, my family lived there for several years when I was young; we had a Japanese governess who spoke nothing but Japanese with us."

At the end of his rope, Bruce said: "And the Scandinavian languages?"

"I'm afraid that my Swedish is a bit rusty, but I can easily brush it up."

David Bruce did the only thing possible under the circumstances— he hired her and then asked her out to dinner.

Fisher Howe often teased David Bruce about having coerced him to work with Evangeline. "He insisted," said Howe, "that he first met her at a Georgetown cocktail party in 1941, a claim which she adamantly rejected. A man of great sophistication and integrity, he was sixteen years older than she. He knew wines. He knew haute cuisine. He was cultured. He spoke with a Tidewater accent and walked with a slight limp, the result of a childhood case of the gout. In 1940 he had been chief representative for the American Red Cross in London, and as a result he knew everybody and was such a knowledgeable and well-respected person that everyone in London society loved him. They invited him to their country homes on weekends. They toasted him at their dinner parties. Despite the rather arduous wartime conditions, he and Evangeline made the best of it."

OSS operative Guy Martin observed that because she was a single lady and an extremely good-looking one at that, "a lot of foreign service officers and Strategic Service types were interested in Evangeline, but she only had eyes for David Bruce." Her attraction to Bruce seemed to be shared by many. He had few detractors. Pamela Harriman, very likely Georgetown's best judge of men, said of Bruce: "David was the most beautiful of men—mentally, physically, emotionally. He was adored and respected by all who knew him."

Born in Baltimore, Maryland, in 1898, David Kilpatrick Este Bruce was the son of William Cabell Bruce, a lawyer and politician who served as United States senator from Maryland from 1923 to 1929. His mother, the former Louise Este, came from one of Baltimore's first families and was active in local civic causes. His older brother, James, would serve as U.S. ambassador to Argentina from 1947 to 1949. David Bruce entered Princeton University in 1915 but left at the end of his sophomore year to enlist in the U.S. Army. After World War I, he attended the law schools of the University of Virginia and the University of Maryland, graduating from the latter in 1921. For the next three years he practiced law in Baltimore but grew bored and in 1924 turned to politics, winning election to the Maryland House of Delegates. In 1926 he joined the foreign service and spent a year as vice-consul in Rome. Returning to the States, he went to work for the Bankers Trust Company in New York and in 1930 accepted an offer to become an executive with W. A. Harriman and Company, Inc., also based in New York. He remained with the Harriman organization until 1939, the same year he published *Revolution to Reconstruction*, a history of America's first sixteen presidencies, and returned to public life, winning election to the Virginia House of Delegates.

David Bruce's relations with the Harriman family, and particularly with W. Averell Harriman, came about largely as a result of his 1926 marriage to Ailsa Mellon, daughter of financier Andrew W. Mellon, then secretary of the treasury and arguably the wealthiest man in the United States. The Mellon connection afforded Bruce not only entrée to the Harrimans and other leading American dynasties but also to a personal fortune that far exceeded the not insubstantial means he already possessed. The couple divided their time between a luxurious penthouse apartment in Manhattan and a baronial mansion in Syosset, Long Island. They had one child, a daughter named Audrey, and lived what appeared to outsiders to be an idyllic existence. Ailsa Mellon Bruce owned a substantial private art collection that she placed partially under the auspices of the National Gallery of Art, in exchange for which David Bruce served until the end of World War II as the museum's honorary director and (with Ailsa) as a member of its board of trustees. There were numerous trips abroad, sailboats, antiques, horses, a gentleman's farm in Virginia, a large town house in Georgetown, African safaris with Ernest Hemingway (with whom David also helped liberate wartime Paris), and dinner parties galore with the cream of New York café society. But contrary to expectations, the marriage ran aground. Ailsa—Drew Pearson once referred to her in his *Diaries* as "the most valuable debutante in town"—began to suffer increasingly severe bouts of depression and withdrawal. In his autobiography, *Reflections in a Silver Spoon*, Ailsa's younger brother Paul Mellon accuses his sister of being "overly introspective" and an out-and-out "hypochondriac." It reached the point where for weeks, having become addicted to sleeping pills, she refused to climb out of bed. Crippled by paranoia, she became seriously agoraphobic. She turned down all social engagements and would no longer leave the house. On those days she did manage to slip out for a few hours, she would either go horseback riding by herself or take long solitary walks along the strand or into the woods. By 1940, with certain members of the Mellon family siding with David Bruce, the couple separated. By 1943 they were estranged, no longer talking, communicating predominantly via their respective lawyers. Knowing that his client stood to gain more in financial terms from a divorce action if Evangeline Bell were temporarily out of the picture, David Bruce's attorney recommended that she be shipped back to America.

In November 1944 Evangeline packed her bags and prepared to leave London. Her sister, Virginia, recalled the occasion as an especially painful period in Vangie's life. "David Bruce," she reminisced, "sent her home to [the] U.S.A. because he was waiting for his divorce (or hoping for it) from his first wife, and he didn't want my sister compromised. I remember very well her leaving England. I think it was late autumn 1944, as my husband and I had gone to Lisbon [Portugal] in August 1944 from London and she stayed a short time with us before taking an airplane back home. It must have been late fall because one day we took the car to Nazaré on the coast, and as it was rather chilly we decided to eat our picnic in the car, which we both preferred anyhow. I know perfectly well what [my sister] did in Washington on her return. . . . She moped, wondering whether David Bruce would get his divorce. . . . She went to [our] uncle in Boston for a bit of the time. I am sure she didn't go back to England. They were married in April 1945."

The marriage took place in Boston's Emmanuel Church, on the periphery of the Public Garden, just three days after a Florida judge granted Ailsa Mellon's request for a divorce judgment on grounds of desertion and mental cruelty. Evangeline Bell's name appeared nowhere in the court documents. Ailsa Mellon never remarried. Ironically, David and Ailsa grew closer after their divorce than they had been before. Whenever he turned up in the greater New York metropolitan area, David called on Ailsa, whose rather unsatisfying life finally ended when she died of cancer in 1969, aged sixty-eight.

Two years earlier—in 1967—Ailsa Mellon and David Bruce lost their only child, Audrey, when she disappeared with her husband, Stephen Currier, on a charter flight from Puerto Rico to St. Thomas. Left behind were three very young Currier children—Andrea, Lavinia, and

Michael—as well as an estate valued in excess of $700 million. David Bruce, by then the father of three children with Evangeline, wanted little to do with his orphaned grandchildren. He categorically refused to take them in. Nobody else among the Bruces, Mellons, or Curriers seemed prepared to jump into the breach, and the three youngsters were placed in the care of virtual strangers, a Yale Law School professor and his wife. When later asked why she thought her grandfather had turned her and her two siblings away, Lavinia Currier, who had become a successful film director, ventured the opinion that David Bruce had absolutely no interest in children or child rearing. There were those, however, who averred that it was Evangeline Bruce—not David—who had problems with young people.

✐

HAVING HAD THE FORESIGHT to purchase one of Georgetown's most gracious town houses in 1939 with his first wife's money, David Bruce now moved into the house with wife number two. Located at 1405 Thirty-fourth Street, between O and P Streets, the early nineteenth-century, two-story, redbrick abode boasted a sizable garden to the rear of the house replete with stone terrace and sunken lawn. The garden eventually contained a number of miniature headstones to mark the burial plots of the family's many pet dogs. On vacations and weekends the Bruces utilized David's so-called gentleman's farm, Staunton Hill, a Gothic Revival mansion overlooking the Staunton River lowlands of Brookneal, Virginia, midway between Lynchburg and Danville. With its unencumbered view of vast uninterrupted acres of wilderness, the structure, built in 1848, had once served as the center of a thriving tobacco plantation. Both homes had become the sole property of David Bruce as per the terms of his divorce agreement with Ailsa Mellon.

In May 1946 Evangeline gave birth to their first child, a daughter named Alexandra, otherwise known as Sasha. A son, David Surtees Bruce, was born in 1948. Their third and last child, Nicholas Cabell Bruce, followed in 1951. Concurrent with the growth of the Bruce family was the continuance of David Bruce's public service career. In June 1947

Truman appointed him assistant secretary of commerce. His old friend and business associate W. Averell Harriman had been named secretary of commerce and therefore was once again his boss. In May 1948 Bruce went to Paris to oversee the European Recovery Program—the Marshall Plan—as director of the Economic Corporation Administration mission to France. There he distinguished himself in helping the French to avert economic chaos by creating a framework for an effective postwar economic policy. A year later he became U.S. ambassador to France. During his service as director of the Marshall Plan, Bruce had made numerous friends among French officials, and he proved equally popular and successful as ambassador. The key to his success, his "secret weapon," as he put it, was his wife—Evangeline Bruce.

The French liked David Bruce, but they *loved* Evangeline. Her reputation among Frenchmen from all walks of life was due in no small measure to her physical beauty, her familiarity with French fashion, her knowledge of the French language, and her interest in French history. In 1939 she had written an article on the French Revolution for *New Oracle*, a British periodical with an interest in politics. In 1940 she had penned, produced, and broadcast a one-hour radio script in French for station WRUL in Boston. After World War II she contributed articles on American subjects for publication in French literary and historical journals. Paris's foremost intellectuals, labor leaders, scientists, economists, businessmen, and policy makers came to the official embassy residence at 2, Avénue d'Iéna for what one visitor termed "long pleasant evenings of perfect food and stimulating conversation, orchestrated almost entirely by Mrs. Evangeline Bruce."

Letitia ("Tish") Baldridge, the well-bred Vassar-educated daughter of a U.S. congressman and a future social secretary to Clare Boothe Luce as well as Jacqueline Kennedy, began her career as social secretary to the Bruces during their ambassadorial years in Paris. "It wouldn't be unfair to say," remarked Tish, "that Vangie served as co-ambassador in tandem with David Bruce. At night she was a star at all the parties, and during the day she more or less managed the embassy, constantly giving the staff things to do. She helped the embassy raise funds for many of the more extravagant ambassadorial dinners. She went around to all the American foreign service wives and encouraged them to become involved in various community-related cultural projects. Vangie Bruce possessed a lot of American know-how in combination with Old World charm. She knew the ropes mainly because she'd been raised as the daughter and then the stepdaughter of diplomats. She was a perfectionist. Her abilities weren't related to money. Yes, she had Porthault tablecloths and could afford the best of everything, but I have seen many wealthy women who simply weren't able to make it cohere. Vangie had it all down, from setting the table to devising the flower arrangements. She knew how to harmonize a room, how to match colors, how to make guests feel wanted. It looked easy, but it was hard work. She had the ability to make things happen, get things done."

One of Tish's responsibilities as social secretary to the Bruces entailed helping with the preparation of guest lists and seating arrangement charts for both official and private dinner parties, in addition to sending out invitations and then monitoring the acceptances and regrets. "All this could sometimes become quite complicated," she said, "as for example the night I inadvertently sat a high-ranking French official next to his wife's lover." The two men evidently spent the evening discussing the traffic patterns of ships in the Suez Canal. And then there was the South American diplomat who turned up for dinner with both his wife and latest mistress in tow. So as not to favor one over the other, they sat the two women near each other and put the diplomat at another table in a separate dining room.

"I also remember," said Tish, "this very annoying, very haughty woman in Paris who for two years had been badgering us to send her a dinner invitation. The Bruces despised her. She had gobs of money and important social connections, so Vangie finally relented and instructed me to send her an invitation to the next function. The problem is that although I invited her, I forgot to add her name to the guest list. At the appointed hour she appeared at the front door in a huge chauffeur-driven Rolls-Royce. She had on all of her diamonds. But because her name didn't appear on the 'Plan de Table,' the butler couldn't seat her. Hearing a commotion emanating from the front hallway and immediately understanding what had occurred, Vangie rushed out, embraced the dowager, and brought her back into the dining room. 'My name isn't on the guest list,' the woman kept saying, her face crimson with rage. 'Of course it's not,' Vangie responded, not missing a beat. 'That's because you're the guest of honor. You're the most important person here tonight, and we want to pay tribute to you and entertain you.' That said, she quickly rearranged the table and sat the bewildered woman directly to her right. The entire protocol seating arrangement went out the window. For the rest of the evening the butler and waiters scurried around in a state of confusion. Somehow the chef managed to dredge up another serving of roast duck. Once again Vangie had saved the day. The disgruntled woman left the Bruces that night with a big smile on her face."

Franklin D. Roosevelt Jr., the son of President Roosevelt, attended several parties at the American embassy in Paris during the period when the Bruces held sway. "Vangie Bruce," he said, "was much more than an ambassador's wife. She was an exceedingly gifted and dignified woman, yet at the same time modest and unpretentious. She had great elegance but it was a simple elegance, the elegance of another age. 'Elegance,' she once said, 'is merely a state of mind.' She was also extremely cultured. I recall hearing that the American cultural attaché in Paris constantly deferred to her on questions of taste and was eventually dismissed because she knew more than he did.

"On the physical side, Vangie looked like a Gainsborough portrait. She had these great gunboat feet, very long and slender. She was unusually tall and regal looking. 'At least I'm shorter than Charles de Gaulle,' she used to say. De Gaulle stood six feet, seven inches. The French couturiers adored Vangie—Christian Dior, Balenciaga, Chanel. They would give her their latest line to wear just to have her be seen in them. I remember a costume ball in Paris in 1951 given by Marie-Laure de Noailles to which Vangie went dressed as Toulouse-Lautrec's bookkeeper in a flaming red wig, a boned collar, and a voluminous black gown designed by Dior. It turned out she was nearly nine months pregnant with her third child and gave birth only a day or two later."

Franklin Roosevelt Jr. spent a weekend with the Bruces at a cottage in Versailles that French officials had lent them as a vacation getaway. "It was a simple little house in the middle of a park," Roosevelt explained, "but the Bruces enjoyed it because it enabled them to escape for a while from the endless grind of embassy receptions and dinner parties. Also, because of her hectic weeklong schedule, Vangie had little time for her children. So weekends in the Versailles cottage afforded her the opportunity to be with her kids, to picnic and play with them—and to play with David as well."

Charles Whitehouse, who in subsequent years became American ambassador to Laos and Thailand, observed that "the Bruces enjoyed a relationship with the French I never imagined could be conveyed upon an American ambassador and his wife. It was a period—1949 to 1952—when French governments came and went with dizzying and deceptive speed, and each time a new government was being formed an emissary would be dispatched to the American embassy to ask the Bruces whether the replacement government would be acceptable in Washington.

"What made David and Vangie Bruce so well liked and respected among the French was their shrewdness and lack of sentimentality. The French perceived them as real people. They weren't syrupy or warmhearted in that very typical, simpleminded, Norman Rockwell-ish way, which in France—and much of the rest of Europe—is taken as downright vulgarity. That's not to say that they weren't a charming couple. David was wildly funny, and Vangie could vamp with the best of them. She was flirtatious as hell. But all this only augmented the image."

cᴀ

DAVID BRUCE WAS RECALLED to Washington in April 1952 to serve as undersecretary of state, the number two man at the State Department under Dean Acheson. Although he resigned his position with the advent of the Eisenhower administration, the new president soon found work for him. For two years, beginning in February 1953, while his wife and children remained behind in Georgetown, Bruce served as American observer at the interim committee of the European Defense Community (EDC) and as American representative to the European Coal and Steel Community. The two groups had been formed essentially to help Western European countries draw together into a more unified military and economic conglomerate. Despite the ambassador's unremitting efforts, his countless trips back and forth across the Atlantic, the plan was eventually disbanded as unwieldy and unworkable. Bruce's participation in the enterprise marked his first and last failure in the field of diplomacy.

During the mid-1950s, while living in the Thirty-fourth Street Georgetown home, Evangeline Bruce established a reputation as one of Washington's most vibrant and influential behind-the-scenes personalities. She gave frequent dinner parties, inviting guests into a home filled with exotic plants and fragrant flowers (the British later named a rose after her), the windows dressed in silk, the walls painted in deep, rich shades of red, yellow, brown, and orange. The interior of the house resembled a stage setting. Sally Reston, a frequent visitor, commented on Vangie's abilities to successfully orchestrate and coordinate a social occasion: "At parties, you would watch in awe as she dashed from group to group making certain that all the guests were enjoying themselves. If she saw someone who looked a little uncomfortable or out of place, she would rush over and start a conversation with them. She was a terrific listener and knew how to draw people out of themselves. Nevertheless, Vangie didn't exude the kind of easygoing friendliness that people might have expected—or even preferred. She wasn't spectacular at cocktail hour chatter. She was more earnest than that. She was insightful. She knew her politics and could hold her own with virtually anyone. I think, though, that her unwillingness to register concern for people or subjects that didn't interest her was too often mistaken as snobbery and standoffishness.

"Being forthright and frank, Vangie represented a kind of heroine to the ladies of Georgetown. She had backbone. If, for example, she disagreed with an opinion put forward by Joe Alsop or Phil Graham, she wouldn't hesitate to say as much. She fought back. Lyndon Johnson is a case in point. Phil Graham, a steadfast supporter and trusted friend of Johnson (he once gave LBJ money to help defray the cost of a new home in Washington), used to have him over for dinner. Aware of the liberal sentiments of most Georgetown denizens, he would talk nonstop about the need for tolerance and understanding when it came to certain disenfranchised minorities, particularly the blacks. He would castigate his fellow politicians for their long silence on civil rights issues. Although she heralded LBJ's civil rights platform, Vangie took issue with his style, his mode of presentation—his fist-thumping pronouncements, patronizing attitude (especially toward women), and accusatory tone (with respect to other politicians). In her eyes, LBJ was a political opportunist who espoused whatever he thought his audience (or constituents) wanted to hear. 'Lyndon's as much a bigot as the next man,' she argued. She never relented on that point, not even in 1957 when Johnson managed to bulldoze the first civil rights legislation through Congress. Needless to say, her views on Johnson didn't endear her to Phil Graham. Phil greatly admired David Bruce—as did Lyndon Johnson—but Graham and Vangie never saw eye to eye on anything."

Oatsie Charles likewise met the Bruces shortly after they settled in Georgetown. "David and Vangie rapidly became part of the Georgetown scene," said Oatsie. "They donated funds to several Georgetown philanthropic groups and put their house on the Georgetown home-and-garden circuit. Washingtonians paid twenty-five dollars a head—it costs more today--to tour the domiciles of Georgetown's rich and powerful, the proceeds going to charity. Once a year, David and Vangie also threw a reunion dinner for their former OSS comrades. They had a French chef who made a wonderful Mongolian hot pot. And they had the best wine cellar in Georgetown.

"The Bruces weren't afraid to enjoy pleasure. They liked pleasure and they had great fun with it. That's a lost art. Vangie never wore anything that was displeasing to the eye. Yet it wasn't necessarily the latest in French fashion. Unlike Kay Graham, who looked frumpy no matter what she wore, Vangie had a gift for wearing just the right thing. She never threw out her clothes. She might combine an expensive designer blouse with an ordinary off-the-rack skirt she'd acquired years earlier. Something old with something new. She became a leader in the fashion field but without spending bundles of money on her wardrobe. It wasn't a question of money, it was a question of taste."

By anyone's standards, the Bruces constituted an impressive duo. "They were a gay couple, in the best sense of that word," contended Oatsie Charles. "David was hysterical. I recall a dinner that he and Vangie hosted at the Jockey Club in the early 1970s. There were maybe a dozen of us. At the end of the meal, the waiter presented David with the bill and went through a lengthy recitation as to which credit cards they accepted. 'I don't have any credit cards,' David said. 'All I have is cash. May I pay with hard currency?' He said it so apologetically and with such wry humor that we all cracked up."

David Bruce was next appointed American ambassador to West Germany, and served from March 1957 to November 1959. Although the ambassador and his wife were less esteemed in Germany than they'd been in France—perhaps because they were temperamentally less suited to the Germans and the German way of life—they were nevertheless regarded as a most astute and effective diplomatic couple. While in Bonn, they enjoyed close relations with Chancellor Konrad Adenauer. David Bruce resigned his post a year prior to the 1960 presidential election and with his family came home to Georgetown.

Following Vangie's return, friends and associates noticed a slight shift in her demeanor. "She and David began giving these Sunday brunches every few weeks, especially on those weekends when the Sunday Night Supper Club didn't meet," said Polly Wisner Fritchey. "They were a continuum of the Sunday brunches that Phil and Kay [Graham] still had on occasion. But the odd part is that they became insulted if you couldn't come. They weren't understanding in that regard, especially Vangie. She'd hold it against you, no matter what the reason. There could be a death in the family, but if you didn't show you were in the doghouse."

Oatsie Charles observed another change in Evangeline's temperament: "Always attentive to her guests in the past, Vangie suddenly seemed distracted. Among other things, she began arriving late at parties and leaving early. In other words, she'd be at the party, including her own functions as well as others, and then she'd be gone. She'd just disappear without so much as a good-bye. And you wouldn't see her again until the next party."

Jean Friendly, the wife of *Washington Post* executive Al Friendly, would be invited to the Bruces, "and Evangeline would be there and she'd greet you, but always she was looking over your shoulder to see who was more important to talk to than you. It could be quite disconcerting."

In July 1960 at the Democratic National Convention, held that year in Los Angeles, the Bruces (both registered Democrats) initially supported Adlai Stevenson, a noncandidate open to draft. Their distant second choice, John F. Kennedy, eventually won his party's nomination and, to Vangie's dismay, selected Lyndon Johnson as his running mate. When she heard the news, Vangie Bruce broke into tears. Johnson had vied with Kennedy (and Stuart Symington) for the Democratic Party's top spot. Phil Graham, sensing in JFK the same presidential qualities he saw in LBJ, had been instrumental in bridging the gap between them. He, Joe Alsop, and Senator George Smathers had worked, together and separately, to convince Kennedy to put Johnson on the ticket. They labored just as vigorously to convince Johnson, then majority leader in the Senate, to accept the offer. As Bobby Baker, one of LBJ's most trusted aides, put it: "Phil Graham played a substantial role in bringing the two men together. As one of the few people close to both, he was in an influential position. He and Jim Rowe—another good friend of Lyndon's—as well as a few others, were unquestionably that year's kingmakers."

Following John Kennedy's narrow victory over Richard Nixon in that November's presidential election, Phil Graham and Joe Alsop again brought JFK the name of a candidate. This time they recommended that he appoint David Bruce to the position of secretary of state. The president-elect declined, offering the job instead to Dean Rusk, who later wrote, in his memoir As I Saw It, "Public life is tough on the wives and children of those whose names are in the headlines. The job of secretary of state often called for 15- and 16-hour days. . . . Virginia [his wife] and I ate at home with the family about once a month during my eight years as secretary of state, and the children essentially grew up on their own." Such an arrangement would not have suited the mutually codependent Bruces, who, while not often in the company of their children, were otherwise basically inseparable.

On February 2, 1961, two weeks after taking office, Kennedy announced the first of his appointments of ambassadorships, naming David Bruce as ambassador to the Court of St. James's, to replace John Hay Whitney. David Bruce was only too happy to accept. He and Evangeline, who had borrowed a tiara from Lorraine Cooper that had once belonged to Lorraine's mother, would remain in England for all eight years of the Kennedy-Johnson administrations, making—in Lorraine's words—"a smashing success of it." The official diplomatic cables and memoranda sent by the ambassador to Kennedy, assessing the current political situation in Europe, were deemed so well worded and "on the money" that the president regularly read them aloud to members of his staff. Bestowing the ultimate compliment upon him, JFK once referred to David Bruce as "the most eloquent American statesman since Thomas Jefferson."

CHAPTER SIX

THE SENATOR'S WIFE

LORRAINE COOPER AND HER HUSBAND, John Sherman Cooper, the Republican senator from Kentucky, were among a select group of friends who had gathered on the night of January 21, 1961, at Joe Alsop's Georgetown home to celebrate the inauguration of John F. Kennedy. Sworn into office earlier that day, the new president and first lady had spent the evening attending a flurry of inaugural galas and balls. They returned afterward to pass their first night in the White House. Jackie, exhausted from the day's activities (she had recently given birth to their second child), went straight to bed. Jack, restless and wide awake, wandered aimlessly around their new living quarters. He wanted a nightcap but didn't know where the White House staff kept the liquor. Then he remembered that Joe Alsop had organized a late-night party in his honor and decided to go. The Secret Service agent on duty drove him to Dumbarton Avenue in the presidential limousine.

The Alsop celebration was a simple affair: a few friends; a case of chilled champagne; a gently boiling pot of terrapin soup; and in one of the rear bedrooms, a half-dozen scantily clad Golden Girls imported for Jack's pleasure from Las Vegas by Frank Sinatra and Kennedy in-law Peter Lawford. By the time Kennedy arrived several of the other guests, including Phil and Kay Graham, the Bohlens, and Alice Roosevelt Longworth had already gone home. The president stayed until four in the morning. Yet contrary to expectations, he spent most of his time not with the Golden Girls but with the Coopers, discussing future political plans and strategies.

Two days later, by then familiar with the layout of the White House, John Kennedy gave the Coopers a personal tour, pausing in the Oval Office long enough to point out a threadbare carpet—not yet replaced—whose surface was covered with spike marks. "What're all those little holes?" Lorraine inquired. "Ike's golf shoes," said Kennedy. "He wore them in here all the time."

A week after JFK's inauguration the Coopers hosted a private dinner party for two dozen guests in their Georgetown home; the formal affair had been arranged around the appearance of Jack and Jackie Kennedy, who had promised to attend. Bailey Guard, an aide to Senator Cooper, recalled the buzz surrounding the event: "It interested a lot of people, particularly the press, that the first dinner attended by the Kennedys after entering the White House would be at the home of a Republican. It points to the almost sacrosanct friendship that existed between the two couples. In reality they were more than friends. The Kennedys regarded the Coopers practically as surrogate parents. JFK and John Sherman Cooper had more or less come up in the Senate together. They served on the same senatorial committee (Labor and Public Welfare). Kennedy trusted Cooper implicitly. Shortly after JFK became president, he sent Cooper on a secret mission to Russia to try to determine how the Kremlin felt about Kennedy's election. He returned with a message of four words: 'They're not impressed.' Cooper was a Republican but an extremely moderate one. As such, he had any number of friends and admirers on both sides of the political aisle, which helps explain why both *Time* and *Newsweek* recognized him as the most respected senator of his day. As for Jackie, she had known Lorraine Cooper since the late 1940s. Mrs. Cooper served as Jackie's mentor. She and Evangeline Bruce were vital to Jackie's early development. And this helps explain the close alliance that marked the relationship between Lorraine and Evangeline."

Lorraine Arnold Rowan—Mrs. John Sherman Cooper—was born in Pasadena, California, on December 18, 1906. She had three younger brothers, the middle two being identical twins. Her father, Robert Arnold

Rowan, a West Coast businessman, cotton farmer, insurance executive, and real estate developer, had been involved in local Republican Party politics. Her mother, Laura Madeline (Schwarz) Rowan, had become active in civic affairs. One of the most prosperous families in Pasadena, the Rowans occupied the area's largest estate, including vast tracts of surrounding farmland. Lorraine's father died in 1915. Ten years later her mother met and married Prince Domenico Orsini, an Italian nobleman and an official in the Vatican. From 1925 to 1938, Laura lived with her second husband in his Roman palazzo, returning with him to Pasadena when fascists seized and destroyed his home.

Lorraine received her education at St. Timothy's—the same Maryland boarding school that Polly Wisner Fritchey attended—supplementing her studies by spending summers learning languages at schools in Paris, Madrid, and Florence. Dropping out of high school at the end of her junior year, Lorraine returned to Pasadena and embarked on her own reading program. "I loved books but hated school," she later told a newspaper reporter.

It was at a girlfriend's debutante ball in New York that sixteen-year old Lorraine encountered twenty-four-year-old Robert H. McAdoo, the son of William Gibbs McAdoo, President Woodrow Wilson's secretary of the treasury and then a U.S. senator from California. Marguerite McAdoo, Robert's niece, pointed out that "nobody referred to him by his first name. Everyone called him 'Ribs.' Ribs McAdoo. I knew him as Uncle Ribs. He'd gone to St. Paul's and Princeton, interrupting his schooling to serve as a naval officer in World War I; after finishing college he became an investment banker, opening his own Wall Street stocks and securities firm. He and Lorraine were married in 1923, the same year they met. She played an essential role in his early financial success. That was her forte, knowing how to make a man shine. They belonged to the restrictive world of New York high society. Lorraine was the epitome of chic. She knew how to dress and how to carry herself. She never went to college, but she had that certain something which serves to attract people, especially men. Call it charisma, call it magnetism. Whatever it's called, she had it."

Lorraine's closest friend during her dozen years as Mrs. McAdoo was the ultrafashionable Mrs. Harrison Williams. It was she, in the winter of 1935, who introduced Lorraine to Thomas H. Shevlin Jr., the polo-playing New York socialite. The son of a noted Yale University all-American football star, Tommy was several years younger than Lorraine. Adventuresome, boyish, and devastatingly handsome, he instantly appealed to her. Their subsequent affair became grist for the New York gossip mill. The ensuing scandal forced Lorraine's embattled husband to seek a divorce. The divorce became final on June 24, 1936; a day later, in a Miami ceremony, Lorraine became Mrs. Thomas Shevlin. Six months later Ribs McAdoo, thirty-seven, died of pneumonia, although there were those who suggested he had actually succumbed to a broken heart.

Tommy Shevlin's charms were not just physical in nature. The beneficiary of a lumber empire fortune, he owned luxury homes in Manhattan, Palm Beach, Florida, and Cat Cay in the Bahamas, which is where the couple honeymooned. He also counted among his possessions a thirty-eight-foot yacht, a plantation in Kenya (where he and Lorraine frequently went big-game hunting), and a string of polo ponies. Not that Lorraine didn't have money of her own. Her father had left her, as well as her mother and three brothers, a significant trust fund.

Few who were acquainted with Tommy Shevlin could deny that he possessed movie star good looks and a voracious appetite for pleasure, even if the same arbiters also detected within his soul certain undeniable deficiencies of personality and character. Fashion designer Oleg Cassini knew Shevlin from New York, Southampton (L.I.), and Palm Beach. "Tommy was attractive but superficial," said Cassini. "He used to fraternize with the polo crowd, fellows like Winston and Raymond Guest, Laddie Sanford, Aly Khan. Another of his cronies was Porfirio Rubirosa, the Dominican Don Juan. Like Rubi, he was popular with the ladies, but unlike Rubi he had little to say for himself." Doris Lilly, author of *How to Meet a Millionaire,* said of Shevlin: "He was one of those rich playboys that infested the cabarets of New York. Tommy considered himself a sportsman. He used to go trolling for women." Another Palm Beach personage, Aileen Mehle, otherwise known as "Suzy," the future society columnist, came into contact with the Shevlins a bit later. "Tommy Shevlin was a playboy, just like all of them," she said. "I was going out with a playboy myself—Woolworth Donahue, the cousin of five-and-dime heiress Barbara Hutton. That's when I met Tommy and Lorraine. I thought she was what the French call a *belle laide*, which means a good-looking ugly woman. Lorraine was unattractive, but she had great style, great flair, and she took great care of herself. Never could you call her good-looking, but she was colorful and erudite and bright and humorous. She had black glossy hair and white skin and wore wonderful clothes. She brought to mind a Diana Vreeland or the duchess of Windsor. She had that kind of stature and bearing."

Washington journalist Maggie Wimsatt likewise noticed a striking resemblance between Lorraine and the duchess of Windsor: "I happened to be staying with friends in Newport when the duke and duchess of Windsor came to town on what turned out to be their first joint visit to the United States. My hosts had been invited to a small dance, and as their houseguest I got to tag along. And that night the duchess had on a perfectly exquisite blue and-white gown, and Mrs. Lorraine Shevlin had on a perfectly exquisite green-and-white gown. Except for the slight variation in color, the two dresses looked exactly alike, as did the women who wore them. For most of the evening, they stared at each other in dumbfounded horror."

During a separate visit to Newport, while still married to Shevlin, Lorraine befriended Nuella Pell, the wife of Claiborne Pell, Democratic senator from Rhode Island. "The first thing I noticed about Lorraine," remarked Nuella, "was that she had great taste. She had originality, which made itself felt in everything she did. I recall going to her home in Palm Beach one season and having lunch. I don't remember what she served, but I recollect it as having been very special. I later learned that Lorraine had never so much as fried an egg. But she knew about food, which is what counted, and was able to impart that knowledge to the cook.

"Although she tried, Lorraine never had children. She had a cocker spaniel while married to Tommy. She always had dogs. When she moved to Georgetown in the late 1940s, she acquired four Shih Tzu puppies, and they went wherever she went. Her existence with Tommy Shevlin seemed radically different from the life that she lived when married to Senator John Sherman Cooper. I grew much closer to her during the latter phase. She and I were Georgetown neighbors. And one year we ran the Senate Ladies' Lunch together. Every spring the Senate wives gave a luncheon for the first lady. She was president of the organization, and I was vice president. I used to drive her home from meetings. We similarly both belonged to the Red Cross Senate Wives Committee, and we would go to meetings together. So I knew Lorraine as both a senator's wife and as the wife of a socialite. She managed somehow to fit wonderfully into both worlds. She succeeded because she had a sense of things. She had finesse. Just going to her house for tea was an experience to be relished and remembered. There was a timeless quality about her. She was ageless."

The first years of Lorraine's marriage to Tommy Shevlin were full of fun. The couple entertained in their New York apartment, wintered in Palm Beach, visited Hollywood on occasion, and vacationed in London or Paris. In Paris, Lorraine shopped for clothes and took in the fashion shows. In London, she posed for Cecil Beaton, who said to her: "Your face breaks the camera. You should only let me take your picture." The Shevlins traveled around the world, attending polo matches on every continent. But ultimately, perhaps inevitably, the marriage began to break down. Bailey Guard expressed the view that for years "Tommy had been sneaking out on Lorraine, seeing other women behind her back. It's difficult to believe that she didn't know—everyone else did."

By the time America entered World War II, the Shevlins were floundering. Tommy enlisted in the navy and was assigned to duty aboard a destroyer anchored off the coast of South Florida. Lorraine took a cottage nearby and saw her husband on occasional weekends. When the destroyer left for Cuba, Lorraine went to New York. While Shevlin spent much of the war in Havana hobnobbing with Winston Guest and Errol Flynn, his wife worked as a volunteer for the Commission on Inter-American Affairs, under the directorship of Nelson Rockefeller. Rockefeller, a personal friend of Lorraine's, often took her for dinner after work, confessing to her one evening that his greatest ambition in life was to become president (a post denied him when he ran against and lost to Richard Nixon for the top spot on the Republican ticket in 1968). Because she spoke French, Italian, and some Spanish, Rockefeller asked Lorraine to represent the commission at the 1945 U.N. charter assembly in San Francisco. Returning to New York from California, she tried again to cohabit with Tommy, but the magic had long since drained out of their marriage.

Tommy and Lorraine were divorced in June 1947; in July he married Durie Malcolm, a young Palm Beach debutante once rumored to have been briefly (and secretly) wed to John F. Kennedy. The story, which the Republicans attempted to exploit in an effort to discredit JFK during the 1960 presidential campaign, proved to be apocryphal. Jack Kennedy had dated Durie Malcolm exactly once. The truth was that she had been a girlfriend of Joe Kennedy Jr., Jack's deceased older brother, and had remained friendly with several of Jack's sisters.

False accusations notwithstanding, Jack Kennedy evidently continued to be titillated by his purported connection to Durie Malcolm. In *The Dark Side of Camelot*, author Seymour Hersh recounts an anecdote he had heard from Maxine Cheshire, a former society reporter for *The Washington Post*. According to Cheshire, whenever Jack Kennedy attended a dinner party at the Georgetown home of Lorraine and John Sherman Cooper, he would turn to the other guests and announce: "Lorraine and I are related by marriage." And with this, the two of them—Jack and Lorraine—"would die laughing, and nobody else knew what they were talking about."

Early in 1948, Lorraine Shevlin—twice divorced, childless, aged forty-one—made a decision that would change her life: she opted to move permanently from New York to Washington, D.C. She had tested the waters first by making periodic trips to Washington, mostly weekend junkets to visit friends or attend a dinner party. Then, one morning, as she wrote in a 1961 letter to Joan Braden, "I woke up and suddenly knew I'd had enough."

Lorraine McAndrew, the daughter of George Rowan, one of Lorraine Cooper's twin brothers, suggested that her aunt had been "devastated by her divorce from Tommy Shevlin. It hurt her. She wanted to put New York and Palm Beach behind her and begin anew. She hoped to do something meaningful for once, something that would enable her to use her brains. Since she'd always been interested in foreign affairs, Washington seemed the most logical place to go."

She started by subletting a tall but narrow redbrick town house on Thirty-fourth Street in Georgetown, one block from the home of David and Vangie Bruce, both of whom she'd met previously. The Thirty-fourth Street house would one day belong to Madeleine Albright, secretary of state under Bill Clinton. For the moment it served Lorraine as a launching pad from which she would embark on her latest journey. At first she gave a number of small dinners, inviting people she already knew, requesting that they bring along a friend or two whom she said she soon hoped to know. Besides David and Vangie Bruce, Lorraine had grown close to Marie Harriman, the wife of Averell Harriman, as well as Oatsie Charles and Lily Guest, Washingtonians whom she'd known while still married to Tommy Shevlin. Lily Guest had it that when Lorraine arrived in Washington she knew nothing about politics; a week later she knew it all.

"Lorraine Cooper was a true original," said Oatsie Charles. "She had tremendous charm. It just oozed from every pore. She lit up a room and had a drop-dead sense of humor—like David Bruce. She had the ability to put people at ease, make them laugh and feel good about themselves. She was outgoing, upbeat, and optimistic. There was a lyrical quality about her. Lorraine moved like a ballerina. She bristled with self-confidence, knew who she was and had a profound understanding of the world. She immediately wanted to know who in Washington it was important for her to get to know. But at the same time she never sucked up to people simply because they had money or wielded power. She wanted to meet men and women who had something to offer, something to bring to the table. They had to be sophisticated. They had to know how the world worked. Or they had to be knowledgeable in some area that she wasn't. She was that rare creature who yearned to learn something new every day. That, she told me, is what made her life worthwhile.

"She has often been compared to Evangeline Bruce, but Vangie didn't have Lorraine's quick wit or irresistible personality. Lorraine was steadfast, whereas Vangie tended to blow hot and cold. Vangie could be extremely off-putting. People often thought of her as being remote, threatening, a bit haughty at times. Lorraine might have been somewhat intrusive and a little zany, but she wasn't a phony. She never tried to be somebody she wasn't. Vangie and Lorraine were different as well in their approach to fashion. Vangie was the more traditional of the two. Lorraine invented her wardrobe. She was an innovator. She did things with scarves I'd never seen done before. She was the first woman in this country to wear a snood—hood—over her head. Another time she took one of John Sherman Cooper's ties and draped it in a loose knot around her neck, and suddenly a whole new trend got started. She brought back the parasol. She owned a vast collection of silk parasols in various colors. She used to walk around Georgetown holding a parasol overhead. I recall somebody saying, 'Look, there's Lorraine Cooper under an umbrella and it's not even raining.' There's a fabulous photograph, now probably long lost, of her on a rubber raft in the middle of Lily Guest's swimming pool, clutching a parasol in one hand, a cigarette holder and a half-filled cocktail glass in the other. She also used to swim in Averell and Marie Harriman's pool. The Harrimans adored her. She was also, as far as I know, the first woman in Washington to sport the mini- and then the maxi-skirt. The only thing Lorraine couldn't do well is spell. I remember once when Lily Guest and I were dictating a list of names to Lorraine to be used for some charitable affair. 'Don't forget to add Franklin Roosevelt Jr. to the list,' I said. An impish grin crossed Lorraine's face. 'How do you spell *Roosevelt*?' she asked. Lily let out a laugh. 'Are you serious?' I asked. 'Look,' said Lorraine, 'I never voted for his father. Besides, intelligence and spelling ability are inversely proportional. Do you think Einstein knew how to spell?'"

Oatsie Charles recalled going to lunch with Lorraine Cooper and Nancy Dickerson in the early 1950s: "We were discussing the enticing subject of husbands versus lovers, or at least Lorraine was. Nancy, a practicing Catholic and still young enough to be idealistic, seemed a little put off by Lorraine's frankness. At one point Lorraine remarked, 'When we die and go to heaven, I wonder who'll be there waiting for us—our husbands or our lovers?' 'Maybe both,' I ventured. 'God forbid,' said Lorraine. 'I'm hoping for the latter.' "

What cemented the friendship between Lorraine Cooper and Oatsie

Charles was that both were gritty, independent women. They took great pleasure in the acquired arts of smoking and drinking. Lorraine, for that matter, often drank to excess. Alice Roosevelt Longworth walked into Julia Child's Georgetown home before lunch one day to find Lorraine drinking Bloody Marys by the pitcher. "You just sicken me," exploded Alice. "It's so stupid to sit there and drink." Another factor in the Oatsie-Lorraine friendship is that both women were between husbands at the same time. "One summer we found ourselves in Paris," said Oatsie. "We'd been invited to a July Fourth cocktail party at the home of the people who controlled the Mark Cross leather consignment in France. Another guest at the same party was Count Gaston Poluski, an incredibly dashing Polish diplomat. They say that titles are bestowed upon anyone in Poland with an acre of land and three sheep. Still, we were extremely eager to make the count's acquaintance, and in our enthusiasm we probably behaved like a pair of giddy teenyboppers. The count wanted nothing to do with us. Neither did anyone else. At the end of the evening the count left with some girl he'd met, and Lorraine and I went to dinner by ourselves. We spent most of the meal excoriating European nobility in favor of their American counterpart."

Having decided to remain permanently in Washington, Lorraine launched an intensive search for a new residence and found it in a four-story, Federal brick house—built in 1792—at 2900 N Street in Georgetown, only minutes from her first home. At the back of the structure a series of porches spanned the width of the house, looking out on a garden laden with lush foliage and leafy shade trees. Purchased by Lorraine in 1953 at a cost of nearly $200,000 (the equivalent of some $3 million to $4 million on today's real estate market), the house (which occupied a sizable corner lot) soon became a work in progress. Forever adding new furniture and furnishings, the village's newest homeowner showed a predilection for vivid colors—splashes of bright orange and emerald green appeared in the dining room, red roses on white chintz in the living room, and a delphinium blue in the library. Interviewed by the *Washington Star* regarding her decorating prowess, Lorraine provided an appropriately tongue-in-cheek comment: "I insist on having a delphinium blue room in every one of my homes."

Her first dinner guest at the N Street house was John Sherman Cooper, whom she'd initially encountered at a supper party on April 1 (April Fools' Day), 1947, at the Georgetown home of the British ambassador and his wife, Lord and Lady Earlforth. Tall (six foot four), quiet, shy, dignified, courteous, and distinguished looking (with a statesmanlike profile), Cooper had been elected in 1946 to fill the unexpired term of Kentucky Senator A. B. ("Happy") Chandler, who had resigned to become commissioner of baseball. Intent in their first meeting on arousing Cooper's interest, Lorraine had tried in vain to think of something intriguing to say. Finally, with the party about to break up, she zeroed in on her prey and said: "Senator, how is the barley cotton crop doing this year in Kentucky?" Hardly an icebreaker, the question had most likely occurred to her because her father had raised cotton in California. In an oral history that she subsequently recorded for the University of Kentucky, Lorraine observed that Cooper "looked at me quizzically and we parted on that note. I did not see him again for two years."

The oldest of seven children, John Sherman Cooper was born into a family of educators and county judges, in Somerset, Kentucky, on August 23, 1901. Educated in the public schools of Somerset, the gifted student spent two semesters at a local liberal arts college, then went on to Yale, where for two years he captained the basketball team. Graduating in 1923, he entered Harvard Law School but withdrew a year later because of the death of his father. He returned to Somerset to assume responsibility as the head of the family.

In 1928 Cooper was admitted to the Kentucky bar and commenced the practice of law in Somerset. During the same year his political career began with election to the Kentucky House of Representatives. Two terms as chief justice of Pulaski County (1930–1938), at the height of the Depression, strengthened Cooper's growing compassion for the unfortunate and had an immense influence upon his future political concerns. After an unsuccessful bid for the Republican gubernatorial nomination in 1939, he resumed his legal practice. In 1942, at age forty-one, he enlisted and became one of the oldest privates in the country. After completing basic training, he went to officers candidate school at Fort Custer, Michigan, where he met Evelyn Pfaff, an army nurse whom he married and almost as quickly divorced. During the war he served with General George Patton's Third Army, making his way from France to Luxembourg and then to Germany. Viewing the Buchenwald concentration camp soon after its liberation indelibly etched upon his memory the atrocities of war.

While still in Germany, helping to restructure that country's postwar legal system, Cooper was elected circuit judge for the 28th Kentucky judicial district. He had only just begun his term when he decided to step down and enter the special election to fill Happy Chandler's seat, defeating his Democratic opponent by the largest majority ever given a Republican senatorial candidate in Kentucky up to that time. As a freshman senator, Cooper immediately established a reputation as a liberal, often voting against the prevailing Republican line. In spite of his seeming popularity with political leaders, voters, and the press (Joe Alsop described him in the New York *Herald Tribune* as "the only modern-minded Republican senator in this year's race"), he was defeated for reelection in 1948 by Democrat Virgil Chapman. Cooper now joined the Washington law firm of Gardner, Morison and Rogers, continuing his public service career by becoming a delegate to the United Nations General Assembly in 1949, and an adviser to Secretary of State Dean Acheson at the London and Brussels meetings of the North Atlantic Treaty Organization (NATO) Council of Ministers in 1950.

Although defeated in the 1948 senatorial election, Cooper showed himself to be a humanitarian of the highest order. A fellow Kentuckian, Edward Prichard (Phil Graham's old friend and Hockley House roommate), with political aspirations of his own, had departed Washington after the war and returned to his home state. There, as Katharine Graham writes in *Personal History*, "he did an incredibly wrong and foolish thing that ruined his life. Someone came to him and asked him to sign some ballots [in support of Virgil Chapman] with fake names, and Prich did." Convicted of ballot tampering, Prichard received a two-year prison sentence. Ironically it was Cooper, the victim of Prichard's wrongful actions, who intervened in Prichard's behalf, convincing Harry Truman to grant the offender a presidential pardon. Phil Graham's former confidant was released from confinement just before Christmas of 1951, having served only five months behind bars.

As in the case of "Happy" Chandler, Virgil Chapman died in office in 1952, creating a new vacancy in the U.S. Senate, which John Sherman Cooper—already a harsh critic of McCarthy's Red Scare tactics—would again fill, this time by defeating Thomas R. Underwood for the coveted prize. However, in 1954, Cooper's bid for reelection was crushed by Alben W. Barkley, who was a former senator and vice president. Cooper's supporters insisted that their man had lost because he wasn't married. Kentucky's citizenry wanted a family man to represent their interests in Congress. What John Sherman Cooper needed in terms of a political future was a wife.

ﾟ⌒ﾟ

ONCE SETTLED IN her new N Street home, Lorraine began to take a more active interest in the political side of Washington. She took out a subscription to the *Congressional Record*, perused three or four newspapers every day (*The Washington Post*, *The New York Times*, the *Los Angeles Times*), hired a Russian language tutor, attended lectures and read books on every aspect of American history. Each morning she would be on the telephone picking the brains of her friends (Evangeline Bruce, Kay Graham, Lily Guest, Oatsie Charles, and Marie Harriman), gathering information, gleaning data, educating herself on the ins and outs of a town she referred to as the "Heart of Darkness." On the social front she joined the Washington Opera Society and instituted her own Monday afternoon salon, bringing together Washington's leading social and political figures. "She liked the mix of policy makers and the so-called 400, and her sanguine nature appealed to both," said Bailey Guard. "But for all her attention to these two factions, Lorraine wasn't into that awful who's in, who's out, dinner party syndrome. She was too intelligent for that. Yes, she loved people and parties, but she had no esteem for that silly social treadmill so prevalent in Washington. She also had no use for difficult or troublesome guests and made a point of not inviting them, or if they did turn up of asking them to leave," Guard observed. Her salon and her parties were immediately recognized by Drew Pearson as a setting where "Washington insiders can meet other Washington insiders in addition to artists, musicians, writers, businessmen, doctors, lawyers, and other challenging types." Joe Alsop called her salon "the place to be."

One of Lorraine's salon regulars, Jackie Kennedy (then still Jacqueline Bouvier, inquiring photographer for the *Washington Times-Herald*) was dating Massachusetts Senator John F. Kennedy. Lorraine Shevlin and Senator John Sherman Cooper, one of Washington's most eligible bachelors, were something of an item as well. Jackie had been introduced to Senator Cooper by Lorraine in 1952 at the Georgetown home of Charlie Bartlett. Enormously taken with Cooper, Jackie described him as a man of "great kindness and sensitivity, almost Jeffersonian in a way." After the Bartlett dinner, Jack, Jackie, John, and Lorraine often doubledated, going out to restaurants or taking in a movie. Other times the two couples would gather at Lorraine's house for an informal dinner, then move on to the home of Senator and Mrs. Albert Gore for coffee and dessert. Now and again they would drop in on Phil and Kay Graham, or the Bruces when they were in town.

In mid-1953, Jackie and Lorraine met over lunch to discuss their respective relationships. One of their major complaints had to do with time constraints. JFK had recently been elevated from the House to the Senate and now faced a longer work week. John Sherman Cooper was already putting in fourteen-hour days, restricting himself to two nights per week for social engagements. In her oral history, Lorraine remarks: "We said . . . how awful it must be to be married to a man in politics." Then: "In retrospect, I think it was all sour grapes, because I don't think either senator had asked us to marry him at that point. It was very funny because in the end Jackie married Jack and I married John."

The Kennedys married first, the ceremony taking place in Newport on September 12, 1953. A week prior to that date, Lorraine had presented Jackie with a loose-leaf binder containing fifty handwritten tips on how to make a marriage work—"from someone who never has." The last item in the makeshift self-help guide had a prophetic ring to it: "Should your husband feel compelled at some point to cheat on you, either cheat back or buy yourself a diamond tiara and send him the bill."

The Kennedys took a six-month lease on a small house located at Dent Place in Georgetown. After returning from their Mexican honeymoon, Jackie gave her first dinner party, inviting fewer than a dozen guests, among them Lorraine and John Sherman Cooper as well as Jackie's stepfather and mother, Hugh and Janet Auchincloss. Before and after the event, Jackie besieged Lorraine with questions on anything and everything—from what to wear to what to say. Before Jackie would agree to move into the N Street town house that she and Jack eventually bought, she asked Lorraine to look it over and render an opinion. Only after Lorraine gave the place her stamp of approval did Mrs. Kennedy begin to pack her bags.

Until he married Lorraine, Senator Cooper lived at the now defunct Dodge House Hotel on E Street, a short distance from the Senate Office Building; he took his meals and entertained at the elitist Cosmos Club. George Smathers did the same. Lee C. White, head of the FCC under President Kennedy and then an aide to John Sherman Cooper, confirmed that "there were four or five senators, each a bachelor, and they all lived at the Dodge and partied at the Cosmos. And somehow the chicks always managed to find them. Under the circumstances I can understand why some of these blokes seemed a bit reluctant to get married. They were what is known in the trade as an "extra," a gentleman whom hostesses invite to dinner parties at which there are unattached women. In no uncertain terms, John Sherman Cooper was a man about town—and a blasé one at that."

In a documentary film produced by the Kentucky Educational Television Network on the life of John Sherman Cooper, Katharine Graham, one of the interviewees, remarks that "people in Washington were taking book on whether John would ever marry Lorraine. You could get even odds on the wager." By Lorraine's admission, she and John had spoken of marriage on any number of occasions but always to little avail; nothing had ever come of the discussion.

The subject came up once again in 1955, when Secretary of State John Foster Dulles—after conferring with President Eisenhower—approached John Sherman Cooper regarding the possibility of his becoming United States ambassador to India (and Nepal). From Cooper's perspective, having lost his senatorial seat the year before, the offer couldn't have been better timed. The only problem, Dulles explained, was that the post entailed a number of social responsibilities and obligations. "You'll need a helpmeet, someone who can organize the embassy's multivarious social functions. Which brings me to Lorraine Shevlin. I understand the two of you are practically engaged. I know Lorraine. She'd be ideal for this endeavor."

Cooper pointed out that although he and Lorraine had been dating for several years, the idea of marriage had never been fully explored.

"Well, now's the time," said Dulles. "Explore away."

"The thing is that Lorraine owns an exquisite town house in one of Washington's most exclusive neighborhoods, and I live in a ramshackle residential hotel with a hot plate and a closet full of wire hangers," Cooper replied. "I doubt Lorraine will want to move in with me, and for me to move into her place would be tantamount to letting her support me—and I can't do that. I've got too much pride, too much Kentucky mountain pride."

"Ah," Dulles said, "that's where the ambassadorship comes into play. We have just built a brand-new embassy in New Delhi. It was designed by Edward Durell Stone, the New York architect. And this will be your new home. Yours and Lorraine's. That way you don't need to move into her place, nor she into yours. You'll both move into a neutral location. Why not propose marriage to her on that basis?"

And that is exactly what John Sherman Cooper did. The future ambassador popped the question (in a whisper) a few days later during a lull at a Phil and Kay Graham party.

"I'm going to India, Lorraine, and I want you to come along."

"I thought you'd never ask."

The Rowans greeted the wedding announcement with mixed emotions. "For one thing, it was a late-in-life marriage," said Lorraine McAndrew, Lorraine Cooper's namesake and niece. "She was forty-eight, he was fifty-four—and that's always a little tricky. He'd been married before but only briefly; he appeared to be a confirmed bachelor, whereas Lorraine had been twice divorced, her second husband being nothing more than an out-and-out playboy. Putting all of that aside, the family wondered how Lorraine would fare as the wife of a senator and ambassador.

"She had such extraordinary ways. I mean when she took an

overnight train, for example, she brought along her own sheets, her own food, and her own maid. She never traveled with fewer than twenty suitcases." There were other idiosyncrasies. Nora Cameron reported that Lorraine started each day by standing on her head for fifteen minutes. She used only Erno Laszlo skin care products, necessitating a regimen that included black soap, repeated facial lathering and rinsing, wrinkle creams, hand lotions, powdery substances that gave her skin a starched, ghostlike appearance. Cynthia Helms commented on Lorraine's germ phobia, her obsession with cleanliness: "She kept a disinfectant on a hallway table near the front door, and whenever you entered her house she sprayed you with it." Lorraine McAndrew lived with her aunt in Georgetown from time to time and remembered being sprayed not with disinfectant but with expensive perfume—and only when she left the house, not when she came in. "Add to this," said McAndrew, "the prospect of Lorraine's going to India, then one of the world's most impoverished countries, and you can understand why the family might have had certain misgivings. Ultimately my aunt proved everyone wrong."

The wedding of Lorraine and John Sherman Cooper took place on March 17, 1955, at the Pasadena estate owned by Lorraine's mother, the same compound where Lorraine spent her early childhood. "The ceremony was strictly a family affair," said Lorraine McAndrew. "They held the wedding in Pasadena because Lorraine's mother, my grandmother, was dying of cancer and lacked the strength to leave her bed. Her husband, Prince Orsini, had passed away several years before. Mr. Cooper's elderly mother traveled to California for the wedding and so did his brother Richard, who served as best man. Louis Rowan, the youngest of the three brothers, won a coin toss with the twins for the honor of giving Lorraine away. A Congregationalist minister officiated. I caught the bride's bouquet."

Within days of the ceremony the couple took a train from Los Angeles to New York and then sailed for England aboard the S.S. *United States*. In London Lorraine telephoned an old friend, Lady Edwina Mountbatten, the wife of Lord Louis Mountbatten, the former British governor-general of India. Lady Mountbatten asked the Coopers to lunch. Recording their conversation in her oral history, Lorraine quotes

Lady Mountbatten as saying to her: "The best way you can help your husband in his mission is to try to make friends with Indira Gandhi. It isn't going to be easy, but that would be the best thing you could do." Edwina also gave Lorraine a letter of introduction addressed to Prime Minister Jawaharlal Nehru. The letter, when Lorraine presented it to the prime minister, proved particularly significant; Nehru and Lady Mountbatten had once been lovers. Lorraine Cooper would become good friends with Nehru, and their association would in turn be instrumental in John Sherman Cooper's more official dealings with the Indian leader. Regarding Indira Gandhi, Nehru's daughter (and the wife of Feroze Gandhi), she and Lorraine grew so close that they continued to correspond long after the Coopers returned to the United States.

Traveling by plane from London to New Delhi, Lorraine reviewed another document that would help her become acclimated to life in India—a copious set of notes compiled by Evangeline Bruce detailing what duties she could expect to perform as the wife of the American ambassador. David Bruce had put together a similar package for John Sherman Cooper.

Knowledgeable as the Bruces were, not even they could have foreseen all the obstacles and contingencies that the Coopers would encounter, not least of which was a marriage so new that the varnish hadn't yet dried. "It couldn't have been easy," said Joan Braden. "They were both middle-aged and they each had half-a-lifetime of bad habits with which to cope. Neither of them knew how to drive, which meant that the smallest errand demanded an official car and driver from the embassy. From what I heard, John Sherman Cooper had driven up to the time in Germany during World War II when he accidentally struck and killed a pedestrian. In addition, John was habitually late for everything—meals, meetings, parties, whatever. And he never seemed to have any cash at hand. Lorraine had to place a hundred dollars' worth of Indian currency in his pocket every morning so he'd have enough to see him through the day. He snored, and she tended to grind her teeth, so they kept each other awake at night."

Although the American embassy in New Delhi had recently undergone construction, nothing had been done about the American ambas-

sador's residence, which resembled, according to Lorraine, "a Grand
Rapids showroom." Her immediate concern was the redecoration of the
residence's interior, so they could start hosting dinners and receptions.
She spent her first weeks prowling the fabric shops of New Delhi, purchasing hundreds of yards of colorful material, using her own funds once
the embassy budget had been expended. When completed, the color
scheme of their living quarters in India replicated the hues and shades inside Lorraine's Georgetown town house.

Robert Schulman, a biographer of Senator Cooper, pinpointed what
arguably became Lorraine Cooper's most challenging feat in India—
entertaining the masses: "John Sherman Cooper, being a man of the people in a very genuine sense, would endlessly invite on short notice all
sorts of guests, including large groups of elementary and high school students, factory workers and low-level politicians. To accommodate these
impromptu visitors, Lorraine had to revise her whole way of thinking.
She had to be able to set up a function in a matter of minutes, which went
deeply against her basic nature."

On those occasions when John invited school groups—he once
brought in an entire school of six hundred students from Madras—
Lorraine would hand out paper plates and organic crayons. The children
who created the most original drawings received prizes, usually a small
sum of money. The rest of the group ate their meals off their hand-
decorated plates. At the end of the meal there were no dishes to wash;
the kitchen staff could concentrate on food preparation for the next
adult-oriented dinner party. Lorraine credited Elsa Maxwell, the high-
society hostess from San Francisco, with having given her the ingenious
paper plate idea.

"The bottom line with respect to India," said Bailey Guard, "came
down to the old Cold War conflict between the United States and the Soviet Union. Which of the two superpowers could exercise the greater influence over India? Nehru wasn't stupid. He adroitly played one country
off against the other. Ambassador Cooper's strategy was simple: do whatever it takes. In cable after cable he urged the State Department to
support India with financial aid in a number of different forms: loans,
outright funding, foodstuffs, medical supplies, farm and factory equip-

ment, military supplies, and weapons. And as history bears out, Cooper emerged victorious, winning India over as an American ally."

Unlike previous U.S. ambassadors to India, Cooper was not perceived by his host countrymen as "the Ugly American." Senator Mitch McConnell of Kentucky, who later worked as an intern for Cooper, described him as "a gentleman, a genuinely nice man. In certain respects, he may have been too nice." Lorraine Cooper was seen in much the same light. Those in India, rich or poor, whose paths crossed hers seemed fascinated by her effusive, very natural personality. She and her husband were considered a unit, a team, whose two-year stay in India helped create a lasting bond between that country and the United States.

༄

IN *EVIDENCE WASHINGTON*, a volume of photos and text on powerful Washingtonians, Bill Walton compares Lorraine Cooper to Mrs. Lightfoot Lee, the leading lady created by Henry Adams in his first novel, *Democracy*. The comparison, insists Walton, is apt insofar as Adams imbued Lightfoot Lee with all the same "graces" to be found in the person of Mrs. Cooper—"beauty, breeding, intellect and the ultimate one, a comfortable income." If Lorraine Cooper lacked great physical beauty, she more than atoned for it with her other attributes. "And even physically," as Joan Braden points out, "she was more than adequate. She was medium height and slim and had an excellent figure."

The characteristics that Lorraine Cooper exhibited in such abundance were originally thought to be qualities that Kentuckians could never appreciate. Thus, when President Eisenhower put pressure on Ambassador Cooper to return from India and become a candidate for the Senate again in 1956 to fill the unexpired term of the recently deceased Alben Barkley, a number of John Sherman Cooper's staffers suggested that he campaign without his wife. Cooper dissented, and Lorraine became a major factor in his defeat of Democratic candidate and former Kentucky Governor Lawrence Wetherby. In the senatorial election of 1960, Cooper won his first full six-year term, trouncing former Kentucky Governor Ken Johnson by 199,000 votes. In 1966 he surpassed that mar-

gin, defeating John Y. Brown Sr. by some 217,000 votes. John Sherman
Cooper served in the U.S. Senate from November 7, 1956, to January 3,
1973, when he chose not to seek reelection. In large measure he owed his
string of consecutive victories to Lorraine.

Scott Miller, an advance man for Cooper since 1948, noted that "the
first thing Mrs. Cooper did was raise campaign funds by telephoning her
many friends and relatives in Pasadena, New York, Palm Beach, Newport, and Washington. In those days there was no limit on how much
money an individual could give. And since she knew so many wealthy
people, she succeeded in raising a veritable fortune. It was the first time
John Sherman Cooper actually had the means to finance a campaign."

More valuable than her fund-raising capabilities was Lorraine's presence on the campaign trail. Laurence Forgy, an aide and friend to John
Sherman Cooper, had been one of those to harbor reservations about
Lorraine's involvement: "With her silk parasol, pinwheel hat, brocade
dress, and emerald-studded cigarette holder, I thought, 'Oh my God,
they're just going to laugh her right out of the state.' But they enjoyed
her. It was like Marie Antoinette comes to Kentucky. Men, women, and
children stood five-deep on street corners to catch a glimpse of her. They
loved her, they loved her parasol, they loved seeing her. She spoke with a
kind of Tallulah Bankhead intonation. 'Hello, dahl-ing.' They loved that
too. It didn't sound affected coming from her. It wasn't as if she was some
kick-ass Kentucky politician. She didn't have a lot in common with the av-
erage person on the street. But they enjoyed seeing her. They wanted to
shake her hand. After the 1956 campaign, when Cooper's advisers realized what an asset Lorraine could be, they encouraged him to bring her
along on future campaign runs—and not to tone her down. She was always there for him, loyal to the end."

Back from India, the couple and their entourage crisscrossed the
state, driving from one improbably named township to another: Paducah,
Paintsville, Neon, Barbourville, Monticello, and London. Then there
were the more familiar ports of call: Louisville, Lexington, Frankfort,
Bowling Green, and Somerset—Cooper's birthplace, where he maintained a small, furnished apartment for occasional visits. Mostly they
were on the stomp, spending nights at wayward motels and country inns,

Lorraine shampooing her husband's hair with a raw egg to bring out the sheen. She read to him from Nietzsche and Shakespeare so he could interject a line or two from one or the other into his next day's speech. When they weren't stuffing themselves at church picnics or chicken barbecues, they took their meals at roadside diners. And whenever the opportunity presented itself, Lorraine would demonstrate her sense of humor. At the Crossroads Diner on the outskirts of Berea, Kentucky, an angry woman berated her for smoking a cigarette at the lunch counter. "Listen," the candidate's wife replied, "I'm supporting the state's most valuable crop."

One of Lorraine's first endeavors as a senator's wife entailed writing a regular column for a string of Kentucky newspapers. Written in a down-to-earth literary style that any layman could understand, the column kept her husband's constituents abreast of the latest political events and developments. In one of her columns she extended an invitation to her Kentucky readership to visit her at home whenever any of them found themselves in the nation's capital. "They would arrive at her doorstep at four in the afternoon, in time for high tea," reminisced John White. "These toothless, shoeless wags from every hamlet and hollow in Kentucky would show up and spill their guts. The bluegrass state then being one of the most impoverished in the country, their concerns were basic. Employment, health care, and education were the main topics of conversation. And Lorraine Cooper would sit there, sipping her tea, listening, taking notes on a yellow lined legal pad for further action."

After Cooper's election to the Senate in 1956, the question of where the couple would live never came up again. Lorraine's Georgetown house became their home, an ideal location for dinner parties and dances as well as political gatherings and meetings. Besides the usual soirées, the Coopers initiated what soon became a Washington tradition, their annual late spring garden party, an affair for senators and their spouses that gradually grew to include diplomats, Supreme Court justices, Pentagon officials, industrialists, White House staffers, and CIA operatives.

Journalist Don Shannon depicted Lorraine Cooper as "the Mother Confessor" of Georgetown. "She somehow inspired people to talk; this enabled her to collect data that proved useful for her husband's political purposes. She and John Sherman Cooper, for example, were on the best of terms with Frank Wisner, James Angleton, Cord Meyer, and Desmond FitzGerald, all of whom supplied them with constant updates on matters of national security." She also gathered information that had nothing to do with politics and everything to do with matters of a personal nature. Kay Graham, her friend and bridge partner, opened herself to Lorraine regarding the ongoing marital strife she and Phil were experiencing. Vangie discussed her marriage to David Bruce, talking at length and in detail about their respective flings and flirtations. After Jacqueline Kennedy revealed her fear of having to campaign with Jack, it was Lorraine who helped her master some campaign strategies, including the importance of remembering people's names and faces. "If Jack's going to run for president," Lorraine told her, "it will help if you can remember the names of people you meet on the campaign trail. I don't mean some housewife you see once on a reception line in Iowa; I'm talking about minor political officials—a mayor, a judge, a convention delegate. It makes a world of difference to these people if you can address them by name." She advised Jackie to carry little cards with her and to send them the minute she departed a city or town. "Write the card and mail it at once. 'Dear So-and-so, thank you for this or that.' If you don't send it right away, things will pile up and you'll forget."

Robert F. Kennedy, JFK's campaign manager, turned to Lorraine for advice on how best to utilize Jackie in the 1960 presidential primaries.

"Should we bring her down to West Virginia?" asked Bobby.

"Why wouldn't you?" Lorraine responded.

"Because West Virginia's populated largely by coal miners and their wives. A lot of them are out of work. Jackie spent her junior year at the Sorbonne, loves fox hunting and fine china, wears mostly designer fashions from Paris, and has her hair done by someone who charges more for a comb-out than most coal miners make in a month. They'll hate her, and we'll blow the primary."

"Nonsense," said Lorraine. "If they like me in Kentucky, they'll adore Jackie in West Virginia. She's young, she's beautiful, and she's glamorous. That's what Americans want today. They'll turn out in droves just for a gander at Jackie. And they will give Jack their vote."

"Lorraine Cooper was one of the few women I knew in Washington," Evangeline Bruce told the current author, "who was able to overcome the stigma of being a woman in a town notoriously hostile to women. Old or young, married or single, women in Washington were almost always looked down upon. They were considered decorative but dispensable. Being a congressional spouse was particularly difficult, more so even than being an ambassador's wife. It was the kind of thing where a senator's wife would go to a dinner party, be seated next to a journalist, and be asked, 'So what does your husband think?' I can't imagine anyone asking Lorraine such a question.

"Women in Washington used to serve the dual purpose of raising families and entertaining for their husbands. They would visit each other from three to six o'clock every afternoon, arriving by carriage, pressing their visiting cards into the calloused hand of a butler or valet, then settling down to tea and idle ladies' chatter. Dinner invitations usually went out so far in advance that the hostess might be remarried by the time the appointed date and hour rolled around. Lorraine represented a major departure from this kind of old-fashioned social behavior. Women were changing, their roles were changing, and Lorraine Cooper was leading the charge."

Lorraine's flawless instincts proved to be of immense value to John Sherman Cooper. During his years in the Senate he championed programs in such diverse fields as labor legislation; federal aid to schools; coal mine safety legislation; aid to farmers; water resources development; aid to underdeveloped nations; health insurance for the aged; and civil rights. He opposed development of the costly antiballistic missile system; attempts to undermine the Tennessee Valley Authority; infringements upon individual rights. From his position on the Foreign Relations Committee, Cooper was one of the earliest, most persistent, and influential critics of the Vietnam War, capping his opposition to that hopeless campaign by cosponsoring the Cooper-Church amendment, paving the way for an end to hostilities. "Nothing that I have accomplished would have been possible," Senator Cooper told an interviewer from *Time*, "without my wife's backing and encouragement. She is my researcher, editor, publicist, partner, and best friend. She made it all happen."

Lee White observed that "John Sherman Cooper lived in his own little universe, so my role . . . at the time, was to make sure things got done. I soon figured out how to work with him and I discovered I had an ally, because Mrs. Cooper knew how to work him too. . . . She knew exactly how to handle him.

"She would bring him lunch, for example, because she knew what he wanted to eat, could eat, would eat, and how to prepare it and put it together. On occasion she would deliver it herself. On other occasions it would be delivered by one of his drivers."

In her oral history at the University of Kentucky, Jackie Kennedy discusses the "very civilized" dinner parties that the Coopers gave. In the atmosphere that pervaded such parties, "sometimes quite a lot can happen. Contacts can be made, you might discuss something. . . . You might have different foreigners there and then say, 'Gee, that's an idea. Maybe we ought to see each other next week on that,' or whatever. So it can be valuable that way. . . . I always felt that going to the Coopers . . . well, it was joyful but it was never frivolous. Social life . . . is part of the art of living in Washington."

For her part, Lorraine Cooper envisioned life in the nation's capital as something intricate and illimitable. "Washington," she told Bill Walton, "is like those exquisite Chinese boxes that contain another box and then another and another. Each one you open is, you're sure, the last one, but then you find there's still something else, something more inside. You can feel it. . . . I still keep opening new boxes. I begin to wonder if I'll ever open the final one—or if there is one."

CHAPTER SEVEN

DEAD MEN WALKING

MOST CONGRESSIONAL WIVES soon discovered that official Washington had little use for them. Although almost all of these women had played an integral role in the campaigns of their spouses, once they reached the nation's capital they rapidly became expendable. What most congressional wives had in common was a sense of frustration, the feeling that not only was Washington most decidedly a man's town but also that everything in Washington revolved around the political aspirations of the husband. Her needs, her schedule, even her opinions took a backseat to his. Unless she had a profession of her own, the congressional wife was all too quickly relegated to the secondary position of housewife and nursemaid.

Determined to avoid being cast in this unfortunate role, Lorraine Cooper took it upon herself to accomplish in the political arena what her close friend Evangeline Bruce had managed to do in the world of diplomacy. Lorraine would attempt to make herself indispensable to her husband by becoming a partner in his senatorial career, selecting an area of legislation that interested them both, then immersing herself in all aspects of that field. Expanding upon the work she had already undertaken—the Kentucky newspaper column; her involvement in sundry senatorial wives' groups—Lorraine joined her husband's fight on behalf of civil rights.

Secretary of State Dean Acheson (right) and Supreme Court Justice Felix Frankfurter were both Georgetown residents who often walked to work together. (*George Tames, NYT Permission*)

Alice Roosevelt Longworth, daughter of President Theodore Roosevelt, became the darling of Georgetown society. (*CORBIS*)

Perle Mesta, "hostess with the mostess," greets Senator and Mrs. John F. Kennedy at a party. (*AP Wide World Photos*)

Katharine Meyer (Graham),
nine years old, on horseback.
She often rode at the Meyer
family estate in Mount Kisco,
N.Y. (*Library of Congress*)

Philip L. Graham, president and publisher of
The Washington Post, assumed control of the
paper a month short of his thirty-first birthday
in 1946 when Katharine's father, Eugene
Meyer, left to become president of the World
Bank. Suffering from manic depression,
Graham killed himself in 1963. (*AP Wide
World Photos*)

Katharine Graham at her home in 1978. (*Copyright
Washington Post. Reprinted by permission of the
D.C. Public Library*)

With its large expanse of front lawn, the R Street mansion of Katharine Graham in the heart of Georgetown is atypical of most town houses in the area. *(Lisa Friel Photography)*

Brothers Joseph (left) and Stewart (right) Alsop, political journalists, at home in Georgetown. *(Magnum)*

James B. "Scotty" Reston, Washington bureau chief of *The New York Times,* and Georgetown resident. *(AP Wide World Photos)*

Celebrated cookbook author and TV chef Julia Child taught the members of the Cooking Class, a group of Georgetown ladies and subset of the Sunday Night Supper Club. (*Bettman/CORBIS*)

Frank Wisner, husband of Polly Wisner Fritchey, served as chief official at the Central Intelligence Agency. Wisner used Georgetown parties as a listening post. He committed suicide in 1965, two years after Phil Graham ended his life. (*AP Wide World Photos*)

James Jesus Angleton, chief of counterintelligence at the CIA and America's preeminent spy catcher, disliked Georgetowners but haunted their parties to collect data and intelligence. (*AP Wide World Photos*)

Senator and Mrs. John F. Kennedy with their daughter, Caroline, in front of their N Street town house in Georgetown, 1959. (*Mark Shaw/Photo Researchers*)

President John F. Kennedy and Ambassador Charles E. "Chip" Bohlen conferring at the White House. Bohlen advised the president during the Cuban Missile Crisis at a dinner party held at Joseph and Susan Mary Alsop's Georgetown home. (*Bettman/CORBIS*)

ABOVE, LEFT: David K. and Evangeline
Bruce, 1949. (*AP Wide World Photos*)

ABOVE, RIGHT: Evangeline
Bruce, 1962. A perennial
on the best-dressed lists,
Vangie was known for her
big hair, multipatterned
stockings, and the leg-
endary evenings she and
her husband gave in
embassies around the
world, as well as at home
in Washington. (*AP Wide
World Photos*)

LEFT: Evangeline and
David K. Bruce's home on
34th Street in Georgetown.
(*Lisa Friel Photography*)

FAR LEFT: Washington hostess Joan Braden, married to journalist and former CIA operative Tom Braden. In addition to throwing many parties, the couple parented eight children, inspiring the TV sitcom *Eight Is Enough.* (*AP Wide World Photos*)

LEFT: After marrying in 1955, Lorraine and John Sherman Cooper went to India, where he served as American ambassador. (*AP Wide World Photos*)

The home of Lorraine and Senator John Sherman Cooper on N Street. (*Lisa Friel Photography*)

The first private dinner party the Kennedys attended after attaining the White House in 1961 was at the home of Lorraine and John Sherman Cooper. (*Mark Shaw/Photo Researchers*)

LEFT: Mary Pinchot and Cord Meyer Jr. after their marriage in 1945. Meyer later became an important official in the Central Intelligence Agency and was a close friend of James Angleton. (*Bettmann/CORBIS*)

BELOW: Murder scene of Mary Pinchot Meyer, who was accosted and killed while walking along Georgetown's C & O Canal towpath in 1964. Although a suspect was arrested and convicted, theories about her death continue to this day. (*Bettmann/CORBIS*)

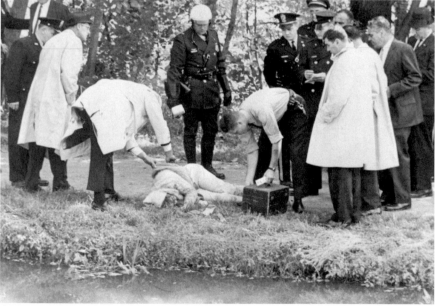

"Kentucky is considered a southern border state," said Mitch McConnell, "and John Sherman Cooper became the first senator from Kentucky—and one of the first senators from the South—to support civil rights legislation. When I worked in his office as an intern, before becoming a senator myself, I couldn't help but notice the constant stream of mail that came in from constituents opposed to his liberal stance vis-à-vis minority rights. One day I asked him how he rationalized his position on civil rights when most Kentuckians were against enforced integration. I'll never forget his response. 'I represent Kentucky,' he said, 'but more than that I'm an American. And in my opinion the time has come for this country to move forward on the issue of civil rights.' " What Cooper didn't tell McConnell was that as an elected official, he deemed it a Jeffersonian conceit to vote according to the dictates of his conscience. If the citizens of Kentucky felt betrayed, they had the perfect right to vote against him in the next election. That they didn't exercise this option revealed the degree to which they respected Cooper, even if they didn't always agree with him.

While assisting her husband with the preparation of a report on the history of civil rights legislation, Lorraine noticed that Senator Cooper had hired only one African-American to serve on his staff. No other southern senator had done even that much. If Cooper intended to spearhead the civil rights movement in the South, he would need to serve as a role model by employing additional minority personnel. At Loraine's behest, Cooper dispatched Merom Brachman, his chief of staff, to Louisville, Kentucky, to conduct interviews with prospective candidates. "I interviewed eight or nine people," said Brachman, "and one stood out above the rest. Dora Jean Lewis was quick, bright, personable, and pretty. She'd been employed by a former Jefferson County judge and was eager to come to work for Senator Cooper in Washington. So we brought her in and made her an office manager. Lorraine gave her a big party to announce to the world that the race barrier had once and for all been broken among senators from the South."

In mid-1962 the Coopers invited Martin Luther King Jr. to their home for dinner. King felt that John Sherman Cooper, more than any of his Senate colleagues, could convince President Kennedy to speed up the implementation of his civil rights package. Having previously chided JFK for not acting decisively enough, Cooper (despite his friendship with the president) renewed his commitment to the cause by again voicing dissent with what he termed "the tedious pace at which the Kennedy administration has moved in enforcing federal law in support of race equality." King further suggested that Lorraine Cooper, with her abundance of social contacts, approach several of her friends in the press to encourage additional publicity of a positive nature on behalf of the movement. Lorraine contacted Phil Graham, already considered practically a lobbyist for civil rights legislation. His latest crusade involved a front-page *Post* story exposing Washington's Metropolitan Club for having refused to seat a black ambassador who happened to be the dinner guest of George Lodge, the deputy secretary of labor and son of Henry Cabot Lodge. The article led to the eventual establishment of the Federal City Club, the first integrated venture of its kind in Washington. In 1957 Graham had backed the passage of Lyndon Johnson's civil rights legislation in Congress, as well as Eisenhower's decision to send federal troops into Little Rock, Arkansas, to enforce the integration of the city's public school system. In 1960, again using his newspaper as a bully pulpit, he had led the campaign to integrate Washington's municipal swimming pools and tennis courts.

Phil Graham's habitual use of the front page of the *Post* for what many construed as pure editorializing was criticized in certain quarters. He was lambasted for being adversarial, for reporting the news from his own narrow vantage point. And while his heart had almost always been in the right place, from a strict psychological perspective his unaccountable behavior had by this juncture progressed to dangerous proportions. Frantic, frenetic, and sped up, he struck many of his friends as a man of boundless energy. Others recognized in his desperation the telltale signs of somebody suffering from a chronic mental condition. Once a master at deflating the pomposity of so many wounded Washington egos, he now exhibited a number of these same ego-related problems himself. At a Georgetown dinner party one evening in late 1961, Graham had words with John F. Kennedy. "You're too young for the job," said Phil. "You'll need my input." To which the president replied: "After you get elected dogcatcher, sonny boy, you may tell me what to do."

At the same time that he suffered from the manifestations of what would later be diagnosed as a severe bipolar disorder, in this case manic-depressive illness, Graham showed himself to be what he had always been: a brilliant businessman. After Eugene Meyer's death in 1959, much of the rest of the Washington Post Company's corporate stock went to Phil and Kay Graham. As titular head, Phil's main objective had been to make the *Post* profitable—a feat that Meyer had barely been able to accomplish. Having previously purchased a pair of television stations in Miami and Jacksonville, Florida, Graham presently acquired two additional network TV affiliates in Washington, D.C., and Hartford, Connecticut, in addition to a few new radio stations to add to those the company already owned. He purchased *ARTnews* and a handful of other highly regarded specialty publications. He established (together with Otis Chandler, owner of the *Los Angeles Times*) the very lucrative Los Angeles Times–Washington Post News Service, which began with a base of thirty subscribers and soon encompassed large and small newspapers all over the world. He also pulled off one of the most successful business ventures in the annals of American journalism, buying *Newsweek* in 1961 from the estate of Vincent Astor (as well as from Averell Harriman, who was a minority shareholder in the magazine) for only $750,000 in cash as part of a complicated $15 million stock transfer venture, which included the purchase and immediate resale of two radio stations in San Diego, California, percentage points in a television station, and assorted bank loans. He made Osborn Elliott, already an editor at *Newsweek*, editor in chief. Elliott "loved" Phil Graham, saying of him: "When he felt well, his smile could light an avenue." Within weeks Graham fired half of *Newsweek*'s editorial staff, labeling them "a bunch of drunks and incompetents." To lend the magazine greater credibility and make it a worthy competitor of *Time*, he convinced Walter Lippmann to become a contributor. For a package deal totaling nearly one million dollars, including a life insurance policy and new car for his seventieth birthday, Lippman signed on with both *Newsweek* and *The Washington Post*. The only other

Post writer Graham hired at such a premium was Joseph Alsop. But on the whole money wasn't an issue. Those magazine editors and writers who remained on staff received generous pay increases. Ben Bradlee, the Washington bureau chief, was encouraged to hire new talent to cover national news. He promptly employed War Just and Jay Iselin, two of the very best.

For somebody on the brink of extinction, Phil Graham still enjoyed stretches of amazing resilience and productivity. Besides his usual duties at the *Post* and the increased workload that came with the acquisition of *Newsweek,* he joined the board of the Rand Corporation, originally an advisory group to the U.S. Air Force that investigated such public policy issues as national security and atomic energy. In 1962, he accepted a presidential appointment to become chairman of COMSAT—the Communications Satellite Corporation—a semipublic, government-sponsored organization that held regular meetings in New York. And in Washington, he continued as head of the Federal City Council, more powerful in scope and influence than it had ever been. He had better moments in his private life as well. At his daughter's coming-out party on December 26, 1961, guests recalled how handsome he and Lally looked as he waltzed her around the ballroom. Polly Wisner Fritchey told a friend that father and daughter "were the best-looking and most dynamic couple I've seen in years." Lally, like her mother before her, attended the Madeira School before matriculating college.

When Lorraine Cooper met with Phil Graham in the summer of 1962 to discuss civil rights, she found herself in company not with the dynamic family man or the vibrant power broker, but with a figure whose mind and body seemed nine-tenths submerged in cement. "He was practically comatose," Lorraine wrote to Evangeline Bruce in London. "I believe I caught him in the down cycle of his roller-coaster ride through hell. I couldn't get through to him. I understand he's in therapy, but I don't know with whom."

Since October 1957 Phil Graham had been a patient of Leslie ("Les") Farber, a Washington psychiatrist who subscribed to few of the standard practices of his profession. He eschewed medications (with the exception of certain sedatives such as Miltown, to which Phil had actually been addicted), didn't believe in electroshock therapy, encouraged his patients to drink (not heavily but enough to relieve symptoms of anxiety), and led them to believe that they could "cure" themselves by reading existential literature. "Every rule of psychiatry was broken," Kay Graham railed in *Personal History*. "He did more harm than good." In the same volume, she admits that she too became a patient of Dr. Farber, on frequent occasions consulting with him during periods when her husband wasn't. Yet for all her complaints, it somehow never occurred to her to place Phil (or herself, for that matter) under the care of another physician, not at least until it was too late in the game to do any good. In Farber's defense, it should be pointed out that the use of lithium, which is today commonly used to control the mood swings of those suffering from manic-depressive illness, was then only in its experimental stages in this country. As for electroshock therapy, it too had not yet been refined to the point where it was used on any but the most radical cases. And while Graham may well have fit into this category, he had developed a personal antipathy toward its use, having seen its effects on several of his friends. Even had Dr. Farber recommended that Phil undergo electroshock therapy, it is doubtful he would have agreed.

Lorraine Cooper next saw Phil Graham on the evening of October 16, 1962, at a Joe Alsop dinner party. On this occasion, as opposed to the last, Graham, evidently in the manic phase of his illness, could not stop talking. The party had been arranged by Susan Mary Alsop, a descendant of John Jay, first chief justice of the United States, and the widow of Bill Patten, an American diplomat attached to the U.S. Embassy in Paris. Patten, formerly Joe Alsop's roommate in college and always one of his closest friends, had died in 1960. After discussing his homosexual proclivities in a letter to Susan Mary, Joe asked her to marry him, assuring her that together they would reign as one of Georgetown's great royal couples. The two knew each other well. Whenever Joe visited Paris, he had stayed with the Pattens. Aside from Evangeline Bruce, Susan Mary knew as much about French culture as anyone Joe had ever met. Reflecting on his proposal for several months, she finally accepted and sold her house in

Paris. To make room for her, Alsop installed a garage for her car (like John Sherman Cooper, Joe himself didn't drive) and subdivided the second level of his home into two separate but adjoining residential units— his and hers. In January 1961, sixteen years after leaving Washington for Paris, Susan Mary returned, placed her two teenage children in New England boarding schools, and joined her new husband to become, as Joe had promised, one of Georgetown's main social attractions, particularly during the glory days of Camelot when Georgetown, mirroring the upscale atmosphere of the White House, was at its absolute majestic best. Although she and Joe gave hundreds of dinner parties during the Kennedy years, Susan Mary Alsop always considered the affair on October 16 one of the most historically (if not socially) significant.

"I gave it on short notice," she said. "President Kennedy wanted to confer with a couple of Soviet experts because of the problems we were encountering in Cuba. The two specialists were former British Intelligence agent Isaiah Berlin and Chip Bohlen, the recently appointed U.S. ambassador to France. Kennedy insisted on speaking with Berlin and Bohlen in an informal setting. Had they met at the White House, the president would have had to explain their presence to the press. So he asked me to arrange the party and provided me with the guest list. (Aside from the Alsops, the Bohlens, the Coopers, the Kennedys, the Grahams, and Isaiah Berlin, the group included the French ambassador and Madame Hervé Alphand.) The irony of the situation is that on the morning of October 16, Kennedy had been shown CIA surveillance photographs of the Soviet installations on Cuba. It marked the onset of the Cuban Missile Crisis. The gathering took on a whole new meaning."

Kennedy interrogated Berlin and Bohlen at length that evening, soliciting their views on the subject of Russian foreign policy. What were Russia's intentions in Berlin and Cuba? What, if anything, would Khrushchev and the Soviets do in a crisis situation if push came to shove? The president took Bohlen out into the garden to converse alone with him. He quizzed Berlin after dinner, asking him many of the same questions. Berlin and Bohlen independently voiced the opinion that in the event of a showdown, if the question ever arose as to the use of nuclear weapons, they believed Khrushchev would back down. It was on the basis of their views that Kennedy mapped out a game plan to deal with the crisis.

During the dinner Phil Graham carried on as if he were the in-house Soviet specialist, talking until hoarse and drinking until drunk. Although Phil seemed visibly and audibly out of control, John Kennedy (and most of the others) treated him as though he were perfectly fine. Besides Lorraine Cooper, the only person taken aback by Graham's comportment was Isaiah Berlin. Discussing the October 16 gathering in an oral history he conducted for the John F. Kennedy Presidential Library, Berlin reported that after the president and first lady left that night, Phil Graham began acting in an even more peculiar fashion. "He went on and on and on," observed Berlin. "Not that he said anything of very great significance. I've never seen a man . . . more excited."

While Phil Graham carried on with shrill and frenzied energy at the Alsops, his wife responded by retreating behind a hard shell of silence. Kay Graham had all but grown accustomed to her husband's shifting and conflicting mood swings· the sudden euphoria versus the morbid depression. Not yet fully aware of the severity (or cause) of his suffering, she continued to attribute his behavior to alcoholism—and to her theory that success had been handed to him on a silver platter. His achievements at the *Post* had not provided much in the way of satisfaction; with each new acquisition, his responsibilities only increased—as did his stress level. Kay would sometimes listen to him prattle on for hours in a futile effort to buttress his sagging spirits or allay his soaring anxieties. In return, he practically ignored her. When she told him (around the time they purchased *Newsweek*) that she'd been diagnosed with tuberculosis and needed immediate medical attention, he refused to believe her. From time to time he carried on about the president. Envious of John Kennedy's aura and style, he once said to Russ Wiggins: "I'm better looking and more intelligent than Jack. I do better with the ladies. So why is he president?" Katharine Graham likewise had her issues with JFK. In conversation with Joan Braden, she expressed the view that although she admired Kennedy's politics, on a personal level he struck her as a confirmed male chauvinist. "He looks straight through me," said Kay. "Or he looks at me and his eyes glaze over. I'm certain he thinks of me as nothing more than a middle-aged housewife. There's no role for a woman like me in Kennedy's Washington."

ɔ✦o

THE LIFE THAT KATHARINE GRAHAM fooled herself into thinking she loved—or at least, in *Personal History,* claimed she loved—came to an abrupt halt in the late afternoon of December 24, 1962. At approximately 5 P.M. on that date the telephone rang at the Graham residence in Georgetown and Kay picked up, not realizing that Phil had answered it in another part of the house. Listening on her end of the line, Kay overheard a conversation between her husband and a woman whose voice she did not recognize. They talked to each other (Katharine Graham writes in her autobiography) "in words that made the situation plain." Waiting until they had hung up, she confronted Phil and demanded to know if what she had surmised was true. "It is," said Phil. With their children up and around for the Christmas holidays—except for Lally, who had gone on a ski trip—nothing more was said; nothing more needed to be said.

The voice at the other end of the line had belonged to Robin Webb, a slim, blonde, girl-next-door type from Sydney, Australia, who worked as a stringer for the Paris bureau of *Newsweek.* "She was attractive but no bombshell," said Russ Wiggins, who met her briefly later that year. "She struck me as matter-of-fact and down-to-earth but also a bit on the wild side. Her family seemed to have some inherited money. Her father was a leading police official in Sydney. She wanted to be a full-time reporter, and like many a youthful reporter, she used four-letter words unsparingly, as if that were the cool thing to do. Frankly, she seemed an unlikely choice to become the next Mrs. Graham, but for whatever the reason or reasons, Phil became fixated on her. Within weeks of meeting her, he gave her a credit card and opened a joint checking account. The bills were coming back to The Washington Post Company. Frederick 'Fritz' Beebe, chairman of the board of directors, received instructions, presumably from Kay Graham, to go ahead and pay."

They had been introduced by Larry Collins, *Newsweek*'s Paris bureau chief, on November 3, 1962, during one of Graham's visits to the French capital, where he had gone on behalf of COMSAT. In need of a secretary to take notes during a meeting, Graham asked Collins to send somebody from *Newsweek*. After some hesitation, Robin Webb volunteered. Two days later, after Graham arranged a visa for her, she flew to New York to hand deliver a COMSAT-related letter from Graham to William Paley at CBS. She was met at the airport by Phil's limousine and driver, who presented her with twelve dozen bouquets of roses, courtesy of "the Boss." She had been instructed to stay in a suite Phil kept at the Hotel Carlyle on Madison Avenue. (It is perhaps noteworthy that John Kennedy maintained a similar suite in the same hotel and used it in much the same way that Graham used his: for assignations with women of all kinds.) A day after Robin's arrival in the States, Phil followed, met his wife in New York and returned to Washington with her; less than twenty-four hours later, he flew back to New York for an editorial meeting at *Newsweek*. Following the meeting he collected Robin at the Carlyle and whisked her off for a long weekend at Glen Welby, the Graham family's vacation retreat in Virginia. "And so it began," Kay Graham remarks in *Personal History*. "I don't know how long she stayed in the United States, but when she returned to *Newsweek*'s Paris bureau, she was discreet about the relationship with Phil, though it was clear, according to Larry Collins, that she was on cloud nine." Around the Paris office, having met and conquered "the Boss," Robin came to be known as "the Popsie."

By the beginning of 1963 Phil Graham had become the talk of Georgetown. "It wasn't just his romance with Robin Webb," said Russ Wiggins, "but rather his overall demeanor. At the *Post*, for example, he picked on everyone. There were some incredible blowups and explosions of temper. He would just suddenly go off like a geyser—yelling, screaming, telling us what a bunch of 'frigging, dumb-ass jerks' we all were. His language, always a bit salty, turned downright ugly. I wondered sometimes if he'd picked it up from Robin Webb, or whether it was simply another symptom of his illness. On several occasions he threatened to fire me. I was editor of the editorial page at the time and when I refused to publish an absurd editorial he'd written on Cuba, he tried to have me axed. The only reason he backed down is that Alfred Friendly, managing editor of the *Post,* told him he'd quit if I were canned. He would've lost two of his top editors in one fell swoop. There were several other very bizarre episodes. I remember hearing about a telephone conversation between Phil and John F. Kennedy—they must have been debating some political issue, because at a given point Phil lashed out at the president, saying to him: 'Do you have any idea who you're talking to?' And Kennedy responded: 'I know I'm not talking to the Phil Graham I have so much admiration for.'

"At a private luncheon between Phil and British ambassador David Ormsby-Gore, a close ally of JFK, Graham began attacking the president, taking him to task, among other things, for the failed Bay of Pigs invasion of Cuba. 'Kennedy laid the blame for the fiasco on Allen Dulles and Dick Bissell, but in reality the responsibility's his,' said Graham. Ormsby-Gore said something like, 'A president's only as good as the Intelligence he receives.' 'Oh come off it,' Phil yelled. 'I should be sitting in the Oval Office. At least I know what I'm doing.' The meal ended abruptly with the ambassador excusing himself and calling for his car."

For Phil Graham's closest friends it was difficult to accept the discrepancy between him as fallen angel, a haunted deeply troubled man, and his earlier persona, that of the sun king, a brilliant and ebullient icon. George Smathers was dismayed by his decline. "During his early years there was no indication at all of the illness that later ravaged his mind," said Smathers. "As an example of his earlier persona, I remember a famous encounter he had with Pam Humphrey, wife of Eisenhower Treasury Secretary George Humphrey, as they sat next to each other at a Georgetown dinner party. Mrs. Humphrey had brought up her husband's supposedly agonizing choice to give up the benefits of his job as the highly paid head of a large corporation in Cleveland to become a member of the cabinet. Phil Graham looked at his tablemate and said, 'Mrs. Humphrey, making that kind of remark down here in Washington is like belching in Shaker Heights. We think of serving the United States of America as a privilege, not a sacrifice.'

"Those were the days when Phil's grand personality dominated. The later Phil Graham was a man who would never again lead a normal life, knew it, and was therefore at the end of his tether. I saw him regularly until the end. He would either be going a thousand miles an hour, or would seem agonized and isolated. Jack Kennedy once told me he thought that if Phil hadn't gone mad, he could have become president."

When Jack Valenti arrived in Washington after JFK's assassination in late 1963 to serve as press secretary to LBJ, he heard a number of harrowing tales concerning Phil Graham. "Lyndon Johnson had been well aware of the rapid deterioration of his longtime friend," said Valenti. "The day had come when Graham marched into the Oval Office and said to Kennedy: 'You're fired!' He told Vice President Johnson the same thing. At other times he told Johnson that he'd never be president, that his political career was doomed. 'This is the end of the line, Lyndon. You'll always be the number two man.' Deeply wounded, Johnson gradually cut himself off from Graham, though it was painfully clear that these were the remarks of someone who had taken leave of his senses. Very simply, Phil Graham in all his delusion saw himself as master of the universe."

Another friend of Phil's, Secretary of Defense Robert McNamara, who was then feuding with some of the top Pentagon personnel, received a telephone call from Graham in which he mentioned, first, that he was about to marry Robin Webb, and second, that McNamara's altercations with the military were hurting the nation, and he, Graham, intended to bring them all together and settle everything. "Look, Phil," responded McNamara with uncharacteristic humor, "you take care of The Washington Post and I'll look after the Defense Department."

Among the common symptoms of manic-depressive illness that Phil began to display was an increasing inability to censure himself. He was capable of saying almost anything to (and about) anyone. One of his favorite scapegoats was his deceased (and therefore defenseless) father-in-law, whom he vilified at every opportunity; Agnes Meyer, a woman he had seemingly once admired, became an equally inviting target. "As she aged," said Russ Wiggins, "Agnes developed a digestive-tract disorder and was apt, especially after a meal, to pass gas in a very noticeable manner. When this happened during a Washington Post editorial meeting that she attended, Phil let loose with a barrage of insults, embarrassing her by loudly complaining: 'Goddamn it, Agnes, can't you fart at a slightly lower decibel? And what did you eat for lunch? The room's beginning to smell like a hard-boiled egg factory.' " And then there was Kay Graham. In 1961 Phil offered Kermit Lansner, one of his top people at *Newsweek,* a cash loan toward the purchase of a New York brownstone. When Lansner declined, stating that he didn't want to be beholden, Phil responded: "Listen, don't kid yourself, we're all beholden. Have you looked at my wife?"

Graham's friends were most appalled by another of his aberrations, one that came to light as early as 1957 when Phil (in conversation with several *Post* editors) referred to Eugene Meyer, then still alive, as "a wily Jew so full of self-loathing that he attends church instead of synagogue and pretends to be Christian." Graham's freshly minted anti-Semitic rhetoric soon found other outlets. Joe Rauh, Graham's Jewish friend from Harvard Law School and a leading civil rights attorney, spent hours on the telephone listening to Phil discourse on the subject of "Jewish bankers and Jewish newspaper moguls." Another acquaintance, Ella Poe Burling, attended a garden party at Lorraine and John Sherman Cooper's house, at which Phil carried on about "the rich *Yids* who still run Hollywood." Burling found it "truly sad that a man of Graham's status and caliber should resort to such language. I thought the cause of it might have been the resentment he harbored against his Jewish in-laws."

Although there were those—such as writer David Halberstam—who felt that Phil Graham's anti-Semitism was a direct product and reflection of his illness, "something which would not have developed had he remained healthy," others saw it as a distinct defect of character. Two of Katharine Graham's biographers—Tom Kelly and Carol Felsenthal—cite myriad examples of Phil Graham's anti-Semitic and anti-Zionist outbursts. His most offensive slur may well have been directed at his wife. "I absolutely believe that [Phil] called Kay a kike," remarked Carol Felsenthal. In *The World of Oz,* an autobiography by Osborn Elliott, the former *Newsweek* editor recalls a luncheon with several of the magazine's top staff people at which Phil drank, swore, made capricious promises, then poked "cruel fun of his daughter, Lally," saying of her, "[She's] pretty bright for a little Jew girl." Truman Capote, whose friendship with Kay Graham dated to 1960 when they were introduced by Babe Paley, informed an interviewer for the *Washington Star* (November 1978) that he considered Phil Graham "a bad number—something about the [southern] cracker with the big gapped teeth . . . something about his total non-Jewishness that appealed to [Kay], there would always be some rebel in a family like that." Capote went on to say that "Kay was always attracted to WASPs—all the people she's attracted to are cut from the same cookie . . . the men she thinks are attractive all come out of the same jar."

Capote told his friend film producer Lester Persky that he had spotted Phil Graham with Robin Webb in the late winter of 1963 at a Park Avenue cocktail party in Manhattan. "Phil and Kay had split," said Capote, "and at this gathering he practically had his hand inside her dress. They were standing in a corner of the room and he was all over her."

The "split" between Phil and Kay occurred on January 12, 1963, approximately three weeks after Kay's discovery of her husband's infidelity. At first, in the wake of the intercepted telephone call, Phil had assured his wife that although he loved Robin Webb, he intended to break it off with her ("I'll send her away") and preserve his marriage. In typical male manner, he also took the opportunity to unburden himself to his wife, divulging details of some of his past liaisons with women, including several of Kay's professed friends. He admitted propositioning Joan Braden, though she had been sensible enough to turn him down. He said nothing about Nancy Dickerson or his lengthy affair with Constance Noel. Nor did he tell her about the Swedish stewardess he'd met on a flight to Europe years before and whom he still saw on occasion or about the parade of female staffers at the *Post* whom he had previously seduced. Although her husband's confessions of debauchery wounded her deeply, Kay wanted desperately to preserve her marriage. Attempting to maintain a semblance of normalcy and to conceal their marital woes, the couple continued to socialize with family and friends. One friend, Ina Ginsburg, observed that "when they weren't socializing, Phil would often sit at home and cry. He would absolutely break down and weep. Kay would quickly try to drum up a dinner engagement for them or a foursome for indoor tennis. She and Phil played tennis together, and this would sometimes cheer him up."

One evening, returning home from a party at the Felix Frankfurters,

Phil rebuked Kay for looking so glum during dinner. The following day—
January 12—they argued. Phil packed a bag and called for a cab. Kay followed him out of the house in her nightgown, imploring him to return.
He passed the night in his office at the *Post,* drove up to New York in the
morning, and moved into his suite at the Carlyle. Robin Webb flew in
from Paris to join him. They spent several days shopping, attending the
theater, going to parties and out to dinner. One frigid, snowy afternoon
he drove her around town in his convertible with the top down. They
went to Brooks Brothers, and within minutes Phil left the store holding
three shopping bags full of men's dress shirts, which he began handing
out to passers-by on the street corner.

While in New York, Graham met up with Otis Chandler (of *Los An-
geles Times* fame) and his young, attractive wife Missy (currently Marilyn
Chandler De Young). Like Phil, they were about to leave for Phoenix,
Arizona, to attend a meeting of the Associated Press. Graham graciously
invited them to fly to Phoenix with him aboard a private jet owned by the
Washington Post Company. His companion on the trip would be Robin
Webb.

"We were confused," said Missy, "because we'd been chummy with
Phil and Kay for several years. We'd heard about Phil's mental state but
didn't realize how far it had progressed—or that he'd dropped Kay for
somebody else. So we telephoned Kay in Washington, and she asked us
to keep an eye on Phil."

They flew first to Sioux Falls, South Dakota, where (according to *Personal History*) Phil had agreed to speak before the chamber of commerce
and meet with the publisher of the *Sioux Falls Argus Leader,* a newspaper he had hoped to purchase. Another passenger on the flight, Senator
George McGovern of South Dakota, noticed that Phil seemed to be "behaving strangely," an impression evidently shared by the Chandlers. They
were greeted in Sioux Falls by the publisher of the paper, who remarked
that he'd heard only the most wonderful things about Phil. "And I hear,"
responded Graham, "that you're a real son of a bitch." Not surprisingly,
the newspaper deal fell through.

Following his chamber of commerce speech Phil rejoined Robin

Webb and the Chandlers on the second leg of the flight. "Shortly after takeoff," said Missy Chandler De Young, "an extraordinary event took place. Phil suddenly wrestled me to the floor of the cabin, rolled on top of me, and started making suggestive movements with his torso, at the same time trying to kiss me. Otis had to pull him off. It was more than clear at that moment that Phil had gone mad. He was crazy."

Once the two couples reached Phoenix and checked into their hotel, Otis again telephoned Kay. He said nothing about the airplane incident, informing her only that he and Missy had taken the suite next door to Phil's and that they had hired a private security guard to look after Phil during the meetings slated to take place prior to the final banquet and swearing in of a new AP board of directors. For the next two days neither Phil nor Robin emerged from their quarters, their sole contact with the outside world being the room service operator from whom Phil ordered two cartons of Parliament cigarettes (he had a two-pack-a-day habit), a dozen bottles of champagne, and a large box of Trojan 4Xs. Their first public appearance came at the Sunday night banquet. Ben McKelway, editor of the *Washington Star* and president of the AP, had begun his keynote address when Graham rose from his seat, walked straight to the lectern, and pushed the speaker aside. In a flurry of four-letter words, he denounced the AP as "a body of guileless, gutless, good-for-nothing motherfuckers." Besides attacking the press in general, he singled out certain individuals among those present for special mention, calling them names and deprecating their professional credentials. He then turned his attention to the subject of "Sex and the Oval Office," wondering aloud why nobody in the press had "blown the lid" on President Kennedy's "sexual exploits" in the White House. "Not one of you has any balls," he told them. In addition to the almost daily White House swimming pool orgies, "my pal, the president," he went on, "is having his way with another friend of mine, a gorgeous Georgetown artist and socialite named Mary Pinchot Meyer." Graham's announcement was greeted by a stunned silence. That not a single story or gossip item appeared in any newspaper, magazine, or tabloid as a result of Graham's outburst seems nothing short of miraculous. Evidently, in the early 1960s, the same ground rules that applied to the privileged private lives of American presidents extended to the very public lives of psychotic newspaper magnates as well as their Georgetown socialite lovers.

Equally amazing was the fact that for some twenty minutes, while Graham rattled aimlessly on, nobody did anything to stop or interrupt him. "It was a pitiful performance," said Missy Chandler, "too painful to acknowledge. We just sat there and watched." Only when he began to unbuckle and then step out of his trousers did somebody step forward. Emily McKelway, Ben's intrepid wife, having seen and heard enough, took Graham by the hand and guided him back to his seat. Otis Chandler, aided by the security guard he'd hired for the occasion, managed to lift him off the ground, carry him out of the banquet hall and back to his suite. From there, Phil began telephoning old friends and family members, many of whom he hadn't seen or spoken with in years. One call went to his wife. In her autobiography, Kay writes that her husband put Robin Webb on the phone and that Robin said to her: "I do love him, but you were there first." If the intensity of Phil's behavior shocked or frightened Robin, she never mentioned it—to Kay or anybody else. He later called his daughter, Lally, at the time an undergraduate at Radcliffe. She and her brother Donald, a freshman at Harvard, flew from Boston to be with their father. At some point that evening, Phil phoned the White House and asked to be put through to the president. "Phil," said Otis Chandler, "you're not disturbing President Kennedy, are you?" "He's a buddy of mine," insisted Graham, "and I want him to meet Robin when we return to Washington."

Graham placed still another telephone call, this one to Ed Prichard in Kentucky. Presently married and working in the field of public education, Prich recognized the seriousness of the situation from the strain in Phil's voice. Indebted to Graham for having raised funds for his legal defense during his term in prison, Prich contacted several acquaintances from his days in Washington, one of whom remained on solid terms with Lyndon Johnson. Apprised of the turn of events, Johnson notified Kennedy. Missy Chandler confirmed that her husband also contacted Kennedy. Presumably reacting to both telephone calls, JFK dispatched a government plane to Phoenix to bring Phil Graham back to Washington.

The morning after the banquet, before the arrival of *Air Force Two*, Phil decided to take a swim. Leaving Robin Webb behind, he walked over to the hotel's outdoor pool and there encountered a couple of women he happened to know from Washington. One was Marie Ridder, whose husband controlled the Ridder Newspaper Group. "I'd gone swimming with my cousin-in-law, Janine Delano, a cousin of the Roosevelts," said Ridder. "Janine was a rather blonde, classic, very attractive girl, a good deal younger than most of the women attending the AP convention. So was I. We were standing at the edge of the pool in our bathing suits. That's when Phil Graham appeared. He came over to us and he shoved Janine up against a nearby wall and pinned her there. He called her a bitch. Then he turned to me. 'And you're a whore!' he hissed. It was scary. It was physically scary because there was nobody else around and you had no idea what he might decide to do.

"I've often wondered what set him off. He didn't pick us at random. I think he had a reason. We were young and attractive, the wives of successful newspaper publishers. Maybe that had something to do with it. In any case, a few hours later his doctors arrived and took him away, after forcibly injecting him with sedatives, in a straitjacket."

The incident, coupled with his sexual attack on Missy Chandler, lends credence to Evangeline Bruce's contention that Phil Graham had at various times been both verbally and physically abusive toward his wife, that their relationship had been far worse than Kay had ever been willing or able to admit.

Dr. Les Farber had boarded the government plane in Washington. With him when the air transport landed in Phoenix was another psychiatrist, Dr. Ian Cameron, whom he had brought in on a consultant basis. They had decided that if Graham refused to board the plane voluntarily, they would resort to force. When the first method failed, they tranquilized him, thrust him into restraints, and carted him off. The next dramatic scene coincided with the plane's arrival at Washington's National Airport. Spotting an ambulance waiting in a small terminal with a team of emergency medical personnel, Phil broke loose and began to walk away. He had to be collared and brought back by Donald and Lally, who were part of the group trying to help him. He was transported first to the psy-

chiatric ward at George Washington University Hospital—a facility he depicted as a virtual snakepit—and from there, several days later, to Chestnut Lodge Hospital, a private sanitarium in Rockville, Maryland, approximately twenty miles from Washington. Dr. Cameron, it turned out, was on the Lodge's medical staff.

Aggrieved and deeply embarrassed by the public's general awareness of her disintegrating marriage, Kay Graham turned to Lorraine Cooper for support. Expecting (in her own words) "the sympathy and commiseration of a friend," Kay was taken aback by Lorraine's abrupt candor. In so many words, Lorraine assured her that in the long run she would be better off without Phil.

"What do you mean?" Kay asked.

"Don't you realize what he does to you?" said Lorraine. "Don't you realize he puts you down all the time, that you're the butt of all the family jokes?"

"Loraine, Phil is ill. I'm sure you see that, don't you?"

"Don't say that, Kay. Everybody says that when their husband leaves them. I should know. The same thing happened to me."

In defense of her devotion to Phil Graham, Kay refers to herself in *Personal History* as a "one-man dog."

After less than a week at Chestnut Lodge, Phil received permission to leave the hospital for several hours each day to visit Les Farber for therapy sessions. It was in Les's office that Kay saw her husband again. She drove back with him to the Lodge and saw him once more the following day. Their lengthy conversations convinced her that he was on the road to recovery. On January 31, 1963, she wrote to their friend Cy Sulzberger, of *The New York Times,* that "things [are] working out." But things weren't working out. On February 4, released by Farber from the sanitarium, Phil traveled to New York with Edward Bennett Williams, a well-known Washington attorney and longtime adviser who in the past had also been somewhat friendly with Kay Graham. Now Phil retained him as his personal lawyer, giving formal notice of his intention to divorce Kay and marry Robin. He had another plan as well: he intended to take over *The Washington Post,* wresting its ownership from his wife and her family. He would accomplish this feat in much the same way he had ac-

quired *Newsweek,* essentially by taking out bank loans and by using *Post* money to buy back his wife's stock in the paper, after which he and Robin Webb would be in charge. Having lost her husband, Kay perceived herself as being in imminent danger of losing the family business. She saw the plot as a "logical aspect" of Phil's illness and was determined, despite some initial trepidation, to protect her rights—and those of her children, whom she hoped would one day run the paper. Conferring with her mother, who was even more adamant than her daughter about retaining control of the *Post,* Kay hired Whitney North Seymour, a senior partner with the powerful law firm of Simpson, Thacher & Bartlett. Given Phil's current mental state, Seymour felt confident that the takeover plot would never work. In the throes of his mania (and intermittent bouts of despair), Phil Graham also undertook the preparation of a new will, leaving one-third of his entire estate to Robin Webb, the remainder in trust for his four children. Shortly thereafter he told Edward Bennett Williams that he wanted the will revised again so as to leave two-thirds of everything to Webb and only one-third to his children. Aware that Graham was probably legally incompetent, his judgment impaired, Williams failed to execute the second testament and later acknowledged that the first would never survive the scrutiny of a probate judge.

Joan Braden, who had previously thwarted Phil's efforts to seduce her, thought the attempted *Washington Post* seizure "one more example of his utter madness. Although he had helped make a first-rate newspaper out of what had once been seen as pure fish wrap, and even though he controlled a small majority of the *Post's* voting stock, the enterprise clearly belonged to the Meyers. They had backed the paper financially, sinking millions of dollars into it, purchasing the *Times-Herald* to eliminate the competition and then moving the *Post* into a new building. Phil's attempt at a takeover represented the most blatant display of chutzpah I have ever seen." Joseph Alsop, having also had his fill of Graham, weighed in with his own assessment, describing the couple's marriage (in an article he decided at the last minute not to publish) as "socially and sexually asymmetrical. Phil Graham has for years belittled his wife's appearance, Jewish heritage, intelligence and domestic skills, while simultaneously enjoying the many benefits derived from her family's fortune, not the least of which are a Georgetown mansion and a sprawling country estate in the foothills of Virginia. Having been made publisher of a large metropolitan newspaper simply because he married into the family that owns it, he now endeavors to bilk the family out of its holdings and investments in an effort to take control of the paper." When Agnes Meyer learned of Phil's plan, she too took umbrage. In a rare demonstration of sympathy for her daughter, she gave an enormous bash for Kay (in Kay's home), inviting hundreds of guests. Agnes fully supported her daughter's efforts to regain control of *The Washington Post,* going so far as to counter Phil's altered will by eliminating him totally from her own last testament.

Not long after his release from Chestnut Lodge, Phil took Robin on a trip to Europe. He had instructed Arnaud de Borchgrave, an editor at *Newsweek,* to arrange a reception at the Connaught Hotel in London for the magazine's (as well as *The Washington Post's*) team of foreign correspondents. De Borchgrave, who once characterized Phil Graham as "mesmerizing," did as asked. The reporters flocked in from around the globe and were treated to a stirring welcome address by Graham in which he attempted to establish himself as the once and future owner of the entire media corporation, at the same time introducing Robin Webb as his intended future bride. De Borchgrave paid a stiff penalty for having orchestrated the gathering. After Phil's death and Kay's takeover of the organization, it became clear that Arnaud's days at *Newsweek* were numbered.

While in London, Phil contacted Isaiah Berlin and Pamela Berry, whose husband, Michael Berry, owned the *London Daily Telegraph.* Like Berlin, the Berrys had known the Grahams for years, and although they had always admired Phil, they owed their allegiance to Kay. Phil nevertheless visited with Pam Berry at home on three separate occasions, twice with Berlin in a West End hospital where he was recuperating from heart surgery; neither Pam nor Isaiah would agree to meet with Robin. (After Phil's second visit, Berlin wrote to Joe Alsop in Washington that while "Graham had achieved a great success, he seems intent on throwing it all away.") Phil also contacted David Bruce, the American ambassador, suggesting that he and Robin join David and Vangie for lunch. The Bruces responded that while they would gladly receive Phil, they had no intention of socializing with Robin Webb. Phil met briefly with David and took exception when Bruce began criticizing the CIA for its poor judgment calls regarding American foreign policy. An argument ensued, and the two men parted on strained terms. One afternoon Graham drove out to Regent's Park to meet alone with Vangie at the official ambassadorial residence, Winfield House, a three-story, thirty-five-room, pink brick mansion that Barbara Hutton had given to the U.S. government after World War II. "He tried to change my mind about getting together with Robin," Vangie told the current author. "I told him that everything considered, I shouldn't actually even be getting together with him although I was. But that's where I drew the line. I refused to be introduced to his girlfriend. As a result, David and I received a rather insulting letter from Phil, accusing us of discourteous behavior and poor manners." On their next visit to Washington, the Bruces had dinner with Kay and encouraged her to hold on to *The Washington Post*, to refuse Phil's request for a divorce until he surrendered his claim to the newspaper. In one of his diary entries, David Bruce described the entire affair—the impending termination of Phil and Kay's twenty-two-year marriage—as "inexpressibly sad."

On arriving back in the States, Phil picked up where he had left off, establishing legal residence in the Hotel Carlyle, installing Robin (as advised by his attorney) in her own Manhattan apartment, an arrangement that she soon aborted in favor of living openly with Phil at the Carlyle. She busied herself by taking up photography (Phil bought her the best available equipment) while penning occasional articles for *Newsweek*. The couple spent their weekends at a farm in Virginia that he had bought the year before with financial help from Kay; he was now in the process of landscaping and refurbishing the property to look like nearby Glen Welby. They traveled to Florida, where Phil introduced her to his family, then vacationed in Puerto Rico. Whenever they visited Washington they stayed in a large house Phil had acquired on Foxhall Road. Both in Washington and New York they gave frequent dinner parties to which only Phil's most trusted comrades (and employees) would be invited, including Charlie Paradise, his private secretary at the *Post*, and Jim Truitt, who at one point had been on the payroll of both *Newsweek* and the *Post*, and who served Phil as a kind of glorified right-hand man. Phil's daughter, Lally, went to one of the New York gatherings, but feeling uncomfortable she departed early. (In her correspondence of that period, she refers to Robin Webb as "the girl.") Al Friendly attended several of the parties as a professional courtesy, but his wife, Jean, refused. Sally Reston and Luvie Pearson similarly balked, whereas Scotty Reston and Drew Pearson showed up now and again.

Tyler Abell pointed out that his mother, Luvie Pearson, "had a serious interest in maintaining her friendship with Kay. In the event Phil and Kay divorced, there was a question as to what would become of the *Post*. Since Drew Pearson wrote for the paper, it became a matter of hedging one's bets, of keeping on terms with both of them. My mother would spend hours over at Kay's house and then come home with an armload of Kay's old dresses to pass on to others. She referred to them as 'the Graham Collection.' It was a terrible time for Kay. Her demeanor was exemplary. One might say that this was her finest hour."

"She showed great resilience," said Oatsie Charles, who convinced Kay to accompany her and Polly Wisner Fritchey to New York that spring to attend the ballet. Kay balked at first but finally relented, agreeing that the outing would be good for her. The venture backfired. Before the ballet, the ladies were having dinner at "21" when Leonard Lyons, the entertainment columnist, came over to their table and said to Kay, "I understand you're getting divorced and that your husband's off with another woman. Care to comment?" The question upset Kay. To make matters worse, when they reached the theater they discovered that their tickets were for the following day. Unwilling to return, they paid a small fortune for third-rate seats to that evening's performance.

"An additional problem," Oatsie continued, "is that Frank Wisner, Polly's husband, was also suffering from manic-depressive illness and, if anything, was in even worse shape than Phil Graham. He'd recently been relieved of his duties with the CIA. My husband and I had gone small-game hunting with the Wisners in Spain, and the idea of Frank wandering around in the thicket with a loaded shotgun made me very nervous. I thought he might blow his own head off, so I suggested that somebody from the hunting party remain with him at all times. It seemed uncanny that Kay and Polly, already great friends, should both have husbands suffering from the same crippling mental condition and that they should come to a similar end."

Frank Wisner's mania centered on World War II. He spoke incessantly about Hitler and Hitler's henchmen. His friends and former associates, men like Desmond FitzGerald and Dick Bissell, to say nothing of his wife, were shocked and saddened by his condition. "He seemed quite ill at times," remarked Polly Wisner Fritchey. "It was doubly sad because Georgetown during the Kennedy administration had become such a beguiling place to live. A younger, livelier crowd had moved into the area. Hostesses had become friendly social rivals as to which of them could give the best dinner parties. But because of Frank's condition, it was impossible for us to enjoy the whirl. He would be all right for a while, but before long he'd be flying again or down so low that he couldn't get out of bed. I often felt the only person I could turn to for support and understanding was Kay Graham."

In early June Phil Graham took Robin Webb to California to introduce her to the small staff that made up Newsweek's Los Angeles bureau. Carolyn Michaelis, whose husband, Tim Bishop, was one of a half-dozen Los Angeles–based staffers, observed that "Phil was apparently taking Robin on a cross-country—for all I know around-the-world—jaunt to introduce her as the next Mrs. Graham, while, of course, he was still married to Katharine Graham. They reserved a private dining room at Ciro's and had this little dinner party for Newsweek staffers and their spouses, most of whom already knew Kay Graham, which made it extremely awkward for everyone.

"Robin wasn't exactly a hot babe, but she was cute and had an interesting accent. She seemed lively and was years younger than Phil and appeared to be absolutely taken with him. I'm convinced she really thought he was going to leave Kay Graham for her. She wasn't at all the bleached blonde, gold digger type, and I remember feeling sorry for her because Phil, though attractive and magnetic, was obviously under great emotional strain. It was so bizarre, putting everyone on the spot, making us meet the 'new Mrs. Graham,' his zooming around the room with her, talking incessantly. It was frightening in a way. Robin had been taken in, I guess, and captivated by this charismatic, manic personality, and maybe, being young and naive, she felt she could help him. She would be the one to save him. As for the very public way in which Phil conducted the affair, I suppose that was an expression of his great indignation at being nothing more than the Meyer son-in-law."

Within days of their return from Los Angeles, Phil Graham crashed, his extreme mood shifting yet again from exuberant to desolate. Although Robin Webb could cope to some extent with the manic highs, the depressive lows took the kind of patience she hadn't so far developed. On June 19, in a state of near mental paralysis, Graham gathered three of his most trusted companions—Al Friendly (who was keeping the *Post* afloat in Phil's absence), his brother Bill, and Edward Bennett Williams—and notified them that he wished to resume his marriage with Kay. While Robin Webb, perhaps grateful for the opportunity to get away, was sent back to Paris, Phil rejoined his wife in their R Street home. He lasted only a day before returning (voluntarily) to Chestnut Lodge. Although he remained friendly with Dr. Farber, he had replaced him as his therapist with a staff psychiatrist at the Lodge. Dr. Ian Cameron also continued to see him as a patient.

Sally Reston recalled, "Kay was ecstatic about Phil's return, less happy about his condition. She visited him nearly every day, frequently bringing along a picnic lunch. The hospital had a tennis court, and they would sometimes play a set or two. Other times Kay invited friends along, such as Robert McNamara and his wife, Margy, and they'd simply talk or maybe play a game of bridge. My husband had hired Donald [Graham] as an intern in his office that summer and Kay would provide Phil with periodic updates on his progress. It was the same year that Lally worked at *Newsweek*'s Washington bureau. The two younger boys were at sleepaway camp. Phil was full of guilt and remorse. His actions over the last year or two had hurt everyone: his wife, his children, his friends, his associates. And now, by dropping Robin Webb, he had undoubtedly hurt her as well. But the common perception, at least as communicated to me, had it that Phil was slowly recovering. The hospital staff felt hopeful, as did Kay, that by midfall Phil would be out and back at the helm of *The Washington Post*."

Russ Wiggins had heard just the opposite. "Al [Friendly] went out there to see him toward the end of June and came back with a rather discouraging report. He'd never seen Phil in such bad shape. 'We need you at the *Post*,' Al told him. 'Let's get you the hell out of here and back where you belong.' Phil said nothing for about ten minutes, but when he finally spoke, he said: 'You're wasting your time, Al. It's no good. Nothing coheres for me. I'm not going anywhere.' Al was concerned, especially when he heard that Phil wasn't taking any medication. He knew enough about hyper-mania and manic depression to know that pharmaceuticals were an essential part of the recovery process, and when drugs didn't work, patients were often subjected to electroshock therapy. Phil did neither one nor the other. 'I can't understand it,' Al said to me. 'They're much too lax about his treatment.' Al felt strongly that Phil's doctors ought to have put him on some form of medication, and he blamed Kay Graham for being so passive."

Al Friendly went to see Phil one last time. It was the third week of July, and Phil told him he'd been given permission by his doctors to spend an upcoming weekend with Kay at Glen Welby. He wanted to escape the stifling atmosphere of the hospital. Given what Al had seen and heard during his previous visit, he thought it premature for Phil to leave the sanitarium, even for a few days.

One of Graham's last visitors at Chestnut Lodge was Osborn Elliott. Finding his employer in a positive frame of mind, Elliott saw nothing wrong with his going to Glen Welby for a weekend and even thought he would soon be out of the hospital and back at work. In the course of Elliott's visit, Phil said to him: "Sometimes, when you've shat on as many people as I have in the past year, you wonder if you shouldn't call it quits. But now, while I can't yet *see* the shore on the other side, I know it's there—and I think that's a sign of progress, don't you?"

Always convincing when he wanted to be, Phil had begun talking about the possibility of a Glen Welby visit in mid-July. After a good deal of discussion, the medical staff at Chestnut Lodge sanctioned the request. The sole dissenter, Dr. Ian Cameron, had been privy to past conversations with the patient about suicide and felt that he wasn't yet stable enough to leave the hospital grounds. Although Cameron expressed his views to Kay Graham, she relied more on the nonmedical opinion of Phil's lawyer, Edward Bennett Williams, who envisioned the visit as the first step in getting Graham back into circulation.

On Saturday, August 3, 1963, Phil's driver picked him up at the hospital, drove him to the R Street house—where they were joined by Kay—then took them both to Glen Welby. The couple lunched on the back porch, chatting and listening to Beethoven. Looking out on emerald pastures, Phil commented on his love for Glen Welby, the pleasure he felt at being able to come home again. He spoke plaintively of how badly he had treated Kay, how good she had always been to him, how unworthy he felt. Following their meal, they decided to take a nap and climbed the stairs to the master bedroom on the second floor. At a certain point Phil stood up and announced that he wanted to rest in one of the other bedrooms. A few minutes later, Kay heard an ear-splitting gunshot blast that seemed to come from somewhere downstairs. Her first thought, she later told Drew Pearson, was that Phil might be shooting groundhogs in the garden. Then she had another thought. Racing downstairs, she headed straight for the guest bathroom (inside the guest bedroom). Phil Graham had perched on the edge of the bathtub, loaded his 28-gauge shotgun with a single birdshot shell, propped the firearm against his head and fired. Blood and brain matter had splattered against every wall. His body had slumped into the tub. Everything considered, it seemed like a thoughtfully chosen place for such an ending, somewhere that would be more contained and easier to clean than some other part of the house.

⁓

IN THE LATE AFTERNOON of August 3, President Kennedy sat on the top deck of the *Sequoia,* the presidential yacht, as it sailed the Massachusetts coastline. Seated next to him was John Kenneth Galbraith, the Harvard economist and American ambassador to India. "Besides a skeleton boat crew, a presidential aide or two and a pair of Secret Service agents," said Galbraith, "the only passenger aboard ship was Joe Kennedy, the president's father, who was resting in a cabin below. Kennedy and I were discussing Vietnam, and he was talking about the eventuality of pulling out. Then, out of left field, he brought up Phil and Kay Graham. I knew Phil but only slightly. He had championed several of my books in the *Post*. Just then an aide appeared and said something to the president. An emergency call had come in on the ship-to-shore: Phil Graham had killed himself earlier that afternoon. The news upset Kennedy. He excused himself and went below to brood."

The Grahams employed two full-time farmhands at Glen Welby. One called the county sheriff's office, while the other notified the local coroner. The coroner arrived after the sheriff and several hours later took away the body. Al and Jean Friendly turned up and drove Kay back to R Street. "What am I going to do now?" Kay had asked them. "You're going to take the joint over," Al had responded, meaning she would run *The Washington Post*. That evening a wave of well-wishers dropped in at R Street, not one of whom Kay would remember with the exception of Lorraine Cooper. She told Lorraine she thought Phil had killed himself partially because of the unspeakable pain he had been forced to endure since the onset of his illness, coupled with his growing awareness that the malady he suffered had no cure and would inevitably strike again. He had obviously planned the whole thing well before returning to Glen Welby, manipulating his psychiatrists into believing he was well enough to go home for a few days. He had similarly impressed his wife, so much so that it had somehow never occurred to her to remove his hunting rifles, shotguns, and ammunition from the premises. This glaring oversight gave rise to an inside joke among *Washington Post* and *Newsweek* reporters to the effect that if Phil—at age forty-eight—hadn't pulled the trigger, his embittered spouse would have done it for him.

Although she claimed in *Personal History* that events "seemed hazy" at the time, Kay Graham evidently had the presence of mind to meet (on August 5, two days after her husband's suicide) with the board members of the Washington Post Company in order to assure them that she had no intention of selling the family business, that she planned to carry on either by herself or with the help of her children—eventually, of course, she hoped her children would take over completely. She also spent time with Scotty and Sally Reston, who had interrupted a European vacation to return for the funeral. President Kennedy attended the August 6 cere-

mony at Washington's National Cathedral, as did a number of other administration luminaries, such as Robert McNamara, Robert Kennedy,
Douglas Dillon, and Roswell Gilpatric. ("Who could have imagined," said
Gilpatric, "that JFK himself would be dead less than four months later?")
A private burial took place afterward at Oak Hill Cemetery. "You can just
wheel me across the street," Phil had once kidded his wife regarding the
cemetery's proximity to their house. He had procured their burial plot
years earlier via a fellow parent at St. Albans, the prestigious preparatory
school where the Grahams had sent their sons. "Of all the mourners,"
said Sally Reston, "none seemed more bereft than Edward Prichard."
Looking back on her husband's suicide, Kay Graham would tell television
talk show host Larry King in 1997: "That was very tough. But everybody—I think, almost everybody—has something very tough to deal
with. Maybe not like that, but something very tough." As for Robin
Webb, she soon left *Newsweek*'s Paris bureau and returned to Sydney,
where she eventually met and married Alan Edwards, an Australian
diplomat. The couple later had a son and moved to Canberra, Australia.
Katharine Graham's only meaningful comment about the woman who
had stolen her husband's affections was that she, like Kay, had "to be considered a victim."

Neither Phil's father, who had suffered a serious stroke, nor Kay's
mother, vacationing with the Drew Pearsons and her granddaughter,
Lally, aboard a sleek white yacht in the Aegean Sea, went to the funeral.
At the last minute it was agreed that Luvie Pearson would fly to Washington with Lally, while Drew and Agnes remained aboard the chartered
vessel. A day after the funeral, August 7, having decided to "get away
from everything," Kay sent her two younger sons back to camp and flew
to Istanbul with Luvie and Lally to join her mother midcruise. The aban-
donment of her sons, including Donald, at a time when she should have
been there for them, was an act she claimed she would come to regret.

In his *Diaries,* portions of which remain unpublished and housed at
the Lyndon Baines Johnson Presidential Library, Drew Pearson calls Phil
Graham's suicide "not unexpected." Summarizing his feelings about
Phil's violent demise, Pearson writes (August 4, 1963): "It ended a long

and tragic saga of a guy who began with nothing, married a wealthy girl, inherited tremendous power and let power ruin him. He went so far in trying to rid himself of the girl whose family made him that he became the laughingstock of the newspaper world and never could have staged a comeback."

A day later, August 5, Drew Pearson's diary entry reads: "I put Agnes [Meyer] to bed last night after dinner. She was still mourning for Phil and saying how much she loved him. The irony is that he hated her, used to scoff at her, once threatened to cancel my column because I praised her. Last summer Lally remarked: 'Grandmother's really nice. I always thought from Ma and Pa that she was terrible.' "

Lally, Luvie, and Kay arrived in Istanbul on August 8 and were met at the airport by Drew and Agnes. That evening the group rejoined the yacht and set sail for Bulgaria, Romania, and Greece. Also on board was Clayton Fritchey, a newspaperman and former deputy chairman of the Democratic National Committee. Currently director of public affairs for the United States Mission to the United Nations, Fritchey was a womanizer with a long list of lovers, including Scottie Fitzgerald, the daughter of writer F. Scott Fitzgerald and a journalist in her own right. Mostly, according to those in the know, he sought the company of wealthy women.

Although Kay Graham had money, the thought of becoming instantly involved with a new man didn't appeal to her. Still, according to Drew Pearson's diary entries for the dates in question, Kay evidently found the cruise a pleasurable experience. "We drank and ate until 2 A.M.," Pearson writes on August 12. "I think Kay had a good time. It has been a real relief after the strain of the funeral." Other entries recount late-night dance parties and daytime mainland sightseeing excursions. On August 25, two days before Kay's departure for the States, Pearson writes: "This trip has been a healthy one for Kay. I think she's pretty well over the shock of the suicide."

Several weeks after the Pearsons returned to Georgetown, Luvie gave a ladies' tea at home for a dozen friends. Bess Abell, Luvie's daughter-in-law, walked in on the gathering and recalled that "several of the ladies were remonstrating about 'poor Kay, poor Kay Graham, it's just so sad.

Poor Kay.' And Luvie finally interrupted them. 'Poor Kay, my ass. She's rich, she's in great shape, and now she's also one of the most powerful women in Washington. I wouldn't feel sorry for her if I were you.'"

Clayton Fritchey continued to pursue Kay off and on for the better part of a year, but meeting with stiff resistance he turned his attention elsewhere, eventually pairing off with Polly Wisner, whom he married in 1975, ten years after the suicide of Frank Wisner. Ironically, Wisner killed himself in the same manner as Phil Graham. Wisner's manic-depressive illness made itself felt for the first time in late 1956, the year of the failed Hungarian Revolution. An ardent opponent of Soviet expansionism (Wisner orchestrated an anti-Communist coup in Guatemala in 1954), the CIA official returned from a tour of inspection in Vienna—the closest outpost to the Hungarian frontier—and immediately began to experience a series of wild mood swings and erratic behavior. As Russian tanks rolled into Budapest, he alarmed his friends by sending them long, rambling letters delineating the drawbacks of communism. "He sounded like Joe McCarthy and J. Edgar Hoover combined," noted Sally Reston, whose husband had been the recipient of one such epistle. "He developed a number of strange habits. He told the same stories and jokes over and over again, often to the same person. He became obsessive-compulsive about his work, putting in eighteen-hour days, six and seven days a week. In December 1956 he went into a catatonic depression which ultimately led to a psychotic breakdown." On the advice of several old CIA colleagues, including Desmond FitzGerald, Wisner took sick leave from the Agency, committing himself to the Sheppard Pratt Hospital, a mental institution near Baltimore, Maryland, where he remained for six months and underwent electroshock therapy. According to Thomas Powers's biography of Richard Helms (*The Man Who Kept the Secrets*), Wisner subsequently told FitzGerald: "Des, if you know what you'd done to me, you could never live with yourself." Although Wisner found some relief from his condition, he soon suffered a relapse. Attending an Independence Day party at Paul Nitze's country home in Virginia, he drank too much and became involved in a number of heated political disputes with other guests, at one point heaving a heavy glass ashtray against a door. He became so frenzied at the affair that Dick Bissell had to drive him home. On the way, Wisner carried on for nearly an hour, describing in tremendous detail some silk fabric his wife, Polly, had recently purchased in Thailand. A similar incident took place at the Washington home of French Ambassador Hervé Alphand, Wisner on this occasion making a minutely detailed comparison between the American pastime, baseball, and the international sport of soccer. Wisner took another medical leave from the Agency, placing his chief of operations, Richard Helms, a future CIA director, in charge of the department. This time he entered the psychiatric wing of Johns Hopkins University Hospital, where he again underwent a series of electroshock therapy sessions. These treatments, unlike those at Sheppard Pratt, seemed only to aggravate his condition. He lost whole chunks of his memory and spent whole days railing against Adolf Hitler. Phil Graham spent one hour with him and swore he would never expose himself to electroshock therapy of any kind.

In 1959, as his condition continued to decline, Wisner was removed by his old mentor, Allen Dulles, as head of the CIA's clandestine services division and installed as British station chief. His wife, setting up her London salon in a large and elegant house at Milton Crescent, was criticized (in the press and by friends) for "pushing" her husband beyond his limitations. Their social schedule was frenzied. Cognizant of the gossip, Polly told an interviewer for the London Times that "while people are saying that I'm driving him crazy for social purposes, that's not true. This is what Frank wants. It's his idea. For years, parties and social get-togethers have been the way he gathers information and intelligence."

To make matters worse, Wisner came down with hepatitis and had to be hospitalized. Back on the job, he managed to feud with local government dignitaries, a practice that culminated in his calling a British cabinet minister at 3 A.M. to dictate the press release that, in his opinion, the minister ought to have delivered earlier that day. Recalled to Washington in late 1961, Wisner was replaced by Archibald Roosevelt, who subsequently told colleagues that his predecessor's personal files represented "the work and thoughts of a madman." Soon after his return, he received a visit at his Georgetown home by the Coopers. Lorraine Cooper wrote to Vangie Bruce that she and John had "come upon Frank pacing back and forth in the garden behind his house. He was in his pajamas and was loudly muttering to himself. When John asked him what he was doing, Frank said he was rehearsing a speech he planned to give at a dinner party later in the week. For all his madness, he is still visited by the likes of Randolph Churchill and Malcolm Muggeridge, both of whom dropped in on Frank just the other day. John, however, believes that Frank is a very sick man, and has been for quite some time."

With his mental health in jeopardy, Wisner spent a good part of the next few years in and out of mental wards. In the late spring of 1965 he had surgery for a painful stomach hernia. Weakened and depressed, he moved out to the family farm at Galena, Maryland. Her awareness heightened by the suicide two years earlier of Phil Graham, Polly telephoned their household employee at Galena and asked him to remove all of Wisner's hunting rifles from the house. The employee complied but overlooked a 20-gauge shotgun that belonged to one of Wisner's sons. On October 29, in what turned out to be an uncanny replay of Graham's final act, Frank Wisner, fifty-six, found the weapon, placed it against his right temple, and pulled the trigger. Because of the secrecy surrounding his work for the CIA, his suicide remained a mere blip on the radar screen, rarely mentioned except within the confines of Georgetown's leading drawing rooms. The nature of Wisner's death reawakened in Kay Graham the painful memory of her own husband's demise. She would later reflect in *Personal History* on how "eerie" it had been to find her life and Polly Wisner Fritchey's "following so much the same pattern."

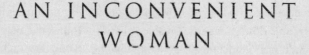

AN INCONVENIENT
WOMAN

THE ASSASSINATION OF President John Fitzgerald Kennedy on November 22, 1963, in Dallas, Texas, brought to an abrupt halt one of Georgetown's most fertile periods of social activity. "There were so many parties during the thousand days of Camelot," said Kennedy White House press secretary Pierre Salinger, who lived in Georgetown, "that they all blend into one. Camelot was one big, endless party." Referring to the encroachment of the Vietnam War, Ambassador Charles Whitehouse called Camelot "a beautiful sunset before an endlessly bitter night." Of JFK's many friends and admirers none was more anguished by his death than John Sherman Cooper. The Kentucky senator subsequently served on both the Warren Commission and on the committee selected by Jacqueline and Robert Kennedy to select a site and raise funds for the John F. Kennedy Library. Regarding his service on the Warren Commission, Senator Cooper publicly expressed dissatisfaction with the commission's findings, terming the group's 1964 report "premature and inconclusive." In no uncertain terms he informed Jack's surviving brothers, Robert and Teddy, that, having personally examined thousands of shreds of documentation, he felt strongly that Lee Harvey Oswald had not acted alone. When he expressed these same sentiments to Jackie, she responded: "What difference does it make? Knowing who killed him won't bring Jack back." "No, it won't," responded Cooper. "But it's important for this nation that we bring the true murderers to justice."

Ten days after the Kennedy assassination, when Jackie and her two young children—Caroline and John Jr.—vacated the White House and moved temporarily into the Georgetown home of Averell and Marie Harriman, at 3038 N Street, John and Lorraine Cooper were among the first to welcome them. In mid-December they gave a small dinner party for Jackie at their home, and a few days later they attended a crowded cocktail party in her honor at the F Street Club. They were also present at a buffet luncheon at the Harriman house organized for the former first lady by Bobby and Ethel Kennedy. President Lyndon Johnson, a guest at the same function, found himself shut out by the distinctly pro-Kennedy crowd. "Nobody would talk to the poor fellow," said Joan Braden. "They considered him an interloper, a usurper of the throne. Finally Lorraine Cooper broke the ice and joined LBJ on the sidelines. And once that happened, others gradually went over to him and made him feel at home. Johnson kept turning up at these affairs and inviting Jackie to visit him and Lady Bird at the White House. Her imprimatur was what he most needed to legitimize his administration. But the last place Jackie wanted to be was back in the Executive Mansion. 'It's much too soon,' she told me."

In January 1964 John Kenneth Galbraith, who had made the arrangements for Jackie to stay with the Harrimans, helped her locate a Georgetown house of her own. On his advice, she paid $195,000 to acquire a fourteen-room, three-story, fawn-colored brick Colonial at 3017 N Street, across the street from the Harrimans. Built with twelve-inch-thick walls circa 1794, the house was fronted by a small grove of old magnolia trees. Jackie's initial choice of Georgetown as a place to reside was predicated to some extent on the fact that she and Jack had enjoyed living there during his years in the Senate. Jack had also lived in Georgetown as a bachelor, while Bobby and Ethel Kennedy were part-time residents before moving to McLean, Virginia. Jackie's mother, Janet Auchincloss, currently owned a home in Georgetown and often volunteered to baby-sit for her grandchildren. The problem with Jackie's new house was that it was raised high off the sidewalk by several flights of steps. It was easy to see into the first-floor windows, which meant that the draperies had to be kept drawn. The interior of the house, devoid of sunlight, had a gloomy feel to it. Not unexpectedly, Jackie had become Georgetown's number one tourist attraction. To the dismay of her privacy-seeking neighbors, the former first lady's arrival transformed the once quaint and quiet village into a raging casbah. Morning, noon, and night the streets were clogged with people eager to catch a glimpse of the young widow and her two beautiful children. They lined up on both sides of N Street, climbing trees and standing on the hoods and roofs of cars, double parking, obstructing traffic, screaming, gesticulating, chanting Jackie's name like a mantra. They sat on the steps of her house, eating their lunch, tossing the leftovers into the gutter. At night they slept in their cars, buying their meals from street vendors hawking an array of fast-food products. The press likewise camped out at Jackie's front door, hundreds of reporters and photographers from around the world, pencils poised, cameras focused. Whenever Jackie emerged from her house, the Washington police and Secret Service agents assigned to her detail cordoned off the street and cleared a path for her. Women would break through police lines in an effort to grab and hug the children as they came and went. On one occasion an elderly female from Iowa took hold of Jackie's hair and refused to let go until knocked to her knees by a burly policeman. The tour bus companies placed the first lady's N Street house on their sightseeing itineraries. Double-deckers rumbled up and down the boulevards at all hours. After ten months of torment, Jackie listed her house with a Georgetown Realtor and made plans to purchase a luxury cooperative apartment on Fifth Avenue in Manhattan, opposite the Metropolitan Museum of Art, where she felt she could reside with a greater degree of anonymity.

While still in Georgetown, Jackie occasionally met with an old friend, a journalist and experimental artist from Georgetown named Mary Pinchot Meyer, the former wife of CIA official Cord Meyer. Talented, worldly, articulate, and attractive, Mary was a descendant of the Pennsylvania Pinchot family that produced a two-term Republican governor, Gifford Pinchot, and which, over the years, amassed considerable wealth and political influence as the founders of the Bull Moose Progressive

Party. Amos Pinchot, Mary's father, had helped establish the American Civil Liberties Union and the controversial America First Committee. The older sister of Tony Bradlee and sister-in-law of Ben Bradlee, Mary's true footnote to history may have been her twenty-two-month affair—January 1962 to November 1963—with John F. Kennedy. Her relationship with President Kennedy, charted and chronicled by Secret Service agents in log books both in the White House and at its tollgate, was more than simply that of lovers. A trusted companion who frequently sat in on Oval Office political huddles between the president and his aides, she was also the woman JFK chose to be with on the night after Marilyn Monroe's body was discovered at her home in Los Angeles. The question most often asked about the Mary Meyer affair was whether Jackie had any knowledge of it. Although pure conjecture, the best answer came from Joan Braden, who knew Jackie well enough to be aware of her astute sensibility. "My guess," said Joan, "is that she knew about all of Jack's extramarital relationships but never attached much importance to them. If anything, she may have felt closer to Mary because of their shared knowledge of JFK. They experienced the same sense of loss. They were also quite good friends in their own right. During Jack's days as a senator, Mary and Jackie would take long walks together around Georgetown. After the assassination they renewed their friendship, often meeting for lunch or just to talk."

If Jackie didn't know about the affair from the start, she almost certainly heard about it as a result of Phil Graham's lunatic outburst at the Associated Press dinner in Phoenix in early 1963. Although nothing appeared in print at the time, Jackie had more than adequate contacts to merit a descriptive firsthand account. Although she probably knew of the affair, she and Mary had a sustained relationship of their own. They were in many ways very much alike and had far more in common than a shared affection for John F. Kennedy. Both were women of exceptionally good appearance and social background. Both wore manners and charm like a second skin, though both were standoffish and somewhat reserved. Both craved independence and personal authority, although they lived at a time when society tended to dismiss these qualities in a woman. Raised on the leafy Pennsylvania estate of Grey Towers and in a luxury apartment at 1125 Park Avenue in Manhattan, Mary (like Jackie) attended Vassar, made her debut in New York society, married well, and had children. Her marriage in 1945 to World War II hero Cord Meyer Junior slowly deteriorated into a contest of wills, particularly after the former "New World Order" advocate became a gung-ho Cold Warrior. The marriage fell apart completely in 1957, following a December 1956 accident in which Michael Meyer, their nine-year-old son, was struck by an automobile and killed. The marriage, already tarnished by sexual affairs on both sides, ended in a 1959 divorce.

Barbara Miller, a 1944 Vassar graduate and former Georgetown resident, remembered Mary "because even though she was a year or two ahead of me, we dated the same man at Vassar, William Attwood, a future ambassador to the U.N. and the eventual publisher of New York *Newsday*. In addition, Mary and I lived in the same dormitory at Vassar: Cushing Hall. Mary's younger sister, Tony, also a student at Vassar, lived there as well. I recall the first time Mary and I actually met. It was a Saturday and almost everyone had gone away for the weekend. It was lunchtime, and since nobody else was around I joined her at the same dining hall table. She had a pretty face with rounded features and rosy cheeks. She wore her hair pulled back, bangs in the front. She possessed a pleasant smile and spoke quickly, although she didn't say much. Toward the end of the meal she remarked that she usually stuck around campus on Saturday afternoons because that was the day they served baked beans and brown bread, both of which she loved. Thereafter whenever our paths crossed, she would stop and exchange a few words. Nothing intimate, but she wasn't snobbish or unfriendly.

"I learned a good deal about Mary from William Attwood. Bill seemed mesmerized by her. He liked her aura. He liked the Pinchot name. He'd known her since his prep school days at Choate. She attended Brearley in New York, and he'd invite her up to Choate on big dance weekends. That's where she first encountered John F. Kennedy. The future president was nothing more than a skinny, fresh-faced Choate upperclassman in those days. He and Mary knew each other but only from afar."

Miller also happened to be acquainted with Cord Meyer, Mary's husband-to-be: "Cord and his twin brother, Quentin, known to everyone as 'Monk,' were undergraduates at Yale, class of 1943, when I met them. I'd been dating Quentin's roommate. Quentin once came by sailboat from Greenwich, Connecticut, to visit me on the North Shore of Long Island. Both brothers were war heroes. Quentin gave his life at Okinawa; Cord joined the Marine Reserves and lost his left eye at Guam when a hand grenade went off in his face. After the war he became a peace activist with a group called the United World Federalists. In 1953, on the basis of supposed leftist associations, Meyer was refused security clearance by the FBI. The CIA, which he had joined two years earlier, suspended him. He fought the charges and was reinstated within six weeks. When I encountered Cord again in Washington following the termination of his marriage, he wasn't quite the same nice, idealistic young fellow he'd been during his college days at Yale. Like James Angleton, he's a guy who spent too many years harboring official secrets, an avocation that evidently does something to a man's soul."

After her graduation from Vassar, Barbara Miller married a U.S. foreign service officer whose early retirement led the couple to Georgetown, where he started his own real estate firm. "We lived in Georgetown," Barbara observed, "and over the years I occasionally spotted Mary Meyer strolling down the street or sitting at the counter of Morgan's Pharmacy, sipping a milk shake and flipping through a magazine. Then, in the early 1960s, I bumped into her at a small dinner party in Wayland, Massachusetts, outside Boston, at the home of Joy Kidder, a Vassar classmate of mine. As I eventually discovered, this was the period when Mary and John F. Kennedy were engaged in their clandestine love affair. Although I never quite saw her sex appeal, I could fully understand how a man might find her attractive. Physically, she reminded me a little of the actress Jean Seberg. She had a wonderful figure and short blonde hair. She seemed cozy and cuddly. Men liked her, and she liked them.

"What struck me most about her at the Kidder dinner was how animated she appeared. She responded to the conversation, wasn't at all retiring, demonstrated a light, flowing wit. She was dressed casually in a skirt and sweater, while the rest of us were more formally attired. But that only added to her allure. She was most definitely the life of the party."

A few weeks later Miller ran into Mary again, on this occasion in Montrose Park. "I was standing there with a friend, Helen Chavchavadze, the beautiful socialite with whom Jordan's King Hussein once fell in love, and we were chatting away when Mary appeared. She must have seen us but didn't stop to talk. She had a faraway look in her eyes. I thought to myself and I remember saying to Helen, 'There goes Mary. I wonder if anything's wrong.' Helen evidently knew Mary fairly well. 'She's painting now,' said Helen. 'She had an affair with her mentor, Kenneth Noland.' A successful abstract artist, Noland had recently moved from Washington to New York, effectively ending the relationship. 'Mary's unpredictable,' Helen added. 'She's an intellectual and a curmudgeon. She seems always to be going against the grain. She's unconventional, a nonconformist, but some very impressive people seem to admire her.'

"Helen went on to describe how popular Mary had become with members of the Georgetown set, particularly Joe Alsop, Kay Graham, and the Coopers. For years she'd been a regular at Alice Roosevelt Longworth's house as well as at Hickory Hill, Robert Kennedy's spread in Virginia She'd once stripped naked at an RFK party and jumped into the swimming pool, encouraging others to follow suit. An insomniac, she frequently spent the wee hours at Martin's or Clyde's—two of Georgetown's more popular watering holes—sipping bourbon while discussing politics and art with close pals."

Like most Georgetown residents, Barbara Miller heard all the cocktail hour chitchat concerning the Cord and Mary Meyer divorce. "I belonged," she said, "to something called the Waltz Group, not to be confused with the Dancing Class, although both drew their memberships chiefly from the select corps of social revelers whose home base was Georgetown. The Meyers also belonged. Cord Meyer began coming to every event by himself, particularly after his divorce. The group met once a month from November to May at the Sulgrave Club, located near Dupont Circle. Live bands played jazz, swing, the polka, and of course the Viennese waltz. There was a lot of drinking, but nobody boozed quite as much as Cord Meyer. He would stand at the bar with a drink in hand, chain-smoking, the smoke from the cigarette curling up and around his glass eye. He would talk endlessly about stuff that I never knew or cared about. Or he spoke about himself and about God, truth, the universe, all those universal subjects so popular with drunks. The only subject he never discussed was Mary Meyer. I had the feeling he was still very much in love with her. He could be extremely annoying. He would cut in when you were dancing. He would seek me out and then talk on and on. I would try to tune him out. People would see him and say, 'Oh God, there's Cord! He's smashed again!' To a degree I think he was on the make. He courted me, though in a rather awkward fashion. He could be very argumentative. He'd say something to me and I'd respond and he'd say, 'I would take issue with that.' I'd want to dance, but he'd trap me in some dark corner and lecture me on world politics. Because he'd had too much to drink, his words came out in a slur, and when he danced he'd trip over his own two feet."

After her divorce from Cord, Mary inherited a share in her family's multimillion-dollar dry-goods business and used it to establish her career as an artist. She and her two remaining sons moved into an antique-crammed Georgetown town house at 1523 Thirty-fourth Street. With the encouragement of Ben and Tony Bradlee, Mary converted their garage, located adjacent to their 3325 N Street home, into an art studio. Under the watchful eye of Ken Noland, she became an active participant on the Washington arts scene, a proponent of what became known as the "Washington Color School," exhibiting brightly colored geometrical designs at the Jefferson Place Gallery. Joe Alsop and Lorraine Cooper were among the first to buy her canvases. In a letter to Evangeline Bruce, Lorraine described the "new" Mary, the no-longer-married Mary as distinctly "Bohemian and glamorous, a Brett Ashley type." Her sister, Tony, labeled her "a free spirit, way ahead of her time." Jim Truitt, perhaps her truest friend and confidant, revealed how, while vacationing on the Italian Riviera with her sister, she spotted a dashing Italian nobleman on his yacht, swam out to meet him, and discarded her bikini in the water before climbing aboard. Still married at the time, Mary told her husband of the affair, describing it as "sexually satisfying but involving no deep emotion." It was Truitt, Phil Graham's amanuensis at the *Post*, who initially told his boss about the Mary Meyer–JFK relationship, precipitating Phil's indiscrete public announcement. It was also Truitt, in 1976, who broke the story nationally, selling it for a thousand dollars to the *National Enquirer.*

The JFK–Mary Meyer affair, about which Ben and Tony Bradlee claimed to know next to nothing, began innocently enough but soon took on the nuances of any desperate liaison, one in which Mary assumed the role of "the dark lady of Camelot—Jack Kennedy's last true love." Blair Clark, a broadcast journalist-turned-politician (in 1968 he managed Eugene McCarthy's run for the presidency), recalled the night he accompanied Mary Meyer to a White House dinner dance. "I'd known Mary for quite a while," said Clark. "I didn't know her in the biblical sense, but I'd known her for years. I knew Jack equally well, and in fact it was I who introduced him to Frank Sinatra. Still, it surprised me to learn that Mary Meyer and JFK were anything other than friends. I say this because I'd heard an interesting story about Mary. It took place at a dinner party in the home of Scotty and Sally Reston. Arthur Krock of *The New York Times*, a guest at the same party, told me what happened. After dinner the men were all seated in the dining room, smoking cigars and drinking cognac, and the women had gathered in the living room. Mary refused to join the ladies. She sat on a staircase talking to another woman. Within earshot of the men she said that every woman there wanted to sleep with Jack Kennedy. She was referring to the wives of all the men gathered at the Restons that evening. She said it disdainfully, as if she felt the women were being rather foolish.

"So I didn't know anything and I don't think the Bradlees did either. I'd been friendly with Ben Bradlee since our undergraduate days at Harvard. I would usually see the Bradlees whenever I found myself in Washington. One night we were all invited to a dinner party at the Kennedy White House. Mary was going to go as well, and Ben Bradlee suggested we all go together and that I escort Mary. Which is what I did. There was nothing in the atmosphere that night to indicate that we were going to a tryst. It was one of those dancing parties for approximately 125 people, mostly friends. It was a purely social gathering. Jackie Kennedy was there. Yet at a given point during the dancing, Jack and Mary disappeared. They were gone for half an hour. Inadvertently, as I learned later, I'd served as Jack's 'beard.' Not that he needed one, because they usually met on those occasions when Jackie absented herself from the White House. From what I could determine, JFK's affair with Mary was serious in nature. Unlike the preponderance of his lovers—and there seemed to be no end to them—Mary was his intellectual equal. He regarded her as far more than a roll in the hay. Under slightly altered circumstances, Mary might have become first lady instead of Jacqueline Kennedy."

Although Ben Bradlee claimed to know nothing about his sister-in-law's liaison with the president, in his book *Conversations with Kennedy*, he writes that in early February 1962, soon after the relationship began, JFK said to him, not for the first time: "Mary [Meyer] would be rough to live with." According to the same passage, Bradlee, "not for the first time," agreed. Such presumed familiarity with Mary Meyer on the part of John F. Kennedy must have raised a red flag in the mind of the future executive editor of *The Washington Post*. One of Kennedy's closest friends during Camelot, Bradlee was surely aware of the president's voracious appetite for multiple bed partners. Given Kennedy's predilection, his personal commentary on Mary Meyer left little to the imagination. "If Ben Bradlee didn't know about the affair," said Roswell Gilpatric, a State Department official during the Kennedy administration, "he must have been either completely blind or a full-fledged moron, neither of which he struck me as being."

Pierre Salinger forged his own friendship with Mary Meyer, and although he too claimed to have known little about her affair with Kennedy, he did share with Blair Clark the estimation that "she possessed great qualities and massive dignity and could have succeeded in any number of careers." Another friend of Mary's, Nancy Dickerson, who on occasion dated Cord Meyer following his separation from Mary, thought her "one of the most interesting women in Washington."

The degree of closeness attained by John Kennedy and Mary Meyer can be gauged by several factors, including a 1963 trip the president made with Mary and Tony to Milford, Pennsylvania, to meet their mother, Ruth Pinchot, an archconservative and supporter of Barry Goldwater. Another sign of their intimacy, other than the frequency of their meetings (more than forty in the White House and several in her Georgetown home) coupled with his policy of inviting her to high-priority conferences with aides and advisers, was Kennedy's willingness to experiment with drugs in Mary's presence—not just marijuana but also LSD.

Mary's drug source was Timothy Leary, the "acid head" guru of the 1960s, then still a full-time faculty member in the psychology department at Harvard. Mary drove to Cambridge, Massachusetts, to see Leary, with whom she had also at some point been romantically involved. While there, she told him that she and several other Georgetown women— none of whom she identified—had devised a plot to "turn on" the world's political and military leaders with pot and acid in order to make them less aggressive and more peace loving. Specifically she hoped for an end to the Cold War, a reappraisal of American attitudes toward the Soviet Union, and the adoption of an ideology calling for peaceful coexistence between the two omnipotent superpowers. Whether such a plot actually existed, or whether it was simply a figment of Mary's imagination, it did capture Leary's attention. He helped Mary procure the desired drugs and chemical agents. In July 1962, while visiting President Kennedy, Mary took him into one of the White House bedrooms, where she produced a small box containing six joints. They shared one, and Kennedy laughingly told her they were having a White House conference on narcotics the following week. They smoked two more joints, after which Kennedy drew his head back and closed his eyes. He refused a fourth joint. "Suppose the Russians drop a bomb," he said. He admitted to having previously tried cocaine and hashish, thanks to Peter Lawford, at whose Santa Monica, California, beach house he had often stayed in the late 1950s, sampling whatever treats his brother-in-law saw fit to provide. Mary told James Truitt that she and the president smoked pot on two other occasions and once took a mild acid trip together, during which they made love. She similarly told Truitt she felt Kennedy had finally begun to take her political views seriously. A major speech he delivered at Washington's American University in June 1963 echoed many of her propacifist sentiments.

They saw each other for the last time only days before JFK's doomed departure for Texas. His death evoked the same feelings she had for the meaningless demise of her young son. "I lose everyone and everything I love," she told James Truitt. "I wonder who'll be next."

The answer came all too soon. Shortly after noon on Monday, October 12, 1964, fewer than eleven months after the Kennedy assassination, Mary Pinchot Meyer was accosted and killed while walking alone along Georgetown's C & O Canal towpath, three-quarters of a mile west of Key Bridge (named for Francis Scott Key, composer of "The Star-Spangled Banner"). She often strolled the towpath, not far from her studio, during work breaks from her tight painting regimen. She and Jackie Kennedy had taken the same walk together on several occasions in pre-White House days. The ensuing police report noted that at approximately 12:45 P.M. Mary was set upon by an assailant who "evidently" attempted to rob and/or rape her. She screamed and struggled; her attacker fled but not before shooting her once at close range in the chest and again in the left temple. The forty-three-year-old artist died instantly. Cord Meyer had been attending a meeting in New York the day of the murder; Mary's two sons were away at boarding school. Ben Bradlee was thus called upon to identify the body later that day in the city morgue.

Within an hour of the shooting the police had picked up a suspect. Raymond Crump, a twenty-five-year-old African-American day laborer with a wife and four young children, had been found wandering in the vicinity of the crime, his shirt and pants soaking wet. When interrogated at police headquarters, he insisted he'd spent the morning fishing in the Potomac, after which he downed a six-pack of beer and dozed off; he attributed his wet clothing to an accidental tumble off a bank and into the drink. The problem with the fishing alibi was that when captured Crump had no equipment with him. Investigators later located his tackle box and fishing rod at his apartment in Southeast Washington. Crump now changed his story, stipulating that he'd spent the morning with a former girlfriend but had lied because he didn't want his wife to know the truth.

Although Crump's credibility had to be questioned, there appeared to be no motive for the crime. Leo Damore, an author who in the mid-1990s began researching and writing a book on Mary Meyer (he died before completing the volume), discounted robbery as a motive by pointing out that although Crump had spent sixty days in jail the year before for petty larceny, "Mary's purse and pocketbook were eventually tracked down to her art studio, where she had left them before going for a walk. She wore jewelry only on social occasions. There was nothing for Crump to steal, even had he wanted to." Rape seemed an equally unlikely prospect. Through 1964 the suspect had never been convicted of a violent crime. Nor did it seem plausible that a potential rapist would ply his trade in broad daylight at a location clearly visible from any of a number of different vantage points. There had been a witness but not to the crime itself, only to its aftermath. A passing truck driver on Canal Road had heard screams and a shot; pulling his vehicle to the side of the road, the driver ran to the wall along the road, peered over, and saw a man with a pistol bent over the prostrate figure of a woman. Yet the man's description of the would-be killer did not match that of Ray Crump.

"Any way you slice it," said Leo Damore, "Ray Crump seemed a far-fetched candidate for murder." An alcoholic who suffered from occasional blackouts, he stood five foot six and weighed less than 140 pounds. Born in North Carolina, Crump moved to Washington with his family as a young teenager, dropped out of high school, and took odds jobs at construction sites. Although accused of several violent crimes in later years, post-1964, Crump directed the brunt of his frustration and anger at those he knew personally—landlords, girlfriends, and future wives— never at random subjects encountered by pure chance. "He was the perfect patsy," said Damore, "better even than Lee Harvey Oswald." In Damore's informed opinion, "Mary Meyer was killed by a well-trained professional hit man, very likely somebody connected to the CIA. After the assassination of John Kennedy, Mary had become an inconvenient woman, the former mistress of one of the world's most powerful political leaders and the ex-wife of a CIA honcho. The feeling in the Agency was that here's somebody who knows too much for her own good. She knows where all the bodies are buried. She knows the Warren Commission report, released shortly before her death, is nothing but a grandiose cover-up. She knows about the Mafia, the Cubans, and the Agency, and how any one of them could have conspired to eliminate Kennedy." What she didn't know, according to Damore, is that a month after the president's murder, the Agency placed her under twenty-four-hour surveillance, tapping her phone, wiring her house, intercepting her mail, and initiating several break-ins in search of notes and letters to and from JFK and others of equal interest. "Strangely enough," Damore remarked, "it was James Angleton, her former spouse's great confrere and a good friend to Mary, who set the surveillance operation in motion, hopeful of ascertaining exactly how much Mary knew—not just about Kennedy but also about the serried ranks of the Georgetown social set. An inveterate partygoer, Mary was similarly something of an outsider and as such retained the kind of objectivity so valuable even to unwitting CIA informants, Mary included. Nor was it unusual for Angleton to ask Mary directly concerning this or that personage. It was largely her involvement that enabled the CIA, for example, to compile substantial informational files on the drug activities of Timothy Leary."

The day after the towpath shooting, Ben and Tony Bradlee walked over to Mary's Thirty-fourth Street town house and opened the front door. To their utter amazement it was unlocked, and standing in the middle of Mary's living room, a guilt-ridden smirk on his face, was their old pizza-party friend James Angleton. Angleton, not only counterintelligence chief but now also CIA liaison to the FBI, had gotten in by picking the front door lock. He'd been apprised, he told the Bradlees, that Mary had left behind a handwritten diary that possibly contained salacious or compromising entries on John F. Kennedy. Angleton no doubt thought the diary might likewise illuminate the private lives of certain members of the Georgetown community, individuals such as Joe Alsop and Averell Harriman, whose day-to-day activities were already under the scrutiny of the Agency. Above all Angleton hoped the diary might name the proverbial double agent, the Russian mole whose presence in high government circles had thus far gone undetected.

Unable to locate Mary's writings inside her home, Angleton left and showed up again the following day outside her art studio just as the Bradlees arrived. "The three of us searched everywhere but found nothing," said Tony Bradlee. "I returned by myself a few days later and discovered the diary among a stack of my sister's books and papers. There were some references in it to Mary's affair with Jack, although it mostly contained a rash of notes on her artwork." Under the mistaken impression that Angleton would first read and then dispose of the binder, Tony turned it over to him. Instead of shredding it, the CIA official read it and placed it in his personal safe at Langley. Clearing out the safe in the early 1970s, he came across the diary and gave it back to Tony. With Anne Truitt, James Truitt's former wife as witness, Tony destroyed the binder, thereby increasing speculation among conspiracy buffs about its contents.

In the interim, charged with first-degree murder, a penniless Ray Crump had the good fortune to find legal representation in the person of Dovey Mae Roundtree, a brilliant, fiercely independent African-American female attorney wholly devoted to the cause of justice. Investing her own funds, Roundtree, a successful civil rights lawyer, prepared to defend her client. "I was acquainted with Raymond Crump's mother from the African Episcopal Methodist Church," she said, "and I knew her to be an honorable, hardworking woman. I agreed to represent Ray, knowing full well that the odds were stacked against us."

Roundtree had little staff and limited resources, whereas Alfred Hantman, the powerful prosecutor for the U.S. attorney's office, had a sizeable staff and a limitless budget. "What kept me going," said Roundtree, "was the knowledge that if I failed, Ray Crump died." In order to defend Crump, whose wife had left him after his arrest, Dovey Roundtree had to scale the walls of social hierarchy, of power and privilege so prevalent in Georgetown, a world entirely alien to both her experience and that of Ray Crump. "The burden of guilt," Roundtree explained, "was on the state, and in this instance the state had amassed not one shred of tangible evidence to support their case. What became evident early in the trial is that a million eyes were riveted on the proceedings. A lot of people knew more about it than I did. The courtroom was filled with CIA and FBI agents. They were everywhere. They had packed into the National Cathedral to attend Mary's funeral. Their overt interest in the case suggested something beyond the fact that Mary had once been married to a CIA official. It was clear to the jury that the man before them wasn't guilty as charged."

The day Ray Crump walked out of court a free man marked the

resurgence of Mary Meyer's death as a major topic of conversation at Georgetown dinner parties. If Ray Crump didn't kill Mary Meyer, then who did? Barbara Miller observed that "while all of Georgetown seemed stunned by the murder of Mary Meyer, few of us believed that the man they put on trial had done the deed. I always had the feeling, as did others, that the CIA was somehow involved." James Angleton told Joe Alsop in 1966 that the "real" killer was still at large and that, in his opinion, all signs pointed to the Russian mole whose identity Mary had surely uncovered in the course of her frequent White House visits, even though his name didn't appear in her diary. Timothy Leary, on the other hand, informed friends that he suspected James Angleton of being behind the crime. Although Leary promised to launch an independent, privately funded investigation into Meyer's death, he never got around to it. Myrna Firestone, publisher of *Georgetown and Country,* a periodical devoted to portraying life among Washington's rich, conducted dozens of interviews for a future book on the Mary Meyer case, after which she concluded that the CIA played a direct role in "the hit." Nina Burleigh, author of *A Very Private Woman,* a biography of Mary Meyer, thought there was at least a "90 percent chance Ray Crump committed the murder. The trouble is that the evidence against him was circumstantial. So he walked." The trouble with Burleigh's biography can be found in its title, a misnomer if ever there was one, Mary Meyer being anything but "a very private woman." It was her utter lack of discretion and disregard for privacy that most likely led to her untimely demise.

In December 1965 Cord Meyer remarried and moved with his new bride from a house he owned in McLean into Mary Meyer's Georgetown residence. As they had done almost daily for so many years, Cord Meyer and James Angleton continued to lunch together. They usually took their midday meal at the Rive Gauche restaurant, an Agency stronghold, but starting in the late 1960s the two CIA officials began eating at La Niçoise, a small French bistro at 1721 Wisconsin Avenue in upper Georgetown. They sat at the same table each time, table forty-one, in a far corner of the restaurant, in front of a large mirror, with a view of the entire room, including the front door. They discussed the world of espionage—what Angleton called "a wilderness of mirrors"—and, being men of habit, ordered the same meal every day—cocktails, red wine, raw oysters or clams, shad and shad roe, coffee, and cognac. They skipped dessert. At those times when a third party joined them for lunch they would hide a microphone in a small vase of fresh flowers that decorated the table. The conversation would be taped for future reference. The restaurant ordinarily attracted a lively lunch crowd from Capitol Hill. Senator Jacob Javits often found himself seated at a nearby table. "By the end of the meal," he said, "they'd be enveloped in a shroud of cigarette smoke, chattering away like a pair of yentas at a beauty parlor. Angleton did most of the talking. The KGB had infiltrated the CIA. Russian moles had eaten their way into the very marrow of the bone. It was a repetitive story with Angleton. He'd been singing the same song for nearly two decades. Then, in 1974, CIA director William Colby forced the old boy into retirement. Angleton's ultraconspiratorial turn of mind had become more of a liability than an asset. His theories actually damaged the CIA by paralyzing its Soviet section. Through it all, Cord Meyer remained Angleton's most ardent supporter. Their friendship endured despite persistent rumors that Angleton might have had something to do with the death of Mary Meyer."

Cord Meyer gave expression to his support of Angleton in *Facing Reality*, an autobiography subtitled *From World Federalism to the CIA*. In the same volume he comments briefly on the murder of his wife: "I was satisfied by the conclusions of the police investigation that Mary had been the victim of a sexually motivated assault by a single individual and that she had been killed in her struggle to escape." Carol Delaney, a family friend and longtime personal assistant to Cord Meyer, observed that "Mr. Meyer didn't for a minute think that Ray Crump had murdered his wife or that it had been an attempted rape. But being an Agency man, he couldn't very well accuse the CIA of the crime, although the murder had all the markings of an in-house rubout."

Asked to comment on the case by the current author, Cord Meyer held court at the beginning of February 2001—six weeks before his death—in the barren dining room of a Washington nursing home. Propped up in a chair, his glass eye bulging, he struggled to hold his head aloft. Although he was no longer able to read, the nurses supplied him with a daily copy of *The Washington Post,* which he carried with him wherever he went. "My father died of a heart attack the same year Mary was killed," he whispered. "It was a bad time." And what could he say about Mary Meyer? Who had committed such a heinous crime? "The same sons of bitches," he hissed, "that killed John F. Kennedy."

CHAPTER NINE

THE BIG DO

LIKE THE HEROINE in a variation on the Cinderella theme, Katharine Graham transformed herself within a three-year period from the shy, frightened, neophyte president of the Washington Post Company into one of the shrewdest, toughest newspaper and magazine publishers in the industry. In describing how she rose to the occasion, Kay Graham in 1997 told TV talk show host Charlie Rose: "I think that I had a sort of naive doggedness, a sort of ability to hang in. And I suppose I was moderately intelligent. At least, I wasn't retarded, but I wasn't a genius, either, especially not in business."

Power bestowed glamour and style on Kay Graham, but there were numerous testimonials to her precarious beginning. "Kay was forty-six at the time she took over," said Sally Reston. "She was plump, dowdy, and somewhat shy. She hadn't worked in twenty years and suddenly found herself in charge of a huge communications empire. Her role up to then had basically been to make her husband and children happy. She got up and had breakfast with her children and tried to be there for them in the afternoon when they returned from school. Despite her protestations to the contrary, I believe in a way she really enjoyed that role. It was a role her own mother always refused to play, dumping her children off on governesses and baby-sitters. After Phil killed himself, Kay had more than enough money to simply retire and become another boring Georgetown dowager. She could have remarried and lived like a queen. Instead she opted to continue the work that Phil had only begun.

"I remember Kay telling me, two weeks into her new position, that she didn't think she'd make it. 'It's too hard,' she said. 'I have no idea what I'm doing, and I'm too old to learn.' 'Nonsense,' I told her. 'Grandma Moses didn't start painting until she was well into her seventies.' She laughed and said, 'Well, I'm not that old, so I may as well take up art.' "

Years later Polly Wisner Fritchey testified that the transition had been traumatic: "Kay was unsure of herself. Women of our generation were brought up to cajole and please, not to make speeches or bark orders at employees. She gave her first major address at the 1963 *Washington Post* Christmas party. Art Buchwald wrote her an opening joke. Scotty Reston and Joe Alsop helped her write the speech. She practiced by reading it over and over to her children. During her first years on the job she used to attend all the newspaper conferences and conventions by herself, and she would stay in her hotel room because she didn't know anyone and had nobody with whom she could talk. She needed constant reassurance. Vangie Bruce sent her a beautiful letter from England saying that the *Post* was better, more interesting under Kay's aegis than it had been under Phil's. Lorraine Cooper also cheered her on. I recall an upsetting event that took place when a board member rebuked Kay for purchasing an expensive pin for a retiring switchboard operator and using corporate funds to make the purchase; Kay nearly resigned over the incident."

Editors, board members, and company executives found Katharine Graham difficult, moody, and remarkably thin-skinned as well as volatile and unpredictable. There were stories of angry 2 A.M. telephone calls, impatient summonses to her office, and sudden inexplicable demands. "She had endless issues," said Russ Wiggins. "I can't say I held it against her. She'd entered what until then, with the possible exception of Cissy Patterson, had always been considered a man's world. Executives at the *Post* and *Newsweek* prodded and pressed her for decisions that had gone unmade since the beginning of Phil Graham's final year. She wasn't used to standing up before a cluster of men and delivering a speech. I used to have to go over her speeches as many as thirty times to satisfy her. She would send me a draft of the speech, I would edit it, and it would then go back and forth, back and forth. Or I would write the first draft and she would do the editing, and it would proceed in that fashion. Al Friendly, who called her 'Mother' behind her back, led her on countless tours of the building, introducing her to every employee, explaining to her how every piece of equipment worked. Then there was Fritz Beebe, whom she telephoned at least five or six times a day. Fritz used to speak to her the way you would a child. Whenever a problem arose, he would attempt to mollify her. 'Don't worry about it, Kay. We've got it under control. What you need to do is go home and get some sleep.'

"Some of the writers and editors, particularly those who'd been close to Phil Graham, resented her. They saw her as a lady of privilege, somebody born to the manor. With all her money, how possibly could she understand their problems, to say nothing of the man on the street? One day, following a heated *Washington Post* editorial board meeting dealing with salaries, somebody said about Kay: 'What that lady needs is a good fuck. Loosen her up, get the juices flowing.' It typified the negativity that existed when she first stepped in. It reached the point where Clare Booth Luce said to Kay, 'What you need to do is get dressed up and arrive at the office late after you come from your hairdresser. Go in, see people, go to lunch, and leave early. That way you won't irritate the men too much. You can't get too aggressive.' "

Other friends and acquaintances imparted their own tidbits of advice. Barry Bingham, editor of the *Louisville Courier-Journal,* recommended that she hire a speech coach to give her public speaking lessons. Kay complied and additionally signed on for courses in accounting and business administration. "Whenever I see Kay these days," Lorraine Cooper wrote to Evangeline Bruce, "she's weighted down with voluminous textbooks on finance and economics." Missy Chandler De Young recalled that once Kay became involved at the *Post,* she consistently turned for help to Otis Chandler at the *Los Angeles Times.* Once a week she traveled to the New York offices of *Newsweek,* then located at 444 Madison Avenue, to confer with Osborn Elliott. The publication's editor in chief took it upon himself to familiarize Kay with the complex business of magazine publishing. She would sit by his desk, sometimes until late at night, watching him put the weekly magazine together. In his autobiography, *The World of Oz,* Elliott writes: "For all her wealth and new station in life, Katharine Meyer Graham was a pitiful figure in those early 1960s days." One of the problems at the news magazine, according to Russ Wiggins, was that "Kay associated it with Phil Graham and Robin Webb. She thought many on the staff had been disloyal to her in favor of her husband. She harbored resentment against the magazine and probably felt embarrassed that the staff knew so much about Robin and Phil. I once pointed out to her that the magazine had shown a nice profit for the year, and her response was a rather stiff 'Who cares, it's a loser of a publication.' Fortunately, she overcame these feelings and began to cope with some of the magazine's many problems."

Another "mother hen" figure in Kay's life during this period was André Meyer, chairman of Lazard Frères, the influential New York banking investment firm. Cary Reich, Meyer's biographer, remarked that "André would invite Katharine Graham to lunch at Lazard and talk with her about the *Post,* and about her investments. Once, he asked her and Fritz Beebe, whom she'd brought along, if they needed tax shelters. Graham was so naive at this stage that after lunch, she said to Beebe, 'Fritz, what's a tax shelter?' She subsequently gave Lazard half her personal portfolio to manage. When the *Post,* after much soul-searching by Graham, went public in 1971, Lazard handled the offering. Aware of the Graham family's concern about losing control of the company, André set up a system of 'A' and 'B' shares, the family retaining the majority of 'A' shares—which carried with it all the voting power. The family's holdings in the organization intact, Katharine Graham could focus on other pressing issues."

Chalmers Roberts confirmed Kay's initial reluctance to take full control: "It was one woman and ten men, all of whom thought they knew more than she did. And at that point, they all did. She didn't know anything about the paper, the unions, the pressmen. Phil Graham had always dealt with the business end of it but had never apprised his wife. Kay felt insecure because she'd never before addressed these matters.

"Soon after taking over the paper, Kay was invited to appear on *Meet the Press,* a prospect that utterly terrified her. She was so uptight that she asked three or four of us who'd already appeared on the program to hold a practice session for her. The Washington Post Company owned WTOP, so we took her to their television studio and did a mock session in the hope she would gain some self-confidence. She didn't. In fact she wasn't very good on *Meet the Press*. At best you might say she got through it. She never enjoyed making speeches or being interviewed, but over the years she developed poise and ultimately a commanding presence."

Phil Geyelin described Katharine Graham's *Meet the Press* performance as "pathetic—she had lockjaw, she couldn't speak. She was painfully shy in the beginning and depended much too much on the advice of outsiders. Robert McNamara, for example, sold her on a business man ager for the paper who just didn't work out. And she went through two or three managers before she found somebody smart. Most of them patted her on the shoulder and said, 'There, there, now don't you bother your pretty little head.' "

Despite her early reticence, Kay demonstrated flashes of the gradually evolving personality that would allow her to mold herself into one of the lionesses of Georgetown, the proprietress of a vastly influential and profitable media conglomerate. One example involved Judy Oppenheimer, a twenty-two-year-old college graduate who, not long after Kay Graham's takeover of the *Post*, procured a job with the city desk. "I used to wear miniskirts in those days," said Oppenheimer. "It was the wild and wooly 1960s. I rode a Vespa, a motor scooter, to work. One day I was draped over a desk reaching for something in a drawer and my legs were exposed. Katharine Graham happened to pass by at that moment and saw me. She pointed at me and yelled at the editor: 'Get that out of here!' A few days later I was canned. It seemed clear that she was hypersensitive to anything that even hinted at female sensuality because it somehow reminded her of Robin Webb. What surprised me is that she acted with such ferocity. One would have expected her to issue a warning first."

A more telling instance can be found in Kay Graham's dealings with Lyndon Johnson. The 1964 Republican and Democratic national conventions were the first that Kay Graham ever attended on her own, without her husband. Looking back, she would say (in *Personal History*): "I was encumbered by a deep feeling of uncertainty and insecurity and a need to please." Yet following the Democratic Party convention, during a visit to the Johnson ranch in Texas, she watched in dismay as the president vigorously berated Lady Bird for accepting several social invitations without first consulting with him. He continued to yell at his wife until Kay could no longer stand it. "Yes, she did get you into this mess tonight," Graham told the president, "but she also got you where you are today." Johnson then focused his attack on Kay until she finally blurted out: "Oh, shut up!" Later, reflecting on her assertive act, she wondered if she ought to have added "Mr. President."

Although theirs was generally speaking a mutual admiration society, the ties between Kay Graham and LBJ were at times made more tenuous by her new position and Johnson's increasing recognition of her growing power base. No longer simply the wife of a control-conscious press baron, Kay Graham had, so to speak, taken over the throne. Overly concerned with the Fourth Estate's perception of him, LBJ set out to employ any means necessary to win over the widow of his former friend. "On the whole," said Liz Carpenter, press secretary to Lady Bird Johnson, "the president made fun of the, you know, Georgetown ladies, most of whom he knew because he'd been in Washington so long. But with respect to Kay Graham, he went out of his way to please her. He recognized that she and Phil had a lot to do with his success, with his acceptance in the inner circles of Washington. He realized he would have to continue to win her over if he wanted her ongoing patronage."

Jack Valenti, having taken a sublet on a Georgetown residence, observed that although Johnson's friendship with Phil Graham deteriorated at the end, "he remained indebted to the Grahams and as such felt a great fondness for Kay. She was one of the first people he invited to the White House following his ascendancy to the Oval Office. As press secretary, I became friendly with her as well, and on a number of occasions I accompanied the president to her house for dinner. LBJ could be extremely dear to Kay. He'd call her up and say, 'Hello, my sweetheart, how are you today? The trouble with my job is that I can't get to see you enough. I'd like to break out of here and be like one of those young animals down on my ranch. The two of us could just frolic together in the grass.' That's pretty much verbatim what he said to her one day. He liked to flirt with her. The two women he most enjoyed flirting with were Kay Graham and Jacqueline Kennedy.

"Then there was LBJ's less affable side. The president made me his emissary in contacting Kay whenever *The Washington Post* or *Newsweek* ran a story he didn't like. He'd become incensed and say, 'Goddamn it! Get on the horn and tell that woman she's got a bunch of cretins over there writing these stories and it's terrible and I demand a retraction.'

"So Kay and I formed a kind of sideboard duo. We had a good rapport. I would call and say, 'Well, Kay, here I am again. I'm going to have to chastise you.'

"And she'd say, 'What is it this time, Jack?'

"I'd go over the story and she'd say, 'Okay, tell the president that I'm sufficiently chastised.' Then she'd say, 'My God, does he think I read every story that appears in the *Post* before it goes to press?'

"After that I'd go and tell the president, 'Boy, did I ever chew her butt out. She's just about quaking in her boots.'

"Graham and Johnson had their share of humorous blowouts. In late 1964, Lady Bird and the president celebrated at the White House their thirtieth wedding anniversary, inviting old chums like Kay Graham, Joe and Susan Mary Alsop, Abe Fortas, Douglas Dillon, maybe fifty in all. At about midnight, with the party still going strong, Johnson decided to retire. On top of his bed he found an early edition of the next morning's *Washington Post*. Within minutes Kay Graham received word that the president wanted to see her. When she appeared in his private quarters she found him in his boxer shorts, preparing to change for bed. As soon as he saw her he began yelling about an article he had just read. Kay remained silent. About to discard his drawers, Johnson told Kay to shut her eyes. She turned her back to him. 'All right,' he said momentarily, 'you can look.' He had donned a pair of blue cotton pajamas and was about to climb into bed. Without a word, Kay walked to the light switch, turned it off, and left the room. As she retreated down the corridor, the president called after her. 'Kay,' she could hear him scream, 'I'm not done with you!' She kept walking and never looked back.

"The one time, though, that LBJ really went out of his mind—rightfully so, I might add—was over Christmas of 1967. I'd already left the

White House, but at the president's request I flew with him on that celebrated fifty-four-hour, round-the-world journey that took us to Australia
for Prime Minister Harold Holt's memorial service as well as Hawaii,
Vietnam, Thailand, Pakistan, and Italy. In Rome we visited with His Holi-
ness Pope Paul VI and two high-ranking Vatican officials—five of us in
all. The president had arranged the audience to explore the possibility of
the pope's helping to free American POWs currently being held by the
Vietcong. The meeting was cordial, the pope agreeing to explore the situation. The next issue of *Newsweek,* however, characterized the meeting
as hostile, the pope supposedly berating Johnson for America's escalating
military presence in Vietnam. *Newsweek*'s story was untrue; nothing of
the sort had been said.

"LBJ went berserk. I got hold of Katharine Graham and said, 'Kay,
that article is a total fabrication. I should know—I was there. Kay, I was
there!'

"Kay told me that the story had been Osborn Elliott's baby and I
should contact him. So I called Oz Elliott. His response was that the magazine had a stringer in the Vatican and that their information was correct.

" 'Oz,' I said, 'unless that stringer of yours was hidden behind a curtain or beneath the pontiff's robes, which I seriously doubt, how the hell
would he or she know?'

" 'Well,' he responded, 'we trust our stringers.'

"With that I went ballistic. I called Kay back and I said, 'This is outrageous.' And I went on and on and on.

"She said, 'Jack, I believe you. But what can I do? The story's there.
My people swear by it. You tell me otherwise. You're probably both right.
I believe you, but I also believe Oz. I have to believe him—he works for
me. So I am truly between a rock and a hard place. It's just one of those
things.'

"She was so understanding and sympathetic that in the end my heart
went out to her. I realized there really wasn't anything she could do. As
for Lyndon Johnson, even though he was unhappy with *Newsweek,* he
wouldn't allow it to color his relationship with Katharine Graham. That's
how it was between them."

Osborn Elliott remembered the incident. "Valenti called me up. I guess we went back and forth for about fifteen minutes, half an hour, and we both stood by our guns. The whole thing reminds me of that old saw which goes something like this: 'There are three sides to every story—mine, yours, and the truth. And the truth lies somewhere in between.' To Katharine Graham's credit—and this is what made her such an outstanding newspaper and magazine publisher—she always supported her own people."

In mid-1964 Osborn Elliott accompanied Kay on the first of several trips they made together to Europe and Asia, the main purpose of which was to further familiarize her with the intricacies of the magazine trade. In London she met with *Newsweek*'s British bureau, dined with Prime Minister Harold Wilson (whom she'd first encountered the year before in Washington), visited with David and Evangeline Bruce, saw Isaiah Berlin, and did a taped TV interview for BBC's *Tonight Show* in which she performed only slightly better than she had on *Meet the Press*. In Paris she met with Chip and Avis Bohlen, ate dinner with Cecil Beaton and Philippe de Rothschild, had her hair done by Alexandre, and resisted buying French fashion originals because she felt that "dressing down" in off-the-rack clothes conferred a more professional look. She shopped for leather goods in Rome, had cocktails with Lady Diana Cooper, and was feted by former Washington socialite Judy Montagu, who introduced her over dinner to Gore Vidal. She returned to the States in time to help organize her daughter's wedding to Yann Weymouth, an architectural student at MIT. They were married at the U.S. Naval Chapel in Washington with a reception at Kay's home in Georgetown. Lally's brother, Don, gave her away. She wore a Mainbocher gown given to her by Agnes Meyer. Katharine Graham would later write in *Personal History* that "although the marriage lasted only a few years, out of it came two marvelous grandchildren, Katharine and Pamela Weymouth, my oldest granddaughters."

Early the following year Katharine Graham and Osborn Elliott (together with his wife) went to Kyoto and Tokyo, Japan, where Kay socialized with business and political leaders, agreed to be interviewed by the *Japan Times*, then met with the emperor and empress of Japan (as well as Prime Minister Sato). She also met with Jim Truitt, who had moved from Washington to become Japan bureau chief for *Newsweek*. In the course of her conversation with Truitt, she expressed her concern that he had acted as a "procurer" for Phil Graham, introducing her husband to sundry women, a role that Truitt denied playing. From Tokyo they flew to Saigon, capital of Vietnam, where Kay met with U.S. Army officers, including General William Westmoreland, whom she describes in a composite letter to her children as "an inarticulate soldier type of a peculiar kind. If he is bright, it is as a technician because he certainly doesn't communicate." She asked Westmoreland about a *New York Times* article on the increasing desertion rate of American soldiers, a report that he denied but which two U.S. Army captains confirmed. In the same letter she recounts eating dinner with several *Newsweek* correspondents in a small French restaurant "beside a beautiful river with boats" where people, including water-skiers, "get shot at all the time by nearby snipers." Saigon, she concludes, "is dramatic and unbelievable, the most fantastic jumble of peace and war." The group rounded off their journey with stops at Cambodia, Thailand, India, and Hong Kong. They were in Hong Kong for the Chinese New Year. A firecracker exploded only a few feet from Kay on a crowded street corner. She jumped. She said afterward it had reminded her of the gunshot that killed her husband.

At the beginning of July 1965 Kay returned to London, visited Oxford, then flew to Paris for lunch with French staffers at *Newsweek,* and again had her hair coiffed by Alexandre ("who, this time, quite literally shaved my head"). She flew back to London to attend several dinner parties. Most evenings in England, she wrote to Russ Wiggins, a supporter of the war effort, were spent defending America's Vietnam War policy. "The British are so awful about it," she complained, "I find myself defending equally violently."

While in London Kay stayed at the American embassy as a guest of the Bruces. Another embassy guest was Adlai Stevenson, whose close connection over the years with Kay Graham's mother had drawn him equally close to Kay. The two had been seen together so often in recent months that the tabloids and gossip columns buzzed with rumors of a pending betrothal or, at the very least, a torrid affair. Despite his benign appearance, Stevenson enjoyed a reputation as a consummate ladies' man. In her memoir, *Power at Play,* Washington columnist Betty Beale, one of Stevenson's legion of lovers (he referred to them as "the harem"), attested to his aptitude for romance. His long-term affair with the very beautiful but married Marietta Tree, who was also staying in London at this time, has been as well documented as an earlier affair she once enjoyed with film director John Huston. Caroline Seebohm, Tree's biographer, observed that "Kay Graham told friends that Adlai had a crush on her and had come to London primarily to see her." Stevenson did see her. On Sunday night, July 11, he appeared in her bedroom and stayed, Graham told Seebohm in an interview for the Tree biography, "for at least an hour, leaving behind his necktie and reading glasses." Three days later, on July 14, while on a leisurely stroll around town with Marietta Tree, he suffered a massive heart attack, collapsed, and was pronounced dead on arrival at St. George's Hospital. That evening a sad and subdued Marietta Tree and her wealthy British diplomat husband, Ronald Tree, dined at the embassy with David and Evangeline Bruce. "Marietta was distressed that Kay had just handed her Adlai's tie and glasses, left behind in her room several nights earlier, the implication being that something untoward had gone on between them," Vangie would tell the current author. "Although I have no way of knowing, I would venture that nothing beyond a passing flirtation took place. Even so, I thought Kay's timing a bit insensitive. I always felt her to be slightly jealous of Marietta. In a way, we all were." When Caroline Seebohm asked Katharine Graham if she had ever been romantically involved with Adlai Stevenson, she received a noncommittal response. "I will neither confirm nor deny," said Graham.

Borden Stevenson, Adlai's son, pointed out that his father "had often showed an interest in, and been affectionate toward, the daughters of his lady friends, including Marietta Tree's daughter Frances FitzGerald and Agnes Meyer's daughter Kay. He was just as interested in Kay's daughter, Lally. It doesn't mean that he necessarily had illicit relations with all of them."

Another incident, similar in scope, occurred in 1970 when Aileen Mehle ("Suzy") announced in her New York *Daily News* society column that Katharine Graham was going to marry Edward Heath, the new British prime minister. "It was the biggest mistake I ever made," admitted Mehle. "The story got picked up everywhere, generating instant headlines: 'Czarina of American Publishing to Wed British Prime Minister.' The item had come from somebody that I and my editor at the *News* considered an unimpeachable source. So we decided to go with it.

"The next day I received a telephone call from Katharine Graham. 'Aileen,' she said, 'I do know Edward Heath but we're mere acquaintances. The story's untrue. Who told you? Walter Annenberg? I *know* Walter Annenberg told you, he's always had it out for me.' "

One of the wealthiest men in the world, Walter Annenberg succeeded David Bruce at the onset of the Nixon administration as American ambassador to Great Britain. He and his wife, Lee, had at one point been friendly with Kay Graham. They admired her dignity in the face of her husband's deceitfulness and his deteriorating mental state. After his suicide they spent several weekends with Kay and supported her decision to assume control of the family newspaper. Then, in 1968, Drew Pearson wrote a scathing attack on Annenberg for the *Post,* questioning his qualifications to serve as ambassador to the UK. Annenberg called Kay and asked her to print a correction. When she refused on the grounds that the column was an opinion piece, the Annenbergs became enraged. To make it up to them, Kay decided to throw a party in their honor. Among the other guests who gathered at Graham's Georgetown house to celebrate the new ambassador to Britain and his wife were Lorraine Cooper and Evangeline Bruce, neither of whom liked the Annenbergs. Vangie had been condescending to Lee when the two met for the first time in London. The new ambassador, claimed Evangeline, wasn't willing to give the Bruces adequate time to leave Winfield House, the official ambassadorial residence. Lee, for her part, claimed that the Bruces were dragging their feet. Encountering each other again at the Graham celebration, the two ladies exchanged angry glances. When Walter Annenberg tried to engage Lorraine Cooper in conversation, she brusquely asked him if he could afford to take over the London embassy. The Annenbergs left the party at the earliest opportunity and never again spoke to Kay Graham. He remained so embittered that he considered commissioning a biography of Phil Graham, with particular emphasis on his mental illness and womanizing. Ultimately he decided against it.

Walter Annenberg, however, had not been the source for Aileen

Mehle's erroneous story on Edward Heath. " 'No, Kay,' I told her. 'Walter had nothing to do with it. But I feel terrible about this. I feel awful. Not just for you but for me. I hate being wrong. Let the *News* print a retraction. Let us make it up to you.'

" 'No,' Kay responded. 'I don't want a retraction. Let it stand.' At this point she said something that amazed me. Remember, this was before *The Washington Post*'s Watergate exposé made her a household name. 'Aileen,' she said, 'you've made me a *star*. My picture's on the front page of every newspaper in Europe and North America. I *love* it!' "

∾

BY 1966 KATHARINE GRAHAM had begun to find her footing. She felt more certain in her role as head of the Washington Post Company. The year before, after taking Ben Bradlee to lunch at the F Street Club, she had transferred him from *Newsweek* to the position of deputy managing editor (and four months later, managing editor) at the *Post*. "It was the first time," said Russ Wiggins, "she had paid for a man's lunch. In many ways Ben reminded her of Phil Graham. Like Phil, he had an inquiring, razor-sharp mind and an enduring vision. He had the same kind of off-the-cuff roughness, even in the way he dressed: mismatched shirts, ties, and jackets, everything rumpled and the wrong color. Kay trusted him implicitly. In 1968, he became executive editor and head of a one-man show."

Having secured the future of her business, Kay felt free to pursue other occasional endeavors and to demonstrate her growing sense of independence. In January 1966 she did what no woman in Washington had ever done before: she threatened to walk out on a dinner party when the host, in this case Joseph Alsop, asked his male guests to remain behind for coffee and cognac, while consigning the women to a bedroom, where they would presumably discuss family life. In the past, women who balked at the tradition had been asked to leave the house. But Kay, who worked as hard as any man, put down her foot.

"Joe, I'll have to excuse myself," she said. "I'm not going off with the women. I'm not doing it. I have a newspaper to get out in the morning."

Alsop implored her to stay. "I'll keep the group together," he promised. He did, and she stayed, putting a serious dent in a social custom that had long outlived its usefulness.

Robert McNamara attended the same dinner party. "I was there that evening," he recalled, "and I don't remember ever going to another dinner at which the men and women were separated. Kay Graham changed all that."

At a subsequent Joe Alsop dinner, Bobby Kennedy attacked Kay for an article on Jackie Kennedy that had recently appeared in the *Post*. The piece took issue with the former first lady for leaving Washington and losing touch with some of her former Georgetown friends, including the Coopers. Bobby said sharply to Graham: "You have lost your husband too. You should know better. It hurts Jackie to think of Washington. That's why she left, and it's the reason she finds it difficult to maintain some of her former friendships." The comment upset Graham. "Bob," she responded, "I own the paper, but I don't personally write or even read all the articles that appear in it." As she said it, tears rolled down her cheeks. Watching all this, Joe Alsop shook his head and mumbled, "It's like a young nephew rebuking his rich old aunt."

In March 1966 Kay Graham and Polly Wisner Fritchey, the latter still recuperating from her husband's recent suicide, took their youngest sons on a midsemester ski vacation to Switzerland. While their children schussed down the icy slopes, Kay and Polly hiked the slippery mountain trails, debating what they might have done differently to thwart the perils of the manic-depressive illness that had robbed them of their spouses.

One morning the subject of old age came up. Kay walked several paces behind her friend. "Polly, I've been thinking about how to grow old gracefully," said Kay. "I've been studying Averell Harriman and Alice Longworth, who've done it beautifully, and I think I know the answer."

"What is it?" Polly asked.

"We have to read a lot," Kay replied, "and not drink."

For a while all Kay heard was the crunch of Polly's steps in the snow. Finally, she asked, "When do we have to start?"

On July 28, 1966, Kay attended Jackie Kennedy's thirty-seventh birthday party at Paul and Bunny Mellon's weekend retreat on Martha's

Vineyard. Others at the function included Bobby and Ethel Kennedy, Teddy and Joan Kennedy, David and Evangeline Bruce, the Averell Harrimans, the Robert McNamaras, Arthur Schlesinger, Richard Goodwin, Kenneth (Jackie's hairdresser), and interior decorator Billy Baldwin. John Kenneth Galbraith, also in attendance, sat next to Katharine at dinner. "We spoke about Martha's Vineyard. Kay was considering buying property either on the Vineyard or at Nantucket. She said she found it difficult to visit her farm in Virginia, because it reminded her of Phil Graham's suicide. In the end Jackie and Kay both acquired homes on Martha's Vineyard."

Later that summer Kay Graham and Polly Wisner visited Saratoga Springs, half an hour from Albany, New York, to take the mineral baths and bet the horses. Franklin Roosevelt Jr., a guest at the same hotel as the ladies, recalled that "Kay handed me a gift one afternoon, a copy of Truman Capote's *In Cold Blood*, which she'd just finished reading herself. A friend of hers, Capote had recently announced his intention to throw a huge bash in Kay's honor. It would be the party of the decade and would redefine society, just as Mrs. Astor's invites had defined society during a previous era. He intended to hold it in the Grand Ballroom at the Plaza Hotel in New York. Guests from around the world would come dressed in black and white, as in the Ascot scene of *My Fair Lady*. They would wear masks, and at the stroke of midnight unmask themselves. Capote, it seemed, had somehow become convinced that Kay was still in agony over Phil Graham's suicide, which is why he wanted to give her a party in the first place."

A short time later Capote met with Kay and Polly at "21" in New York to review his plans. Film producer Lester Persky, a pal of Capote's, joined them for dessert. "Kay understood," said Persky, "that the party was really about him, not her. He needed a guest of honor, somebody accomplished and well known—but not *too* well known—around whom to wrap the party. He couldn't have thrown it for a supercelebrity like Jackie Kennedy because then the party would have been about her, not him. For Kay Graham it represented a kind of strange, glittering, midlife coming-out party, an official end to her period of mourning and at the same time an introduction to the world of New York high society. Truman asked her in his famous falsetto to invite twenty couples from Washington. The remainder of the approximately 540 invitees would be friends of his. He spent a full five months planning the event. He used to carry one of those schoolboy composition books around in which he would jot down the names of potential guests. The list kept changing. And it kept growing. The process never stopped. He would expunge old names and enter new ones, like some kind of deity deciding who should live and who should die. And, in a manner of speaking, if you weren't on his damn list you were as good as dead, at least socially. People who weren't invited did leave town or said they were going. Everyone with even the vaguest pretense of social accomplishment said he or she was invited, whether they were or not, and when the entire list was finally published, the fibbers were caught out. People would call Capote at his apartment in the U.N. Plaza and beg him for an invitation. Tallulah Bankhead was a case in point. He invited her but only after making her wait until the very last minute. And this party, which was officially known as the Black and White Ball but which I once heard Truman call the 'Big Do,' became the main topic of conversation at every dinner party and cocktail party between New York and Los Angeles. For several months the gossip and society columnists wrote about little else. Nobody but Truman knew the names on the final guest list. He refused to divulge this information to anybody. The mystery only heightened the occasion. Finally, the day before the event, he released the full list to Charlotte Curtis of *The New York Times*, which published it. Truman made about a million and a half lasting enemies over the party.

"Kay, Truman, and I convened again a week later, this time at a French café on the East Side, to discuss the food and entertainment situation. Truman had hired Peter Duchin, Averell Harriman's godson, to provide the music. Even though the dinner would consist only of chicken hash and spaghetti, instead of filet mignon and caviar, the total cost was considerable. It included roughly four hundred bottles of Taittinger champagne.

"After mapping it all out, the three of us left the café and headed for a party at Halston's place in the Olympic Towers. I believe this marked the first time Kay Graham had ever met Halston. Martha Graham, among others, was also there. At some point Truman sat between them on a sofa, Katharine on one side, Martha on the other. 'I feel like a Graham cracker,' he quipped. He then proceeded to drink himself into a stupor. Halston would soon become Kay Graham's designer. From about 1970 to the day he died, she relied on him almost entirely for what she wore. By her own admission, before Halston she'd been one of fashion's hundred neediest cases, a perennial on Mr. Blackwell's worst-dressed list. Her only other major fashion adviser during these years was Diana Vreeland."

The Big Do took place on November 28, 1966. Kay had a French dress—a Balmain design—copied at Bergdorf Goodman, a plain white crepe with slate-colored beads around the neck and sleeves. Halston fashioned a mask to match. Kenneth, whom she'd gotten to know at Jackie Kennedy's birthday party, did her hair and makeup. A number of the invitees attended smaller dinner parties held by other invitees the same night as the Big Do. Capote and Graham dropped in on the festivities at the Fifth Avenue home of William and Babe Paley. Among the guests at the same dinner were the Bruces and Coopers.

Writing about the fabled evening in her column for the Kentucky newspapers, Lorraine Cooper remarked that she had put on a "five-year-old white dress that I had given to my niece and taken back for the occasion (it unfortunately needed a trip to the cleaners), with a twenty-nine-cent black Halloween mask like John's. I was amused to see the next day that *Women's Wear Daily* hadn't noticed this and had given me three stars for my costume."

The competition, she vouchsafed, had been stiff: "The cast at dinner included practically every best-dressed woman on the fashion list, starting with Babe Paley. The Maharani of Jaipur wore white silk; Gloria Guinness wore a shimmering white beaded dress with long sleeves; Mrs. Gianni Agnelli, whose husband owns the Fiat Motor Car Company of Italy, was in a dress that looked as if it was made of cobwebs with dew scattered all over it, and a headdress of thin white feathers; Princess Lee Radziwill, the sister of Jacqueline Kennedy, was in silver sequins; the wife of the former ambassador from Brazil, a best-dressed list regular, wore black velvet with a silver mask made by Dior that looked like a glorified Christmas tree."

Right after dinner, Lorraine continued, "we went to the Plaza and were confronted with huge crowds in the streets and in the halls of the hotel that seemed to me to be as big as a football game at the University of Kentucky. One had to skip rope over the television cables and luckily my mask, which had slipped, kept me from being blinded by the flash-bulbs of a hundred cameras, as we groped along trying to avoid the phys-ical hazards. A dozen New York policemen, a half-dozen Plaza Hotel security guards, and a pair of Secret Service agents were posted at strate-gic locations to monitor the crowd. Once past the scrimmage line, we ar-rived at the ballroom where everyone presented separate admission cards—to keep out the gate crashers—and all could enjoy the marvelous spectacle of a throng of more than five hundred people, made up of artists, writers, foreign dignitaries, politicians, social figures, actors, busi-ness tycoons, and New York's best-looking women.

"The old Plaza ballroom is decorated in white and gold and, to give more color to brighten the black and white dresses, Truman had scarlet tablecloths on all the round tables scattered around the ballroom floor, with gold candlesticks twined with miles of green Similax.

"All ages seemed to be enjoying themselves. Alice Longworth, who almost never leaves Washington, came up for the party and labeled it 'the most exquisite of spectator sports,' a line which The New York Times used as the headline for its spread on the event.

"There were the most improbable pairings. I saw Walter Lippmann in deep conversation with Kenneth Lane, who designs those huge fake earrings that everybody wears. Former Ambassador John Hay Whitney was whirling around with Fred Astaire's sister, Adele. The former Mar-garet Truman and the present Lynda Bird Johnson were busy chewing the fat. Arthur Schlesinger Jr. and William F. Buckley, neither of whom are short men, kept dancing with taller women. Marianne Moore, the poet, took a spin around the dance floor with McGeorge Bundy. Frank Sinatra, looking like the Lone Ranger behind his black eye mask, watched his much younger wife, Mia Farrow, twist most of the fast numbers with publisher Bennett Cerf and Bennett's son, Christopher."

(Frank Sinatra's presence at the ball was itself bizarre, given his well-known hatred of the press. Some fifteen years later, during the Reagan administration, the crooner would corner Kay Graham in a Washington nightspot and excoriate her. "You're an ugly bitch!" he growled at her on the latter occasion; she responded with a demure and classy "Thank you very much, Mr. Sinatra.")

Peter Duchin called the Black and White Ball " 'A Night to Remember,' the most incredible collection of personages and celebrities I've ever seen in one place at one time. If it wasn't the party of the century, it came pretty close. Somebody called it 'the Last Great American Party. The Last Gasp!' The guest list included names no less illustrious than Averell Harriman, Leland Hayward, Claudette Colbert, Jerome Robbins, Anita Loos, Rose Kennedy, Jacqueline Kennedy, Alfred Gwynne Vanderbilt, Joe Alsop, Gregory Peck, David Merrick, Candice Bergen, and Mike Nichols. The ballroom was candlelit. The men wore dinner jackets, the women wore evening gowns, everything black and white, with masks made of feathers, fur, and flowers. Truman and Kay Graham were in their glory."

George Plimpton, who first stayed at Kay Graham's house when visiting Washington in 1961, commented that "the Black and White Ball commanded more media attention than the Beatles when they stayed at the Plaza. Actually it was more like a pageant than a party, somewhat self-conscious, a congress of peacocks strutting about and showing their colors."

Drew Pearson attended the ball but wrote an acidic column the following day, criticizing its decadence in the face of the country's complex racial, financial, and social problems. Still, the Big Do was not without its moments. At four in the morning, as the affair began to wind down, one of Capote's doormen from the U.N. Plaza showed up to help the author cart off a few mementos he wanted for his apartment. Having grown up in the nation's capital, the doorman had always been a huge fan of *The Washington Post*. Capote introduced the doorman, who was still in uniform, to Kay Graham and suggested that they take a turn around the dance floor. Peter Duchin struck up the band. At the end of the number, the doorman thanked Kay for allowing him "the biggest thrill" of his life.

✺

"I USED TO GET MOST of my best story ideas at Georgetown dinner parties," said Rowland Evans, whose syndicated newspaper column— written in conjunction with Robert Novak—first became popular during the Vietnam War era. "Since our column ran in *The Washington Post*, we could always depend on Kay Graham to provide us with leads and suggestions. She had contacts in almost every area of the federal government and would share her contacts if it meant bringing in a better story. If you needed to speak to a certain congressman or senator or somebody close to the president, Kay would arrange a dinner and make the necessary introductions.

"Another great source for story ideas were my Georgetown neighbors, the Coopers. With the help of their four servants, Lorraine Cooper gave catered luncheons and dinners that were skillfully prepared by the cook, a Latino named Delia Valesquez. I once heard Lorraine say that if the word *hostess* was going to be her epitaph, she would refuse to die. Still, she loved planning a party and approached it as though organizing an old-fashioned military engagement, with attention paid to logistics, rationing, and deployment of troops. She was aided in her quest by her husband, Senator John Sherman Cooper, who never admitted that the impossible isn't possible and whose idea it had been to invite all of the Republican senators—eighty-four in those days, counting wives—to a once-a-year garden party, an event that soon encompassed the entire Senate as well as other noteworthy Washingtonians. On occasions such as this, the Coopers would set up a twelve-foot-by-twelve-foot outdoor dance floor consisting of three pieces of plywood, which during the winter sat in their garage. This little object became something of a Georgetown character. During the summer months, anyone giving a garden party for themselves or their children would telephone Lorraine and borrow it. Then there were the indoor parties she gave for exactly twenty-four guests. Since there wasn't room enough for that many in any one room, she'd clear all the furniture out of the dining room and set up twelve tiny tables for two along the walls. She found some rose-flowered chintz and made a dozen matching tablecloths and put one candlestick and one rose on each table. It looked very nightclubby, which is the effect she wanted to impart. After each course, the gentlemen moved to the next table, so by the time coffee was served everyone had sat with at least four dinner partners."

John Sherman Cooper had the distinction of being among the first of a growing number of senators who, as early as 1967, began to comprehend the futility of America's position in the Vietnam War. On May 15 of that year he spoke to the Senate on the government's need to open a dialogue with North Vietnam concerning the subject of a peaceful settlement and an end to hostilities. It was a powerful statement by a man who placed personal principles before the latest political poll.

A week after Cooper's speech, Lorraine telephoned Rowland and Kay Evans, his wife, and invited them to a small dinner party. Also in attendance was Secretary of Defense Robert S. McNamara, who had become a great favorite in Georgetown. "McNamara had always been tight-lipped in the past," said Evans, "but on this occasion he delved into some of the exotic, often outlandish weaponry and secret programs that the Pentagon had been planning for Vietnam. One of their stranger projects called for the implementation of an electronic surveillance operation whereby a high wall or barrier would be built around the borders of North Vietnam. Thousands of electronic sensors would then be air-dropped at regular intervals along the outer perimeter of the wall. The wall plus sensors would presumably enable us to detect and monitor Vietcong troop movements and incursions. And this wonderful little invention would cost the nation a mere billion dollars!

"We ran two columns on the prospective surveillance operation, which I assume is what McNamara wanted us to do. But even the Pentagon must have seen the folly of the operation, because it simply never materialized."

The Pentagon indulged itself in a variety of fantasies. At a Georgetown dinner party given by David and Evangeline Bruce in 1969, following their return from England, Evans overheard a high-ranking Pentagon
official describe another phantasmagoric military plot. "This Vietnam-era
scheme," said Evans, "involved the importation of hundreds of schools of
piranha, the man-eating fish from the Amazon River, which would then
be planted in the rice paddies of North Vietnam. The theory was that
once the piranha devoured five or six rice farmers, nobody would dare
work the paddies and the country's most vital food source would be lost."

Ward Just, chief correspondent in Vietnam for *The Washington Post*,
experienced a similar reaction to Defense and Pentagon types. Recalling
a dinner party he attended at Robert McNamara's house in the Kalorama
section of Washington, he said: "Joe Alsop invited me to come and
express my sentiments about the war. He fully realized I'd become skep-
tical about our chances to win. God knows, we weren't making any head-
way. We were at a stalemate. And that was the best face you could put on
it. Stalemate would be considered optimistic. If anything, we were probably losing ground. So I walk into the house. There's McNamara and his
wife, Joe and Stewart Alsop and their wives, a couple of senators and
their wives, a few Pentagon officials and three or four Defense Department biggies. The talk at dinner is general. Over dessert the subject is Ho
Chi Minh and Vietnam. Joe Alsop is discussing the domino theory [a
term he coined to describe, how the Communists—after they conquered
South Vietnam—planned on taking over the world, including Japan,
Hawaii, and California]. So now the men and women separate. The men
walk into McNamara's study, where the talk about Vietnam becomes
more detailed and more intense. Discounted completely is the possibility
that Vietnam was nothing more than a localized struggle, a civil war between North and South. It's also clear that nobody wants to hear from
me. It becomes obvious to me that the dinner has been staged to get me
on the team, to turn my head so my reports to the *Post* more closely follow the party line.

"What's more, they're all digging into their pockets and pulling out
these documents containing the latest set of facts and figures. Somebody
claims to possess documents stolen from the enemy. They're grasping at

straws. All these Pentagon and Defense people, led by McNamara, are justifying the continuation of the war. There isn't any idea so outlandish they can't propose it, ponder it, and in extreme cases, implement it. These guys aren't the ones who are bleeding and dying over there. Most of them have never set foot in Vietnam. And they're not the least bit interested in hearing from anyone who actually has."

Although he didn't raise his voice at the McNamara dinner, Joe Alsop had by this time become a caricature of himself, shouting people down who had the temerity to disagree with him about the war, often accusing them of being Russian spies, Commies. Biographer Robert Merry noted that "Joe was a complete hawk. And since he had a controlling nature, it was either his way or the highway. If anybody said anything at a dinner party that irked him, he started screaming and cursing. He was an alcoholic as well, which only added to his behavior. He fought with virtually everyone, including Susan Mary, whom he constantly vilified in public, and Stewart, whom he stopped inviting to his parties. The two brothers reconciled, but the marriage between Joe and Susan Mary dissolved. After twelve years of marriage, she moved into the exclusive Watergate apartment complex and then into a Georgetown town house that had formerly belonged to her mother. And while she and Joe continued to co-host at each other's affairs, they never again lived together. After Joe's death in 1989, she virtually refused to speak about him."

"Joe had always been contentious," agreed Polly Wisner Fritchey, "but by the mid-1960s he had begun acting irrationally. I remember hearing about a 1967 dinner party he gave for several CIA officers as well as a few young antiwar enthusiasts, including Frances FitzGerald, the daughter of Desmond FitzGerald and Marietta Tree. The party took place shortly before Desmond's death, the result of a heart attack suffered while playing tennis with the British ambassador and his wife. Frances, who went on to write *Fire in the Lake*, kept offering sensible arguments as to why the United States ought not to be involved in the Vietnam War. She knew of what she spoke because she'd been there for most of 1966. Joe became so exercised that he left the dinner table, then returned and had a fit. It reached the point where he had to be restrained from physically assaulting one of the youthful dissenters.

"He began fulminating about the war at a dinner party that I gave later that year. He kept it up for the duration of the meal, filibustering whenever anyone tried to interrupt. At the end of the evening, a woman I didn't know very well said to me: 'How can you invite that boor into your home?' I had to explain that I remained loyal to my closest friends even if I didn't always agree with their politics."

In 1970 Art Buchwald wrote a play, *Sheep on the Runway*, that ridiculed a columnist named Joe Mayflower, who is clearly a parody of Joe Alsop. "Joe Mayflower," said Buchwald, "creates a little war in a far-away land so he can write about it. Unfortunately, Joe didn't appreciate the sentiment and threatened to sue. He dispatched his attorneys to the theater to see if they could close the show. He warned his friends that if they went to see the production, they would no longer be invited to his house. So they went in disguise.

"Things became a bit hairy because I used to bump into him all the time at Georgetown parties. It's a small town, a company town, and people talked. It's a town of leaks and spin and all that stuff, and if you didn't know the right people you didn't get your story. I was writing humor, not hard news, so I went to parties primarily for social reasons, to have fun. Joe Alsop went to gather information and to try and ferret out those who opposed the war. The end of the war marked the beginning of his end, which in turn marked the beginning of Georgetown's ultimate decline. It was a bad time in America. You had the assassinations of Martin Luther King Jr. and Robert F. Kennedy, the race riots, the failed peace initiatives. Walter Lippmann left Washington for New York. Jackie Kennedy left New York for Aristotle Onassis. Then you had Richard Nixon. Joe Alsop's favorite guest of honor during the Nixon years was Henry Kissinger, his last great hope for a reversal of fortune in Vietnam. But even Kissinger couldn't be counted on to perform a miracle."

If Joe Alsop attempted to browbeat the opposition into submission, Robert McNamara employed charm, particularly with regard to Katharine Graham. In a nutshell, the secretary of defense attended her dinner parties while at the same time administrating an increasingly unpopular Vietnam War campaign, one that Graham was stubbornly supporting on the editorial pages of the *Post*. Anytime McNamara found the editorials insufficiently supportive, or the body count reports too high, he would telephone Kay for a "clarification" session or dispatch McGeorge Bundy to the paper's offices to "set the record straight." Bundy, a special assistant for national security to both Kennedy and Johnson (and also a resident of Georgetown), was invited by Graham to attend a number of editorial board luncheons, several of them at her house. As McNamara's henchman, he attempted to influence the *Post* wherever and whenever he could. In 1969, he and McNamara handpicked the *Post*'s new president, Paul Ignatius, a former Pentagon official, secretary of the navy, and assistant secretary of defense from 1964 to 1967. Lacking relevant journalism experience, Ignatius lasted only two years at the *Post*. Nevertheless, given this set of facts, it would be fair to say that McNamara's friendship with Kay Graham had profound social policy implications. At least up to a point. In the final analysis, she placed the rigors of journalism above and beyond her cherished friendship with McNamara.

It was during Ignatius's second year at the *Post* that Graham enjoyed her first major success as a newspaper publisher. In mid-June 1071, going against the advice of the newspaper's general counsel and the misgivings of Robert McNamara, Kay assented to the *Post*'s serial publication of the Pentagon Papers, seven thousand pages of purloined material painstakingly gathered by Daniel Ellsberg, a former State Department, Rand Corporation, and Pentagon employee under Robert McNamara, and Ellsberg collaborator, Anthony Russo. What made the printing of the Papers in *The Washington Post* a particularly valiant act was that *The New York Times*, Ellsberg's first choice, after running an initial installment, had been enjoined by the federal government from further publication of the material. Although the same fate awaited the *Post*, Graham persevered. The release of the confidential archival documents, an internal history of the lies and secrets concocted and circulated by the Pentagon and executive branch in transacting the Vietnam War, set in motion a chain of events that included a landmark Supreme Court decision, the arrest and criminal prosecution of Ellsberg and Russo, the crimes of Watergate, the downfall of Richard Nixon, and the inevitable end to a non-winnable, catastrophic war.

∽

"GETTING *THE WASHINGTON POST* to change its editorial policy on Vietnam," said Ward Just, "was a little like turning the *QE II* in the opposite direction. It had to be done bit by bit." The same can be said for Kay Graham's transmogrification from shy housewife to plucky C.E.O. It took time. It involved a reeducation process, an understanding of the political system both as it applied to government and to the world of big business. As a woman in a man's world, she had to master the art of pushing without shoving, of stepping on toes but not on feet. "She'll never succeed," predicted soon-to-be disgraced Vice President Spiro Agnew, who rapidly discovered the degree to which he'd underestimated her might.

Beyond the publication of the Pentagon Papers, the early-to-mid-1970s found Kay Graham involved in at least three events that helped test the full measure of her resolve. The first, a strike on the part of forty-six female employees at *Newsweek*, began in 1970 and lasted until 1973, at which time there were some fifty-five female staffers. Ironically the strike came about in March, just as the magazine was about to publish its first cover story—entitled "Women in Revolt"—on the women's liberation movement. Ignoring the women staffers at *Newsweek*, Osborn Elliott turned to reporter Helen Dudar of the *New York Post* to write the piece. The issue landed on Kay Graham's desk accompanied by a letter from the women at *Newsweek:*

> *Women have rarely been hired as, or promoted to, the positions of reporter, writer, or editor; they are systematically by-passed in the selection of bureau correspondents and are routinely given lower title and pay.*

The letter also complained that the women's lib cover story had been written by a female journalist from a publication other than *Newsweek*. The women registered their grievance with the Equal Employment

Opportunities Commission, signed on with ACLU attorney Eleanor Holmes Norton (a tall, dynamic black woman who was eight months pregnant at the time), held a press conference, filed a lawsuit for sexual discrimination, and created a total furor in the press. *Newsweek* had the distinction of being the first media organization to be confronted by the women's movement. Kay Graham responded by asking her male executives, "Which side am I supposed to be on?" They assumed she was joking, but she wasn't. "She was a feminist," *The New Yorker* later concluded, "in spite of herself."

Soon after the strike began, Kay Graham met for lunch in New York with Jacqueline Kennedy, ostensibly to discuss *Newsweek*'s coverage of Ted Kennedy and the Chappaquiddick affair, about which the Kennedys felt the magazine had written harshly. They then talked about Jackie's marriage to Aristotle Onassis, and her travels back and forth between Skorpios and New York, where her children were currently enrolled in school. Finally the subject of the strike came up. "I don't go for all that," said Jackie. "I had no trouble finding a job years ago as an inquiring photographer at the *Washington Times-Herald.*"

Kay Graham stared at Jackie in disbelief. "Oh, Jackie," she said, "don't you remember when we would be in the White House sitting at the feet of Jack and Phil, saying nothing, just looking up to them?"

The women at *Newsweek* remained unconvinced of Kay Graham's supposed feminist leanings. Lynn Povich, a researcher at the magazine, noted (in an oral history conducted for Columbia University) that Graham refused to participate in negotiations with the striking women, pointing out to them (by letter) "that the men in charge of *Newsweek* . . . would be the ones dealing with the suit." During a meeting of the women and their attorney in Osborn Elliott's office, somebody noticed that Kay Graham happened to be in the building. According to Povich, Eleanor Holmes Norton "put her notebook down . . . and said, 'I want to stop this meeting right now and I want to request that Kay Graham join us. . . . This is a suit that affects her. She's a woman owner of this company. She should be here listening to what these women have to say. We're not continuing this meeting until she gets here.'

"So Kermit Lansner, the number two guy [at *Newsweek*], gets up from his chair . . . and goes walking out of the room and tries to find Kay Graham, and ends up dragging her back into this meeting. You can imagine how she felt about it. So Eleanor made some speech to her about, 'Now, Mrs. Graham, you're the owner of this magazine and we feel that you should listen and be part of this,' and so on and so forth."

Kay Graham stayed and listened as the women discussed what they considered a typical slight toward them, namely that Val Gerry, the magazine's reporter to the U.N., had been excluded from an important luncheon that *Newsweek*'s editors had arranged for its two male U.N. writers and a number of U.N. personnel.

"So we were raising this issue," said Povich, "showing how women were so excluded that they weren't even invited when they were the ones covering the beats, and Kay Graham said that she was sure that it was just an oversight and probably that there just hadn't been enough chairs at the table, and that after you had all the editors and the two writers who always covered the U.N., and then you had the U.N. guys and their press secretaries, there just weren't enough seats at the table to invite Val. Eleanor had never witnessed anything like this before. Afterward, . . . she said, 'It may be a better thing that Mrs. Graham is not in these meetings.'"

Although an agreement was negotiated several months later, it took far longer to implement the document. Consequently, a new lawsuit (for breach of contract) was filed in the spring of 1972. This time *Newsweek* was represented by a team of Washington lawyers headed by Joseph Califano (a partner with Williams & Connolly, Edward Bennett Williams's firm) and the women by a soft-spoken but tough attorney named Harriet Rabb. "This is ridiculous," Kay Graham purportedly told her lawyers when served with the latest suit. "We can't keep having this go on and on. I want you guys to do something about it." By early 1973, a second agreement had been carefully worked out, with specifics on the recruitment, promotion, and fairer pay of women. And this time around, *Newsweek* lived up to its promises.

Eleanor Holmes Norton, who eventually moved from New York to Washington and became a nonvoting delegate to Congress from the District of Columbia, made her peace with Kay Graham. "She began inviting

me for dinners at her Georgetown home and for visits to her country estate on Martha's Vineyard," said Norton. "I understood the position she
adopted during the *Newsweek* strike. As owner of the magazine, she had
no choice but to support *Newsweek's* managerial policies. But in reality
she backed the feminist movement and was giving sizable chunks of
money to Gloria Steinem to help establish *Ms.* magazine. She joined a
local group of female reporters in successfully protesting the membership regulations of the all-male Gridiron Club. If not an outspoken activist, she became involved in the movement on a number of levels and
became a role model to thousands of young, aspiring female journalists."

The *Newsweek* agreement had not yet been finalized when a more
urgent situation came up, one that would shape not only the future of
The Washington Post but also the future of the country. On June 17,
1972, five men were arrested inside the Watergate headquarters of the
Democratic National Committee while attempting to retrieve surveillance equipment they had installed in the same offices three weeks earlier. The significance of this event went unnoticed at first, so much so that
the story assignment at the *Post* went not to a veteran at the national desk
but to two fledgling reporters named Carl Bernstein and Bob Woodward,
both of whom worked for the metropolitan section of the paper. What
they would learn was that the five-man crew, known within the inner
sanctum of the Nixon White House as the "plumbers," had originally
been formed to discredit Daniel Ellsberg, who, in Richard Nixon's eyes,
had betrayed the country by releasing the Pentagon Papers. Attempting
to retrieve his psychiatric records, the gang of five had broken into the
Beverly Hills office of Ellsberg's psychoanalyst. That break-in and other
governmental wrongdoings destroyed the legal case against Ellsberg.
The plumbers, however, survived to run other nefarious White House errands. Their break-in at the Watergate eventually caused Richard Nixon
to commit obstruction of justice, the cover-up of which led in 1974 to the
threat of his impeachment followed by his formal resignation, Gerald
Ford's ascendancy to the highest office, and his pardon of Nixon.

The entire adventure has been captured in books and films. Perhaps
the most illuminating document is a relatively obscure thirty-minute interview Kay Graham gave in 1997 to C-SPAN television ("Breaking the

Watergate Story"), in which she admits the extent of her paranoia during
the years 1972–1974—her fear that "Deep Throat" was merely a mani-
festation of Bob Woodward's all-too-fertile imagination, her fear that she
was being followed, her fear that certain telephones at the new *Washing-*
ton Post building at 1150 Fifteenth Street NW (they moved in 1972)
were being tapped, her fear that Nixon would succeed in blocking the
Washington Post Company's Florida television-station licenses, her fear
that she (and her company) would be repeatedly audited by the IRS, her
fear that they were "being led down a garden path and that [they] would
soon have the ground cut out from underneath." Aware of the consequences if the newspaper fouled up, Kay experienced a return of her old
insecurities. "I didn't sleep very well," she admits. "I went to lunch with
Bob Woodward and asked him about Deep Throat. He looked so stricken
that I withdrew the question. I still don't know the answer. It's the only
secret that anybody in Washington has ever kept." (Woodward, previously a U.S. Naval Intelligence officer, would be accused of having inaccuracies, unsupportable suppositions, and outright lies in several of his
future books; conversely, many critics believe that Deep Throat either
didn't exist or was simply a term devised to indicate that Woodward and
Bernstein depended for background information and fact-checking purposes on several unnamed sources. Katharine Graham biographer Tom
Kelly asserts that "there is no question . . . that Bob Woodward is a
spook." Curiously, despite a seeming lack of evidence, the same accusa-
tion has been made at least once against Ben Bradlee.)

Kay had other fears and qualms as well. She constantly wondered
why other newspapers, such as *The New York Times,* didn't pick up on
the *Post*'s stories. "We had a wire service," she observes in the C-SPAN
interview, "but our leads on Watergate went unreported elsewhere. I'd
confront Ben: 'If we're right, why isn't anyone else picking up on this?'
He would reassure me, but the next day I'd be back with the same question." At one point, Richard Nixon supposedly formulated a plan geared
at having a consortium force a hostile buyout of the *Post,* complete with a
stockholders' lawsuit if Graham refused to sell. At another point, during a
meeting with henchmen H. R. Haldeman and John Ehrlichman, Nixon
(on tape and in a manner reminiscent of Phil Graham at his worst) railed

against "that Jew bitch over at the *Post*." Aside from Nixon's shrill invec-
tive, there was Attorney General John Mitchell's fiercely worded, now
classic "Katie Graham is going to get her tit caught in a big fat wringer."
Even André Meyer, certainly no enemy, was concerned enough to warn
Kay that if she persisted with her campaign she could be at physical risk.
George Shultz and Henry Kissinger, members of the Nixon administration, were frequent guests at Graham's house. Both men lived in Georgetown and both attempted to encourage their neighbor to become more
supportive of Nixon. "Look at what he accomplished in terms of foreign
policy," Kissinger told her. "And consider the danger of having McGovern in the presidency." His protestations fell on deaf ears. In *RN*, Nixon's
autobiography, he remembers having received a report from Kissinger
quoting Graham's explosive statement: "I hate Richard Nixon and I'm
going to do everything I can to beat him." She had made the comment to
Stewart Alsop, another Nixon loyalist.

"In retrospect," according to Henry Kissinger, "credit must go to Kay
for persevering with the Watergate story. She had everything to lose.
After all, she owned the newspaper. I enjoyed her gatherings both before
and after Watergate. After he became president, Nixon hated the whole
idea of Georgetown parties and did nothing to endear himself to the
ladies who ran Georgetown. As a result, they didn't invite him. I can't say,
though, that he dissuaded me from going. Maybe he thought I could convince Kay to call off the dogs. He was certain she had a personal vendetta
against him and maintained that her newspaper read like one long editorial page, that they did their editorializing on the front page. I went to
Kay's parties to relax and also to try to get the basic philosophy of the administration across. It might have helped Nixon had he attempted to befriend the ladies of Georgetown. But I couldn't convince him to do it, and
I would never have tried."

Nixon did maintain ties with one prominent Washington hostess,
Anna Chennault, the Chinese-born widow of American World War II
hero Claire Chennault. Well connected both in Washington and Saigon,
she became a liaison between Nixon and the South Vietnamese government in an effort, or so she thought, to bring peace to the region. "But
instead of ending the war," said Chennault, "Nixon prolonged it. The re-

sults were tragic. He was totally a political animal, not the least bit interested in partying. He didn't understand that in Washington, at least, partying is part of the political process."

Around the *Post* newsroom, Graham's resolute stance on Watergate
won her a nickname; following Nixon's resignation, she became known as
"Katharine the Great." Bob Woodward and Carl Bernstein penned *All
the President's Men,* a best-seller based on the events leading up to
Nixon's downfall, which became a major motion picture starring Robert
Redford as Woodward and Dustin Hoffman as Bernstein. Bernstein went
on to marry essayist-screenwriter-novelist Nora Ephron, while Woodward purchased a four-story Georgetown town house, not far from Kay
Graham's R Street mansion, thus joining blockbuster authors Herman
Wouk and Kitty Kelley as a "G-town" resident. If Watergate put Kay Graham on the map, it elevated Ben Bradlee to superstar status. If Graham
put her fortune on the line, Bradlee risked his reputation. His instinct
and drive were the ingredients that kept the coverage alive.

There were those who felt that the *Post,* despite its ultimate success,
had stooped to new journalistic lows. "We double-sourced everything,"
Kay Graham assured C-SPAN. But that didn't always seem to be the case.
Many of the newspaper's claims with regard to Watergate were based on
testimony from unidentified or anonymous sources. "Lady luck obviously
smiled on Kay Graham," said Sally Reston. Betty Beale recalled a 1979
Georgetown dinner party, where she and Kay were seated at the same
table. Deborah Davis's unflattering biography of Graham (*Katharine the
Great*) had just been published. "Like many publishers," said Beale, "Kay
had a strange fix on the world. She could write about anyone, bring down
a president, but nobody could write about her, which was doubly weird,
since she had also been a journalist and believed, I assume, in the First
Amendment. Anyway, in the course of this dinner, she leaned in my direction and said, 'I don't see how that woman could write a book about
me when I didn't give her an interview.' So I said, 'Kay, did President
Nixon give Woodward and Bernstein an interview?' "

The final major hurdle in Kay Graham's metamorphosis from cater-
pillar to butterfly was a 139-day walkout by unionized *Post* pressmen,
during which time she continued to publish the newspaper. The strike

began on October 1, 1975, when union members savagely beat a fore-
man, started a fire, and ransacked the presses. Reporters who decided to
stay on the job were subjected to verbal and sometimes physical abuse as
they crossed the picket lines. The same reporters were rewarded by management at lunchtime when their meals were served inside the building
by waiters in tuxedos. Among the placards displayed by the embittered
pressmen was one that read: "PHIL KILLED THE WRONG GRA-
HAM!" Always blunt and to the point, Ben Bradlee had his own method
of dealing with the strikers. As he walked the gauntlet to the cries of
"scab" and "flak," he raised his middle finger and waved it at the crowd.
Bradlee was giving them the bird. Kay Graham's response was less
provocative but equally emphatic. She leased a helicopter and, using the
roof of the *Post* building as a landing pad, ferried reporters' pages to a
nonunion printing plant. Eventually she hired nonunion pressmen, effectively breaking the union in spite of complaints that this violated the
newspaper's liberal editorial tradition and policy.

Bob Levey, a reporter and columnist for the *Post* and the then president of the union that represented reporters, editors, photographers,
advertising workers, and circulation personnel—1,100 employees in
all—regarded the Kay Graham of that period as "somebody who could be
terribly difficult one minute and extraordinarily humorous the next. At
times she would drink like a sailor. Other times she would be the imperious Marie Antoinette. You never knew who you were going to get. But
she always cared a great deal about the paper. I remember when I covered the State Department one year, I would be invited to dinner at her
house with ambassadors and senators. After two or three glasses of wine,
people begin to loosen up. It becomes that much easier to gather information. It's just amazing how many reporters at the *Post* operated like
that, and still do. To put it another way, nobody went to Kay's house for
the food. You went because of the mix, because of the people you met. If
they were in town, she had them. It's like what Elaine's restaurant in New
York represented in the 1980s. You didn't go there for the food, you went
to mingle.

"Concerning the strike, Kay had little choice doing what she did. According to the union contract in force at the time, the pressmen had the

right to determine how many people would work at the paper on any
given night and who those people would be—and the company could do
nothing about it. The pressmen's union could featherbed all kinds of
stuff, and people were routinely paid to sleep downstairs every night.
That kind of thing. Kay Graham was determined to get that one out on
the table and to beat it down once and for all."

One of the people Kay turned to for advice during the pressmen's
strike was Warren E. Buffett. Buffett, a self-made investments tycoon
from Omaha, Nebraska, currently residing part-time in Laguna Beach,
California, had first come to Kay's attention in the spring of 1973, following the death of Fritz Beebe, when he began purchasing large chunks of
Washington Post Company stock. Within a short period he had become,
with $10.6 million in stock holdings, the company's largest shareholder
outside the Graham family. Suspicious of Buffett's motives, Kay turned to
André Meyer, who in turn launched an investigation into the Nebraskan's
background. What he learned seemed encouraging. Born in 1930, Buffett was the son of a two-term, hard-line Republican congressman from
Nebraska and an overzealous but supportive mother. A child prodigy,
he moved to Fredericksburg, Virginia, with his family at age twelve
and wound up at the Wharton School of Finance and Commerce at the
University of Pennsylvania, before enrolling at Columbia University's
Graduate School of Business Administration. Married in 1952 to Susan
Thompson, the couple had three children and reestablished residence in
Omaha, where Warren took over Berkshire Hathaway and transformed
the company into a private investments firm specializing in undervalued
businesses and corporations. An early profile of Buffett in *The Wall Street
Journal* depicted him as "a man with nerves of steel." A later profile in the
same publication labeled him "a boardroom dynamo."

Kay Graham discussed Buffett with Robert Abboud, a Chicago
banker friend of hers, who knew Buffett and spoke well of him, though
he also advised her to proceed with caution. Donald Graham, having
served in Vietnam and then briefly as a policeman in the Washington
area, and who was now working his way up the managerial ladder at the
Post, had suspicions of his own. It turned out that Buffett had invested

heavily not only in the *Post* but also in the *Boston Globe,* the *Los Angeles Times,* and *The New Yorker.* Katharine wrote to Buffett, suggesting that they meet in Los Angeles, where she planned on seeing Otis Chandler in the near future. She later recalled the encounter, which took place at the *Los Angeles Times,* as "a very pleasantly spent hour." She saw Buffett again during her next visit to Los Angeles, at which time she asked him to join the Washington Post Company's board of directors, eventually appointing him chairman of the finance committee. Thereafter Buffett began flying to Washington to attend the once-a-month board meetings. During his visits, he stayed at Kay's house. Noting that she had certain lapses and holes in her knowledge of high finance, Buffett became her personal tutor, bringing along stacks of fiscal statements and quarterly reports, which he went over with her line by line. He invited her to attend the annual meeting events of Berkshire Hathaway. He was, she acknowledged, "a great teacher." She had started to sound like him at editorial meetings, using business lingo and terminology straight out of *Forbes* and *Fortune.* The *Post* executives felt he was manipulating her and that she was growing far too dependent on him, charges she vehemently denied. Yet her favorite new expression was: "That's an interesting point, let's see what Warren thinks." With Warren by her side, Kay succeeded in enlarging the company and making it far more profitable.

Whatever Buffett's gifts as a financial expert, he remained a man of simple tastes and pleasures. He preferred hamburgers to filet mignon and Pepsi-Cola to champagne. Graham stocked up on peanuts, potato chips, and strawberry ice cream for his visits. Although she gradually spruced up his wardrobe, he ordinarily wore a tattered blue suede jacket and a pair of rumpled gray flannel slacks. Buffett himself used to tell a story about a dinner party he attended at Kay's house shortly after joining the board, which Sally Quinn recounts in her book, *The Party.* Still a social neophyte, Buffett became confused when dessert arrived in a *pot de crème.* Never having seen a porcelain dessert cup with a top, he at first thought the porcelain top was part of the dessert and dug into it with his spoon. It didn't give. He tried again, and again nothing happened. Determined to get at his dessert, he gave it a third and final shot. At this point, to his utter embarrassment, Kay leaned over to him and whispered soothingly in his ear, "It might help if you just remove the top with your fingers."

Drawn to each other as much by their differences as by their similarities, Warren Buffett and Kay Graham quickly became an item. Even their age difference—he was thirteen years younger than she—seemed a point of attraction. They were soon spending more time in each other's company. He visited her at her home on Martha's Vineyard, her farm in Virginia, her apartment in Manhattan. She visited him in Omaha and Laguna Beach. They took frequent trips together. On a lark, they spent one weekend at Niagara Falls. Diana McLellan saw fit to write in "The Ear": "All the way up in New York, they're talking about Kay Graham and Warren Buffett . . . but oh, so discreetly." Liz Smith also took notice: "Warren Buffett, the cynosure of all eyes, has down-home charm, intelligence, and an unaffected manner. Mrs. Graham, his frequent hostess, is wealthy, elegant, and cultured." It seemed almost fitting that after all those years of being cheated on by Phil Graham, she was now engaged in a relationship with someone else's husband, although admittedly Buffett and his wife lived separate lives.

On November 24, 1975, Joe Alsop wrote to Aline Berlin, the wife of Isaiah Berlin, then teaching at Oxford, regarding a dinner party he had hosted the night before. Among the guests were the McNamaras, the Kissingers, and Kay Graham. "The real news of the evening," he remarked, "was the presence of Kay's lover, Warren Buffett. It really is the most extraordinary story." Alsop went on in his letter to describe Buffett's purchase of stock in Graham's company, her initial fears, their first meeting and subsequent romance. "Seeing them together, as I began to do rather early," Alsop continued, "finally made me suspect that they were what you might call 'moony' about each other. A little later, they both decided that indeed they were, and a rather flaming affair has been going on ever since. Furthermore, Kay's children like Warren immensely, while his wife, allegedly at any rate, doesn't object to his spending many a week with Kay in Washington. . . . As you can read between the foregoing lines, the whole thing has given me great delight, mainly because it makes Kay really happy for the first time in ages and I like to see my friends happy."

The letter from Alsop elicited a telephone call from Isaiah Berlin to Kay, congratulating her on her new relationship. Kay became alarmed and, in a state of panic, dashed off a note to Alsop maintaining that while the affair meant a great deal to her, it would probably end if it became "a subject of conversation." She realized that there was talk among people "who don't know what they're talking about," but if the few people "who do know don't talk," she felt she and Warren could "continue to have something great." If it became "tawdry" or found its way into print, it would doubtless "hurt the company badly and hurt Warren's family badly." And neither of them, she added, could stand such a possibility.

Warren Buffett's domestic situation had taken a dramatic turn. Now that the children were grown, Susan Buffett decided to pursue a lifelong dream and undertook a career as a professional chanteuse. Signing up with the William Morris Agency, she performed with jazz and swing bands in and around the Omaha area, finally moving to a small apartment in San Francisco to more actively engage in her new profession. It was an amicable separation. Warren and Susan kept in daily contact by telephone and on occasion still traveled together. Moreover, Warren often attended his wife's appearances and recitals. Alexander Cockburn, a left-wing political journalist then involved with Lally Weymouth, recalled double-dating one night with "Lally's mother and Warren Buffett, the plain, blunt Nebraska billionaire. We went out to a Washington nightclub. Mrs. Buffett, a would-be torch singer, warbled her way through a medley of songs. Everybody seemed to be very cordial with everybody else. What I mean is that there was no discernible hostility between Mrs. Buffett and Mrs. Graham."

If any hostility existed it happened later when Buffett took up with Astrid Menks, a former waitress at Omaha's French Café, where Susan had sometimes sung before moving to San Francisco. Although Warren and Susan remained married and on excellent terms, Astrid moved in with Buffett, and together they set up house. According to Andrew Kilpatrick, Buffett's biographer, "Susan and Astrid got along very well." Kay Graham might have felt otherwise toward Warren's newest companion.

"Kay was too practical a woman to believe that she could ever sustain a marriage to a man thirteen years her junior," said Evangeline Bruce, "but the advent of a new woman in Warren's life must have upset her. She and Warren continued their relationship, but she turned her romantic eye to her old friend Robert McNamara, especially in 1981, following the death of Margaret, Bob's wife."

If Robert McNamara, now the president of the World Bank, held it against Kay that she had published the Pentagon Papers in the *Post,* further tarnishing his already damaged reputation as secretary of defense, he never indicated as much. To the contrary, he was there for Kay, giving her business advice, agreeing to serve (alongside Buffett) on the company board, making constant suggestions as to how Kay should handle her personal finances. Executives at the *Post* came to think of McNamara as Kay's "sacred cow," a title they had previously bestowed only upon Warren Buffett. And as with Buffett, Joe Alsop was once again drawn into the drama. A witness to events, he also served on occasion as Kay's beard. While vacationing at the Homestead, a luxury resort in Hot Springs, Virginia, Alsop received a telephone call from Kay asking him to reserve two guest suites at the resort for Bob McNamara and herself. Alsop did as asked. On October 5, 1981, the hotel's reservations manager, W. Dan Reichartz, sent Alsop a letter of confirmation, stipulating that they had booked "a parlor and bedroom suite for Mrs. Katharine Graham for arrival on October 9 and departure on October 11. Additionally, we have reserved a parlor and one-bedroom suite for Mr. Robert McNamara for arrival on October 10 for one night. . . . I trust that these arrangements are satisfactory." At this juncture, Kay was still romantically involved with Warren Buffett, and they continued to be frequent dinner guests at Joe Alsop's house as well as at the homes of many of Graham's other Georgetown friends.

There were additional sightings. Each summer, before going to Martha's Vineyard, Kay would spend a weekend at the Marlboro Music Festival in Marlboro, Vermont. The festival, which brought together well-known, experienced performers with young and talented musicians of the future, had for years been funded by Katharine's father. During the early 1980s, her companion to the annual event was Robert McNamara. Whenever in Marlboro, Bob and Kay dropped in on John Kenneth Galbraith, who owned a nearby summer cottage. They were on their way to

Galbraith's house one Sunday when McNamara's car, a brand-new Ford, developed engine trouble. Just before it died, McNamara managed to steer it to the side of the road.

"What are you going to do about this, Bob?" asked Kay.

"I'd better look under the hood," he responded, climbing out of the driver's seat and walking around to the front of the car. After fumbling with the hood lock for several minutes, he managed to pry it open. He stared at the engine, scratched his brow, then returned to his seat.

"What's the matter with it, Bob?"

"Damned if I know," he said.

"What do you mean?" ventured Kay. "Weren't you president of the Ford Motor Company before you became secretary of defense?"

"I was," he said, "but I've never seen the front end of a car before."

According to Polly Fritchey, Kay adored Warren Buffett, but she loved Bob McNamara. Alexander Cockburn concurred. "Obviously," he conceded, "she had a thing with McNamara." Graham biographer Carol Felsenthal felt that "Kay might have married McNamara, if only he had asked." Instead, McNamara took up with the younger, more coquettish Joan Braden. Their very public affair—Joan was still married to Tom Braden—once again wounded Kay. When she heard that they were planning to go on safari together, she purportedly said: "I hope it pours." Despite their failed romance, Kay remained unduly loyal to McNamara. In 1995, when he published In Retrospect, a halfhearted apologia on his controversial role in the Vietnam War, Kay threw him a huge bash, spending hours with the cook selecting foods first at Neams Meat Market and then at Scheele's Groceries on P Street. When asked by a reporter from Time why she had celebrated McNamara's book, she responded: "I didn't celebrate his book; I celebrated the man."

CHAPTER TEN

THE MIGHTY QUINN

IN 1968 BEN BRADLEE cornered David Laventhol, an editor at *The Washington Post,* and assigned him the task of helping to organize and launch a new segment of the newspaper, something they planned to call the Style section. It would replace an already existent section called For and About Women. To assist Laventhol in this venture, Bradlee turned to Jim Truitt, recently back from his *Newsweek* bureau post in Japan. The idea of the new section, as Laventhol understood it, was to examine the personal lives and lifestyles of interesting and/or important Washingtonians as well as report on parties, banquets, and recent Washington social developments.

The Style section made its inauspicious debut in January 1969. It covered a number of the social events scheduled in conjunction with the midmonth inauguration of President Nixon. Also, because the Metroliner—an express passenger train connecting New York and Washington—had just started its run, Laventhol decided to include several articles on the resurgence of the railroad as a viable means of transportation. Based on his travels in Japan, Truitt wrote a piece on the bullet train from Tokyo to Osaka. There were additional stories on the history of the railroad in American life and on America's most historic trains.

Kay Graham, wary of the new endeavor from the start, was horrified by what she saw. Richard Nixon was the most lackluster president to take office in years, and what did passenger trains have to do with style? Summoning Laventhol to her office, she proceeded to vent her frustration. In short, she objected to the new section primarily because it contained no social news. "To people in Washington," she said, "social reporting is very important. A good many political and governmental activities take place at Washington dinner parties. That's where people meet each other and connect with each other and talk about some pending bill or the latest presidential appointment or whatever. It really is a critical part of the fabric of life in this city."

Ben Bradlee also heard from Graham and took steps to bolster the new section, adding Nick von Hoffman, a young and talented reporter and editor, to the Style staff. Von Hoffman took note of one of the section's trouble spots. "James Truitt," as he put it, "was totally out of his mind. His countless memos to us contained no margins and were typed in either red or blue as opposed to the customary black." Ben Bradlee evidently concurred. In his autobiography, *A Good Life,* he writes: "Truitt once sat in front of a typewriter for forty-seven hours, making a list of more than a thousand story ideas after I asked casually, 'Where the hell are all the ideas?' " Truitt was soon fired, many thought because he had once helped Phil Graham procure women. Laventhol, who went on to become managing editor, editor, and publisher of *Newsday* and publisher and C.E.O. of the *Los Angeles Times,* went away as well, claiming that he had been interfered with by Kay Graham. (Bradlee likewise felt that Graham was pushing too hard and on one occasion said to her, "I can't edit this section unless you get your fucking finger out of my eye.") Before Laventhol left, in the summer of 1969, he made a critical addition to the Style section staff. On the strength of a recommendation by Bradlee, Laventhol hired a twenty-eight-year-old party reporter named Sally Quinn. Untested as a writer, she would soon prove herself one of the most read and talked about reporters in the history of *The Washington Post.*

Delivered by her maternal grandfather, a well-known surgeon, Sally Quinn was born in Savannah, Georgia, on July 1, 1941, the firstborn child of William Wilson ("Buffalo Bill") Quinn, a lieutenant (three-star) general in the United States Army, and Bette (Williams) Quinn, described by her eldest daughter as "the quintessential southern lady." General Quinn served in Europe during and after World War II, in Korea, as head of the Institute for Defense Analysis, and at the Pentagon, where he was director of public information. According to Sally Quinn's memoir, *We're Going to Make You a Star*, her father was deprived of a promotion and forced into retirement by President Lyndon Johnson, who became enraged by the suspicion that General Quinn had passed highly sensitive military data on Vietnam to Senator Barry M. Goldwater of Arizona, an extremely close family friend, a member of the Armed Services Committee, and Johnson's opponent in the 1964 presidential race. "It was a lesson in politics which I will never forget," Sally wrote. After retiring, General Quinn became a vice president for the Martin-Marietta Corporation, a military hardware manufacturer. The remainder of Sally's immediate family consisted of Donna, a sister two years her junior, and William ("Billy") Quinn, a lawyer and amateur astrologer, born in 1947. Billy, a resident of Phoenix, Arizona, served as Barry Goldwater's attorney during the last seven years of the senator's life.

In an interview with the current author, Billy Quinn characterized his own childhood and that of his sisters as "highly transient. By the time our parents celebrated their twenty-fifth wedding anniversary, they had lived in twenty-seven different cities, mostly on army bases. It was difficult to put down roots, especially with respect to community activities, education, and friends. The experience made my sisters more outgoing, while it made an introvert of me." A typical army brat, Sally Quinn attended twenty-two schools, including five high schools, in the United States, Japan, Greece, Switzerland, and Germany. Dating boys from an early age, she was expelled once from a Swiss finishing school for chasing after a goat herder, and at age seventeen, her family stationed at Fort Lewis, Washington, she fell in love with Kris Kristofferson, then a cadet at the same base. "As a teenager, Sally was extremely bright," said her brother. "She was precocious, sophisticated, and perhaps a bit older than her years. She has always been articulate. And she always had fairly good writing and communications skills, together with good skills of observation. And those are the things, it seems to me, that are the stock-in-trade of a decent reporter."

Politically speaking, Billy observes that his father "was very much a Barry Goldwater conservative, which made for some very interesting discussions over family dinners." Regarding General Quinn's position at the Pentagon, "he was the person who represented the United States Army at social functions in Washington, D.C. Whenever the army needed to make an official presence at some function, and usually those were either diplomatic, with the Embassy Row crowd, or sometimes congressional in nature, they would send my father. My parents had acquired a house just two blocks across the District line in Chevy Chase, Maryland, and virtually every evening, at exactly five-thirty, a black sedan from the Pentagon motor pool would pull up with a driver. And mother and father—my father in dress blues and my mother in an evening gown—would get in the car and leave. And we wouldn't see them again until midnight. And almost every night they would go to two or three cocktail parties and at least one dinner party. This went on night after night. They had a voluminous stack of invitations. Between the embassies and the congressional events and the major corporations and other military functions, they were always on the move. Consequently, they met an amazing number of people in the Washington social and political realm. My father was a very personable guy, real gregarious. People enjoyed being around him. He was sort of a joke-telling, back-slapping Irishman."

Sally Quinn's insatiable appetite for the limelight was very likely an inherited trait, heightened by reports that when she was young, she occasionally substituted for her mother as her father's escort at embassy receptions and dinners, functions that she absolutely relished. Despite their obvious lust for reveling, the Quinns were hardly considered A-list material. "High C is more like it," said former Washington hostess Barbara Howar, a lively southerner from Raleigh who for years had been one of Sally's closest companions. According to socialite Coates Redmon, also a friend of Sally's, Mrs. Quinn was less than C list: "She was a mousy little woman who looked like she came from Podunk. She was nice but dull. You'd never think she was Sally Quinn's mother." The couple's great friends, the Goldwaters, were equally déclassé. "Barry Goldwater during the time he lived in Washington was a big social flop," said Howar. "He and his wife were part of a satellite group and not part of the Alsop-Wisner-Graham-Cooper gang."

The Quinns and Goldwaters evidently had more in common than mere comradeship. It was common knowledge that Bette Quinn and Barry Goldwater were very close friends. The same claim was made by any number of locals, including Warren Adler, publisher of Washington's now-defunct *Dossier* magazine, who observed that "the Goldwaters and Quinns traveled everywhere together. They practically lived together." Others concurred that Sally Quinn's mother and Barry Goldwater were quite intimate. Robert Alan Goldberg, a professor of American history and Barry Goldwater's biographer, reported that while he didn't write about the close friendship in his biography, he did read several letters Peggy Goldwater, Barry's wife, wrote him "in regard to his relationship with Bette Quinn, expressing [unhappiness] and her desire that Barry not see Bette." In the course of his research for the biography, Goldberg interviewed General Quinn. "Quinn," he said, "played a tape recording for me, which I took home and rerecorded. You have to hear it to believe it. Something like *Moon River* is playing in the background, and you can hear a crackling fire and Goldwater is reciting poetry—love poetry. And it's very clear that this was Barry to Bette. So you get the romantic side of Barry. And Quinn plays it for me. 'I want you to hear a side of Barry Goldwater that nobody else has heard,' he tells me." What astonished Goldberg about the recording was that Quinn seemed completely unaware of Goldwater's interest in his wife. "He hadn't a clue that the tape had anything to do with his wife," said Goldberg. "No clue, whatsoever. And Quinn was the guy who, in 1944, was part of Intelligence operations in Europe. After he met with me, I telephoned my father, who'd landed at Normandy in World War II, one of the operations Quinn helped organize. 'Dad,' I said, 'you don't know how lucky you are to be alive.'

"Another time I was interviewing Bette Quinn for the biography—we were in her home—and the telephone rang. 'I bet that's him,' she says. And it was. It was Barry calling. Barry called her every afternoon, and here he was calling again. They were in constant communication and I think had a very, very close, intimate relationship that was a matter of common knowledge. George McGovern brought it up when I interviewed him for the book. Others spoke of it, and Peggy's letters were a sure indication to me as well."

❦

COMMENTING ON THE DEGREE to which Sally Quinn traveled the world while growing up, Nancy Dickerson remarked that "while Sally globe-trotted nearly as much as Vangie Bruce, Vangie appeared to be more European in sensibility, whereas Sally seemed distinctly American. Both ladies were equally adept at giving dinner parties." Aside from periodically accompanying her father to diplomatic functions, Sally gained valuable experience in the social arts during the summer following her graduation from high school, when she worked in the Pentagon's protocol office, helping to arrange luncheons and banquets for military dignitaries. That fall she entered Smith College in Northampton, Massachusetts, and she "came out" as a debutante at the Holly Ball in Arlington, Virginia, over Christmas vacation of her freshman year.

At Smith, Sally majored in theater, indicating on a questionnaire for her vocational guidance counselor that she hoped to become a movie star. In pursuing that ambition, she performed in several student productions, playing the role of Lily Sabina in the senior play, Thornton Wilder's *The Skin of Our Teeth*. She dated frequently, sometimes going out every day of the week. During her summer vacations she worked as an assistant technical librarian at the Institute for Defense Analysis in Washington, D.C., a job arranged by her father. "It was intoxicating to be around real power," she wrote, "to have senators pay attention to you, sit across from famous administration types at little Georgetown restaurants, be invited by ambassadors to visit their countries."

Graduating near the bottom of her class at Smith, Sally procured a two-line walk-on role in a summer stock production of *The Miracle Worker* at the Monomoy Theatre in Chatham, Massachusetts. Then, after being discovered by an MGM talent scout, she was considered for roles in television's *Dr. Kildare* and in the motion picture *Flipper*, but as she relates it, she did not hit it off with the "greasy, fast-talking hustler from Hollywood who interviewed me." She supported herself in New

York, while unsuccessfully auditioning for parts, by modeling and dancing in a club as a go-go girl. "I wanted to be powerful, rich, and famous,"
she told journalist Richard Lee, "but I ended up typing." More to the
point, she nearly ended up stripping.

A member of the Junior League, Sally returned to Washington and
spent time helping to raise funds for charities and philanthropic groups.
She worked briefly as a salesgirl in a trendy Georgetown boutique, traveled to Mexico, and next joined her father in Stuttgart, West Germany,
where he was on military assignment as commanding general of the Seventh Army. While in Germany, when not going out with the junior officers (they dubbed her "the cobra"), she performed with a touring theater
company and worked as a translator at the Mercedes-Benz automobile
company. One of the junior officers evidently appealed to her because
while on a trip to Spain with him, they became engaged. Henry Mortimer, a young Harvard graduate from Tuxedo Park presently serving
with the Seventh Army in Germany, was a first cousin of Amanda Burden
and a member of one of the wealthiest families in New York. Still engaged, Sally returned to the States and for most of the mid-1960s held a
successive variety of jobs, including public relations agent for a Coney Island animal husbandry exposition, assistant production manager for film-
maker Charles Guggenheim, Kelly Girls temporary agency, and social
secretary to Cherif Guellal, the dashing and fun-loving thirty-two-year-
old Algerian ambassador to Washington. Guellal, renowned for his parties, was living (at least part of the time) with a former Miss America in
what had once been Lyndon Johnson's old house. Their nonstop social
activities kept Sally fully occupied.

It was in 1966, shortly before going to work for the Algerian ambassador, that Sally met Warren Hoge, a one-time *Washington Star* reporter
and more recently White House correspondent for the *New York Post*. A
graduate of Yale, Hoge was the same age as Quinn. He shared a three-
bedroom residence on I Street (right off Pennsylvania Avenue, a few
blocks from the White House) with two other journalists, Bill Rice and
David Breasted. Both men were impressed with their housemate.
Breasted considered Hoge "a very attractive guy—tall, suave, bright,
funny. He had a supernatural way with women. He had an eye for them,

and they had an eye for him. He was just a natural. He had a mellifluous voice and was ultra sophisticated. He loved to laugh. I would lean against the wall and listen to him on the telephone. He was dating any number of ladies at the same time, and the way he juggled them made for some colorful stories. It was not for nothing that our house became known as 'the Riding Academy.' "

At the point Warren and Sally first met, she was still engaged to Henry Mortimer. This fact notwithstanding, the protagonists differed as to where and when their first meeting took place. Sally insists it happened at Warren's I Street house during a party Bill Rice gave for the cast members of the Bristol Old Vic and that Hoge's first words to her were, "I've never met anybody so full of shit in all my life." His memory of the encounter is markedly different. "One of my girlfriends at the time was the daughter of an ambassador," said Hoge. "And she happened to be a friend of Sally Quinn, and Sally invited her to one of her parties and she brought me along. The party took place in a basement recreation room at the Chevy Chase home of Sally's parents. Sally looked great with her tan, tawny blonde hair, and slim figure, but there was something about her that went far beyond physical appearance. When we were introduced at the party, I made a snide comment to her. I'd been drinking a bottle of beer, and it was room temperature, and I said: 'Tell me, how do you possibly manage to keep the beer so wonderfully warm?'

"I forget now how she responded, but she picked up on the fact that I was being a bit contentious. I'm not suggesting that mine was a particularly good or clever pick-up line, but it did capture her attention. From the very beginning she had much more sass than she would have had as the wife of a WASP millionaire, although given Sally's background, marrying Henry Mortimer would have jumped her up three or four notches. And while being Mrs. Mortimer would have satisfied her immediate social ambitions, it would never have satisfied her long-range ambitions. On many occasions over the years she has stated and written that being exposed to the field of journalism by way of our relationship changed her life. She just fell in love with my circle of friends and the world they inhabited. Clearly that was her world-to-be."

Whatever the original site and mode of their meeting, it is clear that an instant karma flowed between them. Having broken her engagement to Henry Mortimer, Sally soon began staying over with Warren. David Breasted recalled that "the atmosphere of the place became even wilder after Sally moved in. She loved giving parties and cooking up a big pot of jambalaya, accompanied by homemade Fudgsicles all tumbled into a large sterling silver tureen for dessert. It was all very informal. Nothing fancy. There were no place cards. People would just come over and hang out. Jim Hoge, Warren's brother, the editor today of *Foreign Affairs*, was one of the regulars. We had parties all the time: Valentine's Day, Easter, Halloween, Christmas, New Year's. Every holiday provided an excuse for a celebration. Groundhog Day would roll around and Sally would say, 'Great, let's have a Groundhog Day party,' and she'd come up with a theme, like everyone would come dressed as a groundhog. She was a real party animal. Every young Washington celebrity and journalist would drop by, and some of them would crash overnight. You never knew who you might run into in the upstairs hallway. One morning I spotted Michael Caine, the British actor. It was all good clean fun and nobody got hurt. Our parties were more invigorating than the tired and weary social events that went on among the Georgetown rich. Ours was a much more energetic crowd. We were the next generation of makers and shakers. We did a bit of drinking in those days, mostly beer and wine because nobody could afford the hard stuff.

"Sally fit in because she had always been very social. She'd been doing the Washington party circuit for years. She was intent on knowing who was who, and she had a way of not wasting any time with people who weren't important to her. At the beginning, she would come to see Warren, and I would open the front door and let her in. People would say hello to her, and she would sail right past them. She moved so fast she left them behind in a cloud of dust. Eventually Warren sold his shares in the I Street house and bought something on Twenty-second Street. He and Sally moved from there into a four-room 'bachelor-ette' pad that Sally acquired in a stately old apartment building on California Street (in Kalorama), with a distant view of the Washington Monument. They gave a number of parties there, including one at which Ambassador David Bruce did his utmost to seduce the bewitching Barbara Howar.

"Sally had an old jalopy that she called 'the Fiasco,' because it constantly broke down. She and Warren would drive around town in it," Breasted continued. "Then, in 1970, he moved to New York to become city editor of the *New York Post*. He helped run the newspaper's editorial page. Warren and Sally, meanwhile, continued to see each other on weekends—she would visit him or he would stay with her in Washington. They went on ski trips together. They went sailing with two or three other couples, and the women would take turns preparing meals. When it came to Sally's turn, she made peanut butter sandwiches because she disliked playing the conventional female role. She wanted to make a point. The sailing party wound up docking their boat and eating in a restaurant. Sally wasn't your ordinary, run-of-the-mill wallflower. Before Warren left for New York, he and Sally became formally engaged. They had bought rings and Sally had ordered her wedding gown. They had even picked out a place to live. At the last minute Warren got cold feet. Sally went out to San Francisco to recover and stay with friends. When she returned to Washington, she gave a big party for the son of Barry Goldwater. Her romance with Warren resumed, but I always had the feeling that although he had fallen hard for her, he had no interest in settling down."

Washington journalist Joseph C. Goulden remembered that General Quinn and his wife "were not very happy following the breakup of their daughter's engagement. For that matter, they were never particularly enamored of Hoge. Sally's father insisted that Warren pay back every penny he'd laid out for a wedding that never took place."

In 1967 and 1968 Sally Quinn had worked on two Democratic presidential primary campaigns, first as a Washington, D.C., organizer for Eugene J. McCarthy and then as the northern California assistant media coordinator for Robert F. Kennedy, a position she retained until Kennedy's assassination in June 1968. Later that year Ellen McCloy, who had been one of Sally's roommates at Smith, while working as a special assistant to Richard S. Salant, the president of CBS News, arranged a meeting between Sally and her boss. Salant subsequently hired her to work off camera as an "extra assistant" for CBS News at that summer's Democratic and Republican conventions. According to a media gossip column in *New Times* magazine, it was while working the conventions that Sally came to the attention of Gordon Manning, the director of CBS News. Manning apparently "wanted Quinn" at CBS in New York but hesitated to make her an offer at this juncture on the grounds that she was young and lacked experience in either print or TV journalism. Instead, he telephoned Ben Bradlee, with whom he had once worked at *Newsweek,* and recommended that the executive editor of *The Washington Post* "take a look at Miss Quinn." Although he seems to have had no memory of it, Bradlee had evidently been introduced to Sally in 1968 at the Republican convention in Miami. As Warren Hoge remembered it, the three of them had shared a ride across town to the convention center.

Bradlee had the opportunity to meet up with Sally again less than a year after Manning's call, when she came to the *Post* offices to be interviewed by Phil Geyelin for a position as his personal secretary. After speaking with her for half an hour, Geyelin sent her next door to see Ben Bradlee. As Bradlee put it in *A Good Life:* "I advised him against hiring her, and not just because she couldn't take shorthand. Speaking for myself, I suggested to Phil that anyone that attractive could make work difficult."

A month or so later, Kay Graham let it be known around the office that she remained dissatisfied with the Style section, that parties were the backbone of political Washington, and that the *Post* ought to have on its staff a counterpart to Charlotte Curtis at *The New York Times.* Sally Quinn's name resurfaced. Ben Bradlee called her up and invited her back for another interview, explaining that they needed a party reporter. Like her brother, Sally maintained a keen interest in astrology. Before going in to see Bradlee, she looked up his horoscope and found out he was a Virgo. "So I went in and did my Virgo number on him," she informed Richard Lee.

Ben Bradlee confirmed for her that they were actively seeking somebody to work full-time as a party reporter for the Style section. "Yes, of course. Certainly," Sally answered nonchalantly, trying to appear as composed and in control as possible. "Can you show me something you've written?" asked the editor. "Mr. Bradlee," responded Sally, "I've never written anything, not a word." Phil Geyelin, seated in the neighboring office, couldn't help but overhear the conversation. "Well, nobody's perfect," he shouted. Ben Bradlee laughed, then told Sally that as far as he was concerned, she was hired on a six-month trial basis, the same terms accorded any new *Post* reporter. If the job worked out, a new contract would be negotiated. The final interview, with David Laventhol, was little more than a formality. "Ben Bradlee," said Laventhol, "proved himself a wonderful assessor of talent." As for Warren Hoge, he recalled receiving a late-afternoon telephone call from Sally in which she said to him, "Guess what? I've been offered a job." What Quinn didn't know is that nobody else wanted to report on parties. The position was as low on the totem pole as you could possibly get. Chuck Conconi, a former editor at *The Washington Post*, pointed out that "nobody wanted to report on canapés. Had they, Sally probably wouldn't have been offered the job."

That evening Dorothy McCardle, who reluctantly covered parties for Style, took Sally along to a reception at the Greek embassy. On the way, McCardle offered Sally one tidbit of advice: "The first thing you must do when you arrive at a party is head straight for the bar and have a drink. That way you'll feel more like socializing." As it happened, reporting on parties felt as natural to Sally as getting dressed in the pants suits she so often wore to cover her one physical liability: a less-than-perfect pair of legs. In any case, Sally's wholesome, cheerleader good looks more than compensated for the legs. Nick von Hoffman recalled "asking Sally, whenever she came to work," if he could pat her behind. "Certainly," she would reply. He would pat her rear "and tell her she had the best ass in Washington." More than her looks, Sally came to depend on strategy and cunning. Her forte was getting people to say things they later regretted saying. "She had an almost hypnotic effect on people," said the late Stuart C. Davidson, owner of Clyde's. "She'd look you in the eye, and immediately you'd start telling her the most intimate things. She would go to a party and emerge with the most extraordinary quotes. Her early success had little to do with writing skill. She wrote serviceable prose, but she did possess an eye for the telling detail and an ear for the appropriate phrase. Even as a novice, she had the instincts of a seasoned reporter." Sally covered parties and balls, galas and receptions, fund-raisers and dinners. More than anyone else, it was Warren Hoge who taught her how to write. She would attend a party, take detailed notes, then call him up in a state of panic with all her information at hand and a deadline to meet. Hoge would calm her down and help put the story together over the phone. If her lead was wrong, he'd tell her how to fix it, where to place the quotes, what to play up and what to play down. If he wasn't working late on a story of his own, he'd accompany her to the party and afterward go over her copy and make corrections. He sometimes went with her on out-of-town assignments, among them the 1969 Miss America contest in Atlantic City. But if Hoge taught her the rudiments of how to write, it was Sally who provided the blood and guts. "It was a perfect fit," said Hoge. "Sally and party reporting went together like a horse and carriage. After an initial period of uncertainty on her part, she became quite accomplished." Within months, as her first stories hit the press, Ben Bradlee and Kay Graham realized they had stumbled onto something. Sally's gifts for capturing a scene in print were prodigious. In no uncertain terms, she revolutionized the art of society journalism and party reporting, departing from the rather dull and conventional style demonstrated by so many of her predecessors and peers. "Prior to Sally Quinn," said Rowland Evans, "society reporters wrote very respectful pieces. Everything centered around what was served for dinner. It smacked of boredom. In a town like Washington, where parties are such a vital part of the daily regimen, a real opportunity exists to peek behind the lace curtain, to determine what's going on politically. At a party, in a moment of privacy, with a drink or two in his belly, a politician is bound to let something slip out. And that's where Sally Quinn came in. I imagine that the day Sally Quinn walked into his office for an interview for the position of party reporter, Ben Bradlee took one look and said to himself, 'Aha! Here's my Charlotte Curtis.'" Reflecting on the *Post*'s newest employee, Kay Graham in *Personal History* would call Sally a "first-rate writer" and praise her for "making people feel free to talk with her and then hanging them with their own words."

"I covered parties the way they were, not the way the host and hostess wanted them covered," Sally claimed. "I covered them the way someone in the Metro section covered a crime." Reporting on the follies, fantasies, vanities, and peccadilloes of such social-climbing partygoers and givers as the congressman's wife who excoriated the help because the flambé wasn't in flames, or the seasoned senator from the South who made a play for a cuddly brunette only to discover that he had just propositioned the wife of a fellow senator, Quinn quickly established a reputation for herself as a saucy chronicler of Washington's elite. During the better part of the 1970s—and well into the next decade—she filled the Style section with her cutting, often poignant portraits. At times her stories created news. At one party she attended she coaxed out of a senior member of Congress the expected vote on the antiballistic missile—a secret the *Post*'s national reporters had been trying to ferret out for weeks. Her transformation from ordinary reporter to journalistic personality took form several months into her employment, when she buttonholed Secretary of State Henry Kissinger, who was standing off by himself at a Joan Braden dinner dance, and asked him, "What's wrong? Aren't you a swinger?" Kissinger, who knew Sally's father, joked back that he was a "secret swinger"—a self-epithet that immediately began echoing through the international media. Analyzing the moment from a later perspective, Kissinger told the current author that "I was always afraid of Sally Quinn because she had a reputation as being a killer columnist. For years I used to say that Maxine Cheshire always made me want to commit murder, but Sally made me want to commit suicide. The point is that these leading Washington social and gossip columnists wielded considerable power and influence, much more so than those in any other metropolis." Another personage, Norman Mailer, whose fiftieth birthday celebration she covered in New York, anointed her "Poison Quinn." The careers of Lord Conner, the British ambassador, and his wife were compromised when Quinn quoted Lady Conner, who supported the American war presence in Vietnam, as saying during an embassy reception that "life means nothing" to Asians. Then there was Sally's report on Sandra Gottlieb, wife of the Canadian ambassador to the United States, Allan Gottlieb, who viciously slapped her social secretary across the face in full view of their guests when told that the U.S. deputy secretary of the treasury wasn't going to make it for dinner. The event basically ended the Canadian ambassador's career. He and his wife were recalled soon thereafter.

Quinn's surgical skill at wielding a scalpel-like pen eventually began to catch up with her. She was attacked by NOW (National Organization for Women) for using her feminine wiles to get a story. Her response: "I'm a reporter first and a feminist second. Much of the time I deplore that situation but I will take advantage of it until things change." She angered feminists further when she leaned into a microphone at a convention of journalists and huskily announced that the essence of reporting was manipulation—by flirtation, by plying interview subjects with alcohol, by suggestion of availability. "Being blonde doesn't hurt," she added, giving rise to a slew of hostile articles in the press. Her on-again, off-again friend Nora Ephron castigated her in the pages of *New York* for, among other things, being a publicity hound: "There has been altogether too much written about Sally Quinn." Even Lorraine Cooper took a potshot at Sally when, in May 1974, she encountered Quinn during a supper dance at Sonny and Mary Lou Whitney's estate in Lexington, Kentucky, the night before the hundredth running of the Kentucky Derby. In a letter to Evangeline Bruce, Lorraine observed: "Sally Quinn has . . . spirit but does not always write with accuracy." The accuracy issue raised its head again a year later regarding comments made in print by Sally about gonzo journalist Hunter S. Thompson, who then threatened to sue her for libel. Writing to his attorney, Sandy Berger, Thompson remarked: "I'm getting tired of being libeled, misquoted and generally discredited by those fucking hacks [at] the *Post*." Nancy Dickerson observed that most people, especially members of society, tended to flee the room the moment they saw Sally Quinn enter. "It was as if she felt she could establish her own reputation only by dismantling the reputations of others."

Examples abound in support of Dickerson's contention. In one of her patented *Post* exposés, Quinn set out to sully the reputation of Steven A. Martindale, a thirty-one-year-old Georgetown lawyer and lobbyist (with the prestigious public relations firm of Hill & Knowlton) who had arrived in town from Pocatello, Idaho, and quickly established himself among Washington's social elite. Sally's article on Martindale, a former friend of hers, accused him of being a social climber of the most desperate sort. His one major mistake had been to agree to be profiled by Quinn, who revealed that he had once called up Alice Roosevelt Longworth and told her he was having a party for Henry Kissinger; he then called Kissinger and told him he was having a party for Longworth. Both attended, as did the rest of Georgetown's social lions. Martindale evidently used the same duplicitous method for attracting A-list guests to all his at-homes. Robert K. Gray, Martindale's boss at Hill & Knowlton, noted that Quinn "slashed him to pieces. It was a ruthless piece . . . I'm still surprised he didn't just pack his bags after that and leave town."

Not long after the appearance of the Martindale profile, Sally Quinn wrote a devastatingly negative article about Gaetana Enders, the well-liked wife of Tom Enders, a U.S. foreign service officer and the American ambassador to Canada. The profile, based on interviews Quinn conducted with Mrs. Enders at the couple's Georgetown home and at the Chevy Chase Country Club, is often cited by Quinn's critics as an example of her unfairness. An Italian by birth, Gaetana had founded a refugee organization in Cambodia during her husband's service as deputy chief of mission to that country. Following the fall of South Vietnam, Gaetana had been named by President Gerald Ford as the only woman member of his Committee for Refugees, the group responsible for placing the first 375,000 refugees from Vietnam, Laos, and Cambodia. Titled "Madame Butterfly's Refugees: 'They Love Me So,' " the piece depicted Gaetana as a wealthy, thoughtless woman who had spent months driving around the refugee camps of Cambodia in a chauffeur-driven, bulletproof limousine, attired in designer fashions and expensive baubles, while spraying the odiferous wards of refugee hospitals with cheap perfume. Nicknamed "Butterfly" as a child (a term, according to Quinn, which in Cambodia means "prostitute"), Mrs. Enders had procured domestic positions for some of the refugees, not only in her own household but also in the homes of some of her well-heeled friends, including Joan Braden and Ina Ginsburg. "The Quinn piece made us all look like idiots," said Joan Braden. "It was a complete hatchet job, in my opinion initiated by Ben Bradlee, who more than once had voiced his opposition to anybody bringing refugees into this country from Southeast Asia. But it was Sally who did the dirty work, making Gaetana Enders look like a poor little rich girl in search of a cause. It made her physically ill. But it also backfired, because in the long run it created a backlash. It put Gaetana in such a damning light that it made her look like a martyr. It made her cause more popular than ever. Henry Kissinger, under whom Tom Enders was working at the time as assistant secretary of state for economic affairs, stopped Sally Quinn in her tracks one day and said, 'Why did you do that to Gaetana Enders? She's one of the few people in this country doing something positive about the refugee situation.' "

Sally Quinn's character assassinations helped establish her as a household name in Washington. Readers relished the blood and carnage. A number of journalists, however, along with those figures she had bludgeoned in print—as well as their friends and sympathizers—resented her tactics. "There's a saying around Washington that if Sally Quinn calls you for an interview, you'd better be in Toledo, Ohio, that day—you can't give her an interview," commented Joseph Goulden. Christopher Ogden, Pamela Harriman's biographer and a Washington-based *Time* correspondent, observed that "the seven most frightening words in the English language are, 'First in a series by Sally Quinn.' " Aileen Mehle termed Quinn "hardly in a class with Katharine Graham, Evangeline Bruce, Lorraine Cooper, or any of the other grande dames of Georgetown. I once heard her tell how she loved to dispense *booze* to all her dinner guests. Can you imagine any of the other ladies using the word *booze* as a synonym for alcoholic beverages?" Washington hostess Jennifer Phillips, wife of Laughlin Phillips, owner of the famed Dupont Circle art gallery by the same name, called Quinn "a social terrorist. She's not an arbiter of good manners. She's about the rudest person around. Among those she attacked were Jewish hostesses, homosexual hosts, and so forth. They were shredded by her. Her profiles were absolutely brutal. I soon began to see her as an incredibly evil person." White House correspondent Sarah McClendon remarked that "in England they call people like Sally Quinn strivers." State Department protocol officer Patrick Daly said: "I'd like to know why she's entitled to chew up everyone in sight. Who appointed her the social arbiter of Washington? I don't personally know Sally Quinn and I don't want to know her, because I don't want to pick up tomorrow's newspaper and read horrible, nasty things about myself." Although pleased with her overall performance, even Katharine Graham at one juncture wondered if Sally Quinn didn't sometimes go too far, reflecting that at times she "almost destroyed people with . . . her writing." But it was probably Richard Nixon (in 1973) who sounded the shrillest alarm, dictating a note to H. R. Haldeman that read: "Never invite Sally Quinn. Violated rules and attacked a guest at church." The idea of being banished from the Nixon White House could only have amused Sally Quinn. What had the president meant by saying she had "attacked" someone in church? Simply, it seemed, that she had asked someone a question. Somehow getting hold of the actual memo, she had it framed and eventually hung in her guest bathroom. And to the current author, when asked to comment on her critics, she demurely responded: "Do you mean to say I have enemies out there?"

cso

SALLY QUINN'S PERSONALITY, overdrive ambition, bitchiness, and sex appeal earned her the broadcasting opportunity at CBS-TV, which in late 1973 nearly led to her undoing. Gordon Manning, then news director of CBS, had continued to follow her progress as a print journalist. On June 6, 1973, he met with her for dinner at Cantina d'Italia in Washington to discuss the prospect of having her make the jump to television journalism. What Manning had in mind for Quinn was the coanchor position at CBS Morning News (as American network television's first female anchorwoman) in order to compete with Barbara Walters (technically not an anchorperson) on NBC's Today show. While several other women were also being considered for the job, including Nora Ephron, Quinn was the clear favorite.

Within the week Sally shot a successful pilot and was offered a contract. At the beginning of a mounting publicity blitz by CBS to announce her forthcoming television debut, Sally met with Ben Bradlee and revealed her decision to leave the Post. "It was a difficult lunch for both of us," he wrote in A Good Life. During their lunch, Sally declared that she had fallen in love with him and had been the writer of several anonymous mash notes left in his office over the past year. Bradlee, still married to Tony, and well aware of Sally's ongoing relationship with Warren Hoge, observed that "I was stunned, but flattered." For all the flattery, it never seems to have occurred to Bradlee to ask Sally why, given her frank admission, she would presently leave her job and move to New York, where she planned on living with Hoge in his West Side Manhattan apartment at 118 Riverside Drive. For the record, Ben and Tony Bradlee separated some five weeks after Sally Quinn's departure from the *Post*. There are those who claim that their seventeen-year marriage began to disintegrate long before Sally Quinn made her feelings known, that Tony simply had never recovered from the unsolved 1964 murder of her sister, Mary Pinchot Meyer, and that her ongoing preoccupation with the crime had only added to the couple's problems.

During the week of July 23, just as Quinn was settling in with Warren, *New York* magazine ran a cover story on Sally by Aaron Latham, a future screenwriter who had gotten his start at *The Washington Post* and later married broadcast journalist Leslie Stahl, a one-time, short-lived girlfriend of Bob Woodward. Condescending and chauvinistic, the piece portrayed Sally as a brassy, acerbic blonde bombshell who had clawed her way to the top on the basis of her ability to charm and manipulate men. She was further described as having been hired by CBS for the express purpose of knocking Barbara Walters off the air. A number of Quinn's former colleagues at the *Post* were secretly pleased by the article, particularly the depiction of Sally as a full-blooded coquette.

Warren Hoge, on the other hand, was incensed by the article. "I'll never forgive Aaron Latham for doing it," he said. "It was just such a cheap-assed thing. First he wrote it and then he telephoned Sally and apologized, said he didn't mean to say all those terrible things. What he didn't say is that he was advancing his career at her expense. And he set her up as the competition to Barbara Walters, which was complete bullshit. Barbara and Sally were friends, and remain friends to this day. At one point, Sally is quoted saying something like, 'I'm Sally Quinn, and I'm here to take on Barbara Walters.' She never said that or anything remotely like it. They then quote her as practically comparing the respective penis sizes of various Washington politicians. Here she supposedly says, 'If a senator has his hand on my fanny and is telling me how he's going to vote, I'm not sure I'm going to remove his hand.' So the logical conclusion on the part of the reader is that Sally's willing to use sex as a way to get politicians to talk. The statement was taken completely out of context, but the magazine ran with it. Everything in the story is wrapped around sex. She's again quoted as saying, 'I just wish my legs were better. Maybe I would have gotten on the evening news.' And this set the tone for the remaining promotion of the program. Sally was on the defensive. She had to defend herself against the charge that she'd been brought in solely to knock Barbara Walters off her pedestal. It just wasn't true."

What was true, said Warren Beatty, a friend of Sally's, is that she'd been "made out to be a strong, tough, competitive little cock-teaser," and people "weren't going to like her for it."

Beatty's prediction and the article itself distressed Sally, a situation that Evan Thomas, usually a staunch supporter, attributed to "Quinn's affinity for doling it out, but her inability to take it. That's always been the old girl's problem." Sunny Adler, while preparing a piece on Quinn for *Dossier,* discovered the same thing. "I always admired her," said Sunny, "but I soon recognized just how thin-skinned she is. She wanted the profile written a certain way, and when I deviated in the slightest, she began yelling. In other words, she can't take what she gives."

Another problem was the network's reluctance to do anything to help prepare her for the job. "CBS didn't give Sally any training," remarked Warren Hoge. "It was just unbelievable. She had no voice coach, nobody to tell her what to wear, no instruction on what to do or say. They'd hired a first-time producer, Lee Townsend, who was eventually fired. They also took Gordon Manning, formerly CBS News director, and assigned him to another position. That's how much of a disaster it turned out to be. Sally's coanchor, Hughes Rudd, being a swell fellow, did his best to help. But nobody else said a word. Sally went on the air for the first time in early August with a serious case of pneumonia. She was feverish, nauseated, and had a harsh, painful cough. They took her to the hospital an hour before airtime and administered some kind of Novocain throat spray so she could at least speak. Things went downhill from there."

A number of ailments beset Sally at once. She developed an allergic reaction to the pancake makeup she had to wear for the camera, and her skin broke out in blisters. Because she had to report for work at 1 A.M. (they went on air at 7 A.M.), she had to catch up on her sleep during daylight hours. In *We're Going to Make You a Star,* she attests to a daily intake of two bottles of wine over lunch in order to fall asleep in the afternoon. Her sleep deprivation created several embarrassing situations. One weekend she and Warren Hoge visited Barbara Howar at the latter's vacation home in Bridgehampton, and Sally slumbered at the dinner table. Having developed a stomach ulcer, she had to stop drinking, and as a result had difficulty sleeping. Her elevated anxiety level caused high blood pressure, migraines, and shortness of breath. She suffered moments of self-doubt and depression, often caused by gaffes and faux pas that she committed in front of the camera. When Hughes Rudd mentioned a man being sucked out of an airplane at 30,000 feet, she burst into laughter. Following a film report mentioning that half of the migrant farming families in the United States earned less than $3,000 per year, she giggled while observing, "That goes about a week in New York City."

The situation went from bad to worse. At the beginning of September, Sally bought a copy of *Time* and in the People section saw an item linking Warren Hoge romantically with Amanda Burden. "Sally appeared in my living room," said Hoge, "with her hands on her hips and that look that said, 'Okay, big boy, explain yourself.' It was hardly an important relationship for Amanda, or for me. We went out for several weeks and were seen together, and that's about it. It had no bearing on why Sally and I never married. We were just too young and we were terribly nervous about it. I didn't marry until 1981. I had a problem and it took some shrinkage to work it out."

Because of the unfavorable publicity generated by the Burden affair, Sally moved out of Warren's apartment and into a furnished suite in the Alden Hotel at Eighty-second Street and Central Park West. Once elegant, the Alden had fallen on bad times and seemed a bit seedy. Sally had ensconced herself in her new dwelling when she suddenly had an enormously disquieting telephone conversation with Barbara Howar, who had once worked in television (and would, by coincidence, join CBS after Sally's departure). Their exchange focused on the mechanics of broadcasting:

"You need to keep your eye on the red light," said Howar.

"Red light?"

"For God's sake, Sally. Hasn't anyone told you about the red light?"

"What about it?"

"It indicates which camera you're supposed to look at."

"No," said Sally. "Nobody ever mentioned it to me."

At the beginning of November 1973, Sally flew to London's Heathrow Airport to begin coverage of Princess Anne's impending marriage. Don Hewitt, the eventual producer of *60 Minutes,* had volunteered to direct the wedding segment for CBS. Within five minutes of meeting Sally, he would say: "God, we're going to have fun. London is such a great place to have an affair." Declining Hewitt's offer, Sally was informed by the producer "if you won't sleep with me, I'll sleep with Barbara Walters."

It was from her encounter with Hewitt that Quinn derived the title of her future memoir. If she acquiesced to his sexual advances, he would presumably make her a star; if she didn't, he would do everything he could to make her look bad. As Quinn had it in *We're Going to Make You a Star,* Hewitt made her look terrible. Enraged, she stormed off the set, refusing to do extra film work or interviews. Back in New York, Hewitt called Sally to apologize, at the same time informing her that he didn't "want to read about what happened in England in any fucking book you might write." Convinced that in her role as CBS coanchor she had become "the laughingstock of America," Sally now met with Gordon Manning to map out an appropriate exit strategy.

On December 7 she accompanied Ben Bradlee to a dinner party at Katharine Graham's Georgetown home. To Sally's delight, her former employer, aware that she and Ben were dating, greeted her warmly. Considering her own marital past, it was surprising behavior on Graham's part, or perhaps a subconscious acknowledgment that she herself was now involved with a married man. Having left his marriage for a younger woman, Ben Bradlee—who was generally not a player and had a reputation as being old school—had committed the unspeakable; he had replicated the actions of Phil Graham. Although Kay had never particularly liked Tony Bradlee, she almost certainly would have identified with her situation. She nevertheless went out of her way to make Sally feel comfortable, playing the role of hostess to perfection. For the first time in months, Sally felt at ease, observing in her memoir that it was "like coming home." Listening to some of Quinn's more colorful anecdotes about her experiences at CBS as well as her lament that she had forever damaged her career, Kay suggested in passing that Sally write about it. "If nothing else, it will be therapeutic," said Graham. Penning the memoir did help Quinn overcome the stigma of a major career setback.

In finding her way back to the *Post*, Sally initially accepted a position with the Washington bureau of *The New York Times*, a newspaper too stuffy to fully appreciate Sally's particular talents. When she wrote a freelance article on Alice Roosevelt Longworth for *The Washington Post*, Cliff Daniels, who had hired Quinn at the *Times*, attacked her for taking on the new assignment. Their relations never improved, and Ben Bradlee was soon talking about rehiring Sally at the *Post*.

Donnie Radcliffe, an editor who had come over to the Style section of the *Post* from the Women's section at the *Washington Star*, recalled being stopped in the corridor one day by Howard Simons, the managing editor of the *Post*, and being asked how she felt about the possibility of Sally Quinn's returning to the paper.

"I took it that Simons was acting on behalf of Ben Bradlee in conducting an informal in-house survey," said Radcliffe. "I knew Sally from her previous days at the *Post*. My desk faced hers, so besides editing her copy, I had a front-row seat on the traffic she generated, not the least of her visitors being Ben Bradlee. By 1973, when Sally left the *Post* for CBS, there was no doubt that she had come as close to being a star as a reporter could get. Once Sally left, quite honestly, it wasn't the same around there. We had bright, clever, and accomplished reporters, but none seemed to provide the same pizzazz that Sally had. None of them understood the Washington power game better than she did. So when Simons asked me about rehiring Sally, I thought for a minute and then I remember I said, 'Why not? You don't want her to stay with *The New York Times*, do you?' And of course they didn't."

In February 1974 Sally left her job at the *Times* and resumed her former reporter's position at the *Post*. It appeared to be a perfect arrangement, considering that her latest boyfriend and future husband basically ran the paper. Sally had joined Ben Bradlee in a fourteenth-story apartment he had rented at the Watergate, an appropriate location, considering the building's importance in helping him establish his own journalistic reputation. By moving in with him, Sally again managed to anger a number of her contemporaries. Especially galling to Ben and Sally was Diana McLellan's characterization of Quinn in her "Ear" column as "Bradlee's live-in girlfriend." "I don't know why he objected," said McLellan, "because that's exactly what she was."

The publication in 1975 of *We're Going to Make You a Star* was greeted by a host of critical reviews, many of which claimed that the book's author had blamed everyone but herself for her failure as a television personality. Discouraged by the hostile reception accorded her memoir, she nevertheless announced her return to the *Post* by writing, "I am still fascinated by the society of Washington and I'll continue to write about it. My interest is purely chemical. I might as well be a scientist." In a series of audacious profiles, she proceeded to tear apart a whole new generation of society belles and matrons. Of Washington arts patroness Teddy Westreich, she wrote: "There are a lot of people who don't like Teddy Westreich. They accuse her of being the worst social climber they have ever seen." Vicki Bagley, the then wife of R. J. Reynolds tobacco heir Smith Bagley, was similarly dissected, Quinn observing that "many people who have met Vicki Bagley find her one of the most ambitious young women they know." Vicki, it should be noted, had started a highly successful real estate firm in Washington. Certain select politicians received equally shabby treatment in Sally's writings. Bill Thomas, editor in chief of *Capitol Style* magazine, recalled "an embarrassing story she wrote for the *Post* on Zbigniew Brzezinski, in which she accused him of having left his fly open during the course of an interview, implying that some sort of sexual impropriety had either taken place or was intended. The newspaper had to print a retraction."

Peter Milius, a *Washington Post* editor from 1965 to 1990, remarked that "after Sally got together with Ben Bradlee, she could do no wrong. Her stories ran on for thousands of words, long past their point of interest. Once when I questioned their length, I was told that they were longer than most Style section pieces because they appealed not only to women but also to men. But of course we all knew better than that. They were allowed to stand because no editor had the balls to object. Ben Bradlee was the man! I don't think that Kay Graham cared terribly about Sally Quinn. But she worshipped Ben Bradlee's ass and would've done

anything to please him. He called the shots. She paid the bills. A lot of the
editors at the *Post* regarded it as his newspaper."

༄

AFTER A YEAR AT THE WATERGATE, Ben and Sally moved into a
house at Twenty-first Street, off Dupont Circle, purchased with funds
from the sale of *We're Going to Make You a Star.* "Ben and Sally made
one hell of a team," said Barbara Howar, who attended a number of parties in the new house. "Ben had always been one of the most attractive
men in Washington—and Sally fell madly, madly in love with him. It
didn't matter that there was a twenty-year age discrepancy. He introduced her to his generation of friends, and she introduced him to hers.
Ben always enjoyed meeting young people, and they loved meeting him.
This all began around the time of her troubles at CBS, and also around
the time of Watergate. With Ben's help, Sally rebounded and once again
became a hugely successful reporter as well as one of the town's top social
figures. *Ben and Sally.* After Jimmy and Rosalynn Carter, they were the
most sought-out couple in Washington. They were immensely glamorous. They'd make an appearance and there'd be an immediate craning
of necks. Or they'd host their own gatherings and everyone would come.

"It was an immense love match, a flash of lightning every step of the
way, and since I was Sally's confidante at the time, I was in on it. The only
other person who knew all the intimate details was Edward Bennett
Williams, who had always been close to Ben. 'This is trouble,' he kept saying. 'She'll kill him! She'll kill him!' It seemed a bit shocking at first, especially because they were both at the *Post.* Ben's adage had always been:
'Never fish off the company pier,' which is one reason Sally may have initially left the paper to try her hand at television reporting. For a while,
there was a good deal of gossip mongering: 'He dumped his wife. She's an
upstart, blah, blah, blah.' A lot of it had to do with jealousy."

One of Ben and Sally's first invitations was to the mid-1970s dinner
given by Averell and Pamela Harriman in honor of Senator Frank
Church, who was considering a run for the presidency. Among the last
practitioners of a social custom that had been eliminated in most quar-

ters, the Harrimans still insisted on separating the sexes after dinner. On this particular night, when Pamela Harriman tapped her water glass and announced that the ladies would be joining her upstairs for coffee, Sally kept her seat. Assigned by the *Post* to write a profile of Church, Quinn wanted to hear the senator discuss his political plans. Once the women had gone, Sally followed the men, including Bradlee, into the living room. As she passed Averell Harriman, he pointed at her and said, "Miss Quinn, the ladies will go upstairs." She paused. He became adamant. "Miss Quinn, this is my house, and in my house the ladies go upstairs after dinner." With that, Sally said, "Good night, Governor," turned, and walked out of the house. Ben Bradlee followed. Averell Harriman never again invited Sally Quinn to dinner. By extension, Bradlee was also banished.

Another Washington personality with whom they had their share of problems was Joe Alsop. According to Robert Merry, "Alsop had been rather rude to Bradlee on several occasions, and Ben had little use for him, despite Alsop's intimate ties to Kay Graham. Sally Quinn absolutely despised Alsop. When I wrote my book on the Alsop brothers, I asked her why she disliked him so much. She accused him of being mean-tempered and nasty. She didn't like the way he treated people, the way he cut them down to size. I thought her response a bit odd, given her own tendency to do the same thing. But then that's always the case. We tend to criticize others when they display our shortcomings."

They were similarly at odds with Jackie Kennedy, who regarded Ben as a turncoat for having written *Conversations with Kennedy*. Nor did Jackie seem particularly taken with Sally Quinn. "With women like Quinn around," Jackie told Joan Braden, "I'm glad I no longer live in Washington." Ben and Sally once ran into Jackie at a New York cocktail party hosted by Arthur Schlesinger. The former first lady was leaving just as they were arriving. "I whispered to Sally that Jackie was coming down the street," Bradlee is quoted as saying in Chris Anderson's *Jackie Without Jack*. "I stuck out my hand and said, 'Hi, Jackie.' She sailed by without a word." Another time, Ben and Sally had rented a cabana on the beach at Saint-Martin in the Caribbean. Right next to their cabana was Jackie's. "We spent a week," said Bradlee, "staring at each other until the night we almost collided as we left our cabana to go up to the restaurant for dinner. From twelve inches away, she looked straight ahead, without a word, and I never saw her again."

Ben and Sally were finally married on October 20, 1978, in the chambers of an old Bradlee chum, David Bazelon, chief judge of the U.S. Court of Appeals in the District of Columbia. Katharine Graham, Edward Bennett Williams, and Art Buchwald were witnesses to the ceremony, which was also attended by Ben's three children, his brother, and Sally's parents. Kay Graham, who had carried the bride's floral bouquet on her lap aboard a New York–Washington shuttle flight, doubled as maid of honor. Sixty guests attended the wedding reception. "It didn't hurt that Ben Bradlee was a powerful editor," said Barbara Howar, "but Sally married him for love. He's an impressive man. He has integrity. He calls a spade a spade. He's willing to put his neck on the line. Those are the qualities that attracted Sally and which kept her waiting for nearly six years while he got his divorce and took care of business." General Quinn, no doubt disappointed that his new son-in-law wasn't an arch Republican or at the very least an army officer, nevertheless welcomed him into the fold.

Despite her marriage, Sally insisted on retaining the use of her maiden name. In a 1997 C-SPAN interview to promote her latest book, *The Party*, she referred to Jack Kent Cooke, the multimillionaire co-owner (with Edward Bennett Williams) of the Washington Redskins, as an "absolutely horrible man" because he insisted on taking her around every Sunday during the game and "rudely" introducing her as Sally Bradlee, even though she repeatedly told him to call her Sally Quinn.

On Sunday mornings during the winter and spring Ben and Sally met with Art Buchwald in the back room of the Georgetown Pharmacy, where "Doc" Dalinsky, the proprietor, joined them for a brunch of bagels, lox, cream cheese, and mimosas. The small group often brought along their friends for lively round-table discussions and dissections of the day's news. It was in the course of just such a brunch that Edward Bennett Williams told Ben Bradlee that he was "pussy-whipped," because he had taken to wearing the broad striped shirts Sally bought for him at Turnbull & Asser. The couple soon befriended a neighbor, Nora

Pouillon, owner of Nora's Restaurant, a favorite eatery of theirs. Investing $5,000 in the restaurant, Ben and Sally regularly dined and entertained there. It was at Nora's that Sally Quinn nearly attacked Deborah Davis, author of *Katharine the Great,* a Kay Graham biography that accused Ben Bradlee of having at one time been associated with the CIA. Following a letter of complaint from Bradlee, the book's publisher, Harcourt Brace Jovanovich, ceased its support of the biography. A court eventually ordered the publisher to pay the biographer a hefty six-figure sum for the perceived violation of their contractual obligations. Davis was seated at Nora's one evening when Sally Quinn and Ben Bradlee came down the stairs after dinner. Sally spotted Davis and headed straight for her table. Bradlee managed to grab his wife, restrain her, and yank her out the front door. "He just pulled her out the door," said Davis. "She was going to come up and I don't know what, but he got her out of there."

The couple also entertained in the privacy of Sally's Dupont Circle home. One evening they had an informal dinner at their kitchen table with Carl Bernstein and his wife, Nora Ephron, who was visibly pregnant with their second child. At one point during the meal, Ephron asked if she could have a glass of red wine. Eager to please, Bradlee opened a bottle of Burgundy and passed it to Nora, who had positioned herself behind her husband's chair. Very deliberately and without a word, she proceeded to pour the entire bottle over Bernstein's head. The incident, as Ben and Sally soon learned, had come about because of an affair that Carl was having with Margaret Jay, the wife of British ambassador Peter Jay, which had recently come to Nora's attention.

Nora Ephron included the scene, altering it only slightly, in *Heartburn,* the roman à clef (and motion picture) she wrote about her marriage to Bernstein. Ambassador Jay's reaction to the book and its creator, as expressed to the current author, needs little embellishment: "I have nothing but contempt for Nora Ephron. I think she is a dreadful human being. Her book, in my opinion, was a shameless . . . exploitation of people's misfortunes, including her own children's, in order to enhance her literary reputation. . . . In the process of enhancing her career, she did intense damage to her own children."

In *A Good Life,* Ben Bradlee writes: "[Sally] changed me by showing me there was a life outside the confines of *The Washington Post.*" One of the couple's budding interests, outside journalism, was real estate. "Sally," said Barbara Howar, "had an uncanny gift for assessing the true value of a plot of land with a house on it." In 1979 they built a year-round cabin in West Virginia overlooking the Capon River, a mile from the location of a log cabin that Bradlee had owned since the mid-1960s. They then purchased a recently renovated summer house in Amagansett, Long Island. While vacationing in Amagansett, Sally came across Grey Gardens, a dilapidated, rat-cat-and-raccoon infested, two-acre estate in the Village of East Hampton that more than once had been condemned as unlivable by the Nassau County Health Department. The house, which had been the subject (along with its inhabitants) of a documentary film by the Maysles Brothers—Albert and David—belonged to "Big Edie" and "Little Edie" Beale. The Beales, as the press made amply clear, were related to Jackie Kennedy. Big Edie had been the older sister of Jackie's father, "Black Jack" Bouvier. Her daughter, Little Edie, Jackie's cousin, had remained alone in the house after her mother's death. "My impoverishment and the well-publicized run-down condition of the house," said Little Edie, "became a vast public relations problem for Jackie, who in 1968 had married Aristotle Onassis, one of the wealthiest men in the world. I wanted Jackie to buy the place and then restore it without tearing it completely down. She wanted nothing to do with it. Suddenly along came Sally Quinn, the wife of Ben Bradlee. 'Buy it for me, Ben,' she cooed. And he said, 'You must be out of your eff-ing mind.' But Sally turned on the southern charm and in the end he did buy it, and after a complete makeover the property was featured in *Architectural Digest.*"

Jacqueline Kennedy hated the thought of selling her ancestral manse to Ben Bradlee and Sally Quinn but preferred that alternative to the prospect of having to sink her own money into the rehabilitation of the house. Having all but rebuilt Grey Gardens, Ben and Sally spent each August in East Hampton, hobnobbing with the local cognoscenti, importing their houseguests from Washington, and renting out the house for the remainder of the year. A decade later they bought and restored Porto Bello, an historic house on the Saint Mary's River in southern Maryland, where they stayed on weekends and over short vacations.

While Sally indulged herself with the interior decoration of Porto Bello, Ben spent his time landscaping and working the grounds.

In 1982, anticipating the birth of their first child, Ben and Sally sold her Dupont Circle residence and paid a record $2.5 million to acquire the Robert Todd Lincoln House at 3014 N Street in Georgetown. Built in the 1790s, the town house looked out on a field that ran down to the Potomac. Abraham Lincoln's sole surviving son, Robert Todd Lincoln, chairman of the Pullman railroad company, purchased it in 1912 and lived in it until his death in 1926; his widow lived on in the house until her death nine years later. Actually two structures joined into a single abode, the spacious town house—one of Georgetown's largest—included five bedrooms, two studies, living room, library, dining room, and a housekeeper's apartment over the kitchen. Prior to the Bradlees, it had belonged to Smith and Vicki Bagley. Still smarting from Sally's negative profile of her, Vicki reportedly refused to allow the Style reporter access to the house one afternoon when she came over by herself for another look around. Ultimately, Ben and Sally were the only bidders willing to pay the steep asking price for the house, the highest amount ever exacted up to that point for a private residence in Georgetown. To raise the funds, Bradlee divested himself of a substantial block of Washington Post stock.

Josiah Quinn Crowninshield Bradlee—Quinn Bradlee to family and friends—was born on April 29, 1982. A difficult delivery was followed by the detection of a murmur and its cause, a small hole in the newborn's heart. In medical terms, the condition was diagnosed as ventricular septal defect, or VSD. At the age of three months, weighing a mere eight pounds, Quinn underwent an operation at Children's Hospital that took nearly six hours but proved only moderately successful. There were to be additional surgeries in the boy's future, in tandem with extended hospital stays. Although Quinn gradually regained his physical health, he developed certain learning disabilities, including dyslexia, a speech defect, and a problem with audio processing, all of which made it difficult for him to process information quickly. Special schools helped him cope, but the pressure of trying to please two superannuated, highly gifted parents must have added to the strain—for both Quinn and his parents.

Warren Hoge, currently London bureau chief for The New York

Times and the father of a son nearly Quinn's age, speaks of the difficulties that Ben and Sally faced during Quinn's formative years: "I speak of it only because Sally has gone public with it. She has not tried to hide the fact that Quinn has medical issues. She and Ben both served on boards to help raise funds for the Children's Hospital. Sally has spoken on the subject before groups and over the airwaves. Furthermore, let me say that Quinn is a great fellow, extremely personable, exceedingly valorous. He has gone through so much. As a child, he was always small for his age. For a long time, he had difficulty speaking—it was physiological, something to do with his tongue. But that's behind him now. He underwent six or seven operations. Whenever Ben and Sally drove anywhere, Quinn would turn blue in the backseat and they'd have to take him to George Washington Hospital. It was really a test of an awful lot of things. It hasn't been easy."

Recovering from the CBS debacle seemed a simple matter compared to the obstacles Sally overcame with respect to raising her son. "When you have a sick child," she told Alex Witchell of *The New York Times,* "the career is first to go. . . . But for me that was never a question. I love Quinn, and I want to be with him. Though sometimes I feel wistful, maybe, thinking about the kind of career I might have had. I haven't accomplished very much since he's been born."

As her writing production dropped, so her social schedule—especially her home entertainments—took an upswing. She now possessed the means, the house, and—via her husband—the clout and connections needed to become one of Georgetown's premier hostesses. In essence she became the very symbol of affluence, decadence, and social supremacy that she had so often deprecated in print. What with its plush interior, subdued lighting, spacious rooms, high ceilings, working fireplaces, and professional sound system, her recently purchased red-brick, Federalist mansion in the heart of the most politically powerful district in America made for an ideal party setting.

Eden Rafshoon, the wife of former Jimmy Carter media adviser Gerald Rafshoon, speaks highly of Sally's social skills and her generosity to friends. "Her Georgetown house," says Eden, herself an interior decorator, "is an extension of her inner self. The living room is painted a shade of raspberry, which gives it a highly intimate feeling, particularly in the middle of winter with the fireplace lit. Other rooms are lined with unusually patterned, very decorative wallpaper. There are old paintings, eighteenth- and nineteenth-century antiques, a lot of photographs, memorabilia, books. They have a great library. The house is formal but extremely comfortable. There are huge, down-filled sofas, pull-up chairs, ottomans, benches. So you can have a group of two and you would feel at home. Or you can have 150, and there's a place for everyone to perch. Sally also has a wonderful sense of occasion. She used to have Valentine's Day dances at which she'd serve strawberry daiquiris. On Thanksgiving she would have oyster roasts. If a guest of honor at one of her dinners hailed from New York, she might serve Manhattan cocktails. She had parties at Christmas and on New Year's. She celebrated birthdays and anniversaries. Being from the South, she favored southern cuisine but didn't do the cooking herself. Instead, she would supervise the cook. Currently she employs a house manager, a wonderful woman who once worked for Pamela Harriman."

Ben and Sally's largest bashes usually take place on New Year's. They gave their first on December 31, 1982, a dinner-dance for 120. "It marked the beginning of a tradition that has extended to the present day," said Barbara Howar. "The mix was so name-laden, so A list, it was downright toxic." As opposed to the simple beer-and-pizza parties that Ben and Tony Bradlee threw in the 1950s and early 1960s, the Bradlee-Quinn affairs featured guests standing butt-to-butt, belly-to-belly, politicians and journalists, elegantly turned out in diamonds and black tie, toasting one another with clever, irreverent one-liners, clinking fluted crystal champagne glasses shimmering with well-iced Moët & Chandon as they awaited the call to dinner (buffet-style or sit-down, depending on the crowd size and occasion). In the winter, a fire crackled reassuringly at either end of the long living room. The soft, silky voice of Ella Fitzgerald floated out of ceiling-mounted speakers in the hallway, where Ben Bradlee worked the crowd, greeting people he hadn't seen since the last big party and probably wouldn't see again until the next one. Outside, a long line of black Town Cars and limousines moved slowly forward, as more and more guests arrived, including a five-man jazz combo hired to

play dance music after dinner. Among the latest wave of arrivals were Ted
Kennedy, Daniel Patrick Moynihan, Lauren Bacall, Colin Powell, Vernon
Jordan, Al Gore, Tom Brokaw, Bob Woodward, Mike Nichols and Diane
Sawyer, Larry King, David and Susan Brinkley, Pierre Salinger, Arthur
Schlesinger, Henry Kissinger, Art Buchwald, Alan Greenspan, Tip
O'Neill, Barbara Walters, Nora Ephron, and (of course) Kay Graham.

Sally's idea of the "Quinn-tessential" party (as suggested in her *Party*
book) is something akin to a "critical mass." "You want noise, heat, electricity, excitement," she writes. Unlike other leading Georgetown dowagers, Sally Quinn professes that the reason for her entertainments is
simple enjoyment. There is no hidden purpose, no ulterior motive, no
agenda. "I don't have official parties," she points out in *The Party,* "I have
parties only for fun." At other instances in her career, in multivarious articles and profiles for *The Washington Post,* Quinn has said that *every* party
in Washington has a reason. People work at parties. Parties are the place
to make contacts, see people you can't ordinarily get on the telephone,
pick up or exchange information. In one account, she observed: "Parties
are really invaluable to people who want to do serious business, political
or otherwise, in this town." Is there something disingenuous then about
her claim in *The Party* that her soirées are purely fun-oriented get-
togethers? "Ninety percent fun," she responds to the current author,
"and ten percent business."

In the pursuit of "fun," Quinn has devised a list of commonsense
commandments. "I always think that coffee spoils the fun," she stipu-
lates. "So my advice is, bag the coffee." Along the same lines, she recom-
mends that hostesses "go small" on the hors d'oeuvres: "Avoid big, fat,
greasy, lumpy things that require three or four bites." As for children—
"Keep them out of sight." Above all, it is imperative that the host or hostess enliven the conversation by any means possible. "When all else fails,"
she writes, "talk about sex."

LORRAINE AND VANGIE

REPUBLICAN SENATOR HOWARD BAKER JR. of Tennessee, a distant relation and close associate of John Sherman Cooper, retains a vivid memory of Lorraine Cooper telephoning his secretary in the 1970s and requesting an appointment. "I was minority leader of the Senate at the time," reminisced Baker. "And one day my secretary came in and said that Lorraine Cooper was on the line and wanted to see me. I said, 'Lorraine can come in any time she wants.' So we made an appointment for a Thursday at ten o'clock in the morning, and when the day arrived she showed up. I remember she had on a silk blouse, a tweed skirt, a little jacket, and a tweed hat with a feather in it. She sat down and crossed her ankles and looked at me. 'Howard,' she said, 'do you have any money?' And I said, 'Well, Lorraine, not much but I have some. Why do you ask?' She then said, 'Because you need some new clothes. And I have brought you a list of tailors.' She opened her pocketbook, removed the list, and handed it to me. I looked it over. 'Lorraine,' I said, 'all these tailors live in London.' 'I know,' she responded. 'You need all the help you can get.' With that, she stood up and started to leave. And then she stopped suddenly, turned around, and said, 'And when you're on television, Howard, for goodness' sake stand up straight.' "

Former Democratic Senator Mike Mansfield of Montana, majority leader of the Senate, had his own memory of Lorraine Cooper. "I knew

Lorraine rather well," he said, "because Senator Cooper and I were old chums. We used to eat breakfast together three or four times a week along with Senators George Aiken and Ed Muskie. Anyway, Lorraine appeared in my office one day bristling with news concerning the CIA's acquisition of an old house in Georgetown and the Agency's transformation of the house into a training school for foreign intelligence officers. 'What's wrong with that, Lorraine?' I asked her. 'There's nothing wrong with it,' she said. 'But if I found out about it—and I'm a mere layman— you can imagine what the Russians are doing. They've probably got the place under surveillance inside and out.' I told her I'd look into it and report back to her if I came up with anything. And that apparently satisfied her, because she got up and left. Well, I did have the matter investigated and found out that Lorraine was right—the Soviets had this place clearly in their periscope. The CIA vacated the house and moved the training school to another location."

Because of their annual Senate garden party and his lengthy public service record—seventeen years in the Senate—as well as his popularity with members and leaders of both parties, John and Lorraine Cooper knew everyone and everyone knew them. Lorraine was particularly popular with the other Senate wives, many of whom looked to her as their spokesperson. "Whenever the press needed a comment from the wife of a senator, they turned to Lorraine," said Evangeline Bruce. "The wives themselves turned to her whenever they had a problem or complaint. She always had some words of wisdom, often quite humorously put, to offer them. I recall Ellen Proxmire, the wife of Senator Edward William Proxmire of Wisconsin, at a party complaining to Lorraine that she hadn't gone on a family vacation in more than seven years. 'You'll have plenty of time for family vacations once your husband loses the support of his constituency,' Lorraine responded. 'At that point you'll be able to take all the family vacations you want.'

"I never quite knew when Lorraine was putting someone on. I remember, for example, another senator's wife, quite overweight and not very soignée, and this woman wanted Lorraine to tell her where in Paris to go for the latest fashions. We were at a dinner party in Georgetown and the woman kept hounding Lorraine until she finally said: 'Oh, do go to

Madame Camus at Dior's. She's marvelous, will do well by you and give you good prices. You would be a walking advertisement for them, so they will undoubtedly loan you clothes from the collections to wear on special occasions.'

"Lorraine loved to tease people. It wasn't done in bad faith. It had a soft edge to it. And in the case of this woman, Lorraine finally introduced her to a dietician in Georgetown who turned the woman's life around, helped her to lose fifty pounds, and did wonders for her appearance and disposition.

"Lorraine was the perfect senator's wife and loved playing the role. When John Sherman Cooper left office in 1973–1974 and signed on with the Washington law firm of Covington and Burling, Lorraine went into an immediate funk. She had wanted John to run for reelection. My husband, who in recent years had represented the United States at the Paris Peace Talks and headed America's liaison office in Beijing, felt that having successfully served as ambassador to India in the mid-1950s, John would make an ideal choice as American ambassador to one of the countries abroad. Richard Nixon evidently thought so as well. Once Washington officially recognized the government of East Germany (German Democratic Republic), Nixon selected him to serve as the first American ambassador to that country. Nixon was forced out of office before he could make the actual appointment. And there the matter rested until Lorraine began beleaguering Henry Kissinger to move ahead with the appointment. Because of the tense political dealings between Washington and Moscow, Kissinger wanted to delay the appointment. But each time she encountered Kissinger at a dinner party, she would bring up East Germany. She was relentless. 'Will somebody please get that woman off my back,' Kissinger is purported to have said to one of his aides. So the matter finally went to President Ford, who signed off on it. The next thing I heard was that Lorraine had begun studying Russian and German in preparation for the trip."

Scott Miller, a lawyer and friend of John Sherman Cooper, recollected that the appointment "surprised people, insofar as the senator, which is what everyone called him, didn't drive, couldn't speak more than a few words of German, was in his midseventies, and couldn't hear very well. He could never get his hearing aids to work properly. The strange thing is that he was known as the Great Listener. When he set his mind to it, he could communicate extremely well with people, which I suppose is one of many reasons they wanted him in East Germany. Another reason is that he'd spent time in Germany after World War II and therefore had a working knowledge of the country."

In October 1974 career diplomat Brandon H. Grove Jr. was dispatched by the State Department to East Berlin to open the East German embassy. The Coopers arrived in East Berlin three months later. East Germany, then occupied by the Russians and known in diplomatic circles as the "other" Germany, represented a high-priority assignment. "It was the powder keg," according to Grove, "of the Cold War crisis."

Grove's other assignment in East Berlin entailed the procurement of a proper residence for the Coopers. The East Germans first showed him a small house, bordered on three sides by a large cemetery, with tiny rooms and a Pullman kitchen. "It's not possible," Grove told the real estate people. "The Coopers have two butlers, a personal maid (who doubles as their cook), a laundress, and a special assistant." The entire group had checked into the Linden Hotel on the historic Unter den Linden Strasse, where they remained for the next two months. Exasperated by the difficulty of finding more permanent housing, Lorraine at one point threatened to return to the States; her husband talked her into staying. It was one of the few times in their marriage that witnesses heard them argue.

"The East Germans were actually eager to help," said Grove. "We were definitely a big catch. America's presence in East Berlin conveyed the idea that we approved the reality of two Germanys. With the help of the East Germans, I eventually found the Coopers and their retinue a place at a diplomatic compound near the center of the city—not far from the embassy—a kind of Levittown for ambassadors. These twenty-five or so recently constructed houses looked like concrete slab shoe boxes, but they were spacious and well suited to entertaining. The house they decided on contained twelve rooms and had a plot of land around it that connected to the land of the next ambassadorial shoe box. Lorraine immediately sensed the possibilities and with her great flair for decorating and landscaping made a stunning and dramatic showcase out of her home—we were, after all, permitted to shop in West Berlin, driving through Checkpoint Charlie to the other side of the wall, where there were plenty of clothing and food shops, hairdressers, furniture, and home furnishing stores, American schools, and the expansive PX facilities of the U.S. Army. Lorraine purchased most of her household furnishings beyond the wall, acquiring damask wall covering, window dressings, and furniture in West Berlin. The walls inside her home were a deep burgundy, which set off the basically white furniture that she acquired. At a nursery in West Berlin she bought a large number of orange trees that lined the outside of the house. J. Carter Brown gathered together and sent her (on loan) a group of paintings from the National Gallery, the Whitney Museum, and the Phillips Gallery. She totally transformed the shoe box. It began to resemble her home in Georgetown. The rest of East Berlin was shabby, gloomy, and depressing. The winter months were particularly drab, so much so that Lorraine began taking Valium to help counter her downward mood swings.

"Entertaining in East Berlin wasn't easy. East German nationals weren't encouraged by the Communist regime to attend private functions. Whenever we contacted local government officials and asked for additions to our guest lists, they would send over the most boring and stodgy Prussian types. Lorraine had no patience for pretentious, dull, obsequious, or stupid people. So, we had to rely on other diplomats for social purposes. Lorraine forged close friendships with the ambassadors of Portugal, Sweden, Great Britain, and Pakistan. She became friendly with their wives and became a kind of unofficial leader of the pack, the way she had become leader of the senatorial wives' group in Washington. Then there were the people who worked in the West German mission and those from our own delegation in East Berlin, the foreign service careerists. We were like a club, a consolidated corps of professionals in a hostile environment. At the end of the day she always managed to put together an interesting and convivial group. She loved to entertain and she did it magnificently.

"She had the ability to motivate those around her. She and I had this game we used to play. When she wanted something done, she would come up to me and playfully pummel me on the chest with both her fists. 'You can do it, Brandon!' she'd say. 'You can get it done!' And of course I'd do my utmost to satisfy her expectations."

Although the Coopers had brought along their own domestic staff, they depended on the locals—as did all the embassies—for part-time help: gardeners, drivers, maintenance men, and others. "We knew that the local help, decent people on the whole, were nevertheless spying for the regime and were obliged to report regularly on the trivia of our daily lives," said Grove. "We were always careful what we said to each other in person and over the telephone, both at the embassy and in the privacy of our homes. Dinner at a restaurant in West Berlin, where we knew we weren't being bugged or taped, was a good place to talk."

The Coopers used additional means to protect themselves against the possibility of being spied upon. At home Lorraine often turned up the volume on the radio or stereo when she and her husband spoke, or when she and others conversed on sensitive matters. At other times she and her husband communicated by passing notes back and forth. Sometimes they simply turned on a fan or opened the refrigerator door, which rattled loudly when the unit was defrosting. They occasionally used hand signals or prearranged code words. Lorraine compared the process to "a game of charades."

Trude Musson had begun working as a summer intern in John Cooper's senatorial office in 1965. Three years later she signed on as special assistant to Lorraine Cooper, for whom she subsequently became very much a surrogate daughter. Living with the Coopers in East Berlin, she returned to her rooms one day and smelled the stale odor of cigarette smoke. Trude didn't smoke; Lorraine Cooper, who did, hadn't been in Trude's living quarters. "Somebody had obviously been in there smoking a cigarette," said Musson. "You never quite got used to it, but you knew you were being watched."

Musson found the entire experience trying but not without an abundance of good humor. As in Georgetown, she said, Lorraine lit dozens of candles whenever she entertained, whether officially or privately. The effect of so much candlelight was not lost on her East Berlin guests. Following a cocktail party for the English ambassador, Musson overheard a

Writer Truman Capote threw the Black and White Ball at the Plaza Hotel honoring Kay Graham in New York on November 28, 1966. Reputed to be the party of the decade, the event marked Graham's first social debut after the 1963 suicide of her husband. *(Library of Congress)*

RIGHT: Lorraine Cooper with dog in East Berlin. John Sherman Cooper was the first American ambassador to East Germany during the mid-1970s. *(AP Wide World Photos)*

Lorraine Cooper had a predilection for vivid colors—splashes of bright orange and emerald green appeared in the dining room, red roses on white chintz in the living room, and a delphinium blue in the library. "I insist on having a delphinium blue room in every one of my homes," she told the *Washington Star. (Copyright* Washington Post. *Reprinted by permission of the D.C. Public Library)*

LEFT: Lorraine Cooper at home. Cooper liked to swim in the nearby Harriman pool, clutching a parasol in one hand, a cigarette holder, and a half-filled cocktail glass in the other. (*Copyright* Washington Post. *Reprinted by permission of the D.C. Public Library)*

RIGHT: Lorraine Cooper, senator's wife and famous for the annual late-spring garden party she gave for senators and their spouses, which gradually grew in size to include diplomats, Supreme Court justices, Pentagon officials, industrialists, White House staffers, and CIA operatives. (*AP Wide World Photos*)

Warren E. Buffett, C.E.O. of Berkshire Hathaway, became a major shareholder in *The Washington Post* as well as a confidant and companion of Kay Graham. (*AP Wide World Photos*)

Secretary of Defense and Georgetown regular Robert S. McNamara also at one point became a close companion of Katharine Graham. (*Copyright Washington Post. Reprinted by permission of the D.C. Public Library*)

President Richard M. Nixon resigned from the presidency in 1974 as a result of the disclosures of the Watergate investigation launched by *The Washington Post*. Nixon's tough-talking Attorney General John Mitchell warned at the time, "Katie Graham's gonna get her tit caught in a wringer," but it was Mitchell who served time in a federal prison for his role in the scandal. (*National Archives*)

Katharine Graham and Ben Bradlee leave U.S. District Court in 1971 after getting the approval to publish the Pentagon Papers. (*AP Wide World Photos*)

Ben Bradlee, 1981. As executive editor of *The Washington Post* from 1968 to 1991, Bradlee became one of Kay Graham's closest confidants and hired his future wife, Sally Quinn, despite her lack of journalistic training. *(AP Wide World Photos)*

Hired at the age of twenty-eight, Sally Quinn was untested as a writer, but she would soon prove herself one of the most read- and talked-about reporters in the history of *The Washington Post. (AP Wide World Photos)*

Sally Quinn at home in 1991. *(AP Wide World Photos)*

Sally Quinn and Ben Bradlee now reside at the redbrick Federalist mansion on N Street that was formerly the home of Robert Todd Lincoln. *(Lisa Friel Photography)*

Secretary of State Henry Kissinger, attending a dinner party at Tom and Joan Braden's, confessed to columnist Sally Quinn that he was a "secret swinger," forever heightening his status as a man-about-town. (*AP Wide World Photos*)

Tongsun Park, lobbyist and Korean businessman, was proprietor of The Georgetown Club and the Pisces club. He became embroiled in "Koreagate," resulting in a 1977 indictment by the Justice Department for bribery of U.S. government officials. Park had connections to the Korean Central Intelligence Agency. (*AP Wide World Photos*)

Senator John Warner and his wife, Liz Taylor, hosting an annual barbecue for Virginia Republicans at their Middleburg residence. (*Bettmann/CORBIS*)

David K. Bruce, then ambassador to Germany, with his family, 1967. (Top, left to right) Alexandra ("Sasha") and wife, Evangeline. (Bottom, left to right) Nicholas Cabeu, David Surtees. Sasha died in 1975 at the age of twenty-nine by a gunshot wound. (*AP Wide World Photos*)

Evangeline Bruce with two of her springer spaniels. (*Copyright* Washington Post. *Reprinted by permission of the D.C. Public Library*)

Averell Harriman is welcomed to a dinner by Evangeline Bruce, 1971. (*Copyright* Washington Post. *Reprinted by permission of the D.C. Public Library*)

Averell Harriman walks with bride-to-be Pamela Digby Churchill Hayward in Washington, 1971. (*AP Wide World Photos*)

Jackie Kennedy Onassis and the Harrimans. (*Bettman/CORBIS*)

Senator Edward Kennedy of Massachusetts (left) and Robert Strauss, chairman of the National Democratic Committee, chat with Pamela and Averell Harriman at a Georgetown party in 1972. (*Copyright* Washington Post. *Reprinted by permission of the D.C. Public Library*)

ABOVE: Newly appointed U.S. Ambassador Pamela Digby Churchill Harriman before the Woman's National Democratic Club in Paris, 1993. *(Arthur Terry/Corbis Sygma)*

LEFT: 3038 N Street, home of Averell and Pamela Harriman. *(Lisa Friel Photography)*

High-powered cosmetics executive Georgette Mosbacher tried to establish herself in the nation's capital but was viewed by Georgetowners as too glamorous and overly ambitious. *(Mitchell Gerber/CORBIS)*

Author, columnist, and would-be Washington hostess Arianna Huffington met with the same fate as Georgette Mosbacher. Following the political defeat of her then-husband, Michael Huffington, in his bid for senator of California in 1994, Arianna deserted Washington and has become a satirical commentator from her home base in Los Angeles. *(AP Wide World Photos)*

Longtime resident Teresa Heinz could become the next dowager queen of Georgetown. Worth approximately one billion dollars, Heinz is currently married to Democratic presidential candidate Massachusetts Senator John F. Kerry. *(Reuters NewMedia Inc./CORBIS)*

Sally Quinn, the youngest member of the Georgetown Ladies' Social Club, continues to give and attend parties, but many Washingtonians have mixed feelings about her role as doyenne, due to the feathers she ruffled over the years as a *Washington Post* columnist. *(Vivian Ronay/FOLIO, Inc.)*

Sally Quinn and Ben Bradlee (rear) at Colin Powell's Washington book party in 1995. *(Vivian Ronay/FOLIO, Inc.)*

President George W. and Laura Bush on their ranch in Crawford, Texas. The Bushes prefer small, intimate gatherings and early nights, putting a damper on socializing in Washington, D.C., and muting Georgetown's influence. *(AP Wide World Photos)*

pair of bewildered local magistrates comparing notes. "I thought the Americans were so rich," said the first magistrate. "I guess they're not," said the second, "because they never seem to use the electricity. They're always burning candles."

One of Lorraine Cooper's major criticisms of East Berlin, in addition to its dour winters, was her inability to procure certain personal items and products that she had easy access to in the States. Writing to a U.S. State Department requisitions agent, she asked him to send "six cyclax 'plumb crazy' lipsticks; vitamins C, E, and B complex; French's Rum Shampoo packets; five cartons of Carlton cigarettes; a new supply of Lazlo products from Saks." In the same letter, after requesting some two thousand folded paper napkins embossed with the official State Department seal, she provided an abbreviated prescription for a successful ambassadorial dinner party. "A party is not thrown, it is given," she wrote. "When I give a party, I try to have a reason for it. It's also important to give the guests something good to eat."

Aniko Gaal Schott, whose then-husband, James Weiner, was counselor for administration in the East German embassy, attended many of the official functions hosted by the Coopers. "Lorraine was the epitome of style and grace," said Schott. "In her very smart, assertive way, she always seemed to get across what she wanted or needed. She brought new life to East Berlin. Here was a geographical area that hadn't seen color in maybe four decades, and suddenly here comes Mrs. Lorraine Cooper in a lavender chiffon dress with her matching lavender chiffon parasol. What a contrast! Lorraine was full of life; East Berlin seemed a terribly melancholy place, everything gray—from the buildings to the people.

"I can't think of anyone who disliked her. Her household employees all loved her. Her two butlers—Michael Hansen and the British-born Michael Mangin—got along famously with her and were practically considered members of the family. She used to visit the wives of the embassy employees every week or two. She wanted to keep us apprised and made suggestions as to how we could reach out to the members of the community and thereby make our presence felt. She always spoke Russian or German to the locals, who obviously appreciated the effort. Whenever she and her husband traveled, they brought back what they called 'trinkets' for the foreign service wives. For example, when they went to Paris, they returned with expensive bottles of perfume. Attached to the gifts were cards that read: 'No need to write thank-you notes.' By the same token, they didn't like to receive gifts. John Sherman Cooper felt that a politician or diplomat should never accept a present from anyone because the motive behind it could too easily be misunderstood. It could be seen as graft, as influence peddling.

"My Hungarian grandmother came to visit us from Budapest in 1975, and John Cooper insisted on meeting her. They discussed politics. 'Who knows,' said the ambassador, 'communism may not last. Don't despair, there's always hope.' "

As per letters that Lorraine wrote to friends during this period, including Barbara Bush, wife of the future president, the Coopers received visits from Kay Graham as well as the Bruces—David and Vangie— whom they in turn visited in Brussels, where David's latest assignment was to serve as permanent U.S. representative to NATO. They attended several receptions at the vast Russian embassy in East Berlin. They hosted actor Richard Burton at a small dinner party. They gave a mammoth July Fourth party, for which they leased a large Shamiana tent from Pakistan, which arrived in dozens of separate parcels and which no one knew how to put up. It took the supervision of a U.S. Army general (from West Berlin) and his entire regiment to erect the tent. Hundreds of children and adults feasted on "peanuts, popcorn, hot dogs, Kentucky ham, doughnuts, apple cider, and cookies, plus the usual. They also set off firecrackers, which are a wonderful hazard to the tent."

In mid-1976, following a dinner party at the Cooper residence, an incident took place that temporarily turned Lorraine Cooper's life around. According to a letter Lorraine later wrote to Evangeline Bruce, she was "attacked and sexually violated" by one of the guests, a middle-aged German businessman "who had seemed perfectly harmless during dinner but was obviously inebriated and semideranged." The assault, the letter continues, took place in the Cooper living room "after everyone had gone home." John Sherman Cooper, not feeling particularly well and with an early-morning appointment ahead of him, had excused himself and gone to bed. The household staff, including Trude Musson, had also retired for the evening, leaving Lorraine (age sixty-nine) alone with the man. "He requested a final nightcap and I stupidly obliged. He is well known in European financial circles. I remember sitting opposite him, discussing German politics, and then suddenly, violently being subjected to his weight." The assailant "had undone his trousers." Lorraine was "too startled and frightened" to resist or even scream. "The only thing I recall is begging him not to harm me."

"It has taken me weeks to gather the strength and courage to tell John what happened," read another of Lorraine's letters to Vangie Bruce. Because of the sensitive nature of Cooper's diplomatic position and the international business connections of Lorraine's attacker, the couple made a conscious decision not to pursue the matter legally. Instead, they suffered in silence and cut short by several months their stay in East Germany, returning to Washington in the fall of 1976, at which time John Sherman Cooper reluctantly rejoined Covington and Burling. Distraught and frustrated by the situation—their inability to see justice done and their reluctance to discuss the case with anyone—the Coopers nevertheless resumed their frenetic social schedule, organizing and utilizing their gatherings at home in Georgetown as a forum for political debate and action. Whenever asked what he'd learned during his stay in East Germany, the former ambassador replied: "I learned that I was right to oppose the antiballistic missile program. It was obsolete before it began. The Communists will merely ratchet up their program and build a missile capable of evading the ABM. And so on and so forth. Besides, if you get down to it, they're more likely to wage war against us using propaganda methods as opposed to tactical missiles. Why must we invest billions of dollars in such an uncertain defensive mechanism?" Asked what she had enjoyed most about East Berlin, Lorraine Cooper invariably responded: "Coming home again."

∽

DAVID AND EVANGELINE BRUCE'S seemingly charmed life ended tragically in early November 1975 with the death of the eldest of their three children, twenty-nine-year-old Sasha Bruce. Married for the last three months of her life to a Greek citizen of questionable background, Marios Michaelides, she died of a gunshot wound to the head, sustained at Staunton Hill, the Bruce family country manor house at Brookneal, Virginia. Initially ruled a suicide, the case was later reopened (Lorraine Cooper and Kay Graham, among others, encouraged the Bruces to hire their own private investigator, which they did), and in 1977 Michaelides was indicted for first-degree murder, bigamy, embezzlement, and grand larceny, having taken and then sold antiques, furnishings, and rare books that belonged to the Bruces. The accused, who claimed that Sasha had promised him the family heirlooms, had returned to Athens and could not be extradited by the United States to stand trial for murder in Virginia.

At the beginning of 1975 the Bruces were spread far and wide. David and Evangeline were living in Brussels. David, their eldest son, was visiting Taiwan, where he had gone to study Mandarin Chinese, while Nicholas, the younger son, had moved to Portland, Oregon. Sasha, until recently, had been living in London, dating numerous men at the same time, making frequent trips to the Continent to hang out with friends, pursuing the "alternative" lifestyle (said Ina Ginsburg) "of a hippie." A magna cum laude graduate of Radcliffe College, Sasha was described by acquaintances as brilliant, stunning, generous, introverted, and informal. She is said to have been the first Bruce ever to wear a pair of jeans in public. She loved books, movies, dinner parties, going on archeological digs in Greece, and driving small foreign sports cars at high speeds. It was in Greece, on the rebound from an earlier romance, that she met Marios Michaelides, a short, slim, twenty-nine-year-old roustabout with no savings, an ingratiating smile, and a bad temper. Not especially handsome, he is described in one newspaper account as having "a long face and rat-like features." He claimed to be a divorced father of one, but public records were inconclusive as to whether he had legally terminated his first marriage. It is known that after Sasha's death, he resumed living with his former wife and child, that she joined him when he went back to Greece, and several years later left him to return to the United States.

Sasha's propensity for "choosing the wrong kind of men," as her brother David put it, went back to her early days in London when she became involved in a series of romances with men whose sole objective seemed to be Sasha's bankroll. Marios Michaelides was no different. When Sasha informed him of her intention to move to Staunton Hill in Virginia and live off her trust fund, her new boyfriend immediately offered to go with her. There, attended to by several family retainers, including a cook and a handyman, Sasha embarked on her latest venture; in keeping with her father's fantasy of one day becoming a gentleman farmer, she decided to raise chickens, an endeavor that, while not profitable, would at least keep her busy. Without hesitation, she also agreed to marry Marios. Her parents, unhappy with that decision, suspicious of their son-in-law's motives, refused to attend the ceremony, which took place on August 8, 1975, at the Charlotte Courthouse before the county clerk.

The newlyweds had little in common. They argued incessantly. Michaelides proved to be a domineering, manipulative tyrant who, on occasion, resorted to physical force to control and punish his wife. When neighbors asked Sasha about a mass of black-and-blue marks on her arms and legs, she told them she'd fallen down a flight of stairs. The coroner's report revealed that there were bruises and cuts, old and new, over a substantial portion of her body. Eight weeks into the marriage, Sasha consulted an attorney regarding the possibility of having the marriage annulled, a step that would have eliminated Marios as a potential beneficiary of her considerable estate. It is likely that Michaelides knew of his wife's intention to dissolve their marriage. Then came November 7 and the discovery of Sasha amid a clump of old gnarled firs, her body lying half-crouched under low branches and bleeding from a deep wound in her right temple. A .22-caliber pistol lay under her body. On reopening the case, investigators concluded that the placement and position of the gun, coupled with the improbable angle at which the bullet entered her head, precluded the possibility that Sasha had inflicted the wound herself. The motive connecting Michaelides to the crime was his awareness that his wife intended to terminate the marriage as soon as possible. The expected loss of revenue, the investigators concluded, had catapulted the would-be killer into action.

Sasha lived but thirty-six hours after paramedics drove her by ambulance to nearby Lynchburg General Hospital. Her father hurried to her side—having flown to Washington from Brussels the day before for a meeting with President Ford—and sat in her room until she died at 1:15 A.M. on Sunday morning. He had telephoned his wife in Brussels, and she had made plans to join him. The first person she called after speaking with her husband was Lorraine Cooper in East Berlin. Lorraine offered to return to Washington with her, but Vangie declined.

Virginia Surtees, Vangie's sister, was walking her bulldog in the street just outside her London flat, "on that November morning at 7:30 A.M. I was just below my bedroom window, which was open, and I heard the telephone ring. I thought it could only be an emergency so I bundled Fortinbras upstairs . . . and waited. My sister telephoned almost immediately from Heathrow, where the airplane had broken down, and was waiting to [take her] to Washington. She told me about the tragedy. I said I'd come out to Heathrow at once and fly with her. She said not to, that she could only keep *firm* if she was alone. . . . She missed her connection from Washington for another to Lynchburg, so David met her and they flew down together. The next day she telephoned me and told me all the details and a bit later about the funeral. They came over here almost immediately [after the funeral] and I went round and David and my sister talked and talked about it. My sister suffered grievously for her daughter's death, [although after that day] she didn't talk about it very much. We were brought up in an atmosphere of having to maintain a stiff upper lip. There is enough misery without bleating about it."

While in the Washington area the Bruces saw few of their friends. They were able to stay at their Georgetown house, although they had leased it out to foreign service officer Sylvia Clark, who thought the couple "distraught but not distraught-looking. They were too sophisticated to let their feelings be seen." The funeral remained a private, family ceremony. Marios Michaelides attended and tearfully professed his eternal love for Sasha. Afterward Vangie visited with Susan Mary Alsop. Marietta Tree flew in from New York to join them. Susan Mary later wrote to Marietta: "What a help it was to have you come down the day before. I know that all you said will sink in to Evangeline's poor broken heart and remain with her." Susan Mary Alsop continued to be one of Evangeline Bruce's strongest supporters. When *The Washington Post* ran a series of articles on the Bruce tragedy, Susan Mary felt they had portrayed Vangie in an unfavorable light. In response, she wrote a letter defending Sasha's mother and then hand-delivered it to the *Post* offices. "I wanted to make certain they intended to publish it," said Alsop.

That the Bruces felt compelled to leave the scene of the crime as soon as they did and flee first to London and then to Brussels became fodder for a press eager to hold them responsible, if only indirectly, for their daughter's misfortune. "They had remained on their pedestal for so long," said Polly Wisner Fritchey, "that people were eager to knock them down. They were the perfect couple, as close to blueblood as you get in America. If this could happen to them, to one of the most powerful families in the country, then it could happen to anyone. Vangie being British-born, the English press went no easier on them. They couldn't escape the story. It followed them around like a shadow."

If anything, David Bruce received more favorable coverage than his wife. Friends attributed his retirement the following year to the strain he felt from Sasha's death, the strain that came from holding his sadness within. "He used to drift through his wife's parties like a ghost," said Nick von Hoffman. "He gave the impression that he wasn't the least bit interested in their guests." A year after his retirement, two years after Sasha's death, in December 1977, at age seventy-nine, he passed away. The same friends blamed his death on the publicity surrounding the reopening of the investigation into Sasha's presumed murder. The results of the investigation proved fatal to a man whose distinguished diplomatic career had progressed outside the bounds of unwanted gossip and innuendo. According to reports that now peppered the press, Sasha Bruce, despite her intelligence and good looks, had been a morose, troubled, rebellious teenager with drug problems, depressions, and low self-esteem. She had a long history of masochistic relationships with lovers and boyfriends who physically and psychologically abused her. She had threatened suicide on several previous occasions, which left the case open-ended and shrouded in mystery. Many of the articles, including a *Life* cover story, intimated that while Sasha adored her father, she had never been fond of her mother, that mother and daughter were highly competitive with each other and often didn't communicate for months at a stretch—and on those occasions that they did communicate, they usually argued. The press, which in the past had almost always championed the Bruces, now turned against them. Evangeline Bruce was depicted as a cold, negligent, uncaring mother who placed her own interests before those of her children. Ambassador David Bruce was seen as a remote and distant figure, a man so caught up in himself and his image that he had no use for children. Like his wife, he saw his own offspring only when it suited him.

Sasha Bruce's untimely death became the topic of the day among Georgetown's smart set, a newsworthy counterpoint to the murder of Mary Pinchot Meyer a decade earlier. The most argued aspect of the case, aside from the actual cause of Sasha's death—was it murder or a suicide?—had to do with the relationship between Vangie Bruce and her children. Opinions ran the gamut, starting with Jennifer Phillips, a friend of Vangie's: "I know how she felt about her children. They were hard to love, particularly as they grew older. I knew her three children, and it seemed to me very clear that what they were suffering from was not parental neglect, not the fact that Vangie hired nannies to look after them. (All rich people have nannies.) Not that she chose her duties to her husband over her children. There were just [problems] there that you couldn't do anything about. Both of her sons had problems as well. I know she tried to do what she could do, given her own limitations as a human being. And I certainly don't think that what has happened to her children is the result of anything that she, or her husband, did or didn't do. I really, truly believe that. I wouldn't hesitate to say that Vangie was a bad mother, if that's what I believed. It might in part have been the age. The 1960s and 1970s were difficult times. But, of course, many young people survived those years. You can only do what you can do as a parent. My point is that what happened to Sasha didn't happen because Vangie didn't care about her. It happened because of Sasha."

Rowland Evans similarly considered Evangeline "a caring mother, although not a completely hands-on mom. But she took pains to organize the lives of her children. For example, when the kids were young and David Bruce was ambassador to Germany, she wanted a nanny who was fun to be around. It would be difficult enough for them in Germany. So she hired a French girl from a good family who was called Yoyo. And Yoyo turned out to be wonderful with the children and stayed with the Bruces until they left Germany. And Vangie constantly gave Yoyo ideas of things to do with the children. So she was certainly concerned about them."

More common were the voices of those who subscribed to the notion that Evangeline, as a result of her inattention, had somehow contributed to Sasha's demise. "Vangie wasn't exactly the maternal mother type," said Nuella Pell. "She wasn't there for her children," remarked Betty Beale. Ella Poe Burling observed that "Vangie's manners were wonderful. Her thank-you notes must have been written and mailed on the way home from whatever party she had attended. They came too promptly. Yet for all that, she wasn't at all a good mother. She placed her social activities higher on the totem pole than her children, who paid the ultimate price for her lack of mothering skills. She recreated in her own household the same bad relationship she had endured with her mother."

Vangie's harshest critic was probably Joan Mellen, author of *Privilege: The Enigma of Sasha Bruce* (1982), an in-depth examination of Sasha's final years. "In writing the book," said Mellen, "I interviewed a number of people about the Bruces, including Wendy Wisner Hazard, the daughter of Frank and Polly Wisner and one of Sasha's earliest friends. What Wendy and others told me about Evangeline Bruce is that she lacked consistency in the way she related to her children. She ran hot and then cold. She would withdraw her affection and then she would give it. She would be nice to Sasha for a bit and then suddenly not nice. And this is how she behaved with all three of her children. She threw everyone off balance. The children never knew what was going to happen or what to expect. This must have been very terrifying for them."

In an interview with the current author, Hazard drew a different picture from that which she evidently communicated to Mellen. "Sasha and I knew each other when we were little kids," she said. "We rode horses together, played baseball, basketball, what have you. We were tomboys at that stage. Mrs. Bruce was wonderfully high-spirited. She started something called the Thursday Club. On Thursday afternoons after school a bunch of Sasha's friends would go to her house to play and wreak havoc.

Mrs. Bruce would look in on us from time to time to make sure we weren't getting into trouble. And then she'd make us a spaghetti dinner. She cooked it herself. While we ate, she would tell us stories, fairy tales that she made up. She had a great imagination, and it was just enthralling for us. Her dogs were always around. She loved dogs. She had these springer spaniels, and when any of them died she would bury them in the garden, marking their graves with miniature tombstones bearing the deceased canine's name. As we grew older she used to invite us to her outdoor functions. We would run around and talk to the other guests, making pests of ourselves.

"On occasional weekends I would go with them to Staunton Hill. I remember one night when we were about ten and we were telling each other scary ghost stories. There were three of us—Sasha, myself and another of our little friends—and it was late at night and very dark outside. We got into bed to go to sleep, but every time the floorboards creaked we would start to scream. And then something snapped or banged against the window, and we leaped out of bed in absolute terror and ran across the lawn, which is how you got from one part of the manor house to the other. Mrs. Bruce opened the door on her end of the house, and the three of us ran into her bedroom. She started to laugh. 'Come on, girls,' she said, 'you can sleep with me tonight.' And so we all jumped into her bed and fell asleep.

"Mrs. Bruce was more playful than her husband, but Mr. Bruce was probably the most distinguished and elegant man I have ever known. He was deeply intelligent and had a marvelously wry sense of humor. He and his daughter, my great friend Sasha, adored each other. Through her, we all came to adore him. But he was reserved, and I think we all approached him with a great sense of awe and respect."

In writing her book on Sasha Bruce, Joan Mellen approached Evangeline Bruce directly. "I wanted to interview her," said Mellen, "so I telephoned her. We spoke briefly, but she was guarded because *Life* had published what she considered an objectionable article about Sasha and the Bruce family. Her lawyer, Edward Bennett Williams, who seemingly represented half of Georgetown, dissuaded her from suing the magazine for libel and invasion of privacy on the grounds that such a suit would be prohibitively expensive and would only prolong her personal suffering. After our initial conversation, she called me at home from time to time and we would chat. She told me that if I agreed to see Edward Bennett Williams first, she would grant me an extended interview. I believe what people tell me, so I went. I was greeted at his Washington law firm by two of his minions. After a few minutes Williams himself came out, approached me, and said, 'If you reprint one word of that *Life* article in your book, we'll sue the living hell out of you.' That's all he said. Mrs. Bruce never spoke to me again. She did, however, contact John Sargent, chairman of the board of Doubleday Books and an old friend of hers. My book was being published by Dial, an imprint then under the Doubleday banner. She evidently asked Sargent to cancel my book contract, which of course he couldn't do. But in the end the book received little publicity.

"She pulled several other maneuvers. Bruce somehow got hold of the manuscript prior to publication and sent Dial a letter citing inaccuracies and a demand that certain changes be made. Her brief was accompanied by a vast compilation of handwritten notes. I believe the publisher incorporated a few of her suggested changes, including Evangeline's claim that she had been devoted to Sasha, proof of which was provided by the fact that she frequently took her daughter to the store for ice-cream cones."

What irked the Bruces more than Joan Mellen's book was that she willingly traveled to Athens to testify in the extradition case against Marios Michaelides. The purpose of the hearing was to determine whether enough hard evidence existed in the case to merit the return of a Greek citizen by the Greek government to the jurisdiction of the United States to stand trial for a capital offense. According to David S. Bruce, the son of David K. E. and Evangeline Bruce, Mellen "flew to Greece to testify on Michaelides's behalf." Sasha's brother further remarked that Mellen confided to a friend of his that she had testified because she "needed the money," the inference being that she had been paid off. Bruce also suggested that "Michaelides had told Mellen in an unguarded moment what had really happened at the time of Sasha's death, and she [Mellen] suppressed it so she could create [in her book] a false drama and mystery."

Responding to Bruce's allegations, Mellen pointed out that "I never testified on behalf of Michaelides. The hearing in Greece wasn't a trial, simply a forum to determine whether there should be a trial. I wasn't paid a penny for my testimony. Nor did Michaelides ever confess to me as to what actually happened to Sasha. Throughout my two meetings with him, which he accorded when I went to Greece, he maintained his innocence. In my book, I was left to draw my own conclusions. In the end, the Greek government considered putting Michaelides on trial themselves, rather than agree to an extradition process. But as we know, although he remains a fugitive from justice in the United States, in Greece Michaelides is considered innocent of any wrongdoing. Had he admitted his guilt to me, I obviously would have put it in the book. It would have made for a sensational ending, a solution to a case that even today remains unsolved."

David S. Bruce's charges against Mellen are perhaps best explained by the frustration he felt in trying to bring Michaelides to justice. "My original sentiment," he said, "was that Sasha committed suicide. An investigation into the circumstances behind her death demonstrated otherwise. My father was extremely reluctant to push the envelope. He couldn't face up to the possibility of a Michaelides trial, because he felt the family name would be dragged through the mud. My mother bowed to my father's wishes and my younger brother, Nicholas, felt too shattered by Sasha's death to fight for Michaelides's extradition. I became the sole member of the family willing to act. I remain incensed that nothing came of the case, that my sister's alleged murderer remains at large."

The writer Dominick Dunne encountered Evangeline Bruce only once but took away from their meeting a lasting memory. "It took place in the late 1980s or early 1990s," said Dunne. "We met on the Concorde, going to London, and we were seated next to each other. We had never met before, but I recognized her and she recognized me. We were both reading. Without looking up from her book, she said to me, 'We have something in common, Mr. Dunne.' And I said, 'I know we have, Mrs. Bruce.' We had each had daughters who were murdered. My daughter, Dominique, had been killed by a boyfriend in 1982. And she had Sasha. And that's a topic of conversation you have very rarely in life. It's something you can't easily talk about, but it's also something you need to talk about. And we talked. We talked about it all the way to London. It was a release for both of us. Because we had both experienced the same kind of loss, neither of us had to be embarrassed about letting go."

"I think Evangeline Bruce carried her sorrow to the grave," said Barbara Howar. "I think she blamed herself for what happened to Sasha more than I think she should have. Sasha Bruce went astray on her own. Nothing that her parents could have done would have saved her."

In charting a course of recovery from the deaths of her husband and daughter, Evangeline Bruce began devoting much of her time to fundraising on behalf of Christ Church in Georgetown, the parish with which the Bruces had long been affiliated, as well as a Washington program for troubled youth that she had heard about from Lorraine Cooper. Begun in 1974 as an outreach program, the organization had been founded by Deborah Shore, a social worker, who remembered her first meeting with Evangeline: "She breezed in as elegant as can be, wearing a beautiful long black cape, with that flawless alabaster skin of hers. I felt like curtseying. She wanted to do something, she said, to memorialize her daughter. While at Radcliffe, Sasha had become involved in community work for troubled teenagers, so this seemed an area she felt would be meaningful. Mrs. Bruce was very gregarious that day, but there was no doubt in my mind that she was suffering. A few weeks later an envelope arrived from her containing a check for $25,000. And that was only the beginning."

The money helped the organization open the Sasha Bruce House, a round-the-clock shelter for young people, with five resident counselors and a number of youth-oriented programs. Vangie enlisted the help of her wealthier friends to further the cause, sponsored galas and movie screenings, and made the project a focus of her life. Her detractors, however, accused her of spending far more time working for the shelter than she had ever allotted to her daughter. Although her sons were still around, they at first offered little by way of solace. Nicholas had become a janitor in Philadelphia while David returned to China to study Mandarin. He later married and had a child, moving to Georgetown at the same time that he turned Staunton Hill into a glorified bed-and-breakfast. But for the most part, the brothers were estranged from each other and also from their mother, visiting her only on the most select occasions.

The loss of her loved ones did in a sense humanize her. The occasionally haughty, sometimes snobbish diplomat's wife ("bitchlike," according
to Joan Mellen) had become a kindly, empathetic, thoughtful widow. At
her own parties she lobbied influential political guests on behalf of a national health plan as well as a plan to raise the country's minimum hourly
wage, issues that had never interested her in the past. Seated next to
Henry Kissinger at a Kay Graham soirée, she asked him what he knew
about the 1976 Lockheed scandal (in which the Lockheed Corporation
had paid a high-ranking Japanese official over $2 million in bribes), then
launched into a monologue on Robert McNamara, Lyndon Johnson, and
Richard Nixon, accusing all three of acknowledging privately that the
Vietnam War could not be won, yet publicly exhorting American troops
into action. When Kissinger observed that David Bruce had also been
aware of these facts, Vangie responded, "Yes, but my husband tried to
end the war—the others tried to keep it going."

After the death of David and Sasha Bruce, the friendship between
Evangeline and Kay Graham grew closer than it had ever been. Kay knew
the pain that resulted from the loss of a spouse. And like Vangie, she
knew what it meant to have an independent, headstrong daughter. The
relationship between Kay and Lally Weymouth, always tenuous, suffered
a further setback when the owner of the *Post* bypassed her daughter and
chose Donald, her eldest son, to become the newspaper's publisher. Her
other two sons showed no interest in entering the family business. Bill
had pursued a law degree and moved to California, where he soon married and started a family. Stephen, the youngest and most vulnerable of
the children, confronted a drinking problem by entering a substance
abuse program and then relocated to New York to enter a graduate program in English literature. Lally, a gifted historian and journalist who had
written several books, including a biography of Thomas Jefferson, as well
as articles for both *Newsweek* and the *Post,* lived in Manhattan (and the
Hamptons) and threw frequent parties to which she invited the leading
members of the New York literary establishment; at one such bash Gore
Vidal and Norman Mailer nearly became involved in a fistfight. Lally's
unpredictable political convictions ran the gamut from radical liberalism
(or "drawing room liberal," as some called her) to hard-core neoconser-

vatism. Her boyfriends followed suit. In the wake of her divorce, she dated a variety of men, ranging from the Marxist writer Alexander Cockburn to right-wing columnist George F. Will. Lally's inconsistent nature, as opposed to Donald Graham's plodding steadfastness, became a contributing factor in Katharine's decision to prepare Donald to eventually take over her position. Another likely factor had been Lally's loud opposition to her mother's growing dependence over the years on men like Robert McNamara and Warren Buffett, to say nothing of Ben Bradlee.

Easily the most volatile of the Graham children, Lally reacted to her mother's snub by approaching *The Washington Times* for a berth as a political columnist. The newspaper, owned and funded by the Unification Church (Reverend Sun Myung Moon), was by this juncture *The Washington Post*'s only major Washington competitor. Arnaud de Borchgrave, then editor of the *Times* and never a great favorite of Katharine Graham's, while pleased with Lally's inquiry, asked her if working for the competition might not be construed as an act of defection. It seemed clear that Lally was using the opposition as a way to even the score with her mother and as leverage to get her mother to hire her as a full-time political columnist at the *Post*. The incident mushroomed into a full-scale family feud, with Donald Graham finally working out the details for an employment agreement whereby Lally's byline would appear regularly in the Outlook section of the *Post*. She also traveled and wrote articles for *Newsweek*.

One of the points of contention between mother and daughter had been Lally's father, Phil Graham, who had frequently told Lally as a child that her mother was "uncultured" and that she (Lally) could outshine her. For years after Phil's suicide, his daughter somehow held her mother to blame, as if there had been something that Kay could have done to prevent her husband's final action. Despite their frequent squabbles, Lally—unlike Sasha Bruce—was able to transcend their differences. In times of need, she fully supported her family. When Carol Felsenthal's critical biography of Kay Graham appeared, occasioning a positive review by Ronald Steel in *The Washington Post*, Lally fired off a long, effusive letter defending her parents' marriage; the *Post* printed the letter in its entirety. When *Vanity Fair* published an excerpt from the same biography, Lally contacted Ina Ginsburg and asked her to write a letter to the magazine condemning the article. Another writer, Lynn Rosselini, author of a well-researched five-part series on Katharine Graham for the *Washington Star,* ran into an even more irate Lally Weymouth. "I was engaged to Graham Wisner at the time, the son of Frank and Polly Wisner," said Rosselini. "The Wisners and Grahams were great friends, so when I contacted Lally Weymouth in New York and asked for an interview, she agreed. I went up to New York and we had what I thought was a good interview. I saw her again at a dinner party at Polly's house. I was there with Graham, and Lally was seated at the same table. Graham asked her, 'Why do you think the *Star* is doing this series on your mother?' And she just took off like a rocket. The series hadn't even run as yet and we'd had this nice interview, and she had no reason to be mad at me. But she's an odious woman, totally off-the-wall. She was practically foaming at the mouth, yelling at me, saying that the only reasons I'd do a profile of her mother were personal advancement and money." When Rosselini and Wisner married, neither Lally nor her mother would attend the wedding ceremony.

Following Donald Graham's takeover as publisher of the *Post,* Katharine stepped back from the newspaper and became more active in other areas. In anticipation of a trip to China, she met with CIA director Stansfield Turner as well as with Evangeline Bruce, who provided her with introductions to many of the people she'd known in Beijing. During the Iran hostage crisis, Kay flew to Egypt to meet with the deposed shah. She agreed to serve on Willy Brandt's Independent Commission on International Development Issues, attending meetings in Germany, Switzerland, Mali, Malaysia, France, and Austria. She became increasingly active in local Washington politics, supporting Home Rule, while backing the controversial Marion Barry for mayor. At a United Nations postvictory press conference, Barry pointed at Katharine Graham and said: "I'm mayor of Washington, D.C., mainly because of that lady over there." "And don't you forget it!" she responded. After Barry's drug conviction and the public airing of his extramarital sexual adventures, Kay and *The Washington Post* came out against Barry. "Barry deceived me," Kay Graham told Evangeline Bruce one afternoon over lunch at the latter's home.

"The worst thing about him," added Vangie, "is his open disdain for the white community. He only adds to the already existent racial tensions that pervade Washington."

Following the late-1976 return to Georgetown of the Coopers, friends of Lorraine noticed that she had undergone a change. Still suffering from the trauma of being sexually assaulted, she developed several strange habits. Evangeline Bruce recalled walking down a Georgetown street with Lorraine, "and she kept turning around and looking behind her. 'What's wrong, darling?' I asked her. 'I think we're being followed,' she said. Beside myself, I don't think anyone knew about her troubles. Ironically, she and I found ourselves enmeshed in a common twist of fate: Lorraine couldn't bring herself to prosecute the man who'd violated her, and I remained powerless to do anything about the man who had killed my daughter. I told Lorraine about a psychiatrist I knew in New York. 'He can help you, darling,' I said. 'Well, then,' she answered, 'if he's so good, why don't you go?' She had a point. Given Phil Graham's mental history, I don't suppose either one of us had much faith in psychotherapy."

Evangeline Bruce, then in her sixties, spent her evenings perusing books in her bathtub and even had a special shelf installed over the tub to house her reading glasses. Along with a number of other women, she dated William Paley but grew weary, as she put it, "of competing with half the women in the world, most of whom are thirty years my junior." She was occasionally escorted to parties by J. Carter Brown, who recalled "her understated sense of humor. She did extremely funny imitations of people, including Jackie Kennedy and Pamela Harriman." An early riser, she frequently gathered her garden tools and walked over to Oak Hill Cemetery to tend the graves of David and Sasha. She was not without her darker moments. Recalling his interview of her for his book on Joe and Stewart Alsop, Robert Merry remarked that she became "surprisingly hostile whenever the name of an old friend cropped up." John C. Whitehead, deputy secretary of state under George Shultz and the second husband of Nancy Dickerson, had a similar reaction, noting that "she could be quite arch and outspoken at times. She developed a mania against certain Jews, which made itself felt now and again." Oatsie Charles found her "bright and vibrant, but she could be a major bitch, very difficult and nasty. Even her friends were aware of this. She'd be eating dinner at somebody's house and in the middle of the meal she'd suddenly stand up and leave. No explanation, no excuse, no good-bye. This practice became more and more prevalent with the passage of time."

Vangie passed part of each summer with Marietta Tree in the Tuscany region of Italy and, in later years, the Provence district of France. She also spent time at a flat she and David Bruce had maintained since 1969 at the Albany, one of London's most prestigious apartment buildings, manned by doormen in top hats and white gloves. R. W. Apple, who owned a small cottage an hour outside London, frequently attended Vangie's parties at the Albany. "She gave famous Sunday brunches both in London and Washington," he said, "at which there would be almost nothing to eat. She'd pass around these platters of seaweed with bits of bacon and a few small quail eggs interspersed. And there were no tables—you stood or sat wherever you could. But it didn't matter because the company was always very special. She had an enormous number of friends and usually had several well-placed British, French, and American politicians on hand. She had an A-plus guest list. Yet for all her connections, she struck me as rather unpretentious, especially in the years following her husband's death. She was very natural. I invited her to a luncheon we were having at the cottage one weekend. I told her it was very casual. We were going to cook in the back garden. So she took the train out from London to Swindon and a cab from Swindon to the house. She arrived early, wearing the most perfectly pressed pair of blue jeans I'd ever seen. I was preparing tandoori chicken on the outdoor grill and she kept nibbling at it. Finally I said, 'Vangie, you've got to stop or there isn't going to be any left for lunchtime.' She made a face like a little kid who'd been caught with her hand in the cookie jar."

Nuella Pell recalled Evangeline's Georgetown brunches: "They took place in this wonderful drawing room with curtains by John Fowler. She served these little nests with quail eggs in them. You kept waiting for a lunch that never came. Of course the guests were great. They alternated from week to week, depending on who was in town. There were the regulars, like Bill and Deeda Blair, British Home Secretary Roy Jenkins, the

Coopers. I once asked Vangie about the food situation, and she said she thought it best for everybody not to eat too much. And that answer seemed perfect."

Whenever Evangeline Bruce and Lorraine Cooper found themselves in Georgetown at the same time, they shared the services of Michael Mangin, Lorraine's British butler. A celebrity among Georgetown retainers, Mangin added to his luster when he agreed to be profiled by *The Washington Post* in 1982, a year after agreeing to become jointly employed. Walking back and forth the six blocks between the two households, Mangin and his two West Highland terriers maintained living quarters in both homes. He had a private telephone line, and the same number rang in both places. An expert in all facets of housekeeping, the butler spoke solemnly to the *Post* reporter about the pratfalls of tarnished silverware. "The silver has to be cleaned properly," he said. "You certainly can't put tarnished silver on the table. And you can't clean it beforehand. The heat and humidity get to it, particularly during the summer in Washington, and it tarnishes so quickly. It simply has to be polished the day of the party. Some days I'm just up to my elbows in silver polish." Mangin went on to tell the *Post* how fortunate he felt to be working for two of Georgetown's most "aristocratic" women, women whose elegance transcended their wealth and power, women who deplored publicity. Their parties were almost never covered by the press, not even by the omnipotent Sally Quinn.

Mangin, who once had worked for the British embassy in Washington, recalled two anecdotes involving Lorraine Cooper. The first was a Cooper dinner party at which President Ford broke his chair and tumbled clumsily to the ground. The second had to do with an enfeebled female guest, a wealthy Georgetown neighbor of Lorraine's, who turned up for a luncheon invitation a day early. "Show her into the dining room," Lorraine told Mangin, while in the kitchen the cook hastily threw together a three-course meal. "It wasn't beautiful," Lorraine concluded afterward, "but it worked."

In early 1979 Lorraine Cooper inadvertently learned that the German businessman who had attacked her in her home in East Berlin had recently died in an automobile accident while on a trip to Italy. "I can't bring myself to gloat over anybody's death," she wrote to Evangeline Bruce, who was then in London, "but the news has set me free!"

Shortly before the 1981 inauguration of Ronald Reagan, Jody Powell, Jimmy Carter's former press secretary, told an interviewer that if he had it to do all over again, he would have arranged for the Carters to have gotten to know "the leading female adherents of the Georgetown power elite." It was this factor, Powell felt, as well as Carter's failure to bring home the American hostages in Iran, that had cost him the election. "The Carters never bothered to embrace the mainstays of the Washington establishment," agreed Nancy Dickerson. "Presidents come and go, but most of us stayed and they did little to endear themselves to the locals. They scorned Washington society. They alienated the press. They created a good deal of resentment, and when they returned to Plains, Georgia, it was as if they'd never been to Washington in the first place."

Apparently the Reagans didn't want to make the same mistake. Before they even left California for Washington, they contacted Katharine Graham—whom they had first met at a governors' conference in California—and invited her to an F Street Club reception they were about to give as well as to one of their first official White House functions. Cognizant of the honor but wary of the gesture, Graham later told friends that "the worst dinner parties in Washington are those given at the White House. Everybody's so impressed with the surroundings that they forget to have fun. The only thing worse are the inaugural galas. If you've been to one, you never want to go to another." Graham returned the favor, so to speak, by throwing her own party at her home in Georgetown in honor of the new president. She eventually became great friends with Nancy Reagan. Distressed by the press coverage accorded her husband's administration, Nancy made Kay a kind of unofficial media adviser, a position that may have clouded the publisher's ability to remain objective, although it should be noted that the *Post* never endorsed Reagan for the presidency, instead backing Jimmy Carter and Walter Mondale. Nevertheless, Nancy often met Kay Graham for lunch, and in the evenings they conferred by telephone. Later Kay invited Nancy to visit her on Martha's Vineyard, a gathering to which she also invited Jacqueline Kennedy Onassis. The first lady's frustrations with the press endured, however, giving rise to an occasion on which she actually grabbed Sally Quinn by the shoulders and gave her a shake.

A mutual friend, Jerome Zipkin, introduced Nancy Reagan to Oatsie Charles, who promptly invited her to lunch. "I immediately liked her," said Oatsie. "A short while later I attended a dinner at the White House. After the meal Ronald Reagan rose and said a few words. Nancy watched him with one of those adoring expressions on her face. Bob Woodward, evidently no fan of the Reagans, made a deprecating remark about Nancy. I took Bob aside and said to him: 'Too bad you don't have a wife or girlfriend looking at you like that.' "

George Will, as well connected as any journalist in Washington, organized an evening for the president-elect and his wife to which he invited those he considered essential to their social success, including Edward Bennett Williams, AFL-CIO chief Lance Kirkland, *Washington Post* editorial page editor Meg Greenfield, former Democratic National Committee chairman Robert Strauss, and Evangeline Bruce. Seated next to Bruce, Nancy Reagan told her she'd always been an admirer and asked if she could visit privately with her and some of her friends. Vangie subsequently arranged an intimate luncheon at her Georgetown home, had the meal catered with health food from Chez Wok, and invited four of her pals: Lorraine Cooper, Susan Mary Alsop, Jessica Catto, and Patricia Haig (wife of Alexander Haig, the newly appointed secretary of state). "I was prepared not to appreciate Mrs. Reagan," said Evangeline Bruce to the current author. "But I changed my mind. By reaching out to us, she was establishing the beginning of a bond. The fact that most of us were either Democrats or, in the case of Lorraine, moderate Republicans, didn't matter."

Aside from Kay Graham and Evangeline Bruce, Nancy's strongest bond seemed to be with Lorraine Cooper. Approximately six months after the mid-1981 attempt on President Reagan's life by John Hinckley, the Reagans attended a private dinner party given by the Coopers. Not only were the streets of Georgetown closed off by yellow vinyl tape and police vans, but Secret Service cars were also parked on the sidewalks to prevent passers-by from entering the area. In addition the Reagans were accompanied by a SWAT team and a food taster. Any confidences that might have been exchanged over dinner were outweighed by the extreme safety measures taken to protect the president. Even Lorraine, always conscientious when it came to such matters, thought it a bit much. "A food taster!" she exclaimed after the couple's departure. "It's not as if we were about to braise Ronald and Nancy's chicken in arsenic."

CHAPTER TWELVE

GEORGETOWN GOES HOLLYWOOD

IN APRIL 1976, Hollywood superstar Elizabeth Taylor arrived in Washington, D.C., as the special guest of Secretary of State Henry Kissinger, whom she had first met during a visit to Israel the year before. Taylor, whose second divorce from Richard Burton had not yet been finalized, saw the venture as a welcome diversion from the tedium of starring in a string of mediocre American- and European-financed films. One event she hoped to attend while in Washington was a gala benefit for the American Ballet Theater to be held at the John F. Kennedy Center for the Performing Arts. In preparation for the trip she had telephoned Halston, who flew to Liz's side at the Beverly Hills Hotel, where she occupied bungalow number eight. In her midforties, with her deep tan and violet eyes, she still bore a strong resemblance to the young Elizabeth Taylor. "She told me," said Halston, "that although she owned a blue gown for her sapphires, a red number for her rubies, a green one for her emeralds, she needed something yellow to match her yellow diamonds. She also wanted a burnt orange gown to go with a magnificent emerald-and-diamond necklace that Burton had given her shortly before their final separation. She wanted a discount, so I offered her the same deal I extended to all my name clients, including Kay Graham—a 40 percent deduction if she allowed me to handle all her wardrobe needs."

Elizabeth wore the burnt orange ensemble the night of the ABT gala. After the performance she, Halston, Liza Minnelli, and Teddy Westreich—who had helped organize the function—clambered into Henry Kissinger's black bulletproof limousine and were driven to the Iranian embassy, along Embassy Row, to attend a late-night, black-tie dinner-dance arranged by Iranian Ambassador Ardeshir Zahedi.

Ambassador Zahedi's extravaganzas—sponsored by the fabulously wealthy shah of Iran, to whose daughter, Princess Shanaz, the ambassador had once been married—were frequently enhanced by an exotic array of party activities, from conga lines and belly dancers to drinking games and recreational drugs. People were still talking about the night Clare Boothe Luce, Marlene Dietrich, and Pamela Harriman rose to their feet and began emulating the undulating movements of the nubile belly dancers engaged by Zahedi for the occasion. Or the party at which a dozen influential male lobbyists were "entertained" by an equal number of high-priced, scantily attired party girls, similarly supplied by the embassy. On the evening that Elizabeth Taylor showed up, 180 guests sat at fifteen round tables in the embassy ballroom, an enormous golden salon topped by an ornately mirrored forty-foot ceiling. While mountains of caviar (from the shah's private stock) and chilled Iranian vodka were offered as the first course, Taylor chatted amicably with several of her tablemates, among them Rudolf Nureyev and former White House chief of protocol Angier Biddle Duke. But it was the gentleman directly to her right, Ambassador Ardeshir Zahedi, his large liquid dark eyes trained on hers, who most intrigued her.

"That was the night," said Betty Beale, a guest at the same function, "when Zahedi and Liz danced together with their arms wrapped around each other. Although she broke away at one point to do the hustle—the latest dance craze—with Massachusetts Senator Edward Brooke, she quickly returned to Zahedi, and by the end of the evening they both had their appointment books and were mapping out their future plans."

Zahedi and Taylor turned up several weeks later at Pisces, Georgetown's newest nightclub, opened the year before by Wyatt Dickerson and

Peter Malatesta, a nephew of Bob Hope and former aide to Spiro Agnew. Tongsun Park, a silent partner in Pisces, also owned The Georgetown Club, an exclusive facility on Wisconsin Avenue that opened in 1966. Park, an ostentatious man-about-town had arrived in Washington from South Korea in 1956 ostensibly to attend Georgetown University. On the one hand a mover and shaker with close ties to the Washington political community, Park was also known as an influence peddler with established connections to the KCIA, the Korean Central Intelligence Agency, which had evidently helped finance several of his ventures. His indictment in 1977 by the Justice Department for bribery of U.S. government officials (with cash and gifts) ended with a slap on the wrist for several U.S. congressmen accused of accepting bribes and with Park's temporary return to his homeland. Koreagate, as it commonly became known, tarnished the image of Pisces. It was still, according to Wyatt Dickerson, "the hottest private watering hole in Washington—and also the fanciest." The club, as its name suggested, featured several saltwater aquariums full of exotic fish in the middle of the dance floor, with a large tank behind the bar, housing a three-foot baby sand shark. The centerpiece of Pisces consisted of a twenty-foot waterfall at the club's entrance, which emptied into a giant goldfish pool on the floor below.

Nancy Dickerson, Wyatt's then wife, happened to be at Pisces the first time Zahedi and Taylor came in. "I already knew about their romance," she said, "because I'd recently given a party for Henry Kissinger. Kissinger had asked me to invite Senator Hugh Scott of Pennsylvania, Senate minority leader, to the same party because he'd wanted to discuss something with him. Henry absolutely believed in the social scene as a way to conduct politics. I remember seeing Kissinger and Scott facing each other, their elbows on the mantel, drinks in hand. They seemed immersed in conversation, but when Henry saw me he started talking about Elizabeth Taylor and Ardeshir Zahedi and what a 'torrid romance' they were having. She'd actually moved into the royal suite at the Iranian embassy, an elaborately decorated cluster of rooms ordinarily reserved for Empress Farah Diba's stateside visits. One conclusion to be drawn was that nobody loved Hollywood and Washington gossip more than Henry Kissinger.

"The night I saw them at Pisces, Zahedi invited me to a caviar luncheon to be held at the embassy the following day in honor of Elizabeth. I attended the luncheon and then saw them again a day later at a gala given by the Bicentennial Year Committee, chaired by former Secretary of the Navy John Warner. At one point, Warner went over and introduced himself to Elizabeth. He asked her for a dance the first chance he got, but she politely declined. She and Zahedi were very much an item. They were inseparable. They went to the horse races, where she was photographed practically seated in his lap. They were seen at a dinner-dance for senators, congressmen, Supreme Court justices, ambassadors, and White House officials at the Chevy Chase Country Club. The sparks that flew between them almost ignited the room."

In their more private moments, Taylor and Zahedi regaled each other with stories of people they once knew. Well aware of Elizabeth's fondness for priceless baubles, the ambassador related the saga of Evelyn Walsh McLean, the enormously wealthy yet sadly misguided 1930s mining heiress and owner of the Hope Diamond, whose idea of fun entailed playing craps with local police officials in the Georgetown precinct house and, while the wagering ensued, allowing her Great Dane to play with her fabulous jewels. One evening the hungry canine devoured a black pearl necklace she had purchased at Harry Winston and recklessly draped around the animal's neck. To retrieve the valuable necklace, the heiress assigned her valet the unappetizing chore of sifting through the dog's daily deposits until, one by one, the pearls reappeared. Once recovered, the pearls were returned to the jeweler to be restrung.

When exactly the subject of matrimony first arose between Taylor and Zahedi is anybody's guess. "I believe Elizabeth mentioned it over breakfast one morning," said Zahedi, "but I'm not really sure. I think I told her she was still married, which precluded any other possibility." The topic seems to have come up again. This time Zahedi sidestepped the issue by pointing out that such a serious undertaking required the permission of the shah. When Elizabeth persisted, the ambassador ordered a wardrobe for Liz at Saks-Jandel in Chevy Chase and arranged a ten-day, all-expense-paid vacation for her in Iran. She intended to confront the shah directly.

To give the journey a sense of legitimacy, Zahedi invited a number of his friends to join Elizabeth, including Cloris Leachman, Connie Stevens, Page Lee Hufty, and Chicago journalist Marion Christy, who recalled their departure from JFK Airport: "There stood Liz in a tacky, breast-revealing striped dress making goo-goo eyes at her man of the moment. Ambassador Zahedi had come to the airport to see her off. There had been some recent rumblings in the press that as soon as the Burton divorce became final, Liz and Ardeshir would walk down the aisle together. The truth of the matter is that the shah opposed the relationship, Zahedi being a Muslim and Liz a converted Jew, a step she undertook prior to marrying Eddie Fisher."

From Taylor's perspective, the trip proved a complete failure. Another American journalist on the tour, Frances Leighton, described Liz's meeting at the Nalvaran Palace, the royal summer residence, with Empress Farah Diba. "The empress held a reception for the group in the palace gardens," said Leighton. "Liz wore a clinging gold sheath with diamonds dangling from her neck, wrists, and earlobes. The empress barely spoke to her. She seemed disgusted by Liz's garish apparel and gaudy jewels. You had to feel sorry for Taylor. She'd come all this way to meet the royal couple in the event Zahedi proposed to her, and they wouldn't give her the time of day." *Zar E Rus*, Iran's leading news weekly, depicted the actress as "a short, big-busted woman with poor makeup skills and totally out of fashion. She is rude, vulgar, egocentric, and an ignoramus so far as cultural matters are concerned. It is difficult to understand why Westerners consider her a film icon."

"Liz was crushed," said Louis Scarone, a New York physician who'd joined the expedition in an effort to convince Iranian dignitaries to contribute to an international health organization he'd just founded. "She couldn't stop crying. It was our last night in Teheran and a farewell dinner had been arranged. Liz refused to leave her hotel room. I spent the evening alone with her. She blamed her failed mission on Ardeshir Zahedi and condemned the shah for treating her so poorly. I told her that the shah was nothing more than a CIA puppet, installed and maintained by the U.S. government. 'In two or three years,' I said, 'he'll be overthrown and they'll bring back the Ayatollah, and nobody will even re-

member what the shah looked like. As for Zahedi, he's a playboy plenipo-
tentiary. He dotes on celebrities. He's a lightweight.' "

Back in the States, Elizabeth moved out of the Iranian embassy and
into a three-bedroom hotel suite at the Sherry Netherland in New York.
She began hanging out at Studio 54 with Halston and Bianca Jagger, partied with Paloma Picasso and Truman Capote, spent her weekends at the
borrowed summer homes of Andy Warhol and Calvin Klein. In June
1976, when Arab terrorists hijacked an El Al airliner that was then used
as a bargaining chip between the Israelis and the Palestinians, Elizabeth
held a press conference in New York and announced her willingness to
be substituted for the hundred predominantly Jewish hostages being
held by Idi Amin at Entebbe Airport in Uganda. Hearing of Taylor's offer,
Henry Kissinger rebuked her, pointing out that her pronouncements
could undermine the delicate balance of negotiations that were already
under way. On July Fourth, while most Americans celebrated the nation's
Bicentennial, a team of Israeli commandos raided Entebbe, freed the
hostages, and returned with them to Jerusalem. Six months later Taylor
capitalized on the event by appearing (in a cameo role) with Kirk Douglas, Burt Lancaster, Anthony Hopkins, and Helen Hayes in *Victory at Entebbe,* an ABC-TV docudrama detailing the events leading to the Israeli
rescue operation. For her fleeting participation in the project the actress
purportedly received a salary in excess of $100,000.

Taylor's next assault on Washington took place on July 8, 1976, when
she arrived to attend a ball at the British embassy in honor of Queen Elizabeth. Lady Frances Ramsbotham, wife of the British ambassador, had
arranged for the British-born actress to be escorted to the event by John
Warner, who appeared at the Madison Hotel in white tie and tails to pick
up his date. Taylor, barely able to recall her previous introduction to
Warner, remembered only "coming out of my hotel bedroom the night of
the British embassy affair and seeing this marvelous head of silky hair.
Then he turned around and said, 'Ah, Miss Taylor,' and I thought,
'Wow!' " She said at another point that her first impression of the fifty-
year-old Warner was that "of an extraordinarily virile, powerful, and
wealthy man," which is precisely the impression he wanted to impart.

The source of his wealth, estimated in 1975 to 1976 at roughly $10 million ($50 million less than Taylor's worth at the time), stemmed from his marriage to Catherine Mellon, daughter of the enormously rich Paul Mellon. Catherine, whose politics became increasingly radical over the years, found herself out of step with her conservative husband. The staunchly Republican Paul Mellon, on the other hand, sided with his son-in-law. Just as the Mellons, in a somewhat similar instance, had once made David K. E. Bruce a wealthy man, they now saw to it that John Warner received a sizable divorce settlement. It consisted primarily of two exceedingly prime real estate properties: a 2,700-acre estate in the Virginia countryside and an exclusive fifteen-room mansion within the boundaries of Georgetown.

Earnest and hardworking, Warner, whose father had been a prominent Washington, D.C., gynecologist, attended Washington and Lee University in Virginia, where he unabashedly solicited dates by scouring the pages of the Social Register and the *Green Book*, the latest editions of which he kept prominently displayed on his desk. He subsequently entered the University of Virginia Law School, dropping out after a year to serve as a commissioned officer in the Korean War. Completing his legal studies, he joined the elite Washington law firm of Hogan and Hartson. After his divorce from Catherine Mellon in the early 1970s, he dated a succession of well-connected women, including Barbara Walters, whom he saw both before and after Taylor, on one occasion telling her: "A woman like you could probably get me elected senator." He asked her to marry him; she declined but told friends, "John's a wonderful lover."

In Elizabeth Taylor he found a similar, if not greater, driving force. Following the British embassy salute to Queen Elizabeth, he and Taylor danced the night away at Pisces. He then dropped her off at her hotel for a few hours of rest, retrieving her later that morning to give her the grand tour of his Virginia spread, Atoka Farm, midway between Middleburg and Upperville. The pastoral landscape of well-kempt fields and meadows bordered by old stone walls, trees, ponds, and creeks reminded Elizabeth of the peaceful English countryside of her childhood. As they approached the long, winding driveway of Atoka, Warner pointed out a yellow, one-story cottage set in the woods high on a nearby rise overlooking the foothills leading to the Blue Ridge Mountains.

"That's Wexford," he said. "John F. Kennedy built it for Jackie so she could escape the White House on weekends. After the assassination, she sold it."

All the land that comprised both Atoka and Wexford had once belonged to Paul Mellon, whose 13,000-acre estate abutted Warner's. The Mellons had given the Wexford parcel as a gift to the Kennedys. John Warner had lived at Atoka with Catherine Mellon and their three children, who continued to visit the farm now that it belonged solely to their father.

Paul Mellon's largesse made itself felt in other areas as well. A substantial contributor of funds to the Republican Party, he used his influence to convince Richard Nixon in 1969 to name Warner undersecretary of the navy. When Nixon subsequently promoted him to secretary of the navy, several presidential aides, including H. R. Haldeman, wondered whether Warner possessed the intelligence and training to fulfill the requirements of the post. Nixon defended the appointment by declaring that "being secretary of the navy is such a nothing job even John Warner can handle it." Another Warner-as-ignoramus anecdote making the rounds had it that when Alexander Haig, chief of staff under Nixon, first spoke to the secretary of the navy about becoming head of the Bicentennial committee, Warner's response had been, "Al, I can't even spell it."

When Elizabeth Taylor heard the Haig story, she dismissed it as a bad joke, insisting that if anything it pointed to John's "wry sense of humor and genial manner." Nor did it surprise her that from the beginning Warner often referred to himself as "just an old-fashioned country farmer," a claim so modest and offhanded that one of his Virginia neighbors responded by saying, "Come on, John. You're the only farmer in the state with a swimming pool in your barn." Liz was as impressed as the neighbor had been with Warner's so-called farm, starting with a twenty-two-room 1816 fieldstone manor house replete with a den reminiscent of the Oval Office bedecked with flags representing each branch of the military, a captain's chair, and an assortment of Bicentennial mementos. Outside, scattered about the property, were the barns that were used for Warner's six hundred head of Hereford cattle and dozen thoroughbred horses, an outdoor pool and bathhouse, trout-stocked ponds, vegetable and flower gardens, smokehouse, tennis courts, and a five-hundred-acre wildlife preserve. The barn-enclosed swimming pool referred to by his neighbor had evidently been covered over with hardwood floorboards and transformed into a ballroom dance floor.

The charm of the rolling landscape, the patterns of courtesy and cohesiveness, were not lost on Elizabeth. Extending her visit, she stayed the weekend and the better part of the following week. She returned a weekend later, and the couple took a picnic lunch by jeep into the surrounding hills. A sudden summer downpour drenched them as they lay in the long grass, hugging each other, discussing plans for a long-term future together. John Warner may not have been a world-class intellect, but he captivated Elizabeth with talk of a world—Washington politics—that was far from Hollywood and largely unfamiliar to her. In her eyes, Warner represented not only the possibility of future happiness, but also the probability of future success. He told her he had already gathered a campaign team to help him run as the 1978 Republican senatorial candidate in Virginia. And one day he might even consider running for higher office, possibly the highest office in the land. "If not me, then who?" he is reported to have said to her.

A lifelong Democrat, Taylor suddenly switched her allegiance to the Republican Party, concomitantly revealing to the press her desire to become "a country farmer's wife." "I feel safe here," she said. "It's been a long time since I felt that way." Despite her political conversion and their marital intentions, Liz remained pro-choice on abortion and a supporter of the Equal Rights Amendment, as well as an opponent of her husband's conviction that women had no business being in the armed services. Although she agreed to stop wearing her "big jewels," as Warner called them, she made it clear that she had no intention of becoming a lockstep Republican. To John's dismay, she even campaigned for other Democratic candidates, joining Shirley MacLaine in New York to help organize a birthday party/fund-raiser for Bella Abzug. She attended another New York fund-raiser for Jimmy Carter and, wearing a golden pearl necklace, posed for photographers with her arm around him.

Influential Republicans (and Democrats) wondered (often aloud) whether Warner's political aspirations could be realized if he married this multidivorced celluloid queen whose daily peregrinations graced every gossip and supermarket tabloid from New York to California. Although Warner's ties to the Mellon family guaranteed him entrance into Washington's highest and mightiest social and political echelons, his future bride would have to win favor on her own merit. Katharine Graham saw her for the first time later that summer at a glitzy White House affair hosted by President and Mrs. Gerald Ford, when several hundred guests gathered in the Rose Garden to be entertained by Ella Fitzgerald, Tammy Wynette, and Roger Smith. She was not impressed by Taylor. "Liz was there with John Warner," Kay wrote to Evangeline Bruce. "She had evidently burned or otherwise injured her right leg while riding on the back of a motorcycle earlier in the day. Hollywood goddess that she is, she kept whining and moaning throughout the performances, ruining the evening for all those around her. I imagine John Warner sees her as a ticket to victory in some future political race, but I can't see why else he'd want her around."

Others expressed a similar viewpoint. Newton Steers Jr., a political adviser to Warner and his best man at the Catherine Mellon wedding, recalled that "there were constant tiffs between John and Elizabeth. I remember a Republican Party fund-raising swimming pool party at which Liz was posing for photographers. After a while, John said to her, 'Honey, they've photographed you in every conceivable situation, but I don't think I've ever seen you photographed on a diving board.' To which she replied very loudly, 'Don't tell me what to do, buster!' At another event, they arrived late, looking rather frazzled. 'She didn't want to come,' John whispered to me, at which point Liz headed for the ladies' room. She didn't come out for about twenty minutes, so my wife, Nina Auchincloss, went in and found her swigging from a bottle of Jack Daniel's. 'What the hell do you see in her?' I asked John. 'Votes,' he said quietly, 'lots of votes.' "

Nina Auchincloss, the half sister of Jackie Kennedy, observed that Elizabeth "seemed extremely curious about Jackie and constantly assailed me with questions about her. I had the sense she wanted to do for John Warner what Jackie had accomplished on behalf of John F. Kennedy—that is, add glamour and panache to a campaign primarily steeped in the drudgery of political infighting and technicalities. I think she thought that Warner had presidential prospects and that she would follow in Jackie's footsteps as a future first lady. He, in turn, regarded her as a high-profile asset, a person adored by the masses who could help him navigate his way through the political labyrinth, first in Virginia and later in his bid for national office."

Warner and Taylor became engaged on October 10, 1976, during the filming in Vienna, Austria, of A Little Night Music, Stephen Sondheim's highly successful Broadway musical. News of the engagement, which followed by six weeks the Haitian divorce of Taylor and Burton (and Burton's remarriage three weeks later to model Suzy Hunt), overshadowed Taylor's uninspired performance in the film adaptation. The engagement ring, designed by Warner, featured red, white, and blue stones — a ruby, diamonds, and sapphire to symbolize the couple's meeting during the Bicentennial year.

John Warner's girlfriend in the months immediately preceding Elizabeth Taylor was Tandy Dickinson, a one-time companion of the controversial Tongsun Park and the future wife of C. Wyatt Dickerson, whose marriage to Nancy Dickerson would soon begin to erode. Tandy learned of Warner's engagement to Taylor not from him but by reading about it in the newspaper. "I happened to be on a transatlantic flight headed for Washington," explained Tandy. "The stewardess handed me a copy of the New York Daily News, and there, on the front page, was a photo of John and Liz with a caption announcing their engagement. When I reached Washington I called John. He confirmed the story. He had fallen for her. And why not? I mean, you're talking about one of the best-known women in the world. What better way to become one of the best-known men?"

They were married on December 4, 1976, atop the same hill in Virginia where they had first picnicked and snuggled during a sudden downpour three months earlier. Warner arrived at the site first, dressed in a dark business suit, accompanied by his teenage son and several personal friends. Elizabeth arrived two hours later, attired in a dress of lavender gray, accompanied by Chen Sam, her press agent, who accidentally set foot in a pile of fresh cow manure. The couple, in something approximating an abbreviated Episcopal ceremony, exchanged rings, vows, and kisses. The following day they left for England on a six-week honeymoon.

In mid-March 1977 the newlyweds sat in Warner's Virginia kitchen and fielded questions put to them by Barbara Walters, who had recently moved from NBC to ABC-TV. Liz, unaware that Walters had once been her husband's paramour, spoke frankly about her ever-expanding waistline, blaming it on inactivity due to a series of mishaps precipitated by a fall from a horse. Continuing her saga, Liz disclosed that Warner's nicknames for her were "Chicken Fat," "My Little Heifer," and "Pooters" (rhymes with "Hooters"), and that her favorite meal consisted of fried chicken accompanied by "a heaping dish of mashed potatoes drowned in butter." "You ought to eat more vegetables for dinner," Warner admonished her.

Nothing was said about the lavish country breakfasts Taylor devoured whenever she accompanied John to the Warrenton Hunt Club, of which he remained an avid member, often joining other members to ride to the hounds. The day before the Barbara Walters interview, Pooters attended a hunt club buffet, downing an array of white jug wines, lasagna, Virginia ham, homegrown green salad, cheeses, biscuits, and a chocolate-covered seven-layer cake. "I had the misfortune," Lorraine Cooper wrote to Evangeline Bruce, "of being present at a hunt club breakfast and having to watch Mrs. Warner graze in near ecstasy on every platter laid out before her." Vangie's response: "I don't know her, but I do him— John Warner is dreadful, one of the dumbest, most uninformed men I've ever met."

Long before he became a senator, John Warner had his share of critics. Francesca Hilton, the daughter of Zsa Zsa Gabor and a former sister-in-law of Elizabeth Taylor (whose first husband was Nicky Hilton), labeled him "a complete macho asshole, the kind of man the feminist movement loved to hate." Frances Bowerstock, sister of Carol Bowerstock, the mayor of Middleburg, worked at Dominion Saddlery. "I've known John Warner since we were both about fifteen years old, and while I have nothing against his politics, I always thought him an arrogant son-of-a-bitch. He and Elizabeth were regular customers at Dominion. She never made any demands, just came in like everybody else, never made herself known. She looked around and waited her turn. She couldn't have been sweeter, nicer, easier to wait on. But when he came in with her, he'd push himself ahead of everybody. 'Do you realize who I'm with?' he'd say, 'This is Elizabeth Taylor, *the* Elizabeth Taylor.' He'd insist that I wait on them first. She'd tell him to shut up and wait his turn."

To keep busy, Elizabeth volunteered to become involved in the annual fund-raiser for Wolf Trap Farm Park, an outdoor performing arts center situated on a lilac-scented tract of land in the Virginia countryside outside the Beltway. Working with Steve Martindale, the public relations whiz kid whose reputation had long since been sullied by Sally Quinn, Taylor managed to round up a celebrity cast of volunteer performers, including Liza Minnelli, Beverly Sills, and Sammy Davis Jr., as well as Halston, who agreed to design the tents and tablecloths for the two-day affair. Despite Taylor's involvement, the June 1977 Wolf Trap benefit failed to attract any of the more generous benefactors who usually contributed to the event.

"They raised less money that year than any year before or since," said Halston. "The big donors, the members of the wealthy Georgetown set, clearly resented Elizabeth Taylor's efforts. Worn and dejected, we drank away our sorrows and went on a midnight joy ride, Liz dressed in a mink coat with a sheer nightgown underneath, while I had on my tuxedo. With Elizabeth at the wheel, we drove to the foot of the Lincoln Memorial. While a cluster of homeless men and women looked on in dumbfounded silence, Liz delivered an impromptu rendition of the *Gettysburg Address*. We then got back in our car and headed for an all-night White Castle, where we ordered chocolate milk shakes, onion rings, and a dozen burgers each. After a while the counter girl, who'd been watching Liz pace back and forth, said to her: 'Excuse me, aren't you Elizabeth Taylor, the famous actress?' 'Yes, I am,' she answered. 'Now where are those fucking hamburgers?' "

By the fall of 1977, John and Liz were in the full swing of political life and were alternating between the Virginia homestead and 3240 S Street, Warner's ten-thousand-square-foot Georgetown residence, a two-story brick house with landscaped, walled gardens and an outdoor swimming pool, half a block from Dumbarton Oaks. A rare Georgetown "modern," Warner's house had been built by Paul Mellon in 1962 and filled with French and English antiques. It contained six bedrooms, nine baths, bow-windowed drawing room, library, twin pantries, fully equipped chef's kitchen, office suite, media and exercise rooms, and a private spa with sauna. Warner had also personally installed a sophisticated room-to-room intercom system similar to the type in use on U.S. naval vessels during the Korean War. And like many a naval officer, Warner took great pleasure in barking orders over the intercom, his voice crackling and reverberating throughout the house: "Now hear this, now hear this . . ." "You can imagine how all this went down with La Liz," said Halston. "Within weeks she insisted the system be dismantled. He didn't argue with her."

Another source of annoyance for the actress was their Georgetown neighbor. Catherine Mellon lived next door, a domestic arrangement that had proved convenient when the couple's children were still young. Now they were older, and the proximity of Warner's former wife didn't sit well with his current spouse.

Occasional setbacks notwithstanding, Elizabeth threw herself into her husband's political campaign, contributing $200,000 of her own money to his war chest, attending fund-raisers, making appearances when and where needed. Hospitalized with a painful case of bursitis, she went to several functions in a wheelchair. She shook the hands of so many well-wishers that she began extending only her right pinky when greeting supporters. "I broke my hand and ass for John," she quipped some time later.

In the middle of their Washington and Virginia activities, the Warners flew to Los Angeles to appear in *Winter Kills,* a black comedy modeled in part on John F. Kennedy's presidency. Warner played the nonspeaking role of JFK, while Elizabeth acted the part of his mistress. For her fleeting appearance, she demanded—and received—the $40,000 lynx coat worn by her character in the film. Commenting on Warner's impersonation of JFK, C. Wyatt Dickerson voiced the opinion that "John's future as an actor was always in grave doubt."

On January 26, 1978, John Warner officially announced his candidacy as the Republican senator from Virginia, simultaneously declaring his intention to raise additional campaign funds by selling off a thousand acres of Atoka in twenty-five-acre parcels. One of Warner's less admiring neighbors, Pamela Harriman, coowner with her husband, Averell Harriman, of a sixty-acre horse farm in Middleburg, reacted by launching a letter-writing campaign, warning local landowners that "if John Warner lives up to his threat, the value of your land will decrease precipitously, and the Virginia countryside will begin to look like Disneyland." Warner's money-making scheme ultimately fell by the wayside.

Despite Elizabeth's direct participation, on June 3, 1978, Warner lost a close election to Dick Obenshain, his popular incumbent opponent. Warner was still mourning his defeat when, ten days later, an incredible event took place: Obenshain's small private airplane crashed near his home in Chesterfield, Virginia, instantly killing the nominee and his pilot. Promising to assume Obenshain's campaign debt, Warner received the grieving widow's endorsement and thus the Republican Party's nomination as senatorial candidate.

Determined to put on an Oscar-winning performance as the candidate's wife, Elizabeth applied herself to the task with a new-found intensity. She joined her husband at a luncheon meeting of the archly conservative Richmond Bar Association, waved to the crowd from the back of a white Cadillac convertible at the annual Charlottesville Dogwood Festival, accompanied Warner to the Founder's Day ceremony at the Virginia Military Academy. Interviewed by People magazine, Elizabeth said, "My job is now with my husband. I love my life in Virginia." As John Warner and his Democratic opponent for the seat, Virginia's attorney general Andrew P. Miller, traversed the state trading barbs and insults, Elizabeth found herself at the center of the fray, attending campaign breakfasts, brunches, lunches, and dinners, as many as six and seven a day. "If I had eaten another southern fried chicken leg or helping of potato salad," said Taylor, "I would have burst." As photographs of her during this period indicate, she nearly did.

It wasn't easy. She couldn't so much as freshen up without drawing a crowd. Women—complete strangers—would follow her into the ladies' room. Somebody once stuck a camera underneath her bathroom stall door and took a photograph. At a campaign barbecue in Stone Gap, Virginia, a chicken bone became wedged in Elizabeth's throat and had to be removed with a pair of forceps at a nearby hospital. The incident gave

rise to a comic skit on TV's *Saturday Night Live* with John Belushi bur-
lesquing an obese Elizabeth Taylor choking to death on a half-eaten
chicken leg. The clownish image of a leading film siren expanding to
nearly twice her normal size impressed itself upon the American consciousness. Elizabeth Taylor had once been the woman that every woman
in America wanted to look like—and now they all did. Joan Rivers, appearing on *The Tonight Show,* reeled off a series of Elizabeth Taylor fat
jokes, which soon became a regular feature of her act. Also in on the carnage was *The Washington Post,* which revealed in an article that the
"often married" Miss Taylor had for tax purposes never relinquished her
British citizenship and was thus not eligible to vote for her husband. A
Doonesbury cartoon in the same paper referred to the Republican candidate as "Mr. Elizabeth Taylor."

On November 7, 1978, Election Day, John Warner eked out the nar-
rowest of victories, upsetting Andrew Miller by less than one percentage
point. Sworn in as a U.S. senator on January 16, 1979, he vowed to "serve
the needs" of his constituency to the utmost of his abilities. Elizabeth, in
her own words, had "graduated" from "candidate's wife to senatorial
squaw."

"Just when she thought the fun would begin," said Phil Smith, John
Warner's new press secretary, "things got tough. Senator Warner was
working his butt off and barely had time for Elizabeth. She insisted on
moving permanently into the Georgetown home and visiting Atoka only
on weekends, the idea being that they would become part of the Georgetown social scene. But it didn't happen. The Georgetown ladies didn't exactly embrace Elizabeth. And Warner never had time. She practically
had to beg him to go out to dinner. In fact, as his press secretary, I saw
more of him than she did."

On her forty-seventh birthday, Elizabeth ended up alone when her
husband called to say he had too much work to take her out for dinner.
Feeling sorry for her, Liz's friend Dominique D'Ermo, proprietor of her
favorite Washington restaurant, Dominique's, brought over a number of
sumptuous dishes (including a chocolate birthday cake) and sat with her
while she dined. "Elizabeth told me," said D'Ermo, "that Senator Warner
had become obsessed with showing up at every roll call vote. He wanted

to maintain a perfect attendance record. He would return home exhausted in the late evening and say, 'Pooters, why don't you pour yourself a Jack Daniel's and go upstairs and watch TV. I'll join you a bit later.' So she would pour herself a drink and watch TV and wait for another day. 'It's as if,' she said, 'John married the Senate, and I wasn't even invited to the wedding.' "

"Liz quickly wearied of the regimen," said Phil Smith. "At one point she spent two weeks at a fat farm—the Palm Aire Spa in Pompano Beach, Florida—but returned weighing more than ever. During the day she'd sit around the swimming pool in Georgetown, basking in the sun, munching junk food, washing it down with booze. She became so bored she began hanging around with Warner's son and some of his pals, ferrying them about in her limousine, accompanying them to a gay club in Georgetown called The Fraternity House. Warner suggested that she become involved with the Republican Women's Committee. 'And do what?' she inquired. 'Fold bandages for the American Red Cross? No thanks.' "

The essential Georgetown experience had begun to sour for Elizabeth. "Washington is the cruelest city in the world for a woman," she told a reporter for *The Washington Post*. Photographed by the *Post* at a French embassy dinner party in a low-cut lavender gown, she received a visit the following day from Hank Lampey, a member of a support group known as Friends of John Warner. Lampey curtly informed her that her attire was inappropriate to her position as the wife of a senator. "It's too purple and too Hollywood," he said. "People are talking."

"And what are they saying, Mr. Lampey?"

"That you're showing off. That you're out of touch with Washington. That you ought to dress down a bit more than you do."

Elizabeth's idea of "dressing down" was to start wearing cowgirl fashions: tight jeans, denim jackets, fancy western boots. The Georgetown Ladies' Social Club did not approve; neither did the Virginia arm of the Republican Party.

To escape further criticism, Elizabeth took off for New York for a week and sought out Halston and Andy Warhol. According to Warhol's *Diaries,* the actress snorted cocaine and admitted that John Warner hadn't slept with her in months. She blamed her husband's libidinal indifference on her weight gain. She blamed the extra weight on an excess of alcohol: "If you're not in government, there's nothing to do in Washington except drink yourself to death."

In early July 1979 the Warners attended the annual senatorial garden party at the Georgetown residence of Lorraine and John Sherman Cooper. Lorraine, in a blue and white Yves St. Laurent cotton plaid whose ruffled hem swept up on one side to reveal a trim and still provocative knee, stood with her husband in their elegantly appointed drawing room. Flicking a colored straw fan back and forth as much to stave off kisses as to circulate the warm evening air, Lorraine greeted her guests with a cautious smile. "Don't kiss me—it's too hot," she warned those who approached with puckered lips. Even so, there were those who managed to bypass the fan, among them Ambassador Ellsworth Bunker and Alexander Haig.

Ted Kennedy appeared. "I'm going to come over and have lunch with you and not tell your husband about it," he whispered into her ear.

"It'll drive my husband crazy," Lorraine whispered back, with a coquettish lift of an eyebrow.

By the time John and Elizabeth slipped past the front door—they were thirty minutes late—most of the guests had wandered into the garden, where a large number of tables had been set to accommodate the crowd. People were trapped in the aisles, unable because of the crush to reach the buffet table and, more critically, the bar.

Having already visited the bar, the Warners took a table next to the makeshift dance floor in a corner of the garden, where they were joined by fellow Virginia Senator Harry F. Byrd Jr. and his wife. Although Liz had taken pains to dress in moderation by wearing a standard blue-gray Halston evening gown, the outfit appeared tight-fitting on her swollen frame. People gawked at the actress, and those who gawked hardest caught sight of the white, square-cut, 33.19-carat Krupp diamond on the ring finger of her right hand, a souvenir from her days with Richard Burton. The diamond had once belonged to Vera Krupp, of the family that made munitions for Germany in World War II.

"It lit up the night," said Senator Jacob Javits, who went over to catch a closer glimpse. "I always think it's poetic justice that a nice Jewish girl like me gets to wear it," Taylor said to Javits, holding up the ring and slurring her words. "In general," he said, "Elizabeth looked a bit out of sorts that evening, unfocused, off-key, as if she'd had too much to drink or taken too many pharmaceuticals." Seated at a nearby table, Evangeline Bruce made a similar observation. "She seemed ill at ease, despite the fact that a steady stream of well-wishers dropped by their table, including Attorney General Griffin Bell and Chief Justice Warren Burger."

Covering the event for *The Washington Post,* society columnist Donnie Radcliffe avoided mentioning Taylor by name, instead writing, "The band played a little night music for anyone able to reach the dance floor. Seated around it, nearly but not entirely unnoticed, were the two senators from Virginia with their wives. Within a short period of time, the group slipped out through the kitchen door."

Liz's sudden departure so vexed Lorraine Cooper, in many respects the ideal senator's wife, that at the next meeting of the bipartisan Senate Wives Committee, to which she still belonged, she publicly attacked the movie queen. Taylor, she claimed, was an unfit senatorial spouse.

Elizabeth, having routinely refused to attend meetings of the group, found few defenders within its ranks. When *Newsweek,* on orders from Katharine Graham, reprinted some of Cooper's comments, it was *The New York Times* that came to Taylor's defense. In an impassioned editorial—"Cleopatra and the Asps"—the newspaper lambasted Liz's tormentors: "But what about the notion that she is not 'fit' to be something called a Senate Wife? What is a Senate Wife? Would Joan of Arc be found 'fit'? Would Florence Nightingale, that frighteningly strong-minded woman, be found 'suitable'? The Senate Wives should be wary of establishing *any* fitness tests. Someone might get the idea of applying them to Senate Wives' husbands."

The editorial did little to bolster Elizabeth's waning social status. Asked by *Time* why she had never invited Taylor to any of her Georgetown gatherings, Pamela Harriman allowed how "Mrs. Warner shows little interest in political affairs. She's evidently unfamiliar with the issues and not interested in learning more about them. I'm certain she would be bored silly at any of my gatherings."

By 1980, Taylor's unhappiness with life as a political spouse was so evident that John Warner, his immediate goal of a Senate job secured, agreed that she should resume a full-time acting career. To begin the process, she taped a snapshot of herself weighing 180 pounds to the side of her refrigerator and embarked on a major weight-loss regimen. After making a brief appearance in the film version of Agatha Christie's *The Mirror Crack'd,* she joined forces with producer Zev Bufman and accepted a role in a Broadway revival of Lillian Hellman's *The Little Foxes.*

Before beginning rehearsals, Taylor became involved in a final political campaign, this one on behalf of a former Hollywood actor named Ronald Reagan. In July 1980, she and John Warner traveled to Detroit to support Reagan's bid for the presidency at the Republican National Convention. Two months later, the Warners honored the Republican presidential nominee and his wife by throwing a GOP fund-raiser at Atoka. Five thousand guests paid twenty-five dollars apiece to mingle with Liz and John, listen to three bluegrass bands, and consume hundreds of pounds of cold cuts, potato salad, baked beans, applesauce, biscuits and butter, as well as thousands of bottles of beer, wine, and soda pop. A dozen large barbecue pits had been dug behind the main house. In each pit a calf turned over and over on a spit while John Warner raced back and forth between pits yelling at the harried attendants he'd hired to do the cooking. An hour into the festivities, a six-car cavalcade formed a semicircle and Secret Service agents bounded out of their vehicles to clear a path for Ronald and Nancy, who alighted from a seventh automobile, waved at the crowd, said a few words into a microphone, climbed back into their car, and were driven away.

Rehearsals for *The Little Foxes* had begun by February 6, 1981, the day Elizabeth attended a White House dinner party to celebrate the recently inaugurated president's seventieth birthday. Also at the dinner were Katharine Graham and Evangeline Bruce, both of whom went out of their way to avoid Taylor. The Reagans were present at the mid-March opening of Elizabeth's play at the Kennedy Center. By April, the actress had moved to New York with the rest of the cast for the Broadway opening of *The Little Foxes* at the Martin Beck Theater. On occasional weekends, John Warner would fly up from Washington and stay with his wife in a suite she had rented at the Hotel Carlyle. According to hotel staff, the couple argued frequently and after a certain point Warner's visits ceased altogether.

On December 21 of the same year, Elizabeth and John Warner formally announced that they were dissolving their marriage. She had already started to date Tony Geary, a thirty-four-year-old actor, while Warner had resumed a relationship with Barbara Walters. Approaching her fiftieth birthday, Liz agreed to be photographed and interviewed by *Life*. The front-cover profile, quoted in part in *The Washington Post*, represented her farewell to Washington.

"Being a senator's wife is not easy," she observed. "It's very lonely, I wouldn't wish it on anyone. I truly loved John. I wanted this to be a life-long run. . . . But once he won the election, it became very unsatisfying. No longer a candidate's wife, there was nothing for me to do except sit at home and watch the boob tube. My life had no meaning. . . . I'm not one of those Georgetown ladies who either gives or goes to dinner parties night after night. . . . People forget that there's a world beyond Washington, the world I so idealistically surrendered and to which I now return."

Reading Liz's declaration of emancipation, Pamela Harriman—in her typically irreverent and ironic manner—would say to Evangeline Bruce: "How the hell will Georgetown ever survive without Elizabeth Taylor?"

CHAPTER THIRTEEN

QUEEN PAMELA

ON MORE THAN ONE OCCASION Nancy Reagan tried to befriend Pamela Harriman by asking her to visit the Reagan White House. Mrs. Reagan had succeeded, after all, in winning the approval of several of the other Georgetown ladies. Pamela Harriman, the wife of Averell Harriman and founder of a political action committee known as Democrats for the '80s (informally called PamPAC), at first resisted all of Nancy's efforts. Four months into the new administration, the first lady once again instructed Muffie Brandon, her social secretary, to approach Mrs. Harriman and request her presence at an intimate White House ladies' luncheon. This time Pamela acceded, but came away from the function somewhat less than elated. "Nancy's shrewd as a fox," she told Joan Braden, "but all she talks about is Hollywood. I had my fill of Tinsel-town while married to my last husband, [actors' agent] Leland Hayward. You know, I've never been very fond of those ladies-only luncheons with all that chitchat and small talk. Still, there's something to be said for being friendly with the enemy, which is why I keep inviting all those hard-nosed Republicans to my own functions." How impressed Nancy Reagan might have been with the woman many now called "the Queen of the Democrats" is difficult to gauge. She did not, in any case, have her back to the White House for several years and then only infrequently.

Pamela Digby Churchill Hayward Harriman, the newest force on the

Georgetown scene, had made it her business to become the *maîtresse*, the guardian angel of the out-of-power Democrats. Although regarded by many of her contemporaries as nothing more than an adventuress, she used her wealth and connections to create, as Sidney Blumenthal wrote in *The New Yorker*, "a social center for the lower orders—chairmen of subcommittees of the House and obscure governors of distant states," one of whom, Bill Clinton, benefited hugely from her support. If Lorraine Cooper had the market cornered so far as Senate wives were concerned, then Pamela Harriman gave her patronage to the rest of Congress. In addition she became a major Democratic Party fund-raiser, an undertaking one Republican senator condescendingly defined as "women's work."

While the Reagans went out of their way to hobnob with Georgetown society, the Bushes—George and Barbara—stuck primarily to their own small, close-knit group of friends. Only on rare occasions did they venture forth to Georgetown dinner parties. They once attended a Sunday night supper at the home of Polly Wisner Fritchey and her second husband, Clayton Fritchey, but apparently didn't enjoy themselves and left early. "The long Republican era of Reagan and Bush, especially Bush, brought a kind of social stagnation to Georgetown," said Polly Fritchey. "And for good reason. Most Republican leaders lived across the Potomac, and the few who did come to Georgetown parties, such as Secretary of State George Shultz and Secretary of Defense Caspar Weinberger, didn't always bring along their buddies. I'm not saying that all social activity ceased at this time, only that the old Georgetown crowd, which had once reigned supreme, no longer exercised the kind of influence they once enjoyed. The single exception may have been Pamela Harriman, who had emerged to become the reigning queen of Georgetown, the Democratic Party's last great hope. She had power and personality. Members of both parties paid homage to her. Otherwise, the political makeup of Georgetown had changed. A whole new generation had taken over, one with decidedly Republican leanings. The newcomers who settled in Georgetown, some only peripherally engaged in politics, did so because it was still the place to be. In the bustle of late-twentieth-century Washington, Georgetown seemed Old World, a slice of American aristocracy."

Among the "new kids on the block" that Pamela Harriman encountered in 1981, ten years after arriving on the scene, were the ex-
travagantly wealthy Freddie and Diana Prince. "They're young, they're
glamorous, they're from Chicago, they're old-money rich," proclaimed
the *Washingtonian,* a monthly publication with an eye for the au courant.
Freddie's grandfather had founded the restricted Myopia Hunt Club in
Massachusetts. The Princes were die-hard Republicans and, as such,
made sizeable contributions to both the Reagan and Bush presidential
campaigns. Interviewed by *The Washington Post,* the couple claimed to
love Georgetown with but two reservations: the overabundance of dogs
and the lack of available parking spaces. The village, they complained,
would not allow them a curb-cut in front of their house. Consequently,
whenever they needed a ride, their "poor" chauffeur had to trudge
countless blocks to retrieve their Rolls-Royce limousine.

Day-to-day existence proved equally trying for Robert and Anne
Bass, whose R Street mansion, adjacent to the Georgetown Library, had
once belonged to Ulysses S. Grant. Known as the "bashful billionaire" in
his hometown of Fort Worth, Texas, Bob Bass had been appointed chairman of the National Trust for Historic Preservation. Despite his title,
within a year of his arrival in Georgetown, he had torn down and rebuilt
the historic Grant mansion as well as a number of surrounding town
houses he had purchased to protect his privacy. Anne Bass's major
lament, like Freddie Prince's, had to do with the scarcity of public parking in Georgetown. So dire was the situation that Bob and Anne had left
behind the supercharged 1938 black Bugatti convertible she had bought
her husband for his last birthday at a cost of $250,000. "That car," she in-
formed a reporter in her lazy Dixie drawl, "is sittin' in mothballs in a
garage somewhere in the middle of Texas."

There were others of course, from Mort Zuckerman (owner, *U.S.
News & World Report*) to John C. Whitehead (number three man at the
U.S. State Department). Serving during Ronald Reagan's second term
in office, Whitehead established relations with several of the leading
Georgetown ladies, particularly Katharine Graham. "We had a steady
Sunday afternoon match on the White House tennis court," said White-

head, "and the way it worked is that Kay and I always played against George Shultz and a female friend of his named Miss Pumphrey, who was twenty years younger than any of us and one hell of a tennis player. She'd just about tear the cover off the ball. Being the kind of guy who liked to win at everything, tennis included, Shultz would invariably manage to pair off with Miss Pumphrey, and Miss Pumphrey would hit these wicked shots at us. To counter, we'd try to hit the ball at Shultz, but she'd cut it off and smash it back for a winner. 'Let's face it,' Kay said to me one day, 'we're never going to beat them.' She was right. Over a period of four years, I don't think we won a single set."

As well as regularly attending Kay Graham's dinner parties, Whitehead was often a guest at the home of Lorraine and John Sherman Cooper. "Because they were Republicans," he said, "they remained very much at the forefront during the Reagan-Bush years. Their gatherings retained the Old World splendor that one associated with Georgetown in its heyday." Another guest at the same functions, Caspar Weinberger, liked the Cooper home "because it seemed comfortable without being opulent. It was not in any sense ostentatious or elaborate. The atmosphere there was conducive to the exchange of ideas and information." Weinberger used the party scene in Georgetown "to help build the image of the Defense Department and also to strengthen and improve the department's relations with our allies. The Coopers, among others, frequently had members of the diplomatic community at their dinner parties. The parties afforded access and the opportunity to discuss things with people who, under normal circumstances, would require a good deal of red tape to get to. It was often easier to thrash out prickly problems in such a setting than would have been possible in a more formal situation."

One of the newer, more outspoken and flamboyant members of the Republican regime to come in with George Bush was the always controversial Georgette Mosbacher. Her husband, Robert Mosbacher, a Houston oil baron, had served as national finance chairman for Bush's 1988 presidential campaign before accepting the post of secretary of commerce. An ardent Republican, Mosbacher owed his present ties in the

GOP to Secretary of State James A. Baker, a fellow Texan whom he had befriended in the 1950s. Baker, in turn, had introduced him to his friend, George Bush. Over the years, Baker and Mosbacher had been among Bush's most devoted advocates—and among his most generous.

Georgette Mosbacher's beginnings had been far more humble. Her father, a bowling alley manager in Highland, Indiana, died in 1954, when she was seven. Having helped raise her three younger siblings, Georgette—statuesque and with a flowing mane of red hair—worked her way through Indiana University before moving to Los Angeles to pursue an acting career. There she met and married Robert Muir, a successful real estate developer. While still married to Muir, but shortly before their 1977 divorce, she accepted an executive position in Fabergé's newly created film production division. Never one to pass up an opportunity, she soon left California and went to New York to work with George Barrie, Fabergé's director, whom she married in 1980. Divorced after less than two years—she accused Barrie of having been physically violent—Georgette met Robert Mosbacher in Houston on a blind date. More than a thousand guests attended their lavish Texas wedding in 1985.

Using her divorce settlement from Barrie, and with access to her latest husband's fortune, the new Mrs. Mosbacher acquired La Prairie, one of the world's most expensive skin-care product lines, with corporate offices in New York. As chairwoman of the $35-million concern, Georgette adopted all the trappings of a successful career woman: designer clothes, expensive jewelry, imposing makeup. In little less than a year she saw the value of her company jump to $50 million. Her most brilliant innovation involved using as models for her beauty products the so-called working rich, women like Ivana Trump and Carolyne Roehm, the well-known designer. Her ambitions aroused by her triumph on Madison Avenue, Georgette Mosbacher arrived in Washington with every expectation of repeating her success.

"Nothing I'd ever done or experienced prepared me for life in Washington, D.C.," Georgette told the current author. "I was like a fish out of water. I simply didn't get it. I didn't know, for example, that in Washington, unlike any other place in the world, perception and reality are one and the same. In other words, the way things appear is the way they are. What seems to be true is true. This is an abstract conception. There are no absolutes in Washington. It is a town in which appearances are everything. Another lesson I quickly learned is that Washington is totally male-oriented. It is the old-boy network to the *nth* degree. They want their women to be neither seen nor heard. That's what they used to say about children. Women in Washington are treated like children. A woman with any degree of power is considered a liability, a threat.

"*The Washington Post* was on my case before I even got there. They ran a Style piece on how I'd flown to Paris in my husband's private jet to buy a sweater at Christian Dior. Much was made of the fact that he had money, that we'd both been twice divorced, and that he was twenty-one years my senior. It reminded me of the kind of reportage you'd expect to find in the tabloids. And that kind of reportage, the skewering of my character, continued throughout my residency in Washington. No matter what I did they managed to turn it around and make me look like a blood-lusting shark. And the irony is that Katharine Graham routinely attended our dinner parties. My mistake was that, unlike Nancy Reagan, I never complained to Kay. Instead I complained to my San Francisco friend Denise Hale, whose advice to me, simply put, was: 'Be yourself!' "

The Mosbachers spent their first year in Washington at the posh Jefferson Hotel, Georgette commuting daily to and from New York, where she continued as CEO of La Prairie. In Washington, they gave and attended frequent parties. "I love to entertain," said Georgette. "I love crowded parties full of interesting people. I customarily sat ten at a table and consulted with the State Department's protocol office to determine a suitable seating arrangement. Rumor had it that the State Department still called on Evangeline Bruce for the last word on such matters.

"I remember Alan Greenspan passing out at one of my parties. It was a hot summer night. He just keeled over and passed out on the floor. I happened to have an oxygen tank on hand, so we revived him and he went right on as if nothing had happened. Another time I had a dinner party to which I invited Republican Party chairman Lee Atwater and speaker of the House Thomas S. Foley. The two men had been feuding terribly, exchanging barbs and insults in the press and on television. In the serene setting of my living room, they shook hands and made their peace, a fence-mending situation that could never have otherwise occurred."

The Washington Post accused Georgette of staging the Atwater-Foley dinner party solely as a means of self-glorification. Self-promotion and personal gain were purportedly the motives behind a series of social events orchestrated by the Mosbachers on behalf of NAFTA, the commercial trade agreement being forged between Mexico and the United States whereby large, multinational corporations would build manufacturing plants south of the border and employ local workers at rates that would significantly reduce the rising labor costs incurred by these corporations. Such a policy, one of several controversial policies that fell under the rubric of what George Bush called his New World Order, worked (claimed the press) against the interests of the American laborer.

"I couldn't win," said Georgette Mosbacher. "Even though NAFTA finally came into existence, I was perceived as the enemy, too glamorous, too flashy, perhaps too attractive to be welcomed into the inner sanctum of what Ronald Reagan once dubbed the Georgetown Ladies' Social Club." Indeed, Georgette was taken only slightly more seriously than Elizabeth Taylor during her Washington phase. "When they weren't writing about me, they were talking," continued Mosbacher. "Sally Quinn talked about me on *Larry King Live*, making remarks that weren't particularly flattering, speaking on national television as if she'd known me all her life. She didn't know me at all. We never met. Anything she knew had to have come to her secondhand. Her comments were deceptive and dishonest, which suggests that her journalism is fraught with these same characteristics. And I'm not the first to make that charge."

One of the few women Georgette Mosbacher admired in Washington was Pamela Harriman. "Despite her strong Democratic Party affiliation, she came to many of my parties. Pamela succeeded in using the old boy Washington network to her distinct advantage, which is how she rose to such grand heights," Mosbacher observed. "She invented what I call 'the Look.' She had the ability to look a man right in the eye and, just with her interest and concentration, make him feel as though everything he had to say was brilliant."

⚮

PAMELA DIGBY WAS BORN just south of London in Kent, England, on March 20, 1920, the eldest of four children. Six years younger than the British-born Evangeline Bruce and three years Katharine Graham's junior, Pamela—like Vangie and Kay—grew up in a world of conspicuous wealth and privilege, on an idyllic country estate, Minterne Magna, comprising more than 1,400 acres. Located in Dorset, the estate (which had belonged to Pamela's paternal grandfather) came with a twenty-person staff, including tutors and governesses for the children. Like Kay Graham, Pamela was raised primarily by servants. Her parents belonged to the tweedy, cushy town-and-country set. Her father, the eleventh Baron Digby, liked to garden and ride horses; her mother collected antiques and also liked to ride. Pamela, who learned to ride at age three, developed into a more accomplished equestrian than either of her parents. Her favorite childhood memories were of the weekend parties her parents gave at the estate, when grown-ups arrived for dining, dancing, and hunting.

In later years, Pamela maintained she'd found life in Dorset tedious and rejoiced when her parents sent her, at fourteen, to Hatfield to attend the all-girls' Downham School. After two years at Downham, she completed her finishing-school studies in Paris, at the same time auditing a course or two at the Sorbonne. In late 1937 she accompanied her parents on a lengthy trip to the United States and Canada, followed by a visit to Munich, Germany, where a family friend, Unity Mitford, made an appointment for her to meet Adolf Hitler, a meeting that Christopher Ogden, one of Pamela's biographers, surmises never took place. "I think an appointment may have been scheduled, but that's as far as it went," said Ogden. "Chances are she enhanced the story later on, after she learned how much Averell Harriman regretted never having met the Nazi leader."

Returning to England, Pamela made her debut in society and began hanging out with the "Leeds Castle set," a group of young British aristocrats known for their fast ways and liberated lifestyle. Plump, bosomy, wearing high heels, and throwing her bottom around, Pamela developed a reputation for being attracted to powerful, older men with means. Nobody seemed surprised when Pamela, still in her late teens, went out one evening with Randolph Churchill, the twenty-eight-year-old son of Winston Churchill. It was on their second date, the following day, that Randolph proposed to her. "He proposed to every girl he met," said Christopher Ogden. "The only difference is that Pamela accepted."

Prewarned by her friends that Randolph was a womanizer, a gambler, and an alcoholic, Pamela nevertheless went through with the marriage, which took place on October 4, 1939. A day after the ceremony, the British press compared the bride to Wallis Simpson, the Duchess of Windsor, referring to Pamela as "the red-haired tart of England." The general feeling was that she had married Randolph purely to attain the family name and gain access to Randolph's father, a sentiment that was shared by Clementine, Randolph's mother, but not by Winston Churchill, who had admired his daughter-in-law from the start, spent a good deal of time alone with her, and frequently had her over for dinner at 10 Downing Street. In October 1940 she gave birth to a son, thereafter known as Young Winston. Shortly after the infant's birth, mother and son were photographed by Cecil Beaton for the cover of *Life*. The accompanying article, subtitled "Pamela Gives Birth to Young Winston, Old Winston's First Grandchild," appeared about the same time that Pamela first met W(illiam) Averell Harriman, the tall, gray-haired U.S. official and future statesman nearly thirty years her senior.

Averell Harriman's credentials spoke for themselves. Born in 1891, he was the son of Edward Henry Harriman, owner of the Union Pacific Railroad, a leading industrialist and one of the wealthiest men in America. After graduating from Yale in 1913, Averell joined the family business and within two years had been named vice-president. Elected chairman of the board of Union Pacific in 1932, he had in the interim formed a shipping company, a merchant bank, and a brokerage firm. His business successes through the worst of the Depression persuaded Franklin Roosevelt, in 1937, to appoint him chairman of the Business Advisory Council, a division of the Department of Commerce. Just prior to America's entry into World War II, Harriman moved into the field of foreign affairs as coordinator of the Lend-Lease Administration, America's financial aid program to Great Britain and the Soviet Union. It was in this capacity that Harriman found himself in London.

The meeting between twenty-one-year-old Pamela and the nearly fifty-year old Averell took place over dinner at the London home of Emerald, Lady Cunard, an American who specialized in British café society, a kind of mentor to Pamela and a personage whose advice on social mores and entertaining would figure prominently in Pamela's future development as a Georgetown hostess. Pamela and Averell were alone in England. Randolph Churchill had joined the British commandos in Egypt. Averell's second wife, Marie, an art dealer who had been previously married to Cornelius Vanderbilt "Sonny" Whitney, passed the majority of her time between Washington and New York. Averell and Pamela, deeply attracted to one another, left Lady Cunard's that evening and spent the night together in his suite at the Dorchester, thus launching a two-year, wartime love match that everyone in British society seemed to know and care about, with the sole exception of Winston Churchill. The prime minister went so far as to entertain Averell Harriman at Chequers, Britain's official vacation retreat for prime ministers, while Pamela was a guest there as well.

In June 1941, soon after the affair began, Winston Churchill wrote to Randolph that his house in Westminster Gardens had been badly damaged by a two-ton German bomb, and that Pamela had moved into a flat at 3 Grosvenor Square with Averell Harriman's youngest daughter, Kathleen (whose mother, Kitty Lanier Lawrence, had been Averell's first wife); Young Winston, the letter added, was being looked after in the country by the family of Lord Max Beaverbrook. Unbeknownst to Churchill, his daughter-in-law spent most of her nights, not with Kathleen in their new apartment, but with Kathleen's father, Averell, who had concocted the living-together arrangement as a cover-up. In addition, Averell and Pamela spent their weekends together at a cottage Averell had acquired with his daughter outside London. The affair lasted until

1943, when President Roosevelt appointed Harriman to become the next American ambassador to the Soviet Union. By this juncture, both Marie Harriman and Randolph Churchill, having been apprised by friends, were well aware of the infidelity of their respective spouses.

The Harriman marriage endured, but by early 1944 Randolph Churchill had initiated divorce proceedings against Pamela. In a May 14, 1944, letter to his father ("My dearest Papa"), Randolph laid out the case against Pamela: "I have long known that she is an excellent mother and have never had any disagreement with her on that score. . . . I have no doubt that you also find her an agreeable daughter-in-law. But the trouble, which you always seem to overlook, is that she declines to be in any way a satisfactory wife. You will only make all of us unhappy if you create illusions about her in your mind."

Randolph's disenchantment with Pamela stemmed not just from her affair with Averell Harriman, but from other affairs that she started after Averell's departure for Moscow. A short-lived fling with William Paley gave way to more serious entanglements with American newsman Edward R. Murrow and American sportsman John Hay ("Jock") Whitney, whose estimated wealth exceeded $125 million. She and Whitney were still involved in 1945, the year her divorce from Churchill became final. The divorce papers indicated that Randolph had also indulged in extramarital relationships, one involving the effervescent American department store heiress and journalist Kay Halle. Halle, a foreign correspondent stationed in England during World War II, moved to Georgetown in 1947 and there, by bizarre coincidence, became involved with Averell Harriman. The affair lasted less than a year. Harriman had earlier returned to London, in March 1946, as U.S. ambassador to the Court of St. James's, a position that enabled him to once more take up with Pamela. But later in the same year he returned to the United States to become President Truman's secretary of commerce, thereby terminating the second installment of his romance with Winston Churchill's daughter-in-law.

Aware that her reputation in England had been severely damaged, Pamela Churchill left a job she'd procured on Fleet Street and in the late 1940s, after a number of tentative trips back and forth across the English

Channel, moved to Paris with her young son. With monies derived from the Churchills, she purchased a sunny flat with a marvelous view of the Seine and filled it with Louis XVI antiques she picked up at galleries on the Left Bank. Before leaving for Washington in 1946, Averell Harriman had provided her with a new car, which she took with her to Paris, and an annual stipend that covered essentials. With her auburn hair, blue, kittenish eyes, creamy skin, and curvaceous figure, she rapidly amassed a male following. She was, as the writer Evelyn Waugh once put it, "a very tasty morsel, indeed." Through Parisian friends she met Baron Elie de Rothschild, the banker, philanthropist, and art collector who headed the French branch of the Rothschild family. That he was also a married man did not prevent him from beginning a five-year relationship with the then thirty-year-old Pamela.

In his Pamela Harriman biography, Christopher Ogden tells of a 1954 dinner party at which Liliane de Rothschild is seated next to the Duke of Windsor. At a certain point, he turns to her and asks, "Do you happen to know which Rothschild is the lover of Pamela Churchill?" "My husband, sir," the baroness responds.

There were others during the Paris phase, most notably the international playboy Aly Khan and Fiat Automobile Corporation chairman Gianni Agnelli, whom she described as "the love of my life." Susan Mary Alsop, then living in Paris, once looked after Young Winston for a month while the boy's mother vacationed in the south of France with Agnelli. "That's how she brought up Young Winston," said Alsop. "She would dump him with friends and neighbors while she went off with one or another of her lovers. Then she would suddenly reappear and cart the boy off again. The strange thing is that they had a surprisingly close mother-son relationship. While in my care, the boy never doubted that his mother would come for him. Like most children of his background, he later attended boarding schools—Le Rosey in Switzerland, Eton in England—and visited his mother on vacations."

Oleg Cassini, who became acquainted with Pamela after she moved to Georgetown, observed that "Elie de Rothschild refused to divorce his wife for Pamela, and Gianni Agnelli eventually married a Neapolitan princess, Marella Caraciolo di Castagneto. The point is that none of the

European men that she knew would marry her, the reason being that she was too obvious in her desires. She wanted power pure and simple. She was interested in power and money, but money primarily as a means of acquiring power. Politics and politically-involved men interested her, but again only as a vehicle, a way of gathering power.

"She appealed to men who possessed power and money, but not only because of her good looks. She was a handsome woman, but she wasn't beautiful enough to bowl over a man simply on the basis of her looks. Pamela's manner is what was so beguiling. She was the last of the great geisha girls. She looked deep into your eyes when she spoke to you. She had a kind of hypnotic gaze that made you feel as though you were supremely important. For those few minutes, you felt empowered, bewitched. That was her aphrodisiac."

Joan Braden, also a proponent of the theory that Pamela had mastered the art of the geisha, said of her: "She exuded sexuality. She had this provocative way of tossing her hair from one shoulder to the other with a quick flip of her head. She was optimistic, self-confident, and ebullient. She had the ability to fixate on a man and convince him that she was utterly enthralled. If you were a male and you were with Pamela, she gave you her undivided attention. It is a trait that few women possess and which few men can resist.

"On the other hand, her early promiscuity did have a deleterious effect on her reputation. She resided in Paris during the 1950s, and although she had long-lasting relationships with men like Gianni Agnelli and Elie de Rothschild, there was the perception that they considered her suitable mistress material but not someone to bring home to Mother. And more than anything, after her divorce from Randolph Churchill, she wanted to marry again."

Pamela did marry again. In 1960, having relocated to New York, she married the fifty-eight-year-old actors' agent and Broadway producer Leland Hayward. One of the most successful agents in the business, Hayward's client list included names such as Clark Gable, Ginger Rogers, Cary Grant, Gregory Peck, and Henry Fonda. Pamela's initial meeting with Hayward had occurred in late 1958, during a visit to New York, when Babe Paley telephoned a friend, Nancy "Slim" Hawks Hayward (later Lady Keith), and asked whether her husband, Leland, would be free to escort Pamela to the theater. Babe, whose spouse, Bill Paley, had earlier succumbed to Pamela, ought to have known better, particularly since her brother-in-law, Jock Whitney, was also a member of "the Pamela Club," as her retinue of male admirers had become known. Oblivious of Pamela's reputation, Slim not only permitted her husband to escort Pamela, she took the visitor under her wing and proceeded to introduce her around town. When Slim went to Spain on vacation with Truman Capote and high-powered Hollywood agent Swifty Lazar, she asked Pamela to "keep an eye" on Leland. Pamela did more than that. Within little more than a year, she had become the new Mrs. Leland Hayward The 1960 wedding ceremony, a hurried affair, took place in Carson City, Nevada.

Lady Keith, who almost never discussed the details of her private life, would offer only one comment with regard to Pamela. "I don't like that woman," she is quoted as saying.

Having sold her apartment in Paris, Pamela invested the proceeds in her own three-bedroom Manhattan co-op at 1020 Fifth Avenue. Leland Hayward paid the monthly mortgage and maintenance fees as well as the semiannual city taxes on the apartment. In addition, at Pamela's behest, he purchased a sizeable country estate at Yorktown Heights, New York, which they named Haywire, after his cable address. Among their first visitors, even before the wedding took place, was Brooke Hayward, one of Leland's children with his former wife, actress Margaret Sullavan. About to marry actor Dennis Hopper, Brooke, a determined actress and model, had misgivings about her father's soon-to-be bride.

"For weeks," she said, "father kept telling me what a fabulous woman he'd just landed. She had great hair and was Winston Churchill's former daughter-in-law. And Churchill, after all, had won the war. I had a vision of some incredibly glamorous creature, I really did. So I was kind of amazed when I finally met Pamela. She was not at all what I expected. She wasn't this ravishing redhead. She was rather dumpy and quite plain. She was wearing a silk Dior dress that didn't quite fit right. In other words, she didn't have any of the class that I expected. I anticipated a dazzling theatrical charmer, rather like Slim or Mother, or his first wife, a beautiful Texas socialite named Lola Gibbs, whom he'd actually married twice. I couldn't understand what father saw in Pamela. Also, she didn't know a thing about anything that interested our family. She knew nothing about the theater. That's not to say she didn't set out to learn. Within a relatively brief period, she learned everything there was to know about the Broadway stage. She could quote the box-office grosses of every theater in New York.

"She was an enthusiastic student and a sly businesswoman. She carried around a notebook, which looked like a small silver box. She would flip it open and make notes, not only on the theater, but also on what brand of cigar or cigarette so-and-so smoked, what kind of Scotch they preferred, that sort of thing. She wasn't interested in what the women were all about. She was interested in pleasing her male dinner guests, providing them with all the comforts of home."

Following her initial encounter with Pamela, Brooke visited her mother in Greenwich, Connecticut. "I'll never forget it," said Brooke. "As soon as I mentioned Pamela by name, Mother said, 'Pamela Churchill? She's a common whore. Your father must be insane.'"

For another visit with her father and Pamela, who were by then husband and wife, Brooke brought along Dennis Hopper. "We arrived at their Fifth Avenue apartment and were ushered into the study," recalled Brooke. "The idea was that we were all going to have a drink and then go out to dinner. Dennis was wearing a new Brooks Brothers suit and raincoat he'd bought for the occasion. As we sat there we could hear Pamela raging away at father about my brother Bill, who was then in the U.S. Army, stationed near Frankfurt, Germany. To celebrate his twenty-first birthday, they'd invited him to go skiing with them in Switzerland. The ski trip never happened. He'd met up with them in England and brought along his girlfriend, a young German lass, a barmaid, who didn't measure up to Pamela's standards. She excoriated Bill for having the temerity to bring her along, and after a few days he returned with his girlfriend to Germany. Now, to compound the situation, Pamela was going on and on about Bill and this 'ghastly' girl, and where did he come off bringing her along to England at a time when Pamela's father, Lord Digby, lay dying— and how humiliating and what a terrible thing it had been. 'Leland,' she shouted, 'how could you possibly have brought this child up? You should have put him in jail.'

"Father kept trying to shush her up. He felt embarrassed. And Dennis was terrified of her, absolutely terrified. By now she was totally out of control. Finally she calmed down and we had our drink, and we went downstairs and climbed into father's town car and drove off to some overcrowded steak joint, where the discussion centered on father's art collection, which Pamela felt he should donate as soon as possible to the Metropolitan Museum of Art, so he could take a generous tax deduction. Dennis then got into a heated discussion with Pamela about the late Jackson Pollock, whose work Dennis and I both admired. Pamela dismissed Pollock outright. With a wave of her hand, she said something like, 'Pollock's nothing but a dirty beatnik.' On this note, Dennis and father excused themselves and went off to the men's room, leaving me alone with Pamela. She smiled at me as she leaned across the table. 'Brooke,' she said sweetly. 'Do you know why we're at this restaurant?' 'No,' I said. 'Why?' 'Because Dennis just doesn't dress very well. It's simply too embarrassing for your father.' I told her that his clothes were brand-new and were from Brooks Brothers, but my words made no impression. 'That raincoat of his,' she went on, 'is the rattiest thing I've ever seen.'

"After dinner, when we were alone, Dennis said to me: 'Your stepmother is out to get you. And I'm part of the problem. She hates me, because she knows I know what's going on. And this is it: she's trying to get you and your brother written out of your father's will. That's why she brought up the business about giving the paintings to the Metropolitan. She'd rather derive some benefit from them now than have his children inherit them after his death.' "

William ("Bill") Hayward, who went on to coproduce the movie *Easy Rider*, added to his sister's portrait of their stepmother: "Pamela opened an antiques shop on the east side of Manhattan in conjunction with Jansen, the posh antique dealership in Paris, but Dad financed the operation, paid the rent, bought the merchandise, hired several sales clerks to assist Pamela. The shop thrived for a while, but Pamela gradually lost interest in running it and the business ultimately went belly-up. The shop's demise didn't stop Pamela from continuing to spend gobs and gobs of

Dad's money. It was stunning to me. I went with her one weekend to a nursery in New York, where she'd buy plants and flowers for the house and apartment. She always had dozens of bouquets of fresh flowers on display, which didn't necessarily please Dad, because he was highly allergic. She spent more money in one visit to the nursery than I earned in a month. I couldn't get over anybody spending that kind of money on flowers.

"I'll say this for her, though: she was one hell of a hostess. If you ever had to stay at somebody's house, you'd want to stay at hers. Your every need was looked after. She had the best of everything—the most beautiful decorations, the most exotic flowers, the greatest food. The food, in fact, was superb. They had an Italian chef and this fellow eventually quit to open his own restaurant. And Pamela was horrified, just horrified, although in time she found a suitable replacement. She had the routine down pat. She'd grown up in that milieu, always surrounded by servants. Consequently, her houseguests were treated like royalty. Each bedroom in their apartment and at their country estate had an electric blanket, and it would be switched on before the guest reached his room after dinner. A pitcher of ice water sat beside the bed with flowers and a bowl of fresh fruit. The bed would be turned down and a little treat, a homemade cookie or imported chocolate bar, would be placed on the pillow. Fresh towels and washcloths of the finest quality were always laid out. Visiting Pamela was akin to staying in one of the world's ritziest hotels."

Leland Hayward once told his son that Pamela was "one of the great courtesans of the twentieth century." He bragged to publisher Bennett Cerf of her prowess in the bedroom, her unique use of ice cubes as a stimulant. When speaking of her to close friends, he often referred to her as *"La Bouche."* "She has," he said, "the best mouth on either side of the Atlantic." "It was a fair trade-off," remarked Rowland Evans. "He afforded her financial security and entrance into New York café society, a sense of legitimacy, something she'd never experienced in Europe, and in return she gave him sexual fulfillment and a wonderful home. Substituting Washington, the same can be said for her marriage to Averell Harriman."

In 1967, after seven years of marriage, Leland Hayward became ill with pancreatitis. Advised by his doctors to go into semiretirement, Leland agreed, against his wishes, to sell the Fifth Avenue apartment and move with Pamela to their country estate, where they continued to entertain but with much less frequency. They retreated almost completely from the chic New York nightlife that had become so essential a part of their lives. After the first flush of excitement, Pamela's interest in show business had also waned. When Katharine Hepburn, a close friend of Leland's, attempted to pay him a visit, Pamela barred her from the house. The same fate awaited other of his actor friends. "Father never liked the country," said Brooke Hayward. "He'd purchased the property only because of Pamela and only to be used on weekends. Now she held him prisoner there. She was completely possessive of him. She called the shots, decided who came and went. Without her permission, you couldn't even talk to him over the telephone. You certainly couldn't see him. There were times when my brother and I were absolutely on the outs with her, and at those times we couldn't get close to father. Nobody could. That great charm of hers was something she could turn on and off like a water faucet. She had all the makings of an accomplished manipulator."

One of the few visitors Pamela welcomed into their Yorktown Heights home during the final days of Leland Hayward's long illness was Truman Capote. The popular writer had grown close to Pamela, frequently accompanying her on shopping trips around New York, making her one of his choice "swans." "Pamela knows how to make a man feel happy, even on his deathbed," he told a reporter two days after his final visit with the Haywards.

Leland Hayward died on March 18, 1971. Following his death, there were accusations by members of his family of improprieties on Pamela's part against her late husband's estate. Leland's children charged her with the theft of jewelry and professional camera equipment that had belonged to them but which had been left with Leland. Some of the camera equipment, according to Bill Hayward, wound up in Young Winston's hands but was later returned. Although named sole beneficiary of the Hayward estate, Pamela complained bitterly to Brooke that she had been left practically bereft. "Your father," she whined, "left me with the country estate and everything in it but with less cash than I had when I first met him." "She made no reference," remarked Brooke, "to the $50,000 she received annually from father's royalty share in *The Sound of Music,* which he produced on Broadway." For his part, Bill Hayward instigated a lawsuit against Pamela but dropped it soon after she married Averell Harriman. Brooke exacted her revenge by writing *Haywire,* a 1977 best-selling tell-all memoir, which depicted Pamela as "the Wicked Step-mother of the West." The title of the memoir and the publicity it engendered convinced the widow to change the name of her country estate to Birchgrove. What the memoir failed to mention in any detail was an affair Pamela had with one of her husband's physicians while Leland lay dying in a private hospital suite at Memorial Sloan-Kettering. The doctor, who later married Grace Mirabella of *Vogue,* squired Pamela to parties and the theater, then dropped her when, shortly after the funeral, she flew off to Palm Springs to visit with Frank Sinatra. Little is known of the visit, but after she left his compound, Sinatra purportedly told friends that he found her "boring, arrogant, pompous, pretentious, and phony." "She's too old for me, she's middle-aged," he said, "and she's got no sense of humor about anything."

Never one to give in to despair or depression, Pamela revisited her old haunts in Paris, and followed this with a cruise of the Greek isles with Loel and Gloria Guinness, to whom she confided that she was considering moving back to Europe. Ashore again, she placed a call to her old flame, Averell Harriman, whose wife, Marie, had passed away six months prior to the death of Leland Hayward. The day after her conversation with Averell, Pamela packed up and returned to the United States. Repatriating to Europe was no longer on her mind.

❧

ONE QUALITY that Pamela Digby Churchill possessed in abundance was strength of will. Whenever she wanted something, nothing could stand in the way. She went all out to get whatever she happened to desire at the moment, beating down every obstacle. What she currently desired was to be with Averell Harriman on a more permanent basis, a wish that she evidently communicated to Truman Capote.

Capote always took credit for having convinced Katharine Graham to throw a dinner party at her Georgetown home to which she invited both Averell Harriman and Pamela, whom she had first met in New York several years earlier. When Capote told Pamela of his plan to seat Pamela next to Averell, she suggested that they be seated back-to-back. It was less obvious and more provocative.

Other than the London period, there had been several additional encounters between Averell and Pamela. The first time was in Paris in 1949, when he was Marshall Plan administrator and he reproached her for ruining her life by consorting with "good-for-nothing" playboys. "They're good for something," she had said on that occasion. "Or should I say, good *at* something." They met again in January 1965, this time at Winston Churchill's funeral. They then flew back to New York together on an Air Force jet provided by President Johnson. They spent much of the flight reminiscing, Pamela relating tales of Young Winston's marriage to Minnie d'Erlanger and her newborn grandchild (the first of four), Averell discussing his years as governor of New York (his nickname was now "Governor") and his various appointments as an ambassador-at-large. Both Pamela and Averell attended Truman Capote's Black and White Ball in 1966, but because they were with their spouses they never spoke at the affair. Leonard Hacker, however, a real estate consultant employed by Averell Harriman, would see them together at a restaurant in Orange County in the late 1960s. "Yorktown Heights," said Hacker, "and Arden, New York, where Averell had his estate, were not far apart. I saw them together in a restaurant, cozily entwined at a corner banquette, not particularly wanting to be seen. I heard that there were other secret meetings between them during this period. They were both married, but both were players. They had that in common."

Peter Duchin, who had been raised by Averell and Marie Harriman, observed that at the time of the Capote-Graham "reunion" party for Averell and Pamela, Averell "had sunk into a deep depression over the death of Marie. They'd been married for forty years, and although both had engaged in their share of affairs, it was on the whole an excellent marriage. Marie had been a Georgetown grande dame, much admired and with an irreverent wit second to none. Without her, Averell felt adrift, and was extremely vulnerable to the romantic attentions of Pamela Churchill. On the night of the party, she leaned into him at the dinner table and worked her magic. They wound up spending a good part of the weekend together."

The following weekend, Peter Duchin and his then wife, Cheray, were staying with Averell. Another guest, having arrived after the Duchins, was Pamela Churchill. One evening after dinner in a restaurant, the Duchins returned and made their way into the darkened living room. "I turned on the light," said Duchin, "and there on the couch, entangled in sexual foreplay, were Averell and Pamela. Her blouse was unbuttoned and her skirt bunched up around her waist. Averell's face was covered with lipstick. He looked ecstatic."

They were married in a private, unannounced ceremony at St. Thomas More Catholic Church, in New York, on September 27, 1971, a year and a day after Marie's death and six months after the death of Leland Hayward. On November 1, as a wedding present to her husband, the bride became an American citizen. Pamela's detractors presently accused her of having personally engineered the party that had brought her together again with Averell. Although she flatly denied the charge, she found it more difficult to counter allegations that within months of the marriage she had taken control of Harriman's "very existence," a charge not unlike that levied against her in the case of Leland Hayward.

Her modus operandi, while not particularly subtle, at first involved a degree of indispensability rather than outright control. Pamela, now fifty-one, made herself an essential part of the eighty-year-old statesman's life, accompanying him on his ceaseless travels from one lavish home to another. Besides the estate in Arden, New York, which Averell was in the process of transferring as a tax-deductible gift to Columbia University, he owned properties at Hobe Sound, Florida, and Sands Point, Long Island, as well as town houses in Manhattan and Georgetown, and a ski chalet at Sun Valley, Idaho, a resort town in large measure created by Averell in the late 1930s to stimulate rail travel west of Chicago. After a year of logging back and forth between homes, Pamela sought to consolidate her husband's holdings. She induced him to sell the Hobe Sound, Sands Point, and Manhattan properties in exchange for a villa at Mango Bay, Barbados, where on previous occasions she had visited with Marietta Tree. She then brought in decorator Billy Baldwin, whom she'd first met during her Paris period, to refurbish the remaining homes, with special attention to the town house at 3038 N Street in Georgetown, a cavernous, two-and-one-half-story brick structure that dated to the 1790s. The house, located five blocks from the home of Kay Graham, included a backyard garden and swimming pool. Pamela went a step further, commissioning Baldwin to redecorate the Yorktown Heights house she had inherited from Leland Hayward. Not yet done, she talked Averell into purchasing Willow Oaks, a sixty-acre farm in Middleburg, Virginia, where she raised and trained horses, including several steeplechase champions. When a hotel chain sought to acquire a large tract of land in Middleburg in order to build on it, Pamela bought it herself and made it available for use by local fox-and hound hunt clubs. Finally, when Averell developed bone cancer, from which he quickly recovered, she had him invest in a private jet.

"Pamela wasn't so much interested in a change of scenery or venue as she was in cutting Averell off from his past," said Peter Duchin. "She was terribly jealous of Marie Harriman. Averell and Marie had spent their happiest days at Hobe Sound. Pamela wanted to erase all memory of Averell's previous marriage. More than once I heard her say, 'I can't believe I let Marie have all the best years.' "

Pamela terminated those household retainers who had worked for Averell during his marriage to Marie and hired a new staff at the N Street house, consisting of two gardeners, two maids, a laundress, a chauffeur, a butler and valet, a full-time cook, a personal assistant, and two private secretaries, one for Averell and one for herself. When asked by *The Washington Post* why she needed so much household help, she responded: "Because it's a large house."

Pamela's lavish lifestyle presently included three maroon automobiles—a Rolls-Royce, a Bentley, and a Cadillac—which she decked out with vanity license plates—PCH 1, PCH 2, PCH 3—as well as custom-made hood ornaments (an ostrich clutching a horseshoe in its beak, a design derived from the Digby family coat of arms). The ostrich and initials likewise appeared on her matchbooks, stationery, notepads, towels, and sheets. Her overnight and weekend guests shared in the luxury, going home with one or more expensive gifts, such as Gucci handbags, Fruit of the Month gift certificates, cases of wine, and terry cloth bathrobes.

Cynthia Helms, whose husband, CIA director Richard Helms, had worked in government with Harriman, thought Pamela "a superb organizer. She knew how to run a house and deploy a staff. She understood the meaning and uses of power. Averell Harriman wielded a great deal of power. He had advised and worked for both Democratic and Republican administrations, and he had served in that capacity for every president from Roosevelt through Reagan. Nobody in Washington had greater clout. Pamela grew into her role, becoming a leader in her own right.

"She could be thoroughly disagreeable but also enormously generous. I recall when she invited us to join her aboard a chartered yacht for a sail down the Turkish coast from Istanbul to Rhodes. It was a marvelous trip, with every amenity imaginable. She had even rented a Mercedes-Benz with a chauffeur to drive down the coast beside us, so that whenever we went ashore to see something or visit with somebody, we had a ready-made ride.

"The day arrived when Averell put his foot down with regard to Pamela's spending. He could be very tight. One time I won a dollar from him at bridge, and he had to leave the room to get it and he was gone a long time. 'He must be digging it out of the safe,' said Pamela. Another time I said to her, 'Pamela, what have you done to the drawing room? It looks wonderful.' And she pressed a finger to her lips to quiet me down. Then she whispered, 'I've sent the chairs and couches out one at a time and Averell knows something is different but he doesn't know what it is.' "

Pamela's most audacious action involved the systematic elimination of many of Averell Harriman's old friends, as well as the expulsion of family members, among them his two grown daughters, Mary Fisk and Kathleen Mortimer, as well as their husbands and children. Averell Fisk, one of Harriman's six grandchildren, visited them shortly after they were married and before they'd sold the Hobe Sound house. "I'd played polo that afternoon and they invited me for dinner and I didn't have time to change, so I was wearing my polo gear when I arrived," said Fisk. "The minute I entered the house, Pamela said, in front of my grandfather, 'Oh, my God, you smell like a damned horse. Get the hell out of here and don't dare come back until you bathe and change your clothes.' She threw me out of the house.

"That was her technique, to humiliate and embarrass members of the family so as to block them out. I remember a second incident that took place a short while later. Averell had won West Point's Man of the Year award. The ceremony consisted of a reception at the commandant's private residence and a dinner afterward at West Point, at which Averell would deliver his acceptance speech, the same speech he'd given on a hundred similar occasions. Pamela invited me at the last minute. I'd already bought two tickets to a Frank Sinatra concert in New York. 'That's all right,' she said, 'you and your girlfriend can attend the reception and still make it in time for the concert. I'm sure your grandfather will understand.' So we drove up to West Point and went to the reception. When it ended, I walked over to Averell and Pamela to say good-bye. 'You mean you're not staying for the dinner?' said Pamela. 'That's so disrespectful. And after all that your grandfather has done for you. You don't give a damn about him.' She carried on like this for what seemed like an eternity, behaving in a very obnoxious manner, making certain that Averell heard her every word. She'd never told him about the Sinatra tickets, so of course he thought I was a terrible grandson, which had been her intention from the start.

"The only person in the family she didn't cut out completely—only partially—was Kathleen. To shut out everybody would have been too much a gesture of disdain, so while she didn't see much of Kathleen, she would speak to her over the telephone. The rest of us were in the dark. We didn't know what to do about the situation. You couldn't just call and say to Averell, 'Let's get together' or 'let's have lunch,' which is how it had always been with Marie. Pamela had gained complete power and control over him. She dictated his every movement. Whereas previously he'd always been fairly independent, that was no longer the case. By controlling him, she could control his money, which is what it all came down to. She was infected by greed. In my opinion, had he been younger and not in mourning over the loss of Marie, he would never have married Pamela."

A coldhearted enemy to some, to others she could be a great friend. Richard Holbrooke, a future U.N. ambassador and Pamela Harriman adviser, when interviewed for an A&E *Biography* segment on Pamela, spoke affectionately and supportively of Mrs. Harriman, lauding her leadership of the Democratic Party at a time when Democrats found themselves far from the center of power. Holbrooke went on to relate details of a conversation he'd once had with Averell Harriman: "Toward the end of his life, the Governor and I were sitting at the country house outside New York and I said to him, 'Governor, is there anything you've ever regretted in your life?' And without a moment's hesitation, he said, 'Not marrying her the first time.' "

Truman Capote found her "enormously entertaining and a devoted ally." Even Bill Hayward had to admit that although he disliked her personally, Pamela had been generous toward his two children, setting up a trust fund to pay for their college education. "Never mind," he said, "that the money belonged to Averell Harriman." She did the same for Young Winston's four children. Young Winston, a Conservative MP, had also benefited greatly from his mother's largesse, so much so that Averell Harriman wrote him an irate letter stipulating that the house he planned to build for himself in the English countryside, and which the Harrimans were financing, was far too extravagant and needed to be toned down.

Sally Reston, a Pamela supporter, said of her: "She was absolutely incredible with Averell. I have never known anyone so attentive and devoted to a man. If she went to some social function by herself and she got home late, she'd wake him up and kiss him, and say, 'I'm back, sweetheart.' When she went away for more than a few hours, she always saw to it that somebody other than the servants was in the house to keep him company. She would call on her Georgetown friends. Kay Graham, who admired and liked Pamela, would go over there to stay with him. No matter what else was going on, Pamela and Averell always had breakfast together in the morning, in her room, in her bed. When his eyesight began to deteriorate, she contacted her friend Thornton Bradshaw, the chairman of RCA, and ordered a nine-foot television set, which she had flown to Washington and installed. As it turned out, he hated the huge screen, but appreciated his wife's efforts. He preferred carrying around this little transistor radio, which he could hold to his ear and on which he would listen to baseball games. In actuality he was a demanding old man, and she met every demand. Pamela was like a chameleon, able to take on the color of a man's particular passions. With Leland Hayward, for example, it was Broadway and Hollywood; with Averell it was politics. She could blend into any environment."

Pamela's sudden political awakening when she was in her fifties and sixties could well have had its origins in her belief that she had squandered much of her youth. By her serious political contributions she probably hoped to redeem herself, salvage what remained of her reputation, although it can also be argued that she cared little what people thought of her. Evangeline Bruce, who regarded Pamela as "an opportunist," wrote to Marietta Tree in the mid-1980s, expressing the view that "until she married Averell, she [Pamela] was a full-blown Tory, a Republican. If she had wed Richard Nixon instead of Averell, he would very likely still be president." But then, as Marietta Tree responded, "she did marry Averell, and her transformation from international swinger and café society hostess to Democratic Party fund-raiser and power broker has been dramatic. And she achieved it through a combination of shrewdness, focus, and determination—the very attributes that made her so successful with men."

Her transformation, which began after her 1971 marriage, was all the more remarkable in that she lacked both an overpowering intellect and a formal education. But her unflagging ambition, combined with the Harriman name and fortune, made up for any shortcomings. Because she recognized her shortcomings, she made it her business to surround herself with influential members of the Establishment as well as young men on the rise—Clark Clifford and Robert Strauss in the former category, Richard Holbrooke and Samuel "Sandy" Berger in the latter—who could tutor her and help with the speeches that she diligently practiced and delivered in Churchillian cadence. Then there was a personal assistant, a woman named Janet Howard, who was so devoted to Pamela and so protective that their alliance at times raised eyebrows. And, of course, she had the benefit of her third husband and chief mentor. Averell Harriman, despite his old-fashioned patrician manner and stuffy reserve (he favored black-tie dinners and engraved invitations), remained one of the premier statesmen of his time, his greatest triumph probably having been his involvement in the Limited Test Ban Treaty, the first major arms-control agreement between the Soviet Union and the United States. Serving him initially as amanuensis, caretaker, and companion, Pamela accompanied him not just on trips to his multiple dwellings but on five separate junkets to the Soviet Union (where he introduced her to Leonid Brezhnev), helped him to draft reports, speeches, and position papers, and acted as his eyes and ears (by the time he turned eighty, Harriman's vision and hearing were severely impaired). In order to stay close to the Jimmy Carter–Soviet Union policy circle, the couple invited Zbigniew Brzezinski, the president's Polish-born national security adviser, to move into an office complex they owned next door to their N Street town house. They offered Secretary of State Cyrus Vance, who later moved to Georgetown, the use of their guest cottage at Willow Oaks. They gave a fund-raiser in Georgetown in support of Marion Barry. They supported whatever political causes Averell Harriman deemed worthy.

Under Harriman's aegis, Pamela scrupulously constructed her political profile with memberships in prestigious public policy groups and organizations. She raised funds for many of these same bodies. She met and befriended foreign policy specialists and think-tank operatives. Most of all she did her homework, poring over whatever documents came her way, becoming conversant with the issues and familiar with the methodology. At dinner parties she would pick the brains of her guests and take notes on political matters that interested her. "To me, a dinner is about something serious," she said. "A dinner party must have a purpose, an agenda." In this, she disagreed completely with Sally Quinn, for whom parties were ideally fun-filled affairs without serious overtones. Closer to Pamela's idea of party giving were the views of Henry Kissinger, who once pronounced that "the hand that mixes the Georgetown martini is time and again the hand that guides the destiny of the western world." Kissinger wrote of Washingtonians in general that "it is at their dinner parties and receptions that the relationships are created without which the machinery of government would soon stalemate itself." Arthur Schlesinger had put it in similar terms. "Do not be deceived by appearances," he wrote. "The strictest purpose lurks under the highest priority. As every close observer of the political system in Washington knows, half the essential business of government is still transacted in the evening."

Pamela instinctively understood the ways of Washington, realizing that the services she provided for the powerful, whether raising funds or providing introductions and making connections, would earn her favors down the line. The political action committee she and her husband founded in 1980, popularly known as PamPAC, was distinguished not so much by the amount of money gathered over its ten years of operation (approximately $12 million) but more for the new style of fund-raising they created by marketing their name and reputation as consummate Washington insiders. Pamela gave ninety-one fund-raisers for PamPAC during its decade-long existence, most of them in Georgetown, with occasional events held at Willow Oaks. Over that span she convinced hundreds of well-to-do invitees to give her $5,000 each to be distributed amongst select Democratic Party candidates of her own choice. In exchange for their donations PamPAC patrons could mingle with up-and-coming politicians or listen to occasional guest speakers such as Congressman Richard Gephardt, Clark Clifford, or Senator Edward Muskie, whom the Harrimans unsuccessfully backed for a presidential run in 1972. For the less well heeled, Pamela threw an annual $25-a-head garden party, which averaged more than a thousand guests, many waiting on line for hours to get in. She impressed her visitors at N Street, rich and not so rich, by creating an intimate and sophisticated atmosphere that began with a wall of photographs of the Harrimans—one or the other and sometimes both—in company with Franklin D. Roosevelt, Winston Churchill, Queen Elizabeth, Charles de Gaulle, Nikita Khrushchev, and other twentieth-century luminaries, followed by room after room filled with the paintings and sculptures of van Gogh, Sargent, Picasso, Degas, Cézanne, Rousseau, and Matisse. In the end, her political action committee was an anodyne for the Democrats. She ran the inn, so to speak. She became a grand symbol for the Democrats, and she helped foster the perception of success for "the party" even in the Reagan-Bush years. Her supporters referred to the 1980s as "Pamelot," a retrospective reference to Camelot.

Chris Matthews, of *Hardball* fame, a speechwriter for Jimmy Carter and an aide to Speaker of the House Tip O'Neill, remarked that "Basically, back in 1981, the Democratic Party had lost just about everything. We lost the presidency when Reagan defeated Carter, and we lost the Senate for the first time in twenty-six years. The Republicans had also made substantial gains in the House of Representatives. All that was left in power was the Speaker, and he had the power, so he was constantly called upon to participate as leader of the party. And then there was Pamela Harriman and PamPAC, and she would hold these soirées in Georgetown. And people like Bob Strauss and Joe Califano and other party biggies, including Tip O'Neill, would show up. It was a test to try to rebuild and restart the Democratic philosophy, the party point of view. And the Harrimans funded it. Pamela gave it pizzazz. She added glamour, having the home that she had and the money and the staff. The last time the Democratic Party women had been instrumental was at the national convention in 1964, but in those days you still had a lot of backroom politicking, and it was mainly a man's game. Pamela's gatherings were thought-provoking and idea-driven. The format was new and different. It was a new approach, a new program. While most of Georgetown's young, idealistic Democrats-in-exile tossed in the towel in the '80s and retreated into their trenches, she set in motion the machinery that would bring the Democrats back into power. And along the way, she supported and promoted a number of political hopefuls, among them Chuck Robb, Sam Nunn, Jay Rockefeller, and Al Gore. And then there was Bill Clinton."

Producer Lester Persky recalled attending a PamPAC affair with Truman Capote at which the guest speaker was Senator George Mitchell. "There were cocktails and a piano player. Then Mitchell discoursed for about twenty-five minutes before dinner," said Persky. "She had set up five tables that seated ten each. We had paid a thousand dollars per person to get in. Of course you could write out another check while you were there and leave it in a basket near the front door. You couldn't give her a chit. It was pay as you go. Pamela wore Bill Blass, and Harriman, a three-piece pinstripe suit. The meal, for which there was a printed menu, which I still have, consisted of green turtle soup, raw Chesapeake oysters on the half shell, fresh South African jumbo shrimp, creamed Maine lobster, rum raisin cake, dinner wines, Colombian coffee, cognac, and cigars for those so inclined. After dinner, Averell toasted his wife and tottered off to play a game of bridge in the library. The rest of the group—investment bankers, lobbyists, labor union leaders, and politicians—followed Pamela into the drawing room, where conversation centered on the disturbing fact that President Reagan had covert U.S. operations going on simultaneously in Libya, Nicaragua, Cambodia, Afghanistan, and Angola. Pamela called Reagan 'another Nixon.' At some point she came over to me and started complaining that women rarely gave money to political causes. 'They don't get it,' she remarked. 'When they're asked, they say, "Gosh, $5,000 is a lot of money." And these are the women on yachts in the Mediterranean.' "

"As Truman Capote and I were about to leave, we spotted Averell Harriman crouched over a table in the foyer. The bridge game must have ended, because he was alone. He had a bunch of checks in his hand. 'Are you all right?' Truman asked him. He looked up. 'What's that?' he said. 'Are you all right?' Truman asked again. 'I'm fine,' he said. 'I'm counting the house, boys. I'm counting the house.' "

Although Pamela Harriman came into her own after Averell's death, on July 26, 1986, at age ninety-four, the will he left behind—with Pamela named as executrix—triggered a legal battle that would haunt her the rest of her days. Even PamPAC, which continued for four years more, did not suffice to take her mind off the skirmish. Averell's last week had been spent at Birchgrove, where Leland Hayward had died fifteen years earlier. At his bedside on the day of his death were his two daughters, Pamela, and Young Winston, who had flown over from England. By the terms of the will, finalized only the year before, Pamela received as a mainstay the $100 million art collection amassed by Averell and Marie (with the understanding that Pamela would pass it on to either the National Gallery or the Metropolitan Museum of Art upon her death). The centerpiece of the collection, Van Gogh's *White Roses* (which Averell had acquired in tandem with his mother), was itself valued at $50 million. In addition, Pamela inherited her husband's $55 million stock and bond portfolio, two oil companies that yielded an annual salary of $750,000 for "managerial services," all of his residential properties, all his personal effects, and the interest on a $6 million trust fund to be distributed among his grandchildren after twenty-five years. The total value of Pamela Harriman's inheritance exceeded $125 million, not including the art collection, which would benefit her chiefly in terms of tax deductions. The rest of Averell's family was more or less cut out, except for four thousand dollars to each of his two daughters plus the interest generated by a separate $30 million trust fund to be controlled by Pamela. It was the last of these bequests that would lead to most of the turmoil.

There was another wrinkle. Averell's daughters and grandchildren wanted the patriarch to be laid to rest next to Marie Harriman in the family plot at Arden, New York. On the day of the funeral, every detail of which had been planned by Pamela (and her assistant, Janet Howard), 750 of the country's most esteemed politicians filed into St. Thomas Episcopal Church in Manhattan to pay their last respects. Following the ceremony, a coffin was indeed delivered to the village cemetery that housed the rest of the Harriman clan. The coffin supposedly containing Averell's remains was in fact empty. The elder statesman's corpse had been sequestered by Pamela and removed to an unknown location, where, for the next two months, it remained in an isolated refrigeration unit, while another plot was prepared four miles from the original site, the new plot to be reserved solely for Averell and Pamela, after her demise. When confronted by the family, the widow pointed out that she was pursuing her executorial rights to dispose of her husband's remains as she saw fit. Pamela had no intention of reuniting Averell, even in death, with either his family or a former wife.

CHAPTER FOURTEEN

WHO KILLED
GEORGETOWN?

"JOE AND SUSAN MARY ALSOP never cared for Pamela Harriman," said Polly Wisner Fritchey, "and I didn't like her very much myself. She had an annoying way of exaggerating her past. She used to claim, for example, how well-educated she was, which simply wasn't true. She did the same with her son. She constantly bragged about Young Winston's academic prowess, how he'd gone to Oxford and become a rising star in British political circles. In fact, Young Winston was a chip off the old block, much more similar in manner and lifestyle to his father than he was to his namesake grandfather. On the whole, he was a disappointment. Margaret Thatcher, for one, couldn't stomach him.

"Which is not to say that Pamela didn't come to the rescue of the Democratic Party at a time when they most needed her. She liked the power game and played it well. Except for the supposed purity of her aristocratic upbringing, she didn't seem to care what people thought of her, which I consider an asset rather than a liability. It enabled her to move ahead in the face of a good deal of resentment. She became a Georgetown princess but only at a point when Georgetown was on the wane. By the mid-1980s, the place had lost much of its former luster. It was still an enjoyable spot to live, but politically speaking, it no longer was the mecca it had been."

Polly Wisner Fritchey's negative feelings toward Pamela Harriman were to some extent shared by Evangeline Bruce. Vangie's son David recalled the evening in 1985 when he and his mother attended a performance at the Kennedy Center in Washington. "I spotted Mrs. Harriman in the audience," he remarked, "and since I'd never met her, I decided to go over during intermission and introduce myself. 'Don't bother,' my mother said. 'Pamela Harriman is interested exclusively in people with power. Now that your father's not with us, we're no longer of interest to her. She won't want to meet you.' I assume, since both women were at the top of the Georgetown social ladder, that my mother felt competitive with her. The truth of the matter is that their social interests differed. Mrs. Harriman's endeavors were purely political in nature. Because of my mother's background, her salon was as much geared to writers and artists as to politicians and diplomats. In that sense it was much more European in its essence, the result of my father having served as ambassador to both London and Paris."

(Regardless of the competitive attitude that Evangeline Bruce appears to have manifested toward Pamela Harriman, it is a matter of record that more than once Evangeline attended Pamela's celebrated fund-raisers. And more than once, she invited Pamela to her Sunday brunches, indicating that the two ladies at the very least had in common the desire to see the Democrats back in power.)

Like Polly Fritchey, Evangeline Bruce saw the 1980s as the beginning of Georgetown's end. "Joe Alsop died in 1989," she said, "but equally telling was the death in 1985 of Lorraine Cooper. Lorraine wasn't so well known outside the domain of New York and Washington, but her death marked the end of an era."

Trude Musson, Lorraine Cooper's personal assistant, attested to the fact that her employer had remained "extremely active" until the day she suffered a massive stroke in October 1984. "Mrs. Cooper continued to make new friends throughout her lifetime," said Trude. "An example would be the alliance that she formed with Phyllis George, a former Miss

America who in 1979 married John Y. Brown Jr., the then governor of Kentucky." Whenever Phyllis and the governor came to town, the Coopers would organize a dinner for them. Phyllis idolized Lorraine. She came to her for advice on Kentucky and campaigning and being married to a governor. Lorraine introduced her to her friends and to people she needed to know in politics and government. It was the early 1980s and Lorraine was still very much on top of her game.

Phyllis George recalled one particular evening "when John Y. and I were hosting a little party at the Jockey Club. We did most of our entertaining there because it seemed such a natural place to promote Kentucky's thoroughbred industry. Jay and Sharon Rockefeller were there, Bill and Hillary (Bill was then governor of Arkansas), Robert Byrd and John Warner of Virginia, Alan Simpson, a very nonpartisan crowd. Lorraine and John Sherman Cooper held court, but the highlight of the evening was when Lorraine joined Bob Hardwick, another Kentuckian, at the piano and sang 'My Old Kentucky Home.' Normally, everyone chimes in for this, but her voice was so strong and sweet, we were all amazed, and contained ourselves until the chorus."

Unlike most other senatorial couples, the Coopers remained in Washington following John Sherman Cooper's retirement from public office. The senator, still active as an attorney at Covington and Burling, and Lorraine, still one of Georgetown's most influential hostesses, were frequent guests at the Reagan White House. In a 1982 letter to Reagan, Jacob Javits, still active despite an advancing case of Lou Gehrig's disease, recommended that Cooper be considered for another ambassadorial post, possibly to Israel. "Surprisingly enough, Lorraine wasn't opposed to the idea," said Evangeline Bruce, "but John refused, probably because of his memory of the horrendous incident that had occurred in East Germany, when Lorraine became the victim of a sex attack."

Vangie remembered attending a ladies' luncheon for Clare Boothe Luce at Lorraine Cooper's house in early 1983. After lunch the ladies repaired to the library. "Perhaps I should break out the cognac and cigars," Lorraine joked, referring to the by-then passé Washington tradition of separating the sexes after dinner. "Lorraine held forth from a sofa in a black taffeta dress," said Vangie, "and I thought how wonderful she looked, her skin peach-perfect and glowing, the result of protecting herself from the sun with all those parasols. She quickly gained control of the gathering. Lorraine had such social flair and good humor. The rest of us, including Katharine Graham, were lightweights by comparison—and this was a pretty extraordinary group of women, if I must say so myself. Clare and Kay were media powerhouses. Others present were Marietta Tree, Nancy Dickerson, and Sally Reston. But we were all simply transfixed by Lorraine. She entertained us as though performing a one-woman show on Broadway."

Late in 1983 John Sherman Cooper fell ill. "He contracted an upper respiratory infection of unknown origin, which didn't respond to antibiotics," said Vangie. "Within a matter of days, it spread. He experienced a great deal of pain. For a while it was touch and go. He was in and out of the hospital. It was the Christmas season, so Lorraine got her nephew, Brice McAdoo Clagett, also a lawyer at Covington and Burling, to escort her on the annual round of holiday parties. But for once, it seemed, her heart wasn't in it."

Clagett agreed that while Lorraine "put on a brave face," she was terribly worried about John. When Cooper finally returned from the hospital, Lorraine hired a private nurse to look after him. The nurse, afraid that the patient would fall out of bed at night, tethered him to the headboard. Lorraine fired the nurse and hired another. By May of 1984, John showed signs of recovery. In June he and Lorraine took a short stroll around the neighborhood. To celebrate, she invited Brandon Grove over to the house for drinks.

Grove, who had worked on Senator Cooper's diplomatic staff in East Berlin and remained friendly with Lorraine, went to the house "and noticed something odd when I first saw Lorraine. Her lipstick was unevenly applied and ran past the corners of her mouth. I didn't give this much thought, although it was unlike her not to be carefully made up."

Brandon and Lorraine sat in the library and talked and sipped champagne. When it was time to leave, the visitor stood up and started toward the front door. "Instead of accompanying me, as she always did whenever I visited," said Grove, "Lorraine turned and walked to the porch outside the library, her back to mine, just standing there." Grove watched her for a few moments, then let himself out of the house. The next morning he received a telephone call from Trude Musson. After his departure, Trude told him, Lorraine had gone into the kitchen for a snack. There she lost consciousness and collapsed on the floor. She had suffered a major stroke. She never regained consciousness. She lingered in a coma for months. Friends, like Evangeline Bruce and Kay Graham, would visit her in the nursing home where John Sherman Cooper had placed her. "We would talk to her," said Vangie, "and maybe she heard. We watched her sleep. She never awoke. She would stir a trifle, or a finger would move. 'I don't think Lorraine would want us to see her like this,' Kay said one day. So we stopped visiting."

Lorraine Cooper died on February 23, 1985, at age seventy-nine, and was buried at Arlington National Cemetery in a plot reserved for the popular Kentucky senator and his wife. To his own amazement, John Sherman Cooper outlived Lorraine by six years. "He felt lost without her," said Lee C. White, Senator Cooper's former aide. "We would occasionally dine together at Billy Martin's in Georgetown, and while he continued to be interested in world affairs, you could tell how much he missed Lorraine." Never able to fully regain his health, Cooper spent his last two years in the same nursing home where Lorraine had spent her last months. He died in his sleep on February 21, 1991, at age eighty-nine, and was celebrated by President Reagan as "one of the most beloved and compassionate American statesmen of this or any other century."

Trude Musson, who had worked for Lorraine Cooper for years, now joined Pamela Kinsey McClelland, special assistant to Vangie, as a part-timer on Mrs. Bruce's staff. When Vangie, having also recently hired an excellent Portuguese chef, expressed concern that her own house at 1405 Thirty-fourth Street was too large for one person, it was Trude who suggested that she acquire Lorraine Cooper's slightly smaller house at 2900 N Street. The transaction completed, Vangie contracted with an interior designer to make certain changes to the house. While she waited, she turned her attention to a project that had occupied her for nearly twenty-five years, a nonfiction book, *Napoleon and Josephine: An Improbable Marriage* (first published in the United States by Scribner in 1995).

A subtheme in the book is the political and social role that women played in France toward the end of the eighteenth century. "It was women," she writes, "who set the tone of the intellectual and political life of the capital . . . as arbiters of ethics and politics and molding public opinion. Women have never had so much power—before or since." One might almost apply these words to the women, like Evangeline Bruce, who ruled Georgetown during the better part of the latter half of the twentieth century.

When she wasn't writing, Vangie continued to raise funds for the Sasha Bruce House, ran her 1 to 3 P.M. Sunday brunches, and attended the theater with friends. At the Washington premiere of *Les Misérables* she told her escort, British journalist Alexander Chancellor, that she liked "anything revolutionary." She didn't like George Bush's suggestion that she invite Colin Powell, then chairman of the Joint Chiefs of Staff, to one of her brunches so he could talk to her guests about the necessity of going to war against Iraq and Saddam Hussein, whose forces had invaded and taken over neighboring Kuwait.

"Philosophically, Vangie supported the Gulf War," explained Joan Braden, "but she didn't appreciate President Bush's attempt to involve her in his attempt to change the public's perception of him as a weak administrator. 'If Bush needs to gain support for the use of force against Iraq,' she told me, 'he ought to approach the Senate and the House, not me. I've always admired Colin Powell, but I don't want him to come over here and preach to us about necessity of going to war. I'd rather he discussed what it was like growing up poor and black in the South Bronx during the 1940s.' "

Three years after the Gulf War, in April 1994, Vangie woke up one morning with a migraine headache and blurred vision. Her general practitioner sent her to a specialist, who took X-rays and then placed her on a regimen of multivitamin pills and injections. A month later the headache returned. The specialist prescribed sedatives and painkillers. The migraines and vision problem persisted, but Vangie, ever the trooper, managed to complete her book, select a suitable cover design, and, with Pam McClelland's help, correct page proofs.

The publication date was March 19, 1995. A book party had been planned in Washington for the following day. Returning by plane from a visit to New York, Vangie suddenly found herself immersed in a world of darkness. She had gone blind. Evangeline's physician, according to her son David, had tragically misdiagnosed the root cause of her ailment. Known as temporal arthritis, the condition involved the progressive inflammation of the cranial blood vessels, especially those vessels located in the forehead region. Usually treatable at (or shortly after) onset, in Vangie's case it had progressed beyond the point of reversal. Frightened and desolate, she refused all visitors, including her sister, Virginia Surtees, who had wanted to fly over from England. "I had to fight to see her two months after she went blind," noted Virginia. "I wanted to see her at once, but she utterly refused to see anyone."

At first she restricted contact with the outside world to the telephone. Gradually she began to receive visitors. Susan Mary Alsop and Katharine Graham would show up regularly and read to her. Margot Hahn, a Washington socialite who taught cooking, "would try things and take them to Vangie, and she would call me up and say—this is after she went blind—'I tasted it at two in the morning and I think you need more paprika.' Marvelous! She never slept. She was so sick, poor thing. She felt so wretched, and so this was a diversion." Sandra McElwaine, a former reporter for the *Washington Star*, also dropped by once a week to read to her. "I read to her from magazines and newspapers," said McElwaine. "She had a small staff and they were usually present. The phones were always ringing in her house. I mean they were just ringing off the hook. You had to stop reading half the time because she would take calls from Arthur Schlesinger and George Weidenfeld and people like that. The telephone calls and visitors helped, but in general she seemed terribly upset about her condition."

Other visitors included Henry Kissinger and Cyrus Vance. Kissinger had once leased Felix Frankfurter's former Georgetown home at 3018 Dunbarton Avenue, before marrying and moving with his new wife, Nancy, into another Georgetown residence at 3026 P Street, surrendering the first address to Cyrus and Grace Vance. Vance had succeeded

Kissinger as secretary of state. The two appeared at Evangeline's house only a week apart. Both men reminisced with Vangie about their days in Georgetown.

"It's still lovely in Georgetown," said Vance, "but it's not the same anymore."

"It never is," responded Vangie. "Things change and so do people, not always for the better."

One evening she attended a small dinner party at a Georgetown neighbor's house. Ella Poe Burling happened to be at the same dinner. Recalling the circumstances, she said: "It was actually a going-away party for another neighbor in the process of moving from Georgetown to Fox-hall Road. You'd have thought the guest of honor was moving to Missouri, rather than to a location a few minutes away. 'Once you leave George-town,' said Vangie, 'you may as well move to Siberia.' Her humor aside, Vangie seemed to be suffering. She told me that what she missed most in her life was dancing. 'I can't dance anymore,' she said. 'I don't see where I'm going.' She had another regret. She had bought Lorraine Cooper's house and had looked forward to moving in. She could no longer make the move, because she didn't know the layout well enough to feel com-fortable there. 'I'd be forever bumping into furniture,' she said."

Sally Reston paid a visit. "We sat in her sunny living room," said Sally, "and I admired her many rare plants and flowers. Then I realized she could no longer see them. She spoke to me about somebody named Tru-man, and at first I thought she meant Truman Capote. She meant Tru-man, the driver of her Cadillac. He was an African-American and had accompanied the Bruces to Beijing and Brussels. Evidently well-known in Washington's black community, he had been with Vangie for more than fifteen years. After his death, several years earlier, she had been grief-stricken. Now she was saying that very soon she would be seeing Truman again, which I took to mean that she expected to die. So I said, 'Come on, Vangie. You'll be here long after the rest of us are gone.' And she said, 'Baloney.' "

David and Nicholas Bruce, her sons, estranged from one another but not from their mother, both visited her at home. David brought along his wife, Janet, and their infant daughter, Vangie's only grandchild. "Mother often felt ill," David remarked, "but she rarely complained, at least not to us. She kept up her spirits by listening to music, the news, and sometimes Books on Tape. She and I used to chat at night on the telephone. But then her health took a turn for the worst. She suffered a heart attack and died on December 12, 1995, at Georgetown Hospital. She was eighty-one years old and was laid to rest at Oak Hill Cemetery next to my father and sister."

☙

PAMELA HARRIMAN DIED IN 1997, two years after Evangeline Bruce. Her life after the 1986 death of Averell Harriman would take a number of unexpected twists and turns. On the cusp of a new career as an ambassador and power broker, she demonstrated that she possessed the same cool, collected political instincts and insights that had once served her late husband so well. Self-educated in the ways and means of Washington, she once told Al Gore Jr. that President Carter's undoing had been his intransigent stance against the Russians, his unwillingness to compromise. It had led to the Soviet invasion of Afghanistan in 1979, to their tacit support of the Iranian hostage situation, and ultimately to a sweeping Republican victory in the next presidential election.

Averell Harriman's death enabled Pamela to achieve the financial independence she had always sought. Moreover, in November 1986, despite the efforts of Ronald Reagan, the Republicans were dealt a stunning midterm defeat. The Senate, previously controlled by Republicans (53–47), currently became a Democratic stronghold (by a 55–45 margin), a reversal that was matched in the House of Representatives. The turnaround justified the existence of PamPAC and encouraged Pamela to pursue some of her other interests. In the summer of 1987 she flew to China, bringing along her own delegation, including Arthur Schlesinger, Richard Holbrooke, and Sandy Berger. On their return to the States, Holbrooke and Berger helped her prepare an op-ed piece for *The New York Times* dealing with China's views of the Soviet Union's newly instituted economic policies. Other trips—to Spain, Turkey, and the Soviet Union—soon followed. She joined the New York–based Council on Foreign Relations, a group that met regularly to discuss American foreign policy (and related) issues. She delivered a series of public addresses on the subject of American foreign policy, one at Georgetown University, another at the Georgetown public library. She organized several conferences. In 1987 she assembled five distinguished American women, including Supreme Court Justice Sandra Day O'Connor and Katharine Graham, for a colloquium on foreign policy. She hosted receptions and dinner parties for foreign dignitaries. Raisa Gorbachev, the Soviet leader's spouse, turned down Nancy Reagan's invitation to a White House tea in favor of a private reception at the home of Pamela Harriman. She asked Jesse Jackson to speak at one of her rallies and suggested that he consider an ambassadorial position as a future career move. *The Washington Post* subsequently described Pamela as "the only Georgetown hostess with her own foreign policy."

In 1988 Pamela bypassed Michael Dukakis in favor of Al Gore as the Democratic Party presidential candidate, throwing several PamPAC fund-raisers for him. She had known Al and Tipper Gore since 1984 and was particularly impressed by Tipper, a photojournalist with a graduate degree in clinical psychology. In 1984 Pamela had backed Gore's successful senatorial bid in Tennessee. To her dismay, however, Gore not only lost to Dukakis in 1988, but in November of that year, George Bush won by a landslide over Dukakis. It marked the fifth time in six elections that the Republicans had emerged victorious.

With Bush's triumph, the social influence of Georgetown's leading ladies again receded. Lorraine Cooper was already dead. Evangeline Bruce spent more time than ever out of the country. Kay Graham, while not a voting Republican, had lost her enthusiasm for liberal causes. Sally Quinn, an unflinching Democrat, had not yet established enough of a power base in Washington to make a difference. Even Pamela Harriman had begun to weary of the grind.

"I'm tired of getting up at 5 A.M. every day and banging my head against a wall," Pamela told society writer Doris Lilly, whom she'd known since her days in Paris. "I hadn't seen her in years," said Doris, "when she unexpectedly called and invited me to spend a week with her at Sun Valley. Now well into her sixties, she looked better than when I first met her, better even than she'd looked as a plump but pretty teenager. She'd apparently just undergone a complete makeover: face-lift, hair, diet, personal trainer, new wardrobe. She didn't mind talking about the face-lift. It had been performed by Dr. Sherrell J. Aston, chief of plastic surgery at Manhattan Eye, Ear, and Throat Hospital. 'You arrive in New York and check into a small but comfortable hotel across the street from the hospital,' said Pamela. 'He does the surgery first thing the next morning. You spend a second night in the hotel and then you go home. After three weeks, you go to your first dinner party and nobody recognizes you. Aston is a genius!' I guess she'd let herself go a bit because she and Averell hadn't had sex in years. He'd been rather feeble toward the end, and it had been trying to look after him and at the same time carry on that whole PamPAC business. After his death, she started seeing J. Carter Brown, curator of the National Gallery of Art. Brown named her to the museum's board of trustees. Much to the horror of Harriman's daughters—they accused her of dissipating the estate—she later gave the National Gallery van Gogh's *White Roses.*

"They seemed an odd couple, because he knew little about politics and she knew little about art. What's more, although they were separated, he was still living in Georgetown with his second wife. He came from an exceedingly wealthy, aristocratic, Rhode Island family—they had founded Brown University—but he himself was a bit on the chintzy side. Whenever he visited Pamela at Sun Valley, he'd go shopping for clothes and charge everything to her account. 'Just send the bill to Mrs. Harriman's attention,' he'd tell the sales clerk. She'd pay, but that sort of behavior probably irked her. Over the years she saw less and less of Brown, often supplementing their affair by maintaining platonic relationships with men like Truman Capote, Tom Foley, and Oscar de la Renta. She also on occasion still saw her old flame, Gianni Agnelli. On the whole, I had the impression that by the late 1980s she'd grown tired of Brown. She'd also become bored by PamPAC and wanted to point herself in a different professional direction."

Although Doris Lilly admired Pamela Harriman, she found her "narcissistic and self-centered." "When you visited with her," said Doris, "you did what she wanted to do." Pamela loved to take long hikes, so her guests were expected to accompany her on her jaunts. She liked to show movies at night, and her visitors were forced to watch the film with her, whether they had already seen it or not. "The most annoying part is that she insisted on controlling the conversation," continued Doris. "If you started to discuss art, for example, she would quickly change the subject."

For his part, J. Carter Brown had mostly complimentary things to say about Pamela. "She was just a very interesting person," he remarked. "She'd been so many places and done so many things and knew so many people. And she had a fund of stories and anecdotes from World War II, from the years in Paris, from her theatrical period with Leland, and finally from her days with Averell in the proverbial eye of the American political storm. She could converse about virtually anything, from French wines to the details of the latest Panama Canal treaty. And when she told a story, she had a real kind of thespian's gift to recreate the voices of the people in the story, so it always sounded very dramatic.

"Like anyone in a position of power, Pamela had her share of critics. They frequently downplayed her intelligence and knowledge, but I can say with certainty that she knew what she was talking about. And she would make sure that you knew that she knew. She was a person of substance, as well. She had informed opinions, an agenda. It wasn't just a question of bringing people together and giving them a good time, though that's what she did best of all. But Pamela was more than that. She saw something that needed to be changed, and she went about changing it. She wasn't infallible, of course. In 1984 she threw a $250-per-person fund-raiser for Gary Hart, whom she saw as a way to regain the presidency. After he got caught in the Donna Rice sex scandal, she never spoke to Hart again. 'He nearly put me out of business,' she said. But she had staying power, and she ultimately succeeded in her mission."

J. Carter Brown's only real complaint about Pamela was that she had promised to leave him Willow Oaks, her horse farm in Middleburg, Virginia, which in the end she declined to do. Bill Rich, her longtime financial adviser, pointed out that she had changed her mind "because she feared that J. Carter Brown lacked the personal funds to properly maintain the property, and she didn't want it to be broken up and sold in smaller lots." At several points during their romance, Brown had raised the possibility of marrying Pamela. But marriage never crossed her mind again. She was determined to die, when the time came, as Averell Harriman's widow. "The only subject we argued about," said Brown, "was her indulgence of Young Winston. Whatever he wanted in the way of money, he would get. He played his mother like a harp, pushing her buttons and sweet-talking her to death. I would tell her to clamp down. She would argue with me and even agree, but then she would visit her son and grandchildren in England and give them whatever they wanted."

Pamela Harriman was a strange combination of utter generosity intermingled with pure money-lust. "I heard it said many times," noted J. Carter Brown, "that she had little affection for other women, primarily because they didn't occupy positions of power. That may be so, but I personally know that she had a special place in her heart for the widows of Washington. She was friendly with and very generous to women like Avis Bohlen, Selwa 'Lucky' Roosevelt, and Millicent West. Pamela's biographers, Christopher Ogden and Sally Bedell Smith, particularly the latter, have produced distorted and unrealistic volumes on the lady, concentrating mostly on the negative, because that after all is what sells books."

Angela Hemingway, the wife of Jack, Ernest Hemingway's eldest son, depicted another aspect of Pamela, that of an eccentric dowager with a grand but highly aggressive manner. "We were neighbors of hers in Sun Valley," said Angela. "Jack invited her over for dinner one evening. She burst into the house and without a word headed for the kitchen, where we had installed oversized refrigerator-and-freezer units covered with a dark cedar wood. She loved the units and couldn't say enough about them, but what amazed me is that she simply, without asking, opened the refrigerator door and started peering inside, I suppose to see how much room there was. Then in the living room she saw this four-foot-high stuffed fox that we had. Its eyes were fashioned out of rubies. You lifted the head and it became a wine cooler. 'That would look smashing in my house in Middleburg,' she said. I thought she might simply pick it up and carry it out with her. In the end, she had me order both the fox and the refrigerator-freezer units for her."

In December 1990, having gradually reduced the number of Pam-PAC events she sponsored each year, Pamela decided to dissolve the organization altogether and instructed her assistant, Janet Howard, to compose a letter that went out to each member of the PamPAC board. "One reason she disbanded PamPAC," said J. Carter Brown, "is that she wanted to play a more hands-on role in the political process, something she couldn't do while Averell was still alive. Stodgy and traditional, he simply would never have stood for it. Now, having befriended Bill Clinton, she thought she had found the candidate who could unseat George Bush and reinstall the Democrats in the White House. He possessed charisma and energy, two qualities she felt Al Gore lacked. She didn't care for Hillary Clinton, once called her 'an overreaching opportunist,' but she nevertheless decided to throw her weight behind Bill Clinton. In her own words, she would make him her 'last great political project.' "

Although Clinton had attended Georgetown University as an undergraduate, he was perceived as an outsider in Washington, an upstart, a zealous ex-governor from a "hick" state whose record of achievement at best had been viewed as mediocre. Pamela became his entrée to Georgetown society, such as it was in 1991. They met occasionally and spoke frequently by telephone, Pamela dispensing funds (from her personal account) and advice whenever and wherever she could. She placed phone calls in his behalf, wrote letters, provided introductions. When the media called Clinton "an ersatz John F. Kennedy," she told a Virginia audience, "Where Jack Kennedy was born to power, Bill Clinton got there all by himself."

In mid-1991 Pamela telephoned Bob Strauss, then serving as American ambassador to Russia, and together they strategized on how to wrest the presidency away from Bush. Strauss arranged a meeting at the F Street Club to include himself, Pamela Harriman, Robert Rubin (vice chairman of the New York investment banking firm of Goldman, Sachs), Senator Bill Bradley of New Jersey, Katharine Graham, and Vernon Jordan (Bill Clinton's good friend and a partner of Bob Strauss's at the Washington law firm of Akin Gump Strauss Hauer and Feld LLP). The main purpose of the meeting was to discuss how Goldman, Sachs could help Clinton. The answer came in the form of money. Goldman, Sachs became one of the single biggest contributors to Clinton's presidential campaign fund, with partners kicking in well over $500,000. The firm went a step further, organizing a series of fund-raising dinners, which netted Clinton in excess of $5 million. Rubin himself donated an additional $275,000 to help defray the cost of the forthcoming 1992 Democratic National Convention to be held at New York's Madison Square Garden. Further donations were made by the law firm of Akin Gump, as well as by many of the firm's clients, including such major corporations as American Express, Bankers Trust New York, Union Carbide, and Xerox. It seemed no accident that Clinton later chose Rubin to become his secretary of the treasury, or that he named no less than five of Akin Gump's attorneys to White House staff positions. Vernon Jordan, serving on the boards of no less than five of Akin Gump's largest client corporations, remained one of Clinton's most trusted personal advisers, a key player in the still looming Monica Lewinsky case. Whatever other failings Clinton may have had as president, the nation's economy was healthy during his administration.

Pamela Harriman did her own behind-the-scenes politicking, raising a fortune in contributions from some of her former lovers, among them Gianni Agnelli. She attended all five days of the Democratic National Convention, cheering Clinton on to victory, then endorsing Al Gore for the second spot on the ticket. In September 1992 Pamela threw her last major fund-raiser, a $10,000-a-head "Day in the Country for Clinton" party at Willow Oaks, raising some $3.2 million for the final phase of the Democratic nominee's campaign. On November 20, following Clinton's successful election, Pamela gave Bill and Hillary a reception at her Georgetown home, inviting many of her friends and acquaintances. Kay Graham attended and later threw a party of her own for Clinton, at which she told a reporter: "Without Pamela Harriman, Bill Clinton would not have been elected." Pamela hosted another bash the night of Clinton's inauguration. Every notable Democrat in town dropped by, including Evangeline Bruce, who greeted the hostess with a warm hug.

In a cover story about Pamela that also coincided with Clinton's inauguration, *New York* magazine dubbed her "Queen Mother of the Clinton Court." It is said, though it has never been confirmed, that Pamela hoped for more than she finally got—perhaps a position in Clinton's cabinet. It has also been said, though never confirmed, that Hillary Clinton didn't want her "in the neighborhood," that is, anywhere near her husband.

Whatever the case, on January 20, 1993, the new president announced her appointment to become the next United States ambassador to France (America's largest embassy abroad).

"I had wanted to send Mrs. Harriman to Britain," Clinton said at a press conference, "but she felt she could be more useful in France. For fifteen years, she has been the blood and guts of the Democratic Party. I don't have to defend her record or appointment. She will succeed."

Pamela had declined Clinton's offer to send her to the Court of St. James's because, she informed friends, she felt the British were still resentful of her involvement with Randolph Churchill, her extramarital affair during World War II with Averell Harriman, and her subsequent sexual deportment as an emancipated woman in France and the United States. The French, on the other hand, were more forgiving, particularly when it came to sexual indiscretions.

In 1948 Perle Mesta had been rewarded for her contributions to Harry Truman's presidential war chest by being appointed American ambassador to Liechtenstein. She returned to the States after a year, resentful that she had missed out on so many exciting Washington parties. For Pamela Harriman, the situation was quite different. Although it wasn't a cabinet post, the assignment to one of the world's most beautiful and historic capitals seemed to complete her voyage and her transformation. The Paris assignment was a symbol of the power and respectability she had finally attained. She had overcome the obstacle of her tarnished past. Admittedly, she had the benefit of having lived in France for a decade and of being acquainted with the language, culture, food, history, and leading societal and political figures of the country. Instead of passing judgment, the sophisticated French tended to view her past as a learning experience, therefore an enhancement. As one *Paris Match* reporter put it: "Pamela Churchill Harriman has turned the scandal of her past into an ornament." By way of contrast, Strom Thurmond, the ultraconservative senator from South Carolina, on learning of her appointment, said: "They're sending the Whore of Babylon to Paris."

The Clintons gave Pamela a going-away party at the White House, and Katharine Graham did likewise at her home in Georgetown. The new ambassador arrived at her Paris post in December 1993. The Ameri-

can embassy and her official residence, at 41, rue du Faubourg Saint-
Honoré, soon housed the invaluable art collection that Pamela, currently
seventy-three, had inherited from Averell. Before leaving Washington,
she had sold her estate at Mango Bay, her property in Westchester
County, and her private jet, and closed down her Georgetown town
house and dismissed her staff, except for Janet Howard, who joined her
in Paris as executive personal assistant (in charge of five matching
appointment books and a computer-generated daily schedule). Ben
Bradlee and Sally Quinn acquired Pamela's housekeeper; Michael and
Arianna Huffington, Washington's newest "fun" couple, hired her cook
and butler. "Georgetown appears to be floundering," the new ambassador told Joan Braden. Washington had been further soured for Pamela by
virtue of a lawsuit she had instigated against Christopher Ogden, with
whom she had begun writing her autobiography. When she decided not
to reveal intimate details of her past love affairs, the publisher demanded
the return of their advance. Pamela withdrew from the project, but
Ogden, having spent dozens of hours taping the subject, opted to go it
alone and produce a biography of the lady instead. Ogden's Pamela opus,
slightly revised, eventually appeared and received critical acclaim.
Strangely enough, although she objected to Ogden's volume, Pamela had
no quarrel with Truman Capote's unflattering portrait of her in *Answered
Prayers*, his semifictional rendering of life among the rich and infamous,
in which, as Lady Ina Colbirth, she is said to have once been raped by
Joseph Kennedy, the father of the president. Capote assured his own biographer, Gerald Clarke, that the Kennedy story appeared verbatim just
as Mrs. Harriman had reported it to him.

Pamela's typical day as ambassador often began with a 5 A.M. breakfast and invariably ran through a late dinner, which almost always revolved around the presence of a guest of honor. She hosted numerous
gatherings, meetings, parties, and briefings. She kept up such a hectic
schedule that she averaged less than five hours of sleep a night. Unable to
keep up with her, members of the embassy staff regularly asked to be
transferred. The strain of running an embassy by herself, without a mate
or spouse, caused enough concern in the White House for President
Clinton to write to her: "But can you handle it solo?" Her response:

"What are my alternatives?" Each July Fourth she held an open house at the embassy, inviting any and all American citizens visiting or living in Paris. On Sunday evenings she hosted screenings of recent American films for her French friends and officials. "The French embraced her as one of their own," said Barbara Victor, an American journalist residing in Paris. "She gave great parties," remarked Robert Wiener, an American producer with the Paris bureau of CNN, who once attended a lavish affair organized by Harriman in conjunction with her effort to introduce California wines into the French marketplace. Needless to say, the French weren't interested. But on the whole, she managed well during a period when Franco-American relations were tenuous and difficult, with issues such as NATO, Botswana, and the Middle East constantly at the forefront. She proved particularly adept at arbitrating the differences that arose between Bill Clinton and French President Jacques Chirac. Chirac, in particular, never a great admirer of America or American politicians, adored Harriman, calling her "the finest ambassador the United States has sent us since Thomas Jefferson."

Christopher Dickey, Paris bureau chief for *Newsweek* and the son of James Dickey, the well-known southern author, observed that "the French liked Pamela because she spoke French well. They liked her glamour. They liked her style. They liked to write about her in the French press. Sometimes when she delivered a speech she would begin to imitate Winston Churchill and people would look at each other. Otherwise she was extremely well received by the French."

Dickey attended a Left Bank dinner party in 1995 for the *International Herald-Tribune* and found himself seated between Pamela Harriman on one side and his boss, Katharine Graham, on the other. "I felt honored," Dickey said, "to be seated between two of the great women of their time. They were a contrast in styles, Kay with her serious, no-nonsense approach, Pamela more at ease and laid-back. The idea of her as a courtesan made sense that evening. Although she was in her mid-seventies, she was definitely an attractive woman. Younger men fell for her all the time.

"My feeling is that her values and interests changed as she grew older. There came a point in her life when she was no longer interested only in the reflected glory that motivated her in her early days. She had to find a way of being herself and still being the person that she had been. I believe this process began while Averell Harriman was still alive and continued after his death. Like Kay Graham, Pamela took pleasure in being her own person and not being at the top only because some man had put her there. It was a similar transformation to the one that Kay had undergone after the suicide of Phil Graham, when she suddenly found herself in charge of a publishing empire."

Less pleasurable for Pamela was the ongoing financial battle that raged with Averell's offspring over the Harriman estate, culminating in two 1994 lawsuits charging Pamela with "gross negligence and willful malfeasance" in her management of trust funds that, under her supervision, had been reduced by more than $30 million. Pamela retained Lloyd Cutler, an influential Washington attorney then married to Polly Kraft, the widow of political columnist Joseph Kraft. Cutler had been a lawyer for Jimmy Carter and was currently doing the same for President Clinton. Another of Pamela's advisors in the case was Linda Wachner, a businesswoman whose name figured prominently in the news several years later when, as director of Warnaco, a large clothing manufacturer, she drove the firm into bankruptcy and left amidst rumors of mismanagement and wrongdoing. Wachner had grown particularly close to Pamela as the result of an altercation between Pamela and Janet Howard. The latter, feeling unappreciated, had quit her job with Pamela and returned to the United States.

"The Harriman family," said Averell Fisk, "was supposed to receive income from several trust funds which, due to bad investments—including $20 million into a Playboy resort in New Jersey—basically disappeared. There was nothing left to distribute. The paperwork on these high-risk transactions was so complicated and profuse that it took months to figure out where it had all gone. Meanwhile she was hoodwinking us on other fronts as well, moving funds out of one account and into another. You needed a road map to follow the flow.

"The problems were compounded when we chose Clark Clifford, a friend of Pamela's, to represent the family as trustee. That is probably the biggest mistake we made, because although Clifford had a name and a reputation, he was as corrupt as they come. This is a man who stole from everybody. When I learned that he'd been indicted for bilking the investors in his own bank, I went to my mother [Averell Harriman's eldest daughter, Mary Fisk] and suggested we dump him. He'd been charging us outrageous sums and doing nothing, while good old Pamela was busy using Mafia-like tactics to defraud us. My mother and her sister, Kathleen, didn't act for a long time. 'Don't rock the boat, there's land out there. We're going to reach shore. Everything will turn out okay.' Finally, we dismissed him and sued him for $1.2 million for malpractice. It was like trying to sue a president of the United States. He hid behind his age. He was, or so he claimed, too old and sickly to be deposed. He was too old to appear in court. And so on. In the end, he outlived Pamela by a year, and he outlived my mother by three years. People still think of him as some kind of American folk hero. In reality, he was nothing but an old crook. We ultimately settled with him out of court for a million dollars.

"Whenever my mother or Kathleen approached their father about his estate, he'd wave them off. 'Don't worry. Everything will be great. Pamela will take care of you.' She took care of us, all right. It's a sad, sad story. My mother took it all very hard. In a true sense, it killed her."

The negative publicity that arose from the case alarmed U.S. State Department officials, who considered Pamela their most visible diplomat. Calling the family war "a Greek tragedy," the ambassador confronted her growing stack of legal bills by placing her Georgetown house (and the adjacent office space) on the market. She sold some of her jewelry and a few paintings that Averell had given her for her own collection. In January 1995, she offered the opposition $10 million to settle the case. They turned it down. "The case just kept going on and on and on and on and on," said Bill Rich. "The family so disliked Pamela that there wasn't much anyone could do to end it." As proficient a swimmer as she was an equestrienne, she worked out some of her anger and frustration by joining the Hotel Ritz Health Club, built around the city's most luxurious indoor swimming pool. She would be driven to the Ritz at lunchtime, but instead of lunch she would swim between thirty and fifty laps a day, depending on her schedule and disposition. According to Barbara Victor, Pamela was having an affair with one of the swimming pool attendants, an athletically built Frenchman young enough to be her grandson. She was in the pool on February 3, 1997, when Jacques Lang, France's esteemed minister of culture, swam by and greeted her with a warm smile. She smiled back. A moment later a sharp pain shot through her body. She dragged herself out of the pool and collapsed onto a chaise lounge. An ambulance rushed her to the American Hospital at Neuilly-sur-Seine, outside Paris, where medical personnel determined that she had suffered a massive stroke. Pamela Harriman, seventy-six, lingered for two days. She died on February 5 without ever regaining consciousness.

Posthumously awarded by the French, the cross of the Legion of Honor sat atop Pamela's coffin as it was carried into Washington's National Cathedral, where a thousand mourners gathered to bid the ambassador farewell. Emissaries from more than forty nations attended the ceremony. The first to eulogize Pamela was President Clinton. "Today," he said, "I am here in no small measure because of her." The coffin was then transported to Arden, New York, and laid to rest in the plot she had reserved for herself and Averell Harriman. The litigation over Averell's estate, which must have seemed endless to those involved, came to a close within weeks of Pamela's death. The family accepted basically the same terms she had offered them a few years before, a sum total of approximately $10 million to compensate for the trust funds she had so irresponsibly mismanaged.

℗

IN JUNE 1987, less than a year after the death of Averell Harriman, as Congress held its televised hearings of the Iran-Contra affair, which threatened to implicate President Reagan in a plot illegally providing arms to both Iran and to the CIA-sponsored Nicaraguan rebels, Katharine Graham invited the Reagans to her seventieth birthday party. Arranged by her daughter, Lally Weymouth, to take place in a government banquet hall, the birthday celebration drew some six hundred guests from the upper echelons of the New York–Washington power syndicate. Feasting on smoked salmon and filet mignon, the invitees consumed five hundred bottles of champagne. Among the more recognizable guests were William Paley, Clare Boothe Luce, Barbara Walters, Arthur Sulzberger, Henry and Nancy Kissinger, Rupert Murdoch, Bob Woodward, Ben Bradlee and Sally Quinn, Nora Ephron, Robert McNamara, and Warren Buffett. "It was," as one guest later phrased it, "a foreshadowing of her funeral."

Between the fish and meat courses, Ronald Reagan danced with Kay to the music of Peter Duchin and his orchestra. After dinner, Reagan took his wineglass to the podium and praised Katharine as a "sensitive, thoughtful, and very kindly person." Then he tipped his glass toward her and, in his best Humphrey Bogart imitation, said, "Here's looking at you, kid!"

Art Buchwald, another guest speaker at the same function, recalled it as "an important day in Kay's life. Anyone who mattered was there to pay homage to her. It was a big deal. She had attained godlike status by this time. So when my turn came at the podium, I began by saying: 'If there is one thing that brings us all together here tonight, it is fear. Cold-blooded fear. Fear that if you are not here, you will never be forgiven.' "

Although Art Buchwald had lighthearted humor in mind when he made his birthday speech, the truth of the moment struck deeper. Kay Graham, at seventy, the queen emerita of Georgetown society, the head honcho of one of America's most influential publishing empires, had the power to make or break almost anyone in Washington. There were exceptions perhaps, but they were few and far between. "Whenever I saw her at the offices of *The Washington Post*," said Rowland Evans, "my first impulse was always to fall to a knee and kiss the back of her hand. She engendered awe. I have a mental picture of her seated at the head of a long conference table, ten men—her top editors and money people—occupying seats on each side. Of course it's true that her good friend Meg Greenfield, editor of the editorial page, was also at the table by this time. But you see my point."

The point is well taken. After Kay Graham's death, the *Los Angeles Times* ran a piece on how Kay struck terror in the hearts of young *Washington Post* foreign correspondents, because when she showed up in their town on one of her world tours—tours she continued to make her entire life—they would be expected to make extraordinary efforts to expose her to the local color. David Remnick, a young *Post* correspondent in Moscow (before he became editor of *The New Yorker*), received a visit from Graham in 1988 and was asked, before her arrival, to find her a hairdresser and show her around. As Remnick himself later wrote in *The New Yorker*, he was all too familiar with the story of a certain Africa-based *Post* reporter who had set up a ballooning safari for Mrs. Graham across the savanna at daybreak. In the middle of the flight, as they watched a herd of elephants tramp across the landscape below, Kay turned to the reporter and said, "You know, I didn't travel all this way to be treated like a fucking tourist!" The forlorn reporter ended up as a recipe checker in the *Post*'s food section.

The tales and stories about Kay Graham as an aging, imperious dowager begin at times to sound like Kay Graham talking about her own mother. In a sense, though she resented, even despised her mother, she seemed in her later period to take on many of the same characteristics. One of her biographers, Tom Kelly, spoke of "a woman with little understanding of what makes the common man tick." Another biographer, Carol Felsenthal, referred to her in her advancing years as "a most unsympathetic figure." Roberta Hornig, a former *Washington Star* reporter, speaks of a harrowing encounter she had with Graham. "We shared the same Georgetown hairdresser," she said. "Jean Paul's salon was located on Wisconsin Avenue, off R Street, and everyone in Georgetown used him. It happened I had an important luncheon one day, so I made a 7:30 A.M. appointment to have my hair done. Well, I'm sitting there and Jean Paul is working away on me, when into the shop walks Katharine Graham. It turns out she has an important luncheon date as well, and so she too has made an early morning appointment with Jean Paul. She's standing there and she doesn't want to wait her turn. Jean Paul tells her that maybe there was a mix-up, but he'll take her after he's done with me. 'What do you mean?' she says. 'That woman is a nobody!' Words to that effect. And he says something like, 'Well, she may be a nobody, but she has an appointment.' At this, she turns and stomps out."

Perhaps the most blatant of the many late-in-life disparagements to emerge about Kay Graham involved a 1991 lawsuit that she filed against Nancy E. Polucci, a native of Martha's Vineyard whose modest house sat in the shadow of Graham's imposing oceanfront estate. "She sued me first under the guise of another neighbor of hers, a brain surgeon named Dr. Gani," said Polucci. "She didn't want the negative publicity, but then she sued me again using her own name. I'm a jogger and the gist of her suit was that I would cross her property to get over to the ocean, where I liked to run. There was a precedence for using the trail that crossed her land, because the Indians on the Vineyard had been using it for years. She had a caretaker and he would let me cross when she wasn't around. Then they put up a No Trespassing sign. And that's when she sued. The upshot of it was that she had money, and I didn't. She didn't like the way I dressed or looked, and she didn't want her fancy friends to catch a glimpse of me on her property. The truth of the matter is that most of the large landowners on the Vineyard allowed people to cross their property. That was the long and the short of it. She objected to me because I didn't have a bankroll. So for years we were in and out of court. Eventually she won the case."

Beyond all else, Kay Graham had strength of will. In 1992, a reporter for *The Washington Post* discovered the existence of a vast congressional relocation site underneath the Greenbriar, a five-star resort in West Virginia. The secret underground bunker had been constructed at the height of the Cold War for the exclusive use of senators and congressmen. Asked by national security advisers not to run the story, Kay was outraged that escape plans had been devised for high-ranking Washington officials but not for the general populous. The article, replete with photographs, appeared in May 1992. In 1995, the elaborate shelter was permanently shut down.

Warren Adler, formerly of *Dossier* magazine, presented another side of the later Kay Graham, a more sensitive side that seemingly emerged only under extreme duress. In the mid-1970s, Adler had written a roman à clef, *The Henderson Equation*, about a woman publisher who brings down a president and at the same time leaves a loaded rifle in the house, which her demented husband uses to blow his head off. "My wife, Sunny, and I had been friendly with Kay, because every winter we would bump into her at a resort called Rancho La Puerta in Baja California (Mexico)," said Adler. "On this particular occasion she was there with Meg Greenfield. When she saw me, it suddenly occurred to her after all these years that I was the author of that book. She spent three hours with me at the swimming pool berating me for having written it. I said, 'Kay, you brought down Richard Nixon back when, so why are you upset about a novel that deals with the same subject?' And she said, 'I didn't bring him down. The son-of-a-bitch brought himself down.' She revealed to me that she was very thin-skinned and very vulnerable, because she began to cry. Then suddenly she screamed, 'And I did not kill Phil.' I was deeply shaken, and I decided never to write a novel again that so closely paralleled somebody's life."

The vulnerability and lack of self-assuredness that had been so much a part of Kay Graham's character in the earlier days of her life never completely dissipated. When she won the Pulitzer Prize for *Personal History*, Meg Greenfield said to her: "You see, Kay—you really can write. You've written a wonderful book."

The success—commercial and critical—that greeted *Personal History* inspired its author to undertake another project, an anthology of her favorite writings by novelists and nonfiction commentators about the nation's capital. Titled *Katharine Graham's Washington*, the volume appeared posthumously (a year after her death on July 16, 2001, at the age of eighty-four). "She said to me once that we had outlived our times," said Polly Wisner Fritchey. "She was badly shaken when Meg Greenfield, her dear friend, died of cancer in 1999." Meg Greenfield had also penned a book, *Washington*, which was posthumously published. Superbly written, it dealt with Greenfield's experiences in the D.C. area starting on the day of her arrival in 1961. Loyal to those who had been loyal to her, Kay Graham went on the road to help promote the book, appearing on television shows and in bookstores. She sent complimentary copies to an assortment of her associates, a list of people ranging from Gloria Steinem to Henry Kissinger.

Nobody was closer to Kay Graham during her final years than Donna Shalala, secretary for health and human services under President Clinton. Shalala lived across the street from Graham in what had once been Kay Halle's town house. Every Sunday they took Shalala's dog for a long walk in Montrose Park. Shalala would drive Kay around town when both ladies did errands or accompany her to a performance at the Kennedy

Center. They would sometimes eat dinner together. Shalala frequently attended Graham's parties, parties that she continued to give until the very end. In previous days, they had played tennis together. On one occasion they'd made a tennis date and then Clinton called Shalala and invited her to play golf. "I told him," she said, "that I already had a tennis date. When I reported this to Kay, she said to me, 'Don't ever make that mistake again. If the president asks you for something, even something as trivial as a round of golf, you do it.' She was serious."

Shalala found Kay to be "a great deal of fun. She was fun because she would mix gossip with politics with substantive discussions. More than anyone else I knew in Washington, she was always growing. If she didn't completely understand the dilemma of the man on the street, she understood the dynamics of Washington. I don't think she much liked Bill Clinton, though she had great respect for the presidency. No matter what she thought of a person's politics, she respected the institutions, the Supreme Court, the Congress of the United States. In my book, she was the last of the great Georgetown ladies."

Donna Shalala's final assessment of Katharine Graham as "the last of the great Georgetown ladies" would find at least one dissenter in the person of Sally Quinn. In July 2001, during her sixtieth birthday celebration at a restaurant in London—the same year as Georgetown's 250th anniversary—Sally informed a guest that she had been in such demand that she "could use a full-time social secretary to keep track of my schedule." In May 2003, Quinn would tell Susan Watters that she (Quinn) was the natural heir to the Georgetown throne vacated in rapid succession (and in recent years) by the deaths of Lorraine Cooper, Evangeline Bruce, Pamela Harriman, and finally Katharine Graham. Watters, Washington correspondent for W, would in turn tell Diana McLellan that in the course of an afternoon spent with Sally Quinn, "her cellular phone never stopped ringing. Sally is invited to more dinner parties than anybody else in Washington. I have to wonder if Sally really isn't Georgetown's so-called last princess."

It didn't hurt, of course, that Sally was the wife of Georgetown's so-called last prince, Ben Bradlee. Nor did it matter that in 1985 she had written a *Washington Post* piece, "Death of the Dinner Party," citing the prohibitively rising cost of food, wine, and servants as the main cause. Buffets were in, sit-downs out. Then, in 1987, Quinn wrote an article (for the same newspaper) proclaiming that the era of Washington's most powerful hostesses had also pretty much passed into extinction. But in their time, Quinn wrote, they were "the ones who made a difference." They were "a special breed of women, reared, schooled, and trained to understand the subtle arts of entertaining."

If dinner parties were dead and hostesses obsolete, what then did Sally Quinn bring to the table? Over what sort of kingdom did she consider she reigned? By 1986 she had taken to creating her own kingdoms in the form of fiction. *Regrets Only*, her first novel, portrayed the fictional existence of Lorraine Hardley, a Georgetown hostess with the mostess whose lifestyle seemed a concatenation of the lifestyles of all the members of the Georgetown ladies' social club. As expected, *The Washington Post* gave the novel a rave, calling it "intelligent and absorbing." It was neither. In fact the book generated predominantly negative reviews. Christopher Buckley, the humorist son of William F. Buckley Jr., writing for *Vanity Fair*, termed the work "clit-erature," which proved particularly vexing for Quinn, since she and Tina Brown, the magazine's editor, were friends. Tina had married her husband, publishing executive Harry Evans, at Grey Gardens, the house that Ben and Sally owned in East Hampton, Long Island. While the review led to a yearlong interruption of Sally's friendship with Tina, it did not dissuade Quinn from writing a second novel. *Happy Endings*, published in 1991, which reaped equally negative reviews.

Quinn's itch for fiction did not end with the written word. In more recent times she attempted to write and produce a pilot for CBS-TV (her former employer) based on Georgetown and the machinations of Georgetown hostesses. Intended as the first in what she hoped would become a weekly series (called *Georgetown*), Quinn found the financing to have the pilot made. To date, however, it has not been shown. Her latest project, or so she has said, is a book that her son, Quinn, is writing with Sally's help. Presumably we will learn from it what it means to be the son of high-powered parents as successful in their chosen livelihoods as Ben Bradlee and Sally Quinn.

How successful Sally Quinn truly is or will become is still, according to Washington attorney C. Boyden Gray, an unanswered question. Owner of one of Georgetown's largest town houses, Gray calls Quinn "a work in progress. Her reputation is still growing. She has not yet attained the stature of, let us say, Katharine Graham. Then again, Georgetown is no longer what it was in Kay's day. Everything is considerably different. I don't know if it's possible any longer to muster the kind of social power that the Evangeline Bruces and Kay Grahams once possessed."

Betty Beale sees Quinn in much the same light: "Sally would like to be perceived as Washington's top hostess, or at least as Georgetown's top hostess. But what exactly does that mean? Georgetown today is different. It is filled with businessmen, students, people in the computer or electronics field. Some of them have money but not much else." Aside from Georgetown's shifting population and its emphasis on youth, there is the appearance of the place. The town houses are still there, regal and charming as ever, but M Street and Wisconsin Avenue, its two major thoroughfares, which intersect at a lively bistro called Nathan's, are lined for the most part with fast-food emporiums, souvenir shops, and retail clothing stores. Georgetown is no longer the Garden of Eden it once was; instead, it is reminiscent in spots of what it had been prior to its sweeping renovation. Land value in Georgetown has remained firm, but the vagaries of the day have finally caught up with the fabled kingdom. Although the architects of the city's Metro system acceded to demands not to construct a Georgetown station, a fair share of "outsiders" and "undesirables" still manage to find their way. In the mid-1990s, Georgetown's cave dwellers were shocked to learn that former CIA Director William Colby had been mugged and beaten up only a block from Kay Graham's house.

What Sally Quinn imagined for herself, if we are to believe the philosophy put forth in her 1997 book, *The Party,* is that she represents a new breed of Washington hostess, one whose parties and gatherings are without ulterior motive, without a stated agenda. She is the self-proclaimed queen of the Georgetown party circuit, but one—in her own words—who is "existentially detached" from overt influence peddling. This sentiment put her in the same league with several friendly competitors, notably Kate Lehrer, wife of the novelist-broadcaster Jim Lehrer, and Cokie Roberts, the daughter of Hale and Lindy Boggs. Cokie, married to newsman Steve Roberts, caters to many of the same partygoers who attend Kate Lehrer's affairs, namely the Washington media crowd, including Andrea Mitchell, Tim Russert, and Robert MacNeill (Jim Lehrer's former broadcast partner). Kate and Cokie, neither of whom lives in Georgetown, tend to give informal dinners, serving beer rather than wine and crab cakes rather than sole. Their parties, while popular and sometimes covered by the press, lack the cachet of a Sally Quinn function. "These days," says Chris Matthews, "you can do no better in Washington than Ben and Sally's annual New Year's Eve bash. No doubt about it. It's like the honors list in this town."

For all Sally Quinn's claims not to believe in "official" parties, parties with a purpose, she seemed unusually preoccupied with the prospect of being excluded from the Clinton administration loop. In 1993, when the new president took office, she wrote two very pointed editorials for *The Washington Post* suggesting that since the Clintons were "from out of town," it would behoove them to "get to know" the "old-line" locals, particularly those who lived in Georgetown. "You must come to us," she wrote, as if the Clintons were the Carters all over again. Her assumption in writing the articles was that Georgetown still mattered politically, or that its political and social importance could easily be restored. Her stance seemed to contradict her earlier expressed sentiments regarding the demise of Georgetown dinner parties and hostesses.

"Sally Quinn is an iconoclast," said Chris Matthews. "I think the Clintons had a hard time with her and I think both sides probably enjoyed the rivalry. Sally is Georgetown, and the Clintons never really clicked in Georgetown. After his inauguration and particularly after the departure of Pamela Harriman, I never saw them at any parties. They were regarded as kind of a hick couple. They didn't fit in. Hillary wanted nothing to do with Sally. Sally was off her scope. As it was, the Clintons had little use for the press, and this too annoyed Sally who, after all, is still something of a journalist."

Sensing that Georgetown was no longer a bastion of political influence, the Clintons stayed away. This did not prevent Ben and Sally from inviting practically every major Clinton official into their home. Within the first year of Clinton's first term, their guests included Al and Tipper Gore, David Gergen, George Stephanopoulos, Dee-Dee Myers, Lloyd Cutler, Laura Tyson, James Carville, Vernon Jordan, Mickey Kantor, and Lee Aspin. Secretary of State Madeleine Albright, a longtime George-town resident, had never been to an "A-list" party until she received a much-coveted invitation to one of Ben and Sally's New Year's Eve cele-brations. She had, she told a friend, finally arrived.

Despite Georgetown's loss of prestige as the hub of social power, there were occasions when the thin line between partying and politics was still crossed. On July 19, 1993, for instance, a number of Clinton offi-cials were dining at the Bradlees'. Also present were several journalists, one of whom, Johnny Apple, still found parties a rich source of material for news stories. "I continued to go," he said, "because I would meet peo-ple who could provide me with information I wouldn't ordinarily be able to get, especially members of the intelligence community. At any rate, on this occasion, which took place early on in the new administration, David Gergen was suddenly summoned to the telephone. He came back a few minutes later looking rather grim and rounded up the other Clinton people—Carville, Jordan, Kantor, Aspin—for a hallway confab. It was just amazing. It was like a tornado blowing through a wheat field. The whole mood of the room shifted and people just started clearing out. The press people at the party—myself, Al Hunt, Walter Pincus, and Evan Thomas—started grabbing our cell phones to try to find out what was happening. The gathering, which began as a seated dinner for forty-eight in honor of *New Yorker* media writer Ken Auletta, broke up within about five minutes and thereafter became known as 'the Vince Foster Dinner.' What had happened is that this was the day that Vince Foster, Clinton's legal counsel, somebody very much on the inside, fell on his sword and killed himself. And until that dinner I'd never even heard of Vince Foster. I'd simply not come across his name."

Sally Quinn's anti-Clinton stance only hardened with the passage of time, reaching its high note with the emergence of the Monica Lewinsky scandal. Wielding her pen, she once more attacked Clinton in print as an unscrupulous, unethical, immoral, and somewhat unbalanced human being, reiterating her point of view as a talking head on *Larry King Live* and other television programs. She spoke eloquently but gave the impression that almost any impropriety on the president's part suited her need to be thrust into the spotlight. Her egocentricity galled those who knew her. Generally speaking, Ben Bradlee's children from his previous marriages had problems with her. So did his stepchildren, who found her autocratic and controlling. Her enemies, almost as plentiful as those who had opposed the controversial Pamela Harriman, were quick to speak out against her. Coates Redmon reported hearing that Sally would talk about how she would live her life after Ben Bradlee's death, and that she routinely uttered these statements in front of her much older husband. There was endless chatter about her growing dependence on astrologers, her frequent conferences with one named Svetlana (a former astrologer at *The Washington Post*) and another named Caroline Casey, as well as Patricia McLean, whom she would pay to prepare her astrological charts and read them to her over the telephone.

Her reputation as a leading hostess was challenged during the Clinton administration by Arianna Huffington, the Greek-born, Cambridge-educated biographer of Maria Callas, whose husband, Republican Congressman Michael Huffington, scion to a Texas oil fortune, lived with her in Washington from 1993 to 1997. An archconservative during her stint in Washington, Arianna was originally inspired by Pamela Harriman, whom she met at the 1984 Democratic National Convention. "I thought she had an incredible capacity for intimacy," said Arianna, "because I'd just met her and she invited me to sit in a box with her and listen to the future. She was totally immersed in politics. I was in my early thirties and she was a grande dame, very open and charming. The convention took place in San Francisco and Walter Mondale was the party's nominee."

What prevented Huffington from establishing herself in Washington in a more conclusive manner was her ever shifting political viewpoint, from right to left and back again. At one juncture an ardent supporter of Republican Speaker Newt Gingrich, she soon began writing critical columns about him. "He cut out one of my columns," she said, "and mailed it back to me. Across the side of the clipping, he wrote: 'Your column is strategically counterproductive.' I framed it and nailed it to the wall."

Unlike Sally Quinn's well-planned soirées, Arianna's parties were spontaneous, her invitations often arriving on the day of the event. Residing in a spacious Foxhall house, this hostess encouraged her guests to bring along their children. "She was regarded more as a character than a dowager," said Sally Reston. "She was eccentric and unorthodox, but no more so than Sally Quinn." Her guest lists, drawn predominantly from the conservative right, included David Brock, John Podhoretz, and Grover Norquist. She preferred keeping company with writers from *The Washington Times* as opposed to those from the *Post*. What finally sank Arianna in Washington was not her husband's expensive defeat in the 1994 California senate race, but his frank confession in the pages of *Esquire* that he was bisexual. Arianna moved to California with their two children and sought a divorce. In August 2003, she again shifted gears and ran for public office as an Independent Party candidate (against, among others, film star Arnold Schwarzenegger) in the recall race for governor of California. It is noteworthy that of all contemporary Washington hostesses, Huffington is the only one who vied for a political seat.

In the years to come, Sally Quinn's primary competition will derive not from another hostess but from the gradually evolving times in which we live. The Georgetown social circuit reached its height in an era when women lacked direct access to the machinery of government. But by the onset of the new millennium, women had gained a solid foothold in the governing process. Two of the most visible members of Bill Clinton's cabinet—the secretary of state and the attorney general—were female, to say nothing of Hillary Rodham Clinton's overt influence on her husband's presidency. The number of distaff members of Congress, both in the Senate and the House, has grown considerably. There is even talk of the possibility in the not-too-distant future of electing a woman president. Under these conditions, hostesses, even high-powered ones, tend to become redundant.

Sally Quinn's other archnemesis has to be the administration of George W. Bush. Bill and Hillary Clinton took their time warming to

Washington social life, waiting a year and a half before they threw their first state dinner, this for the emperor of Japan. But having begun the process, they frequently gave White House dinner parties for several hundred guests at a time, in warmer weather holding them in tents set up on the South Lawn. By contrast, the Bushes have entertained less frequently and with far fewer guests. Here and there they venture out to dinner with friends, frequenting such out-of-the-way restaurants as the Peking Gourmet Inn in Arlington, Virginia. The current Bush presidency is an early-morning administration, much less given to socializing than previous administrations. George and Laura spend the majority of their weekends back at their Texas ranch. What's more, their main Republican staffers and supporters live not in Georgetown but in McLean, Virginia, where they play golf and attend each other's barbecues.

The war in Iraq, the Palestinian situation in Israel, Afghanistan, North Korea, the collapsing stock market, the failing economy, the ongoing threat of terrorism, have all conspired at once to create a dour social climate in Washington. After the events of September 11, 2001, the entire country fell into the abyss of a deep depression. In response to the threat of weapons of mass destruction, Sally Quinn made it her business to learn the ins and outs of home security, even editing a section on the subject in *The Washington Post*. While Sally Quinn researches the various types of oxygen masks available to the American public, another Georgetown hostess, Teresa Heinz, makes plans to campaign side by side with her current husband, Senator John Kerry of Massachusetts, the Democratic presidential nominee for 2004. A handsome, stately woman, Teresa was previously married to Republican Senator John Heinz of Pennsylvania, who was killed in a 1991 airplane crash, leaving his wife an estimated net worth of $760 million, in addition to homes in Georgetown, Boston, Nantucket, Sun Valley, and Scotland. In charge of the Heinz Foundation, an international organization devoted to humanitarian causes, Heinz's good works have earned her the nickname "Saint Teresa." Fluent in five languages, she doesn't doubt that she can become the next first lady, and in the process restore Georgetown to what it had once been. She has only just begun.

EPILOGUE

ONE JULY MORNING IN 2002, approximately one year after the funeral of Katharine Graham, Susan R. Ames, a retired Washington bookkeeper who knew neither Evangeline Bruce nor Kay Graham but admired both, entered the gates of Oak Hill, the Victorian garden park cemetery on the edge of Georgetown, to pay her last respects. It was warm but misty, a fine rain gently glazing the marble headstones along the winding paths that lead to the granite façade of a small chapel half-hidden behind the Graham and Bruce plots a scant fifteen yards apart. Pausing for a few minutes before Kay's grave, Ames placed a long-stemmed, thorny red rose next to an array of floral displays that had been carefully arranged around the periphery of the gravesite. It wasn't too far for Kay to travel in her last journey—directly across from the R Street home she had resided in with her husband, Phil Graham, who had been laid to rest in the same plot following his suicide in 1963.

Ames then walked the short distance to Evangeline Bruce's final resting place in the Bruce family plot and repeated the exercise with a second rose. Also buried there were Vangie's husband, David Bruce, and their daughter, Sasha, whose tragic death in 1975 at the age of twenty-nine had sent shock waves through the ceremonious streets of Washington.

Ames considered the proximity of the graves of Katharine Graham and Evangeline Bruce. The notion of two of the nation's grand duchesses lying practically side by side, close in life but even closer in death, struck the visitor's imagination. There was something absurdly romantic, even mythic about it. The well-manicured landscape of Oak Hill was a suitable setting for the ladies to end their days. The intertwining lives of the two women contained all the elements of a modern-day fable, a timeless saga of power and passion, in which the ladies' social club lived on evermore in a place called Georgetown.

⟡

Memento mori.

EXPLANATION OF SOURCES

THE GEORGETOWN LADIES' SOCIAL CLUB has not been conceived as a book of history but rather as an informal chronicle of a time and a place, with an emphasis on five leading ladies: Katharine Graham, Evangeline Bruce, Lorraine Cooper, Pamela Harriman, and Sally Quinn. In the late 1980s, while writing *A Woman Named Jackie,* my biography of Jacqueline Kennedy Onassis, I discovered that a social history of Georgetown did not exist. While conducting interviews for the Onassis volume, I spoke on several occasions with Evangeline Bruce. She requested anonymity at the time but discussed the possibility of cooperating at a future date on her own biography. Our conversations, predominantly by telephone, continued into the early 1000s, at which time she was writing her own book on France circa 1775. Unfortunately, Mrs. Bruce died in 1995, and I was unable to complete enough interviews with her to pen a comprehensive biography. I did, however, gather enough information to begin work on *The Georgetown Ladies' Social Club.*

As for my acquaintanceship with the other women portrayed in the book, I never met nor spoke directly to Lorraine Cooper. I did, however, meet on two occasions with Pamela Harriman, once at a PamPAC function at her home in Georgetown (after the death of Averell Harriman) and once at a dinner party in New York. I met Katharine Graham on one occasion at a charity event in Manhattan, and later requested an interview with her for this book, which she initially denied. During the last year of her life, she evidently underwent a change of heart. I received a telephone call from her one evening and we spoke for nearly an hour, during which time she answered specific questions. Regarding Sally Quinn, it was she who approached me to do an interview. We subsequently had several conversations over the telephone, in which she replied to queries and spoke briefly about her life. Although she proved engaging, and at times humorous, I felt I could gather more information about her through others than I could directly from her.

Because this book is not an academic study but rather an anecdotal record of the lives of five women who helped run Washington from behind the scenes, I have avoided the use of footnotes and end-of-chapter notes. Instead, wherever possible, I have included source information in the body of the text, occasionally in the form of parenthetical commentary. While this method may strike the reader as an awkward encumbrance, it is far less cumbersome than the use of footnotes or similar devices. *The Georgetown Ladies' Social Club* is based substantially on interviews conducted over a ten-year span. Some 420 people were interviewed for this book alone and are listed alphabetically in the acknowledgment section, which follows. A list of those interviewed includes several interviewees whose interviews first appeared in my earlier books. A few names have been omitted from the list by request of the interviewee, but unlike many other authors, I rarely resort to anonymous sources, in almost every instance naming the interviewee. Interviews were either taped in person or on the telephone. In those cases when the interviewee refused the use of a taping device, the interviewer took detailed notes and later transcribed them. Each taped interview was also transcribed. The tapes and transcriptions will be housed in the author's archive, currently located at the rare book and manuscript collection at the State University of New York at Stony Brook. Regarding correspondence referred to in the body of the foregoing text, such material is located at libraries or in collections listed in the acknowledgments section. In some instances, however, particularly in the cases of Evangeline Bruce and Lorraine Cooper, letters were provided the author by confidential sources. The wide-ranging bibliography at the back of this book includes the names of any and all titles referred to or read by the author.

ACKNOWLEDGMENTS

THIS BOOK WOULD NOT HAVE BEEN POSSIBLE without the help of many individuals and institutions. First acknowledgments must go to my literary agent, Owen Laster of the William Morris Agency, and to my editor, Emily Bestler, and her able assistant, Sarah Branham. I very much appreciate the careful legal reading accorded the book by Felice Javit, Esq. Then I would like to thank Lynn Goldberg and Grace McQuade, for their expertise in publicity and public relations. Elizabeth Hartjens (of Imagefinders in Washington, D.C.) did a fine job as a photograph editor. Margaret Shannon (Washington Historical Research of Washington, D.C.) proved an invaluable resource as an expert in archival research and a specialist in Washington history and lore. Alma Schieren must be acknowledged for her tireless efforts as a transcriber and typist. She was assisted by Judy Boundy. I would like to thank Jim Kozak for his computer expertise. Secretarial support was provided by George Brown and Nils Richards. I am particularly grateful to an able staff of researchers and interviewers that included Charles Cassell, Negin Farsad, Roberta Fineberg, Nadine Granoff, Nina Hein, Francesca Hilton, Jacquelyn Jackson, Susan Kelly, Bruce Millar, Anthony Mizzer, Susan Nahm, Mark Padnos, Ryan Rayston, Tinker Ready, Abraham Velez, Peter Walsh, and Carmella Watkins. Among the main interviewers for this project, I have to acknowledge Lisa Friel, who seemed capable of tracking down virtually anyone and getting them to talk. I am indebted to Steve Hammons, not only for his interviewing skill, but for friendship and encouragement. John J. McLaughlin of Lynnfield, Massachusetts, attorney and national radio commentator, had the connections and ability to interview some of the most notable politicians and personalities in the country, including Henry Kissinger, Arthur Schlesinger Jr., Robert Mc-Namara, Art Buchwald, Caspar Weinberger, and John Kerry. Gerry Visco must be cited for invaluable assistance in a number of areas, among them interviewing, editing, Internet research, computer troubleshooting, organization of material, and writing of photo captions. I am also grateful to her for her friendship and emotional support. My most encouraging reader has always been my mother, Renee Heymann. I must also thank Beatrice Schwartz for her encouragement, patience, and fortitude. Finally, this book would not have been possible without the silent devotion of my favorite Siberian Husky, Chickie.

✍

NUMEROUS ORGANIZATIONS, INSTITUTIONS, and groups provided documents, correspondence, oral histories, and written material. While it is not possible to thank the individuals associated with each organization, I would like to express my gratitude to the following institutions: Franklin D. Roosevelt Presidential Library; Harry S. Truman Presidential Library; Dwight David Eisenhower Presidential Library; John F. Kennedy Presidential Library; Lyndon Baines Johnson Presidential Library; Richard M. Nixon Presidential Library; Gerald Ford Presidential Library; Jimmy Carter Center; Ronald Reagan Presidential Library; George Bush Presidential Library; Bill Clinton Presidential Library Group; Library of Congress Manuscript Division; District of Columbia Public Library (Washingtoniana Division and the *Washington Star* Collection); Georgetown Library (Peabody Room); Washington Historical Society; Washington Preservation Society; Virginia Historical Society; Palm Beach Historical Society; New York Historical Society; Massachusetts Historical Society; Arizona Historical Foundation, Arizona State University (Barry Goldwater Collection); Columbia University Library (Special Collections); Columbia University Law School Library; City University of New York Library Center; New York University Library (Special Collections); Princeton University Library (Adlai Stevenson Collection); Radcliffe Institute, Harvard University, Schlesinger Library (Lorraine Cooper and Marietta Tree papers); Radcliffe College Registrar's Office; SUNY at Stony Brook Library (Jacob K. Javitz and Robert F. Kennedy Collections); Boston University Library (Doris Lilly Archive); Temple University Libraries (Special Collections); Margaret I. King Library, University of Kentucky (John Sherman Cooper Collection); Georgetown University Library (Special Collections); William and Mary University Library (Special Collections); American University Library (Special Collections); George Washington University Library (Special Collections); University of Virginia Library (Special Collections); University of Maryland Library (Special Collections); University of Maine Library (Special Collections); Churchill Archives Centre, Churchill College (Cambridge, England); St. Albans School Library; National Archives; Smithsonian Institution; National Geographic Society; Central Intelligence Agency; Federal Bureau of Investigation; Department of the Treasury; Department of State; U.S. Supreme Court; United Nations Archive Center; New York Public Library; OSS Research Foundation; the Greenbrier Project; Dumbarton Oaks Foundation; the Morris and Gwendolyn Cafritz Foundation; Hilltop Foundation (Marjorie Merriweather Post papers); Celebrity Services, Inc.; Tudor Place Foundation; CBS Television Archives; Academy of Motion Pictures Arts and Sciences; Washington, D.C., Police Department Archives; New York Society Library; Metropolitan Museum of Art, Costume Division; Frick Collection; National Gallery of Art; *Town and Country* Magazine Archives; *W* Archives; *Interview* Magazine Archives; *New York* Magazine Archives; Condé Nast Archives; Time-Life Archives.

❧

AND FINALLY I THANK the many individuals who agreed to be interviewed for this book or who answered questions in writing. While a few requested anonymity, most did not. Among the latter are:

Bess Abell, Tyler Abell, David Abramson, Rudy Abramson, Natalie Adams, Sunny Adler, Warren Adler, Thomas Alexander, Tony Alexander, Catherine Allgor, Susan Mary Alsop, Susan R. Ames, Jan Cushing Amory, Jack Anderson, R. W. "Johnny" Apple Jr., E. J. Applewhite, Dr. Sherrell J. Ashton.

Bobby Baker, Howard H. Baker Jr., Letitia Baldrige, Robert Barnett, Susan Barron, Marion Barry, Charlie Bartlett, Betty Beale, Jo Becker, Jean Viner Bell, Sonya Bernhardt, Deeda Blair, Bill Blass, Peter Blute, Corinne Claiborne "Lindy" Boggs, Avis T. Bohlen, Carol Bowersock, Frances Bowersock, Merom Brachman, Joan Braden, Sarah Bradford, David Breasted, Governor Edward Breathitt, J. Carter Brown, Anthony P. Browne, David S. Bruce, Janet Bruce, Art Buchwald, Nina Burleigh, Ella Poe Burling, Frida Burling, Pat Butler.

Buffy Cafritz, Tracy Campbell, Nora Cameron, Liz Carpenter, Caroline Casey, Linda Cashdan, Charles Cassell, Igor Cassini, Oleg Cassini, Ruth Cavanaugh, Kevin Chaffee, Otis Chandler, Ellen Charles, Oatsie Charles, Margaret E. Cheney, Anna Chennault, Julia Child, Marion Christy, Sharon Churcher, Brice McAdoo Clagett, Marjorie Clapprood, Blair Clark, Sylvia Clark, Alexander Cockburn, Nancy Cole, Chuck Conconi, Maureen Connally, Evelyn Cooper, Esther Coopersmith, Alan Cranston, Mimi Crocker, William Xavier Cross.

John Daly, Patrick Daly, Leo Damore, Stuart C. Davidson, Deborah Davis, Deborah Gore Dean, Alexandra de Borchgrave, Michel de Bourbon, Carol Delaney, Dominique D'Ermo, Robert Devaney, Doda de Wolf, Marilyn de Young, C. Wyatt Dickerson, John Dickerson, Nancy Dickerson, Christopher Dickey, Tandy Dickinson, Timothy Dickinson, John Dizard, Diana DuBois, Peter Duchin, Dominick Dunne.

Edward Eames, James Eichberg, Eleanor Elliott, Osborn Elliot, Gaetana Enders, Rowland Evans.

Douglas Fairbanks Jr., John "Jack" Farrell, Carol Felsenthal, Julie Finley, Myrna Firestone, Averell Fisk, Frances FitzGerald, Ray Flynn, Wendell Ford, Lawrence Forgy, Lisa Friel, Jean Friendly, Clayton Fritchey, Polly Wisner Fritchey.

Zsa Zsa Gabor, Catherine "Kitty" Galbraith, John Kenneth Galbraith, Joan Gardner, Phyllis George, Ann Geracimos, Phillip Geyelin, Shirley Geylin, Alma Gildenhorn, John W. Gill, Roswell Gilpatric, Angele Gingras, Ina Ginsburg, Lillian Glass, John Gleiber, Robert Godwin, Lucianne Goldberg, Robert Goldberg, Doug Golde, Andrew Goodpaster, Suzy Gookim, Joseph Goulden, Caroline Graham, C. Boyden Gray, Robert K. Gray, Meg Greenfield, Brandon Grove Jr., Mariana Grove, Bailey Guard.

Leonard Hacker, Margot Hahn, Patricia Haig, Halston, Steve Hammons, Ann Hand, Charles Hartman, Richard Harwood, Jimmy Hatcher, Charlotte Hayes, Bill Hayward, Brooke Hayward, Wendy Wisner Hazard, Teresa Heinz, Cynthia Helms, Angela Hemingway, Jim Henderson, Don Hewitt, Francesca Hilton, Christopher Hitchens, Warren Hoge, Bill Hoogeveen, George Anthony Horkan, Roberta Horning, Barbara Howar, Fisher Howe, Richard Howland, Arianna Huffington, Marjorie Hunter.

Paul Ignatius, Jayne Ikard, Reed J. Irvine, Jacob K. Javits, Peter Jay, Anne-Hope Johnson, George Jones Johnson, Carol Joynt, Ward Just.

Philip Kaiser, Cynthia Kane, Ron Kaufman, Don Kellerman, Tom Kelly, Kathy Kemper, John Kerry, Ronald Kessler, Billy Kilmer, Andrew Kilpatrick, Henry Kissinger, Joel Klein, Mary Knill, Bill Koplowitz, Milly Kowalski, Polly Kraft, S. Paul Kramer.

Allison LaLand, Joseph Lambert, Nelson Lankford, David Laventhol, Billy Leach, Richard Lee, Chris Lehman, Frances Leighton, Mary Leonard, Bob Levey, Jeffrey Lewis, Doris Lilly, Trowbridge Littleton, Jeanne Livingston, Sandra Loomis, Elizabeth M. Lorentz, Jacques Lowe, Ernest Lowy.

Lynn Magruder, Susan Malbin, Michael Markoff, Jan Marr, Doug Marshall, Guy Martin, Barbara Matsos, Chris Matthews, Barbara Matusow, Marguerite McAdoo, Lorraine McAndrew, Abigail McCarthy, Pamela McClelland,

Mitch McConnell, Jerry McCoy, Dennis McDougal, Sandra McElwaine, Nan McEvoy, George McGovern, Elizabeth "Betty" McIntosh, Ken McKnight, John J. McLaughlin, Diana McLellan, Robert McNamara, Susan Medalie, Aileen ("Suzy") Mehle, Joan Mellen, Robert Merry, Cord Meyer, Victoria Michael, Carolyn Michaleis, Peter Milius, Arthur Miller, Barbara Miller, Scott Miller, Anthony Mizzer, Charles Moffat, Ruth Montgomery, Ted Morgan, Georgette Mosbacher, Helga Moss, Daniel Moynihan, Trude Musson.

Harry Nalatchan, William Neichter, Jack Nelson, Jane Niagra, Grover Norquist, Eleanor Holmes Norton, Robert Novak, Louie B. Nunn.

Christopher Ogden, Michael O'Harro, Don Oldenburg, Tom Oliphant, Judy Oppenheimer, Bill O'Reilly, Alejandro Orfila.

Robert Packwood, Eloise R. Page, Betsy Paradis, Thomas A. Parrot, Lyn Paulsin, Claiborne Pell, Nuella Pell, Charles Percy, Lester Persky, Charles Peters, Mary Ellen Philip, Jennifer Phillips, Antoinette Pinchot, George Plimpton, Nancy E. Polucci, Jan Pottker, Jennifer Pradas, Sharon Pratt, Alan Pryce-Jones, Joyce Purnick.

William ("Billy") Quinn.

Donnie Radcliffe, Eden and Gerald Rafshoon, Tom Rapone, Ryan Rayston, Coates Redmon, Alfred S. Regnery, Cary Reich, Sally Reston, Bill Rich, Mary Kay Ricks, Marie Ridder, Peter Rieves, Ruth Ripley, Peter Rivers, Alice Rivlin, Chalmers M. Roberts, Warren Rogers, William P. Rogers, Franklin D. Roosevelt Jr., James Roosevelt Jr., Lynn Rosselini, Sandy Rovner, David E. Rust.

Faith Sale, Pierre Salinger, Terri M. Sapienza, Louis Scarone, Robert Scheer, Arthur Schlesinger, Daniel Schorr, Aniko Gaal Schott, Stephen Schragis, Robert Schulman, Janet B. Schwarz, Caroline Seebohm, Donna Shalala, Eileen Shanahan, Donald Shannon, Margaret Shannon, John Sherman, Stanley Shipman, Deborah Shore, Ken Silverstein, Alan Simpson, Eileen Slocum, George Smathers, Clifford Smith, Phil Smith, Sam Smith, Stoff Smulson, Stephen Sondheim, Ken Sparks, Delbert Spurlock, James Srodes, Garnett Stackleburg, Ronald Steel, Newton Steers Jr., Jane Stein, Gloria Steinem, Borden Stevenson, Raimund Stieger, Nina Auchincloss Steers Straight, Marianne Strong, Nina Sturgeon, Jeffrey Suchanek, Virginia Surtees, Jane Suydam, Jane Swarthmore.

The Reverend Arnold Taylor, Bill Thomas, Evan Thomas, Gordon Thomas, Nina Totenberg, Noël Train, Stanley Tretick, James Truitt, Sterling Tucker.

Jack Valenti, Barbara Victor, Nick Von Hoffman, Edward von Kloberg, Diana Vreeland.

David Wade, John Walker, John Warner, Paul Warnke, Gerald Warren, Walter Washington, Lynda Webster, Caspar Weinberger, Robert Weiner, Gulley Wells, Millicent West, Lee C. White, John C. Whitehead, Charles Whitehouse, Janet Whitehouse, James Russell Wiggins, Maggie Wimsatt, Lucy Winchester, Elizabeth Winthrop, Jim Wise, Frank George Wisner.

Sandra Yives, Byron Yorke.

Ardeshir Zahedi, Franklyn Zappho, Fred Zucker, Carol Zussman.

BIBLIOGRAPHY

Abramson, Rudy. *Spanning the Century: The Life of W. Averell Harriman, 1891–1986*. New York: William Morrow, 1992.

Adams, Henry. *Democracy, An American Novel*. New York: Penguin, 1994.

———. *The Education of Henry Adams: An Autobiography*. Introduction by Edward Morris. New York: Modern Library, 1996.

Adler, Warren. *The Henderson Equation*. New York: Putnam, 1976.

Akbar, M. J. *Nehru: The Making of India*. New York: Viking, 1988.

Allgor, Catherine. *Parlor Politics: In Which the Ladies of Washington Help Build a City and a Government*. Charlottesville: University Press of Virginia, 2000.

Alsop, Joseph W. *"I've Seen the Best of It": Memoirs*. With Adam Platt. New York: W. W. Norton, 1992.

Alsop, Stewart. *The Center: The Anatomy of Power in Washington*. London: Hodder and Stoughton, 1968.

Alsop, Susan Mary. *To Marietta from Paris, 1945–1960*. Garden City: Doubleday, 1975.

Ambrose, Stephen E. *Nixon: Volume Two: The Triumph of a Politician, 1962–1972*. New York: Simon & Schuster, 1989.

Auburn, Ellis. *The Most Beautiful Woman in the World: The Obsessions, Passions, and Courage of Elizabeth Taylor*. New York: HarperCollins, 2000.

Anderson, Christopher. *Jackie after Jack: Portrait of the Lady*. New York: William Morrow, 1998.

Anthony, Carl Sferazza. *As We Remember Her: Jacqueline Kennedy Onassis, in the Words of Her Family and Friends*. New York: HarperCollins, 1997.

Arms, Thomas S. *Encyclopedia of the Cold War*. New York: Facts on File, 1994.

Aronson, Stephen M. L. *Hype*. New York: William Morrow, 1983.

Ashman, Charles L. *Connally: The Adventure of Big Bad John*. New York: William Morrow, 1974.

Atwater, Maxine. *Capital Tales: True Stories about Washington Heroes, Villains and Belles*. Bethesda, Md.: Mercury Press, 1996.

Auchincloss, Louis. *The House of the Prophet*. Boston: Houghton Mifflin, 1980.

Bach, Steven. *Dazzler: The Life and Times of Moss Hart*. New York: Alfred A. Knopf, 2001.

Bachrach, Judy. *Tina and Harry Come to America: Tina Brown, Harry Evans, and the Uses of Power*. New York: Free Press, 2001.

Baedecker's Paris. Basingstroke, Hampshire, England: AA Publishing, 1999.

Baker, Robert Gene. *Wheeling and Dealing: Confessions of a Capital Hill Operator*. With Larry L. King. New York: W. W. Norton, 1978.

Baldridge, Letitia. *Of Diamonds and Diplomats: An Autobiography of a Happy Life*. Boston: Houghton Mifflin, 1968.

Baldwin, Billy. *Billy Baldwin, An Autobiography*. With Michael Gardine. Boston: Little, Brown, 1985.

Barras, Jonetta Rose. *The Last of the Black Emperors: The Hollow Comeback of Marion Barry in the New Age of Black Leaders*. Photos by Darrow Montgomery. Baltimore: Bancroft Press, 1998.

Beale, Betty. *Power of Play: A Memoir of Parties, Politicians and the Presidents in My Bedroom*. Washington, D.C.: Regnery Gateway, 1993.

Beaton, Cecil. *Self Portrait with Friends: The Selected Diaries of Cecil Beaton, 1926–1974*. Edited by Richard Buckle. London: Weidenfeld and Nicolson, 1979.

Bernstein, Carl, and Bob Woodward. *All the President's Men*. New York: Simon & Schuster, 1974.

Beschloss, Michael R. *The Crisis Years: Kennedy and Khrushchev Years, 1960–1963*. New York: HarperCollins, 1991.

Bingham, Clara. *Women on the Hill: Challenging the Culture of Congress*. New York: Times Books, 1997.

Birmingham, Steven. *The Grandes Dames*. New York: Simon & Schuster, 1982.

———. *The Right People: A Portrait of the American Social Establishment*. Boston: Little, Brown, 1997.

Black Georgetown Remembered: A History of the Black Community from the Founding of "The Town of George" in 1761 to the Present Day. Kathleen M. Lesko, general editor and contributing author; Valerie Babb and Carroll R. Gibbs, contributing authors. Washington, D.C.: Georgetown University Press, 1991.

Blackman, Ann. *Seasons in Her Life: A Bibliography of Madeleine Korbell Albright*. New York: Scribner's, 1998.

Blass, Bill. *Rare Blass*. Edited by Cathy Horyn. New York: HarperCollins, 2002.

Blumenthal, Sidney. *The Clinton Wars*. New York. Farrar, Straus & Giroux, 2003.

Bockris, Victor. *Warhol*. New York: Da Capo Press, 1997.

Boggs, Lindy. *Washington Through A Purple Veil: Memoirs of a Southern Woman.* With Katherine Hatch. New York: Harcourt Brace, 1994.

Boller, Paul F. *Presidential Wives.* New York: Oxford University Press, 1988.

Bowles, Chester. *Promises to Keep: My Years in Public Life, 1941–1969.* New York: Harper and Row, 1971.

Braden, Joan. *Just Enough Rope: An Intimate Memoir.* New York: Villard Books, 1989.

Bradley, Benjamin. *Conversations with Kennedy.* New York: W. W. Norton, 1975.

———. *A Good Life: Newspapering and Other Adventures.* New York: Simon & Schuster, 1988.

Branch, Taylor. *Parting the Waters: America in the King Years, 1954–1963.* New York: Simon & Schuster, 1995.

Bray, Howard. *The Pillars of the Past: The Making of a News Empire in Washington.* New York: W. W. Norton, 1980.

Brenner, Marie. *Great Dames: What I Learned from Older Women.* New York: Crown, 2000.

Brinkley, David. *11 Presidents, 4 Wars, 22 Political Conventions, 1 Moon Landing, 3 Assassinations, 2,000 Weeks of News and Other Stuff on Television and 18 Years of Growing Up in North Carolina.* New York: Alfred A. Knopf, 1995.

Brodie, Fawn M. *Richard Nixon: The Shaping of His Character.* New York: W. W. Norton, 1981.

Brown, Anthony Cave. *The Last Hero: Wild Bill Donovan: The Biography and Political Experience of Major General William J. Donovan, Founder of the OSS and "Father" of the CIA, from His Personal and Secret Papers and the Diaries of Ruth Donovan.* New York: TimesBooks, 1988.

Bruce, David Kirkpatrick Este. *OSS Against the Reich: The World War II Diaries of Colonel David K. E. Bruce.* Edited by Nelson Lankford. Kent, Ohio: Kent State University Press, 1991.

———. *Revolution by Reconstruction.* New York: Doubleday, 1939.

———. *Seven Pillars of the Republic.* Priv. Print. Garden City, N.Y.: Country Life Press, 1936.

———. *Sixteen American Presidents.* Indianapolis: Bobbs-Merrill, 1962.

———. *Window on the Forbidden City: The Beijing Diaries of David Bruce.* Hong Kong: Centre of Asian Studies, University of Hong Kong, 2001.

Bruce, Evangeline. *Napoleon and Josephine: The Improbable Marriage.* New York: Scribner, 1995.

Buchwald, Ann. *Seems Like Yesterday.* New York: Putnam, 1980.

Burleigh, Nina. *A Very Private Woman: The Life and Unsolved Murder of Presidential Mistress Mary Meyer.* New York: Bantam, 1999.

Bush, Barbara. *Barbara Bush: A Memoir.* New York: Scribner's, 1994.

Campbell, Tracy. *Short of Glory: The Fall and Redemption of Edward F. Prichard, Jr.* Lexington, Ky.: University Press of Kentucky, 1998.

Capote, Truman. *A Capote Reader.* New York: Random House, 1987.

Carlisle, Kitty. *Kitty, An Autobiography.* New York: Doubleday, 1988.

Caro, Robert A. *The Years of Lyndon Johnson: Volume 3: Master of the Senate.* New York: Alfred A. Knopf, 2002.

Caroli, Betty Boyd. *First Ladies.* New York: Oxford University Press, 1987.

———. *The Roosevelt Women.* New York: Basic Books, 1998.

Carpozi, George. *Poison Pens: The Unauthorized Biography of Kitty Kelley.* Fort Lee, N.J.: Barricade Books, 1991.

Carrier, Thomas J. *Historic Georgetown: A Walking Tour.* Charleston, S.C.: Arcadia Publishing, 1999.

Carter, Rosalynn. *First Lady from Plains.* Boston: Houghton Mifflin, 1984.

Carville, James. *Stickin' the Case for Loyalty.* New York: Simon & Schuster, 2000.

———. *We're Right, They're Wrong: A Handbook for Spirited Progressives.* New York: Random House, 1996.

Carzon, Jean-Marie. *Paris Larousse.* Translation by S. D. Henderson. Paris: Larousse, 1982.

Cassini, Igor. *I'd Do It All Over Again.* With Jeanne Molli. New York: Putnam, 1977.

Cassini, Oleg. *In My Own Fashion: An Autobiography.* New York: Simon & Schuster, 1987.

Chancellor, Alexander. *Some Times in America and a Life in a Year at the New Yorker.* New York: Carroll & Graf, 1999.

Chester, Lewis, Godfrey Hodgson, and Bruce Page. *An American Melodrama: The Presidential Campaign of 1968.* New York: Viking, 1960.

Chisholm, Anne, and Michael Davie. *Lord Beaverbrook: A Life.* New York: Alfred A. Knopf, 1992.

Christopher, Warren. *Chances of a Lifetime.* New York: Scribner's, 2001.

Churcher, Sharon. *New York Confidential.* New York: Crown, 1986.

Churchill, Randolph Spencer. *Winston S. Churchill: Volume VI: The Finest Hour, 1939–1941.* By Martin Gilbert. Boston: Houghton Mifflin, 1983.

Churchill, Winston S. *Memories and Adventures.* London: Weidenfeld and Nicolson, 1989.

Cigliano, Jan. *Private Washington: Residences in the Nation's Capital.* Photographs by Walter Smalling Jr.; foreword by Sally Quinn. New York: Rizzoli, 1998.

Clarke, Gerald. *Capote: A Biography.* New York: Simon & Schuster, 1988.

Clifford, Clark M. *Counsel to the President: A Memoir.* With Richard Holbrooke. New York: Random House, 1991.

Cockburn, Alexander, and Ken Silverstein. *Washington Babylon*. London; New York: Verso, 1996.

Cohn, Roy M. *The Autobiography of Roy Cohn*. By Sidney Zion. Secaucus, N.J.: Lyle Stewart, 1988.

Colacello, Bob. *Holy Terror: Andy Warhol Close Up*. New York: HarperCollins, 1990.

Collier, Peter, and David Horowitz. *The Kennedys: An American Drama*. New York: Summit Books, 1984.

Collins, Gail. *Scorpion Tongues: Gossip, Celebrity, and American Politics*. New York: William Morrow, 1998.

Collins, Nancy. *Hard to Get: Fast Talk and Rude Questions Along the Interview Trail*. New York: Random House, 1990.

The Continuum Dictionary of Women's Biography: New Expanded Edition of the International Dictionary of Women's Biography. Compiler and Editor, Jennifer S. Uglow. New York: Continuum, 1989.

Cook, Fred J. *The Nightmare Decade: The Life and Times of Senator Joe McCarthy*. New York: Random House, 1971.

Coy, Cissie. *Washington Hostess Cookbook*. Godalming, Surrey, England: Portland House, 1990.

Cronkite, Walter. *A Reporter's Life*. New York: Harper and Row, 1996.

Curtis, Charlotte. *The Rich and Other Atrocities*. New York: Harper and Row, 1976.

Dallek, Robert. *Lone Star Rising: Lyndon Johnson and His Times, 1908–1960*. New York: Oxford University Press, 1991.

Davenport, Elaine, Paul Eddy, and Peter Gillman. *The Plumbat Affair*. London: Future Publications, 1978.

Davis, Deborah. *Katharine the Great: Katharine Graham and the Washington Post*. New York: Harcourt Brace Jovanovich, 1979.

Deaver, Michael K. *Behind the Scenes*. With Mickey Hershkowitz. New York: William Morrow, 1981.

Delany, Kevin. *A Walk Through Georgetown: A Guided Stroll That Details the History and Charm of Old Georgetown*. Washington, D.C.: Kevin Delany Publications, 1971.

Demaris, Ovid. *The Director: An Oral Biography of J. Edgar Hoover*. New York: Harper's Magazine Press, 1975.

Diamond, Edwin. *Behind the Times: Inside the New York Times*. New York: Villard Books, 1994.

Dickerson, Nancy. *Among Those Present: A Reporter's View of Twenty-five Years in Washington*. New York: Random House, 1976.

Ditzen, Eleanor Davies Tydings. *My Golden Spoon: Memoirs of a Capital Lady*. Lanham, Md.: Madison Books, 1997.

Drury, Allen. *Capable of Honor.* New York: Dell, 1966.

Duchin, Peter. *Ghost of a Chance: A Memoir.* New York: Random House, 1996.

Earl Blackwell's Celebrity Register. Towson, Md.: Times Pub. Group, 1986.

Eisele, Albert. *Almost to the Presidency: A Biography of Two American Presidents.* Blue Earth, Minn.: Piper, 1982.

Eisenhower, Julie Nixon. *Pat Nixon: The Untold Story.* New York: Simon & Schuster, 1986.

Elliott, Osborn. *The World of Oz.* New York: Viking, 1986.

Ellsberg, Daniel. *Secrets: A Memoir of Vietnam and the Pentagon Papers.* New York: Viking, 2002.

Ephron, Nora. *Crazy Salad: Some Things About Women.* New York: Modern Library, 2000.

———. *Heartburn.* New York: Alfred A. Knopf, 1983.

Epstein, Edward Jay. *Deception: The Invisible War Between the KGB and the CIA.* New York: Simon & Schuster, 1989.

Evelyn, Douglas, and Paul Dickson. *On This Spot: Pinpointing the Post in Washington, D.C.* Washington, D.C.: National Geographic, 1999.

Eszterhas, Joe. *American Rhapsody.* New York: Alfred A. Knopf, 2000.

Fairchild, John. *Chic Savages.* New York: Simon & Schuster, 1989.

Farrell, John Aloysius. *Tip O'Neill and the Democratic Century.* Boston: Little, Brown, 2001.

Felsenthal, Carol. *Alice Roosevelt Longworth.* New York: Putnam, 1988.

———. *Power, Privilege, and the Post: The Katharine Graham Story.* New York: Seven Stories Press, 1993.

———. *Princess Alice: The Life and Times of Alice Roosevelt.* New York: St. Martin's, 1988.

Fitch, Noel Riley. *Appetite for Life: The Biography of Julia Child.* New York: Doubleday, 1997.

Forgotten Heroes: Inspiring American Portraits from Our Leading Historians. Edited by Susan Ware; with a foreword by David McCullough. New York: Free Press, 1991.

Frantz, Douglas, and David McKean. *Friends in High Places: The Rise and Fall of Clark Clifford.* Boston: Little, Brown, 1995.

From the Secret Files of J. Edgar Hoover. Edited with a commentary by Anathan Theoharis. Chicago: I.R. Dee, 1991.

Gaines, Steven S. *Philistines at the Hedgerow: Passion and Property in the Hamptons.* Boston: Little, Brown, 1998.

Gentry, Curt. *J. Edgar Hoover: The Man and the Secrets.* New York: W. W. Norton, 1997.

Gingras, Angele de T. *From Busing to Bugging: The Best in Congressional Humor.* Washington, D.C.: Acropolis Books, 1973.

Goldberg, Robert. *Barry Goldwater.* New Haven: Yale University Press, 1995.

Goldman, Eric F. *The Tragedy of Lyndon Johnson.* New York: Alfred A. Knopf, 1969.

Goodwin, Richard N. *Remembering America: A Voice from the Sixties.* Boston: Little, Brown, 1988.

Goulden, Joseph C. *Fit to Print: A.M. Rosenthal and His Times.* Secaucus, N.J.: Lyle Stuart, 1988.

Graham, Katharine. *Katharine Graham's Washington.* New York: Alfred A. Knopf, 2002.

Gray, Robert Keith. *Eighteen Acres Under Glass.* Garden City, N.Y.: Doubleday, 1962.

Greenfield, Meg. *Washington.* With a foreword by Katharine Graham and an afterword by Michael Beschloss. New York: Public Affairs, 2001.

Grobel, Lawrence. *Conversations with Capote.* With a foreword by James A. Michener. New York: American Library, 1985.

Grose, Peter. *Operation Rollback: America's Secret War Behind the Iron Curtain.* Boston: Houghton Mifflin, 2000.

Gulley, Bill. *Breaking Cover.* With Mary Ellen Reese. New York: Simon & Schuster, 1980.

Hagwood, Wesley O. *Presidential Sex: From the Founding Fathers to Bill Clinton.* Secaucus, N.J.: Carol Publishing, 1998.

Halbertstam, David. *The Best and the Brightest.* New York: Random House, 1959.

———. *The Powers That Be.* Urbana: University of Illinois Press, 2000.

Haldeman, H. R. *The Haldeman Diaries: Inside the Nixon White House.* Introduction and afterword by Stephen E. Ambrose. New York: Putnam, 1994.

Harris, Fred R. *Potomac Fever.* New York: W. W. Norton, 1977.

Hass, Stephen. *America's Political Dynasties: From Adams to Kennedy.* Garden City, N.Y.: Doubleday, 1966.

Havill, Adrian. *Deep Truth: The Lives of Bob Woodward and Carl Bernstein.* New York: Carol Publishing, 1993.

———. *The Last Mogul: The Unauthorized Biography of Jack Kent Cooke.* New York: St. Martin's, 1992.

Hayward, Brooke. *Haywire.* New York: Alfred A. Knopf, 1977.

Heller, Robert. *Roads to Success.* London: Dorling Kindersley Pub., 2001.

Hendrickson, Paul. *The Living and the Dead: Robert McNamara and Five Lives of a Lost War.* New York: Vintage Books, 1997.

Herr, Michael. *Dispatches.* New York: Alfred A. Knopf, 1977.

Hersh, Burton. *The Old Boys: The American Elite and the Origins of the CIA.* New York: Scribner's, 1992.

Hersh, Seymour M. *The Dark Side of Camelot.* Boston: Little, Brown, 1997.

Hewitt, Don. *Tell Me a Story: Fifty Years and 60 Minutes in Television.* New York: Public Affairs, 2001.

Heymann, C. David. *Liz: An Intimate Biography of Elizabeth Taylor.* London: Heinemann, 1995.

———. *Poor Little Rich Girl: The Life and Legend of Barbara Hutton.* Secaucus, N.J.: Lyle Stuart, 1984.

———. *RFK: A Candid Biography of Robert F. Kennedy.* London: Heinemann, 1998.

———. *A Woman Named Jackie: An Intimate Biography of Jacqueline Bouvier Kennedy Onassis.* New York: Carol Communications, 1989.

Howar, Barbara. *Laughing All the Way.* New York: Stein and Day, 1993.

———. *Making Ends Meet.* New York: Random House, 1976.

Huffington, Adrianna. *How to Overthrow the Government.* New York: Regan-Books, 2000.

Ignatieff, Michael. *Isaiah Berlin: A Life.* New York: Henry Holt, 1998.

Isaacson, Walter. *Kissinger: A Biography.* New York: Simon & Schuster, 1992.

Isaacson, Walter, and Evan Thomas. *The Wise Men: Six Friends and the World They Made: Acheson, Bohlen, Harriman, Kennan, Lovett, McCloy.* New York: Simon & Schuster, 1986.

Jaffe, Harry S., and Tom Sherwood. *Dream City: Race, Power, and the Decline of Washington, D.C.* New York: Simon & Schuster, 1994.

Johnson, Lyndon Baines. *Reaching for Glory: Lyndon Johnson's Secret White House Tapes, 1964–1965.* Edited with a commentary by Michael Beschloss. New York: Simon & Schuster, 2001.

———. *Taking Charge: The Johnson White House Tapes, 1953–1964.* Edited with a commentary by Michael R. Beschloss. New York: Simon & Schuster, 1997.

———. *The Vantage Point: Perspective of the Presidency, 1963–1969.* New York: Holt, Rinehart and Winston, 1976.

Johnson, Sam Houston. *My Brother Lyndon.* Edited by Enrique Hank Lopez. New York: Cowles, 1970.

The Johnson Years. Edited by Nelson Lichtenstein. *Political Profiles,* vol. 4. New York: Facts on File, 1976.

Kaiser, Philip M. *Journeying Far and Wide: A Political and Diplomatic Memoir.* New York: Scribner's, 1992.

Kaplan, Fred. *Gore Vidal: A Biography.* New York: Doubleday, 1999.

Keith, Slim. *Slim: Memories of a Rich Imperfect Life.* With Annette Tapert. New York: Simon & Schuster, 1990.

Kelley, Kitty. *Elizabeth Taylor: The Last Star.* New York: Simon & Schuster, 1981.

———. *His Way: The Unauthorized Biography of Frank Sinatra*. New York: Bantam, 1986.

———. *Jackie Oh!* With photographs by Ron Galella. Secaucus, N.J.: Lyle Stuart, 1978.

———. *Nancy Reagan: The Unauthorized Biography*. New York: Simon & Schuster, 1991.

Kelly, Tom. *The Imperial Post: The Meyers, the Grahams and the Paper That Rules Washington*. New York: William Morrow, 1983.

The Kennedy Years. Edited by Nelson Lichtenstein. *Political Profiles*, vol. 3. New York: Facts on File, 1976.

Kessler, Pamela. *Undercover Washington: Touring the Sites Where Famous Spies Lived, Worked, and Loved*. McLean, Va.: EPM, 1992.

Kirkpatrick, Andrew. *Of Permanent Value: The Story of Warren Buffet*. Birmingham, Ala.: AKPE, 1994.

Kissinger, Henry. *White House Years*. Boston: Little, Brown, 1979.

———. *Years of Renewal*. New York: Simon & Schuster, 1999.

Klein, Herbert G. *Making It Perfectly Clear*. Garden City, N.Y.: Doubleday, 1980.

Kleindienst, Richard G. *Justice: The Memoirs of Attorney General Richard Kleindienst*. Ottowa:, Il.: Jameson Books, 1985.

Konolige, Kit. *The Richest Women in the World*. New York: Macmillan, 1985.

Krock, Arthur. *In the Nation: 1932–1966*. New York: McGraw-Hill, 1966.

———. *Memoirs: Sixty Years on the Firing Line*. New York: Wagnalls, 1968.

Lait, Jack, and Lee Mortimer. *Washington Confidential*. New York: Dell, 1951.

Lambro, Donald. *Washington: City of Scandals: Investigating Congress and Other Big Spenders*. Boston: Little, Brown, 1984.

Lanahan, Eleanor. *Scottie: The Daughter of... The Life of Frances Scott Fitzgerald Lanahan Smith*. New York: HarperCollins, 1995.

Lankford, Nelson D. *The Last American Aristocrat: The Biography of David K. E. Bruce, 1898–1977*. Boston: Little, Brown, 1996.

Latham, Laurence. *The Kennedy Women: The Saga of an American Family*. New York: Villard Books, 1994.

Leary, Timothy. *Flashbacks: A Personal and Cultural History of an Era*. Foreword by William S. Boroughs. New York: G. P. Putnam's, 1990.

Levy, Shawn. *Rat Pack Confidential: Frank, Dean, Sammy, Peter, Joey, and the Last Great Showbiz Party*. New York: Doubleday, 1998.

Lewis, Finlay. *Portrait of an American Politician*. New York: Harper and Row, 1980.

Lilly, Doris. *Those Fabulous Greeks: Onassis, Niarchos, and Livanos*. London: W. H. Allen, 1991.

Logan, Joshua. *Josh: My Up and Down, In and Out Life*. New York: Delacorte Press, 1976.

The London Encyclopaedia. Edited by Ben Weinreb and Christopher Hibbert. London: Macmillan, 1983.

Lowenstein, Roger. *Buffett: The Making of an American Capitalist.* New York: Random House, 1995.

MacPherson, Myra. *The Power Lovers: An Intimate Look at Politics and Marriage.* New York: Ballantine Books, 1975.

Mailer: His Life and Times. Edited by Peter Manso. New York: Simon & Schuster, 1985.

Mailer, Norman. *The Presidential Papers.* New York: Dell, 1982.

———. *The Time of Our Time.* New York: Random House, 1998.

Mangold, Tom. *Cold Warrior: James Jesus Angleton: The CIA's Master Spy.* New York: Simon & Schuster, 1998.

Maroon, Fred J. *Maroon on Georgetown.* Photography and Text by Fred J. Maroon. New York: Lickle, 1997.

Martin, John Bartlow. *Adlai Stevenson and the World: The Life of Adlai E. Stevenson.* Garden City, N.Y.: Doubleday, 1977.

Martin, Ralph G. *Cissy.* New York: Simon & Schuster, 1979.

Marton, Kat. *Hidden Power: Presidential Marriages That Shaped Our Recent History.* New York: Pantheon, 2000.

Matalin, Mary, and James Carville. *All's Fair: Love, War, and Running for President.* With Peter Knobler. New York: Random House, 1994.

Matthews, Chris. *Hardball: How Politics Is Played—Told By One Who Knows the Game.* New York: Simon & Schuster, 1999.

Maxwell, Elsa. *The Celebrity Circus.* New York: Appleton-Century, 1953.

McCarthy, Abigail. *Circles: A Washington Story.* New York: Doubleday, 1977.

———. *Private Faces/Public Faces.* Garden City, N.Y.: Doubleday, 1973.

McCarthy, Denni V. N. *Protecting the President: The Inside Story of a Secret Service Agent.* With Philip W. Smith. New York: William Morrow, 1985.

McCarthy, Eugene. *Up 'Til Now: A Memoir.* New York: Harcourt Brace, 1987.

McClendon, Sarah. *Mr. President, Mr. President!: My Fifty Years of Covering the White House.* With Jules Minton. Santa Monica, CA: General Publishing Group, 1996.

McDougal, Dennis. *Privileged Son: Otis Chandler and the Rise and Fall of the L.A. Times Dynasty.* Cambridge, Mass.: Perseus, 2001.

McIntosh, Elizabeth P. *Sisterhood of Spies: The Women of the OSS.* New York: Dell, 1998.

McKeever, Porter. *Adlai Stevenson: His Life and Legacy.* New York: William Morrow, 1989.

McLendon, Winzola, and Scottie Smith. *Don't Quote Me!: Washington Newsmen and the Power Society.* New York: Dutton, 1970.

McMurty, Larry. *Cadillac Jack.* New York: Simon & Schuster, 1982.

McNamara, Robert S., James G. Blight, and Robert K. Brigham. *Argument*

Without End: In Search of Answers to the Vietnam Tragedy. With Thomas J. Biersteker and Col. Herbert V. Schandler. New York: Public Affairs, 1999.

————. *In Retrospect: The Tragedy and Lessons of Vietnam.* With Brian Van DeMark. New York: Times Books, 1995.

Mellen, Joan. *Privilege: The Enigma of Sasha Bruce.* New York: Dial Press, 1982.

Mellon, Paul. *Reflections in a Silver Spoon: A Memoir.* With Joan Baskett. New York: William Morrow, 1992.

Mendell, Ronald L. *Who's Who in Football.* New Rochelle, N.Y.: Arlington House, 1974.

Merry, Robert W. *Taking on the World: Joseph and Stewart Alsop—Guardians of the American Century.* New York. Viking, 1996

Meste, Perle. *My Story.* With Robert Cohn. New York: McGraw-Hill, 1960.

Meyer, Agnes. *Out of These Roots: The Autobiography of an American Woman.* Boston: Little, Brown, 1953.

Meyer, Cord. *Facing Reality: From World Federalism to the CIA.* New York: Harper and Row, 1980.

Miller, Merle. *Plain Speaking: An Oral Biography of Harry S. Truman.* New York: Berkeley Pub. Corp., 1974.

Moldea, Dan E. *Dark Victory: Ronald Reagan, MCA, and the Mob.* New York: Viking, 1986.

Moon, Vicky. *The Middleburg Mystique: A Peek Inside the Gates of Middleburg, Virginia.* Sterling, Va · Capital Books, 2001.

Mooney, Booth. *LBJ: An Irreverent Chronicle.* New York: Crowell, 1986.

Moorhead, Lucy. *Entertaining in Washington.* Introduction by Arthur Schlesinger Jr. New York: Putnam, 1978.

Morgan, Ted. *A Covert Life: Jay Lovestone, Communist, Anti-Communist and Spymaster.* New York: Random House, 1999.

Morris, Edmund. *Dutch: A Memoir of Ronald Reagan.* New York: Modern Library, 1999.

Mosbacher, Georgette. *Feminine Force: Release the Power Within to Create the Life You Deserve.* New York: Simon & Schuster, 1993.

Nine and Counting: The Women of the Senate. Barbara Mikulski . . . [et al.]; Written with Catherine Whitney. New York: William Morrow, 2000.

Niven, David. *The Moon's a Balloon.* New York: Putnam, 1971.

Nixon, Richard. *The Memoirs of Richard Nixon.* New York: Simon & Schuster, 1978.

Ogden, Christopher. *Legacy: A Biography of Moses and Walter Annenberg.* Boston: Little, Brown, 1999.

————. *Life of the Party: The Biography of Pamela Digby Churchill Hayward Harriman.* Boston: Little, Brown, 1994.

O'Neill, Tip. *Man of the House: The Life and Political Memoirs of Speaker Tip O'Neill.* With William Novak. New York: Random House, 1987.

Oppenheimer, Jerry. *Barbara Walters: An Unauthorized Biography.* New York: St. Martin's, 1990.

O'Toole, G. J. A. *The Encyclopedia of American Intelligence and Espionage: From the Revolutionary War to the Present.* New York: Facts on File, 1988.

Pack, Robert. *Edward Bennett Williams for the Defense.* New York: Harper and Row, 1983.

Paper, Lewis J. *Empire: William S. Paley and the Making of CBS.* New York: St. Martin's, 1987.

Parker, Robert. *Capitol Hill in Black and White.* With Richard Rashke. New York: Dodd, Mead, 1986.

Parrish, Michael E. *Felix Frankfurter and His Times: The Reform Years.* New York: Free Press, 1982.

Pearson, Drew. *Diaries, 1949–1959.* Edited by Tyler Abell. New York: Holt, Rinehart and Winston, 1974.

————. *Washington Merry-Go-Round.* New York: Horace Liveright, 1931.

Perlstein, Rick. *Before the Storm: Barry Goldwater and the Unmaking of the American Consensus.* New York: Hill and Wang, 2001.

Phillips, Julia. *You'll Never Eat Lunch in This Town Again.* New York: Random House, 1991.

Pitch, Anthony S. *A Walk in the Past: Georgetown.* Potomac, Md.: Mino, 1997.

Plimpton, George. *Truman Capote: In Which Various Friends, Enemies, Acquaintances, and Detractors Recall His Turbulent Career.* New York: Doubleday, 1997.

Political Trials. Edited by Theodore L. Becker. Indianapolis: Bobbs-Merrill, 1971.

Pottker, Janice. *Celebrity Washington: Who They Are, Where They Live, and Why They're Famous: Plus Maps, Photos, Movie Locations, and Restaurants.* Potomac, Md.: Writer's Cramp Books, 1995.

————. *Janet and Jackie: The Story of a Mother and Her Daughter.* New York: St. Martin's, 2001.

Powell, Colin L. *My American Journey.* With Joseph E. Persico. New York: Random House, 1995.

Powers, Thomas. *The Man Who Kept the Secrets: Richard Helms and the CIA.* New York: Alfred A. Knopf, 1979.

Pusey, Merlo J. *Eugene Meyer.* New York: Random House, 1974.

Quinn, Sally. *Happy Endings.* New York: Simon & Schuster, 1991.

————. *The Party: A Guide to Adventurous Entertainment.* New York: Simon & Schuster, 1997.

———. *Regrets Only.* New York: Simon & Schuster, 1986.

———. *We're Going to Make You a Star.* New York: Simon & Schuster, 1975.

Quinn, William W. *Buffalo Bill Remembers: Truth and Courage.* Fowlerville, Md.: Wilderness Adventure Books, 1991.

Radziwill, Lee. *Happy Times.* New York: Assouline, 2002.

Reagan, Nancy. *My Turn: The Memoirs of Nancy Reagan.* With William Novak. New York: Random House, 1989.

Reagan, Ronald. *An American Life.* New York: Pocket Books, 1990.

Reich, Cary. *Financier: The Biography of Andre Meyer. A Story of Money, Power, and the Reshaping of American Business.* New York: William Morrow, 1983.

Reston, James. *Deadline: A Memoir.* New York: Random House, 1991.

Roberts, Chalmers M. *In the Shadow of Power: The Story of the Washington Post.* Cabin John, Md.: Seven Locks Press, 1989.

Roberts, Cokie. *We Are Our Mothers' Daughters.* New York: William Morrow, 1998.

Robertson, Nan. *The Girls in the Balcony: Women, Men, and the New York Times.* New York: Random House, 1992.

Rockefeller, David. *Memoirs.* New York: Random House, 2002.

Rodriguez, Elena. *Dennis Hopper: A Madness to His Method.* New York: St. Martin's, 1988.

Roosevelt, Selwa. *Keeper of the Gate.* New York: Simon & Schuster, 1990.

Rowan, Carl T. *Breaking Barriers: A Memoir.* Boston: Little, Brown, 1991.

Rubin, Nancy. *American Empress: The Life and Times of Marjorie Merriweather Post.* New York: Villard Books, 1995.

Rusk, Dean. *As I Saw It.* With Richard Rusk and Daniel S. Papp. New York: W. W. Norton, 1990.

Ryskind, Allan H. *Hubert: An Unauthorized Biography of the Vice President.* New Rochelle, N.Y.: Arlington House, 1968.

Salinger, Pierre. *With Kennedy.* Garden City, N.Y.: Doubleday, 1966.

———. *P.S.: A Memoir.* New York: St. Martin's, 1995.

Schlesinger, Arthur M. *A Life in the Twentieth Century.* Boston: Houghton Mifflin, 2000.

———. *Robert Kennedy and His Times.* Boston: Houghton Mifflin, 1978.

Schoenbaum, Thomas J. *Waging Peace and War: Dean Rusk in the Truman, Kennedy and Johnson Years.* New York: Simon & Schuster, 1988.

Schulman, Robert. *John Sherman Cooper: The Global Kentuckian.* Lexington, Ky.: University Press of Kentucky, 1976.

Seebohm, Caroline. *No Regrets: The Life of Marietta Tree.* New York: Simon & Schuster, 1997.

Shannon, Jasper Barry. *The Education of a Professor: A Study in Failure and Frustration* (unpublished manuscript).

Silverstein, Ken. *Washington on $10 Million a Day: How Lobbyists Plunder the Nation.* Monroe, Me.: Common Courage Press, 1998.

Smith, Florence Pritchett. *These Entertaining People.* New York: Macmillan, 1966.

Smith, Hedrick. *The Power Game: How Washington Works.* New York: Ballantine Books, 1988.

Smith, Sally Bedell. *In All His Glory: The Life of William S. Paley, The Legendary Tycoon and His Brilliant Circle.* New York: Simon & Schuster, 1990.

————. *Reflected Glory: The Life of Pamela Churchill Harriman.* New York: Simon & Schuster, 1996.

Smolla, Rodney A. *Suing the Press.* New York: Oxford University Press, 1986.

Sotheby's (Firm). *The Estate of Ambassador Pamela Harriman. Auction: May 19–21, 1997.* New York: Sotheby's, 1997.

Spada, James. *Peter Lawford: The Man Who Kept the Secrets.* New York: Bantam, 1997.

Sparber, A. M. *Murrow: His Life and Times.* New York: Freundlich Press, 1986.

Srodes, James. *Allen Dulles, Master of Spies.* Washington, D.C.: Regnery, 1999.

Steel, Ronald. *Walter Lippmann and the American Century.* New Brunswick, N.J.: Transition Publishers, 1999.

Stevenson, Adlai Ewing. *The Papers of Adlai E. Stevenson, Volume VIII: Ambassador to the United Nations, 1961–1965.* Boston: Little, Brown, 1979.

Stockman, David A. *The Triumph of Politics: How the Reagan Revolution Failed.* New York: Harper and Row, 1986.

Stuart, Lyle. *The Secret Life of Walter Winchell.* New York: Boar's Head Books, 1953.

Sulzberger, C. I. *The Last of the Giants.* New York: Macmillan, 1970.

Summers, Anthony. *The Arrogance of Power: The Secret World of Richard Nixon.* With Robbyn Swann. New York: Viking Press, 2000.

————. *Conspiracy.* New York: McGraw-Hill, 1986.

————. *Official and Confidential: The Secret Life of J. Edgar Hoover.* New York: Putnam, 1993.

Swanberg, W. A. *Luce and His Empire.* New York: Scribner's, 1972.

Taub, William L. *Forces of Power.* New York: Grosset and Dunlap, 1979.

Theodoracopulos, Taki. *Princes, Playboys & High Class Acts.* Foreword by Tom Wolfe. Princeton: Karz-Cohl, 1984.

Teague, Michael. *Mrs. L: Conversations with Alice Roosevelt Longworth.* Garden City, N.Y.: Doubleday, 1981.

Thomas, Evan. *The Man to See: Edward Bennett Williams, Ultimate Insider, Legendary Trial Lawyer.* New York: Simon & Schuster, 1991.

————. *The Very Best Man: Four Who Dared; The Early Years of the CIA.* New York: Simon & Schuster, 1995.

Thomas, Helen. *Dateline: White House*. New York: Macmillan, 1975.

―――. *Front Row in the White House: My Life and Times*. New York: Scribner's, 1999.

Thompson, Hunter S. *Fear and Loathing in America: The Brutal Odyssey of an Outlaw Journalist, 1968–1976*. Foreword by David Halberstam, edited by Douglas Brinkley. New York: Simon & Schuster, 2000.

Tifft, Susan E., and Alex S. Jones. *The Trust: The Private and Powerful Family Behind the New York Times*. Boston: Little, Brown, 1999.

Toer, Pramoedya Ananta. *The Mute's Soliloquy: A Memoir*. New York: Hyperion East, 1999.

Toledano, Ralph de. *J. Edgar Hoover: The Man in His Time*. New Rochelle, N.Y.: Arlington House, 1973.

Tower, John G. *Consequences: A Personal and Political Memoir*. Boston: Little, Brown, 1991.

Trento, Joseph J. *The Secret History of the CIA*. Roseville, Calif.: Prima Publishing, 2001.

Trento, Susan B. *The Power House: Robert Keith Gray and the Selling of Access and Influence in Washington*. New York: St. Martin's, 1992.

Troy, Thomas F. *Wild Bill and Intrepid: Donovan, Stephenson, and the Origins of the CIA*. New Haven: Yale University Press, 1994.

Truffaut, Francois. *Hitchcock*. With the collaboration of Helen G. Scott. New York: Simon & Schuster, 1984.

Tudor Place Historic House and Garden. *Splendours of Georgetown: 25 Architectural Masterpieces. An Exhibition Presented in Collaboration with the Commission of Fine Arts and the Historic American Building Survey, April 13–December 31, 2001*. Washington, D.C.: Tudor Place Historic House and Garden, 2001.

Tynan, Kathleen. *The Life of Kenneth Tynan*. New York: William Morrow, 1987.

Van Riper, Frank. *Glenn: The Astronaut Who Would Be President*. New York: Empire Books, 1983.

Vikers, Hugo. *Cecil Beaton: A Biography*. Boston: Little, Brown, 1985.

Vidal, Gore. *Palimpsest: A Memoir*. New York: Random House, 1993.

Walton, William. *The Evidence of Washington*. Photographs by Evelyn Hofer. New York: Harper and Row, 1966.

Warhol, Andy. *The Andy Warhol Diaries*. Edited by Pat Hackett. New York: Warner Books, 1989.

Welch, Neil J., and David W. Marston. *Inside Hoover's FBI: The Top Field Chief Reports*. Garden City, N.Y.: Doubleday, 1984.

White, Theodore H. *In Search of History: A Personal Adventure*. New York: Warner Books, 1978.

―――. *The Making of the President 1964*. New York: Atheneum, 1965.

Wicker, Tom. *One of Us: Richard Nixon and the American Dream.* New York: Random House, 1991.

Williams, Tennessee. *Memoirs.* New York: Doubleday, 1979.

Wilson, Robert Anton. *Everything Is Under Control: Conspiracies, Cults, and Cover-Ups.* With Miriam Joan Hill. New York: Harper Perennial, 1998.

Winks, Robin W. *Cloak and Gown: Scholars in the Secret War, 1939–1961.* New Haven: Yale University Press, 1987.

Woodward, Bob. *Five Presidents and the Legacy of Watergate.* New York: Simon & Schuster, 1999.

World Almanac of U.S. Politics. 1991–1993 Edition. New York: Pharos Books, 1991.

Wright, William. *Heiress: The Rich Life of Marjorie Merriweather Post.* Washington, D.C.: New Republic Books, 1978.

Wyden, Peter. *Bay of Pigs: The Untold Story.* New York: Simon & Schuster, 1979.

Yoder, Edwin. *Joe Alsop's Cold War—A Study of Journalistic Influence and Intrigue.* Chapel Hill: The University of North Carolina Press, 1995.

INDEX

ABOUT THE AUTHOR

C. DAVID HEYMANN is the author of one book of poetry and six previous biographies, including *Poor Little Rich Girl: The Life and Legend of Barbara Hutton*; *A Woman Named Jackie: An Intimate Biography of Jacqueline Bouvier Kennedy Onassis*; *Liz: An Intimate Biography of Elizabeth Taylor*; and *RFK: A Candid Biography of Robert F. Kennedy*. The Jackie biography was a *New York Times* number one best-seller and was translated into more than thirty foreign languages. The Barbara Hutton, Jackie Onassis, and Elizabeth Taylor biographies were all made into NBC-TV award-winning miniseries.

The author currently resides and works in New York City.